Praise for *Black Hibiscus*

"Convening a range of scholars of Florida's African American literary and cultural history, *Black Hibiscus* offers a unique engagement with contemporary scholarship marked by clarity of vision and conceptual verve."
—**Keith Cartwright,** professor of English at University of North Florida

"*Black Hibiscus* is a remarkable gathering of essays that causes you to re-encounter Florida as much more than its stereotypes. The collection not only makes you discover writers you may have known little or nothing about such as Albery Whitman and Gwendolyn Bennett, but also enriches your understanding of established authors such as Edwidge Danticat, James Weldon Johnson, Zora Neale Hurston, and Colson Whitehead. The essays range beyond writers to explore artists such as the Highwaymen, West Indian folklore in Florida, the history of the Yamasee, the legacy of the Ocoee massacre, and the Academy Award–winning film *Moonlight*. Be prepared to be enlightened, interested, and entertained."
—**Veronica Makowsky,** professor emeritus of English at University of Connecticut and editor emeritus of *MELUS*

"Through interviews, first-person accounts, and traditional academic essays, *Black Hibiscus* disrupts typical racial and cultural narratives about Florida and shows the centrality of the Black experience to the state."
—**Julie Buckner Armstrong,** author of *Mary Turner and the Memory of Lynching*

"*Black Hibiscus* is an important collection of interdisciplinary essays on Florida's Black cultural legacy. Together these essays offer a diverse exploration of the arts and literature of the Sunshine State; they tell a story about the allure of the exotic landscape with its dark undersides that begins in the colonial past and reaches to the contemporary moment. This book is a rich resource and excellent starting point for readers interested in Florida's central role in the Black cultural experience and imagination."
—**Annette Trefzer,** professor of American literature at University of Mississippi

Black Hibiscus

Black Hibiscus

African Americans and the Florida Imaginary

Edited by **John Wharton Lowe**

University Press of Mississippi / Jackson

A subvention for the color printing was provided by the
Barbara Methvin Endowed Professorship funds at the University of Georgia.

www.upress.state.ms.us

The University Press of Mississippi is a member
of the Association of University Presses.

Chapter 1, "Yamasee African Ties in Carolina and Florida" by Jane Landers,
is reproduced from *The Yamasee Indians: From Florida to South Carolina*,
edited by Denise I. Bossy, by permission of the University of Nebraska Press.
Copyright 2018 by the Board of Regents of the University of Nebraska.

Chapter 9, "African American and West Indian Folklife in South Florida"
by Joyce Marie Jackson, was first published in *South Florida History Magazine* 3
(Summer 1990): 11–18.

Chapter 12, "Black and Blue in Florida: *Moonlight*'s Poetics of Space and Identity"
by Delia Malia Konzett, was first published in *Quarterly Review of Film and Video*
(2021-07-01). DOI: https://doi.org/10.1080/10509208.2021.1946258.

∞

Library of Congress Cataloging-in-Publication Data

Names: Lowe, John Wharton, editor.
Title: Black hibiscus : African Americans and the Florida imaginary / John
Wharton Lowe.
Description: Jackson : University Press of Mississippi, 2024. | Includes
bibliographical references and index.
Identifiers: LCCN 2023039014 (print) | LCCN 2023039015 (ebook) | ISBN
9781496848598 (hardback) | ISBN 9781496848604 (trade paperback) | ISBN
9781496848611 (epub) | ISBN 9781496848628 (epub) | ISBN 9781496848635
(pdf) | ISBN 9781496848642 (pdf)
Subjects: LCSH: African Americans—Florida—History. | African
Americans—Florida—Social conditions. | African
Americans—Florida—Social life and customs. | Florida—History. |
Florida—Social conditions. | Florida—Social life and customs.
Classification: LCC E185.93.F5 B533 2024 (print) | LCC E185.93.F5 (ebook)
| DDC 908.996/0730759—dc23/eng/20230905
LC record available at https://lccn.loc.gov/2023039014
LC ebook record available at https://lccn.loc.gov/2023039015

British Library Cataloging-in-Publication Data available

Contents

Black Hibiscus

Introduction

John Wharton Lowe

Often considered an outlier in Southern Studies, the state of Florida in fact has a rich literary and cultural history, which is increasingly of interest today as our focus shifts from the national to the circum-Caribbean. Florida's Spanish past, its many ports, and tropical terrain are only a few of the state's Caribbean markers. It has also been home to several Native American cultures, and there are still Seminoles living there. What has been scanted, however, is the key roles African Americans have played in Floridian history and culture.

The state's early population boom came from immigrants from the US South, particularly Georgia, and many of them were African Americans. Over the centuries, the state has produced remarkable writers such as Zora Neale Hurston, James Weldon Johnson, and Gwendolyn Bennett. The most recent addition to this list is the amazing Edwidge Danticat, whose relocation to Miami has revitalized the African American literary scene there. The interaction between the state's many ethnic communities has created a unique and vibrant culture, which has had, and continues to have, a significant impact on Southern, national, and hemispheric life and history. Most recently, the distinguished writer Colson Whitehead has set his new novel *The Nickel Boys* in the state, focusing on a notorious Tallahassee reformatory.

This volume begins by exploring Florida's colonial past, focusing particularly on interactions between maroons who escaped enslavement and Native Americans. The role of Blacks in St. Augustine, settled by the Spanish and the oldest still-inhabited town in the United States, will be a special interest. Slave narratives from Florida will receive close inspection. The Afro-Cuban and Haitian diasporas in Florida are a focus, and there will be two clusters of essays, one on Zora Neale Hurston and the other on the recent film *Moonlight*. Only three of the proposed essays have been previously published (Landers,

Jackson, and Konzett). This collection considers the art, literature, music, foodways, religion(s), and folklore of the state's Black communities as well as the complex circum-Caribbean history that has shaped and influenced all of these traditions. Racial struggle—particularly during the long civil rights movement—takes pride of place. Our contributors include literary scholars, historians, film critics, art historians, anthropologists, musicologists, political scientists, and poets. This book will appeal to scholars and students in all these areas, but will also have much to interest general readers. Our essays form a valuable complement and supplement to the excellent 2014 volume edited by Amanda B. Carlson and Robin Poynor, *Africa in Florida: Five Hundred Years of African Presence in the Sunshine State* (2014), which plumbs African elements in Florida history and culture from the early days of enslavement to today's tourist attractions.

•   •   •

African Americans are associated with the South's plantations and are often thought to have arrived on our shores in 1619, as the recent (and controversial) *New York Times* project that uses that date as its signature claims. However, the first African American came to the New World in 1528, when an enslaved African from Morocco, Estevanico, arrived with his master, Panfilo de Narvárez of Spain, landing near what is now St. Petersburg on April 16 of that year. They would travel widely over the course of eight years, reaching what is now Arizona and then Mexico. Estevanico soon picked up basics of Native languages and acted as interpreter for the Spanish explorers. His adventures ended in a Native American village in what is now New Mexico, where the Natives, suspecting him to be a spy, killed him.

Large numbers of enslaved Africans were not imported into Florida until 1687, when many of them escaped their bonds in Georgia and fled south. The Spanish, who had built Fort Mose, just north of St. Augustine, permitted these refugees to settle there as long as they embraced Catholicism. These new Floridians rewarded the Spanish by helping them successfully ward off an invasion by the British in 1740. Until 1763, they helped St. Augustine flourish by providing game through hunting, and working as carpenters and ironsmiths. But the British temporarily conquered Florida in 1763, causing many of St. Augustine's Blacks to join their Spanish employers in Cuba. The British split their new colony in half; West Florida maintained its capital in Pensacola, while East Florida chose St. Augustine. But when Britain finally acknowledged the independence of its former New World colonies in a 1783 treaty, Florida became Spanish once again.

The Atlantic slave trade was forbidden by the United States in 1808; however, Florida was still a Spanish possession, and smugglers found it easy to disembark their human cargo there. Inevitably, the brutalities exerted on the enslaved cause many to run away, often to swamps, and in some cases, to refuge among indigenous peoples. Other escaped enslaved peoples erected a Black fort in western Florida on the Apalachicola River's Prospect Bluff, under the leadership of one Garcia. The over 300 inhabitants of the fort were viewed as threats by the surrounding white communities, who prevailed on the US government to assist them. In response, in 1816, Andrew Jackson supervised the destruction of the fort by two gunboats, killing over 200 men, women, and children. To justify this action, Jackson wrote: "I have little doubt of the fact, that this fort has been established by some villains for the purpose of rapine and plunder, and that it ought to be blown up . . . destroy it and return the stolen Negroes and property to their rightful owners" (Jones and McCarthy, 16). This perceived threat to surrounding states created a campaign for the United States to annex Florida, which was accomplished in 1821. Even after statehood, however, smugglers were able to bring enslaved peoples to shore from Africa due to the state's long coastline and many hidden coves.

The new territory was sparsely populated until the United States offered free land in 1842. Soon settlers were planting crops, which necessitated cheap labor: slavery. In 1840 the Black population of the state was around 16,000, including 844 free people. But on the eve of the Civil War there were 60,000 enslaved Blacks, comprising 45 percent of the total population.

As noted, some runaways—maroons—found refuge with the Seminole nation, and after much intermarriage, there were hundreds of Black Seminoles. The people who became known as Seminoles were originally Creeks who migrated to Florida from Georgia and Alabama in the eighteenth century. They enslaved the Yamassee people they defeated in warfare, and established towns near current-day Gainesville. Their leaders, concentrated in the town of Cuscowilla, were led at first by Cowkeeper, and then by his nephews Micanopy and Billy Bowlegs. At first the escaped enslaved Africans who joined the group were put in bondage as well, but intermarriage led to a merger and increasing numbers of Black Seminoles. All of the amalgamated people were instrumental in helping the Spanish repel invasions from both the British and the United States. But Jackson was persistent, and succeeded in his first "Seminole War" in 1817, burning most of the Native homes in Bowlegs Town on the Suwanee River, followed by the capture of Spanish Pensacola. Subsequently, Jackson became governor of Florida in 1821 when the United States claimed it as a territory. One of his first acts was to try to purge the state of both groups of Seminoles; his actions led to the Seminole groups fleeing to the tip of the peninsula; some voyaged to Cuba and the Bahamas.

A remnant of the people built up their town of Peliklikaha (near present-day Orlando) and established farms, worked by their Black enslaved, under the leadership of Abraham, himself an escaped Black, and an interpreter of the chief Bowlegs. Abraham led an attack on US encampments, instigating the second Seminole War in 1835, which resulted in the removal of the Black Seminoles to Oklahoma. As Jane G. Landers has demonstrated, this inter-mingling of escaped Africans and Seminoles led to a joint history; Black Seminoles eventually took on roles of equality with the blood Seminoles, and for a time, helped keep their new brothers and sisters in Florida (Landers, 115–16). As a result of these complex interactions between the indigenous and maroons, African Americans to the north began to valorize the Seminoles. Eventually, the great Black poet Albery Whitman (1851–1901) wrote an epic poem, *The Rape of Florida* (1884), that mythologized this union of ethnic groups, while depicting the tragic wars with Jackson and his soldiers and the subsequent exile of most Seminoles to Mexico.

When the Civil War erupted, there were only 140,000 people in Florida, and almost half were enslaved Blacks, who worked the cotton fields in north-ern Florida. Very little combat occurred in the state, and Key West stayed in Union hands throughout the conflict, but African American Union soldiers fought in the February 1864 Battle of Olustee (which the Confederacy won). After the war, as was the case in the wider South, Florida's Black citizens were stripped of the franchise and subject to harsh new "Black Codes" laws. But a great leader, Robert Meacham (1835–1902), stepped forward and helped develop the key role of the African Methodist Episcopal Church in Florida. Born enslaved, after Emancipation he became a teacher, as well as a celebrated pastor in Monticello, Florida. He served in the legislature, helped draft the state's constitution, and became superintendent of Monticello schools. His friend Josiah Walls (1842–1905) distinguished himself by serving as the state's only representative to Congress from 1870–76. Walls also established the first Black newspaper in Florida, the *New Era*. Racial violence, however, prompted his move to Tampa, where he ran a shoe shop until his death in 1902. Other Black newspapers served the Black community after the war, including *The Sentinel*, which ran for forty years after its founding in 1870 by Matthew M. Lewey; it eventually became the Tampa *Sentinel-Bulletin*. Yet another Black Floridian, Jonathan C. Gibbs (1827–1874), distinguished himself by serving as Florida's secretary of state and later as state superintendent of schools.

Eventually, Blacks played key—if menial—roles in the nascent Florida tourism industry. One of its first manifestations was the development in the

1860s of special narrow steamboats that could navigate the exotic twists of the Oklawaha River, a tributary to the broad St. Johns. Winding through swamps and tropical jungles, the boats were manned by Black crews who kept the steam engines going, and at night built illuminating fires on the top of the vessels to cast dramatic shadows over the teeming banks. Quite a few celebrities would take passage on these boats, and the journeys provided material for the growing numbers of travel writers, such as Harriet Beecher Stowe, Thomas Bangs Thorpe, Lafcadio Hearn, and Constance Fenimore Woolson. Sidney Lanier, the great nineteenth-century Georgian poet, published a popular early travel book about Florida, which at that time was touted as an ideal place for consumptives like him to mount a recovery. In *Florida: Its Scenery, Climate, and History, with an Account of Charleston, Savannah, Augusta, and Aiken, and a Chapter for Consumptives; Being a Complete Hand-Book and Guide*, he opens the study by declaring that the state "by its very peninsular curve whimsically terminates the United States in an interrogation-point" (1875, 9), an ideal starting point for his musings on the state's bewildering tropical diversity and, often, its inaccessibility. Lanier was writing in the wake of other early travelogues, particularly Edward King's *The Great South* (1875), which trumpeted the author's skill in making "discoveries" in the unknown realms of the mysterious South, through "penetration" and "investigation." As Jennifer Greeson has noted, King and others of his ilk were capitalizing on the vogue for accounts of African exploration by whites; King was thus attempting to situate the South as a kind of "domestic Africa," reaching for a "global reframing" (Greeson, 244). Indeed, another competing book, the two-volume edition of *Picturesque America* (1872–74), published by the aggressive and ambitious publisher D. Appleton and Company, began its compendium of discrete sketches with the exotic "A Journey up the St. John's and Ocklawaha Rivers."

Unsurprisingly, these white travel writers—even Harriet Beecher Stowe, who owned an orange plantation in Florida, and would pen her own travel narrative, *Palmetto Leaves* (1873)—tended to slight African American Floridians, presenting them as servants and minor characters in the broad canvases being limned, which were heavy on flora and fauna and rather light on social and racial realities. Nevertheless, the new hotels, inns, and travel lodges demanded cheap labor, and Black Floridians were employed as drivers, cooks, domestics, and groundskeepers.

As indicated earlier, far from being an "empty state" prior to its incorporation into the United States, Florida had a rich and complex Native history. Early explorers such as De Soto encountered many peoples of the Americas there, and were frequently nourished and sustained by them. The little-known Yamassee Wars of 1715, which united Blacks and Natives in Carolina, led to their joint exile in Spanish Florida, where both groups were enlisted into Spanish military exploits. One of the first African Americans to employ Florida's indigenous people in his works was the aforementioned poet Albery Whitman. While he wasn't familiar with Florida personally, he had studied its history and was aware of the strong bonds that had been formed between enslaved Africans and the state's beleaguered Native Americans. His epic *The Rape of Florida* (1882) provides an invaluable early example of the inter-braided effects of white domination of these two cultures, and a portrait of racial communities interacting with and supporting other groups. The heroic Seminole figures of Alassa, his beloved Ewald, and her father, the Chieftain Palmecho dominate the four cantos, which together comprise 251 nine-line Spenserian stanzas, a formal structure that proves in tension with the violent events of Anglo-Native warfare and ultimate exile for the Seminoles in Florida, an epic journey that parallels the much later "Trail of Tears" that forced Georgia's Cherokees on an often deadly trek to Oklahoma.

The vibrant Black folklife and folklore of the state would be largely unexamined until Zora Neale Hurston took her Chevy coupe into the hamlets and sawmill and turpentine camps in search of "lying sessions," resulting in her pathbreaking collection *Mules and Men* (1935); the resources of this book and her other two folklore collections would enrich her novels: *Jonah's Gourd Vine* (1933); *Their Eyes Were Watching God* (1937); and *Seraph on the Suwanee* (1948). Significantly, Hurston herself migrated to Florida with her family as a small girl, and *Their Eyes* similarly has Janie joining Joe Starks, a Georgian, in his move to all-Black Eatonville, where everything seems possible. Over the course of the novel, readers are taken across the state, to Lake Okeechobee and back; Hurston's folklore collections covered the entire state, from rural hamlets to bustling new cities. *Seraph on the Suwanee* acquainted readers with orange groves, real estate booms, and the seafood industries. Black Florida even had a say in Hurston's startling revision of the Moses chapters of the Old Testament, *Moses, Man of the Mountain* (1939), which is mostly told in contemporary Black dialect, replete with comic episodes straight out of the Florida towns and landscapes, but in the service of an underlying and quite serious discourse on racial leadership.

Of course, Hurston, who trained as an anthropologist at Columbia with Franz Boas and Ruth Benedict, spent years gathering folklore in Florida, and a good deal of it came from the turpentine camps, where most workers were African Americans. For many years, however, these workers were in reality enslaved, through the notorious convict-lease system that began operating in Florida in 1877. Arrested Black men could be sent to these camps where armed guards kept them in check, and often in chains, in order to kept them from escaping. Beatings and murders by guards were common. Convicts were also forced to help build the entrepreneur Henry Flagler's railroad over the islands south of Miami to Key West, which revolutionized the state's burgeoning tourism. Convict lease would only end in 1923 after public outcries.

The keystone for Black higher education in the South was set by Booker T. Washington's Tuskegee Institute, which led to the establishment of other colleges and universities, such as Fisk, Dillard, Morehouse, Spellman, Clark, and importantly in Florida, Bethune-Cookman. Public education, however, was another matter. In 1887 the state legislature of Florida provided funding for the State Normal College for Colored Students in Tallahassee, in order to create a corps of teachers for the segregated Black schools of the state. Eventually, this became Florida Agricultural & Mechanical University, which today is one of the largest and most important public HBCUs.

Like her friend James Weldon Johnson, who spent his last years as a professor at Fisk University in Nashville, Hurston several times took on teaching positions, although her writing ambitions inevitably scuttled all such appointments. At one time, Hurston worked with the celebrated Floridian educator Mary McLeod Bethune at Bethune-Cookman College. Bethune was born in 1875 in South Carolina, the youngest of seventeen children, and grew up picking cotton alongside her family. They were able to send her to boarding school in North Carolina, which enabled her to attend Dwight Moody's Institute for Home and Foreign Missions in Chicago. When no churches would accept her as a missionary, she returned to South Carolina to teach; she married Albertus Bethune, and moved with him and their son to Palatka, Florida. In 1904 Bethune opened a school for girls in Daytona; eventually it became a college and merged with the existing school for men, Cookman, to become Bethune-Cookman College. The school prospered and drew funding from wealthy white donors. Bethune became a leader of many racial organizations, and a confidante of first lady Eleanor Roosevelt. President Roosevelt made her director of Negro Affairs of the National Youth Administration. In 1940 she became vice president of the NAACP, and was instrumental in the creation of the integrated Women's Army Corps. A true Renaissance woman, Bethune also ran a Florida insurance company and wrote for leading Black newspapers. Black Floridians looked to her for decades for leadership and inspiration.

Hurston, however, clashed with Mrs. Bethune and soon left the college. She had already, of course, been a leading figure in the legendary Harlem Renaissance, when her raucous tale telling at fabled rent parties brought a down-home Floridian flavor to the new culture brewing uptown. But she wasn't alone—one of the elder statesmen of the movement was Jacksonville's James Weldon Johnson, her dear friend and fellow Harlem Renaissance writer. Johnson (1871–1938), who became field secretary for the NAACP, also created lyrics for New York musicals with his talented brother, the composer J. Rosamond Johnson. He also wrote the "Negro national anthem," the stirring "Lift Every Voice and Sing." Hurston, too, would write, direct, and stage musicals during her career, almost all of them set in rural Florida. Johnson's diplomatic career as consul in both Nicaragua and Venezuela had a parallel with Hurston's anthropological work in Haiti, Jamaica, and the Bahamas; both explored the connections between diasporan people of color in the circum-Caribbean. Johnson's celebrated novella *The Autobiography of an Ex-Colored Man* (1912) predated the glory days of the Harlem Renaissance, and inspired many of those writers—especially Hurston, who felt a deep connection to Johnson through their love of their home state and its culture. Johnson's lengthy and impressive actual autobiography, *Along This Way* (1933), uses its early chapters to depict a long-lost Black Florida (especially that of Jacksonville, his home city) that featured vibrant folk culture but also an educated and often prosperous Black middle class.

A third member of the fabled New Negroes in Harlem, the poet Gwendolyn Bennett, has been lightly considered in the histories of the movement, and no one before Belinda Wheeler, has focused on the effect Bennett's stay in Florida had on her life and work.

As members of the Harlem Renaissance, Johnson and Hurston (who was a trained anthropologist) were vitally interested in folk culture. As Joyce Marie Jackson reveals, there has always been a rich tradition of African American folklore in Florida, and its several distinctions from larger patterns in the US South make it fascinating, particularly when you factor in the effect that immigration from the Black Atlantic had, as Black people from the Bahamas, Cuba, Latin America, and especially lately, Haiti, brought many contributions to the cultural table. The African-inspired religions of Haiti (vodun), Brazil (Candomble), and Jamaica (Obeah) have contributed to religious rituals and practice, particularly in coastal cities such as Tampa and Miami.

But Florida also produced many other distinguished African American leaders outside the arts; among these we find the founder of the Afro-American Life Insurance Company Abraham Lincoln Lewis (1865–1947); the fabled sculptor Augusta Savage (1900–1962); the electrifying singer and pianist Ray Charles (1930–2004); the first African American four-star general, Daniel "Chappie" James Jr. (1920–1978); and Leander Shaw (1930–2015), the first Black chief justice of the Florida Supreme Court.

Most popular histories of the civil rights movement rightly focus on the Southern Christian Leadership Conference, Rev. Martin Luther King Jr., and events in Birmingham, Selma, Atlanta, Memphis, and Nashville. There were, however, many significant demonstrations and sites of resistance in the Sunshine State, which over the centuries had been a prominent site of slavery, sharecropping, lynching, and racial riots. According to Gillian Brockell, citing research by the Equal Justice Initiative, between 1880 and 1940 more African Americans per capita were lynched in Florida than in any state except Mississippi. Isabel Wilkerson has cited the threat of lynching as a common tool of citrus grove owners in their efforts to manage Black workers (Wilkerson, 150–57).

Well before the civil rights movement, however, racial riots were instigated by whites as a way of keeping rights from African Americans. While there were many we could consider here, such as the notorious Wilmington riot of 1898 (memorialized in Charles Chesnutt's searing 1901 novel, *The Marrow of Tradition*), the most significant such event in Florida occurred in Ocoee in 1920, when that town's African American community was destroyed by angry whites in an effort to shut down Black voting. At least thirty African American citizens were killed; Zora Neale Hurston wrote a report on the event. A second horrific event, the Rosewood Massacre, erupted in January 1923, when a Black man was accused of attacking a white woman. A manhunt led to widespread attacks on the entire Black community, with homes, churches, and stores burned and as many as thirty African Americans murdered.

While the bus boycott in Alabama remains indelible in national memory, there was one in Tallahassee in May 1956, when Carrie Patterson and Wilhelmina Jakes refused to give up the seats they had taken in the designated "whites only" section of a municipal bus. Their arrests sparked a boycott organized by the Reverend C. K. Steel (1914–1980), who would go on to play a central role in the state's struggle over equal rights, including Martin Luther King's participation in the movement to integrate St. Augustine's beaches in 1964.

One of the chief avenues of contestation that made Florida almost unique were the many municipal edicts against Blacks enjoying the state's beaches. Segregationist legislators tried to get around this by designating (usually minuscule) beaches for Black use. While coastal resorts hired Blacks for menial jobs, they refused to allow them access to the adjoining sands. Black businessmen succeeded in buying and operating similarly small beach areas, and the ever-resourceful Mary McLeod Bethune funded and implemented the two-and-a-half-mile Bethune-Volusia Beach near Bethune-Cookman. Another Black beach, Virginia Key in Dade County, hosted celebrities such as Nat King Cole, Lena Horne, and Jackie Robinson; even these stars were denied access to the fabled Miami shores such as Baker's Haulover (Mormino, 310–11). "Wade-ins," the beachfront equivalent of sit-ins, were generated in the mid-fifties, which continued to be necessary as late as the sixties; a famous one attempted to integrate Fort Lauderdale beach on the

Fourth of July in 1961, and a violent confrontation between white and Black bathers on St. Augustine's shores made national headlines.

• • •

This collection doesn't try to cover all these figures and events; how could it? Only a multi-volume project could aim at that kind of comprehensiveness. What we do, however, is focus on some key African Americans and important historical and cultural moments that we believe provide an expanded and illuminating understanding of a rich artistic and social history, one that is inseparable from Florida, national, and circum-Caribbean culture in all its aspects.

Increasingly, in the twentieth century, real estate moguls, bankers, and local boosters mounted a campaign among the nation's elderly, seeking to lure them to retirement properties in the "Sunshine State." While they were ultimately wildly successful—so much so that Florida became known as "God's waiting room," these pitches were not aimed at Black retirees, and only a small number moved to the state compared to the onrush of white elders.

While a record number of African Americans served in the Allied Forces during World War II, the promise of G.I. Bill housing down payments ran up against entrenched racial siloing. As T. L. Redding, an NAACP leader, summed up: "Negroes are regimented generally in neighborhoods where there are located industrial plants . . . 91 percent of the houses occupied by Negroes are of frame construction, most of which are old . . . Colored veterans cannot beat the red tape required by local financing agents to qualify them for GI loans." In 1951 racial bombings further stunted efforts by Blacks to obtain improved housing/homeownership, leading many Black Floridians to leave the state (Mormino, 154). Additionally, rising temperatures and increasing intolerance of uncooled homes (in 1960 only one in fifty Black households had air conditioning) had a negative effect on the retention of Black Floridians (Mormino, 239).

Black neighborhoods also increasingly were targeted as sites for the expanding highway systems of the state. I-95 was routed right through the historically Black neighborhood of Overtown, in Miami, gobbling up eighty-seven acres. A similar fate came to Orlando's Black areas when the East-West Expressway was constructed through its center. Black Tampa met a similar fate, when Central Avenue, the Black business hub, was taken for highways (Mormino, 247).

Black Floridian migrant farm workers were displaced about this time as well, by a flood of lower-paid imported workers; this was especially true in the sugar cane fields (Hamhamovitch, 200). Florida has often been seen as an odd appendage of the US South, differing in myriad aspects; however, for a long time the state was all too similar to its neighbors Mississippi, Alabama, and Georgia in its racial codes. Segregation was practiced in the schools, movie theaters, parks, department stores, and public facilities, sometimes well into the 1960s, despite the milestone *Brown v. Topeka Board of Education* decision of 1954 that putatively put an end to school segregation. Thirteen years after the *Brown* decision, the well-regarded University of Florida in Gainesville had no Black faculty and only sixty-seven African American students (Mormino, 316).

The opposition to Black civil liberties was not only present among whites; the Latinx business leaders of Ybor City met in Tampa in 1955 to oppose the numbers of Blacks moving into the historically Hispanic district. Similar meetings were held in Key West about this time as well (Mormino, 283). The first major Florida civil rights demonstrations erupted in Jacksonville, Tampa, and Miami in 1960. Sit-ins, boycotts, and marches preceded the monumental Civil Rights Act of 1964 that ended segregation in public facilities. The Jacksonville sit-ins at a department store lunch counter, termed "Ax Handle Sunday," were inspired by earlier sit-ins in Greensboro, North Carolina. The appellation came from the students in Florida being surrounded at the lunch counter by Ku Klux Klan members wearing Confederate uniforms and brandishing baseball bats and ax handles. After the initial confrontation, the Klan members rampaged through the nearby stores, attacking any Black person they encountered. The police declined to intervene, and the attacks were ignored by local newspapers (Brockell 2022).

Three years later, in July a similar sit-in at a Woolworth's lunch counter led to the arrest of seven Black teenagers. A local judge offered to release those whose parents signed a statement guaranteeing their children would not take part in further such demonstrations until they were twenty-one. Four of the children persuaded their parents not to sign, and as a result the kids were sent to reform schools. The two boys wound up in the notorious Dozier reformatory near Tallahassee, an institution that became known for torture, rape, and murder of captive youth. "The St. Augustine Four" were not released until 1964.

When the Cuban Revolution placed Castro in charge of that island in 1959, thousands of well-off Cubans migrated to South Florida and profited from generous new immigration policies created by the adamantly anticommunist US government. Significantly, however, very few of Cuba's Black inhabitants were part of this first wave of exiles, or of the "second wave" of those fleeing when Castro permitted so-called "Freedom Flights" from 1965 to 1973. There was alarm, however, when the new Cuban enclaves of South Florida were discovered to include practitioners of Santería, an Afro-Cuban religion similar to "root work," "conjure," Haiti's vodun, Jamaica's obeah, and Brazil's

Candomble. The cult's practice of animal sacrifice fit in with racist stereotypes of African cultures. Soon Cubans became the largest ethnic group in South Florida, vastly outnumbering African Americans.

The situation became more complicated in 1980, however, when Castro shrewdly opened up emigration portals again, but this time including large numbers of those he considered undesirable, especially criminals and mental patients; many of these "traitors to the Revolution" that he termed *gusanos* ("worms") were Afro-Cuban, thus introducing a new racial factor to perceptions of the island's transfers, one that troubled many of the affluent and white earlier exiles. Since the trip to the states were on boats departing from the port of Mariel, these soon-to-be-scored implants came to be known as "Marielitos."

Nor were these immigrants alone in causing consternation among Florida's resident Black population. Sadly, a new influx of exiles from Haiti split the overall Black community, particularly in Miami. US-born Black Floridians resented Haitians who supposedly took jobs away from them, and received various forms of government assistance. There was similar dismay around the turn of the century when new waves of Black immigrants from the Bahamas and Jamaica jostled for basic amenities. Hostilities between groups grew, and many of the new arrivals resented being thought of as African American. The admixture of Mexicans, Nicaraguans, and more Cubans—all now thought of as nonwhite by many—exacerbated the situation.

While the numbers of Afro-Floridians have long since been eclipsed by Latinx citizens, they have maintained prominent positions in government and culture. Black mayors have been elected in Tallahassee, Sarasota, Jacksonville, Gainesville, North Miami, and St. Petersburg, as well as in many smaller cities. As of this writing, one of the state's members of the House of Representatives, Val Demmings, is running for the Senate seat currently held by Marco Rubio, a Cuban American.

Over the past few decades, Miami has rivaled Atlanta and Nashville as a recording center, and many of the rhythms created there have come from the Black community, such as reggae, merengue, salsa, hip hop, and Afro-Cuban jazz.

Like other southern states, Florida has realized the potential posed by the state's African American history and heritage for tourism; in 1992 the state legislature published a booklet, *Florida Black Heritage Trail*, detailing 141 sites that reflect that history.

Miami has always been a hot spot for racial confrontation in Florida. There was racial rioting in Miami in 1968, 1980, 1982, and 1989. The influx of waves of Cubans—who received special treatment by the US government—created resentment among many in the Black community. But this group is by no means homogenous—for decades the Black community has been composed of migrants not only from Georgia and the upper South but also from the Bahamas, Cuba, Jamaica, Nicaragua, Colombia, and most recently, Haiti and Puerto Rico, especially after hurricanes and earthquakes devastated those islands. Despite a supposed common racial background, some of these groups—especially Haitians—have tended to stay in their own communities, and of course language constitutes a barrier between more recent migrants and the existing African American community. For many years of the early twentieth century, restrictive zoning policies kept Black citizens within Miami's Overtown area; in the thirties and forties the Ku Klux Klan hung effigies and burned crosses to frighten Blacks who dared to attempt living in white areas. In the early fifties dynamite bombings were added to the mix. Then redlining practices led to the creation of Liberty City in 1937, another Black ghetto. Urban planners subsequently routed the new Interstate 95 right through Overtown, devastating the community; its business center was decimated, and over 30,000 Black citizens were displaced, leaving only 8,000 (Mohl, 331). So called "second ghettos" developed in Opa-Locka and Carol City in the sixties and seventies.

Bennett, Hurston, and James Weldon Johnson are the starry figures in the state's twentieth-century literary pantheon, but the tradition continues today, especially in the work of the Haitian immigrant Edwidge Danticat, whose 2019 *Everything Inside: Stories* makes use of her now-hometown of Miami. Other, (so far) less famous African American writers who feature Florida in their work include Tananarive Due from Tallahassee, who specializes in horror, suspense, and historical fiction. Her 1997 *My Soul to Keep* employs a Florida version of the supernatural. Leonard Pitts, a nationally syndicated columnist for the *Miami Herald*, came out with a thriller in 2015, involving a newspaper background and a white supremacist terror conspiracy. Erica Dawson, in 2018's *When Rap Spoke Straight to God*, garnered national attention for her book-length poem centered on myth, religion, and Black womanhood, one that builds on her Florida roots.

The state has produced a plethora of important nonfiction studies by Black Floridians, particularly those that rehearse the state's African American history, such as Ersula Knox Odom's *African Americans of Tampa* (2014). But perhaps the most spectacular young Floridian writer of late has been Tarell Alvin McCraney, a Yale PhD born in Liberty City. The recipient of a MacArthur "genius" award (among many others), his dramas include *The Brother/Sister* trilogy of plays—*In the Red and Brown Water*, *Wig Out!*, and *Choir Boy*—but most significantly *In Moonlight Black Boys Look Blue*, the basis of the Academy Award–winning film *Moonlight*, which we honor in this collection with two essays. McCraney wrote the screenplay for the movie and was the recipient of the Academy Award for Best Adapted Screenplay. In 2019 he followed this up by writing the screenplay for the film *High Flying Bird*, which was directed by Steven Soderbergh. Because of the keen interest in this film, and its multiple uses of African American Florida, we feature a cluster of essays that assess *Moonlight* from a variety of angles.

• • •

This collection begins with the early days of La Florida, when Spanish settlers brought enslaved Africans to the East Coast. Inevitably, runaways (who would become known as maroons) sought refuge in the tangled swamps and undergrowth surrounding settlements, and this brought them into contact with the then numerous indigenous people of the interior. We are fortunate to have an essay by one of the leading experts on both Native and African Floridians, Jane Landers. She has written extensively on so-called "Black Seminoles," and here considers the complex interaction between the Yamassee people and Black maroons, a relationship that began in South Carolina and continued when the two peoples migrated to Florida. The essay rehearses the early history of Florida's African Americans, especially those who served in the Spanish militia. Both the British in the Carolinas and the Spaniards in Florida employed Native Americans and Africans in their recurring combats; the British invaders killed many indigenous people, wiping out many Native settlements. Landers show how the abuse of the Yamassee in the Carolinas by bands of traders, and the failure of the British to free Black militiamen, led to increased numbers of immigrants from both groups to the lands around St. Augustine. Inevitably, the two peoples mixed, creating a new caste the Spanish termed *mustee*. When abuses of the Natives in Carolina—including enslavement—led to the Yamassee War, enslaved Africans joined their indigenous neighbors against the British and became members of the Yamassee Confederacy; the amalgamated group migrated to Florida, settling in ten towns set out by the Spanish in the periphery of St. Augustine. The conjoined peoples were important elements in the Spanish forces during the War of Jenkins' Ear (1739–48). This moment in Florida history concluded, however, with the British acquisition of Florida through the Treaty of Paris in 1763; the Spanish relocated all subjects, including the mixed Yamasee/African community. Sadly, many of the Yamassee died soon after relocation.

Florida took the starring role in one of the most important African American epics of the nineteenth century, Albery Whitman's *The Rape of Florida* (1882), which also focused on the union of Native and African Americans, as it dramatized the tragic removal of the Seminoles from Florida after the two Seminole Wars (1817–18 and 1835–42). José Felipe Alvergue rereads this long poem as "reparative ontology," concentrating on Whitman's complex merger of poetics and politics. He follows Whitman's tracery of a sylvan paradise, one that sustained and inspired Creeks, Seminoles, and, subsequently, Black Seminoles after the incorporation into that people of maroons escaped from bondage. We come to understand Whitman's deconstruction of white authority and sanctity, as racial outrages erupt during the Seminole wars. "Speech acts of witness" make a forgotten history come alive again. We see how Whitman's astute and unusual use of Spenserian stanzas—formal and regular—enclose a violent and traumatic history, creating a powerful tension that animates every part of the epic. Alvergue shows us Whitman's attempt to make his story specific but ultimately universal. Lasting reverberations of this epic emerge when Alvergue turns to contemporary efforts to diminish minority communities in Florida, a sad parallel to the displacement of ethnic "others" in *The Rape of Florida*. We also become informed of the racial turmoil in the state during the period of the poem's composition, which clearly motivated Whitman; poor white farmers were pitted against a Black majority in northern Florida, while Jim Crow laws were being passed by the state legislature. Again we see these factors compared with displacement efforts of our own time. We conclude by pondering the difficulties of the supposed "happy ending" of the epic, when the heroes Atlassa and Palmecho embrace their roles in Mexican exile, but we also are reminded of the power of the epic's rehearsal of a dark chapter in Florida and national history as a reparative moment in the reconstruction of settler-colonial annals.

Paul Ortiz reconstructs an address he gave in Ocoee, Florida, on the hundred-year anniversary of the terrible massacre of Afro Floridians that took place there on Election Day, November 3, 1920. As he recounts, Zora Neale Hurston wrote a short account of the tragedy for the Federal Writers' Project publication *Florida Guide*; but it wasn't printed, because she told the history from the viewpoint of the town's Black citizens, as does Ortiz. When they tried to vote, there were fights, resulting in whites taking July Perry, a Black man accused of murdering two white men, from jail and lynching him. The mob burned the Black community down and killed thirty-five residents. Ortiz links this event with others occurring in other southern states as Blacks tried to cast ballots. He also situates the massacre within national and international contexts. As he points out here, the tragedy has a part to play in vital educational programs today, in a time of resurgent racism and voter suppression. Ortiz's background as a widely published historian of the Florida civil rights struggle, and the current director of the Samuel Proctor Oral History Program at the University of Florida, makes him an ideal choice for reconstruction

of the event, its reverberations, and its relation to the age of Black Lives
Matter. Ortiz begins this reconstruction by going back to the work of Lester
Dabbs, W. E. B. Du Bois, and later historians who led the way in uncovering
the many racial conflagrations of the American 1920s, when the ballot was
jealously guarded by both the Klan and myriad numbers of ordinary white
citizens, many of them prosperous merchants who feared competition. But
the story of the massacre has to include the determined and brave work of
the African American voter registration movement that emerged after World
War I, which involved Black Floridians from every economic and educational
level. This was a prefiguration, Ortiz shows us, of similar movements in the
1960s, but it was strengthened by a rich heritage of Black resistance that began
with escapes from bondage during the Seminole Wars. Ortiz links legendary Florida African Americans such as Mary McLeod Bethune, James Weldon
Johnson, and A. Philip Randolph with the unsung heroes of Ocoee such as
July Perry and Moses Norman.

After Zora Neale Hurston, Florida's most notable Black writer of the
twentieth century clearly is James Weldon Johnson of Jacksonville. The son
of a West Indian mother, he always understood the strong Caribbean heritage of his native state. It has been argued that his monumental novel *The
Autobiography of an Ex-Colored Man* (1912) constitutes the opening salvo of
the fabled Harlem Renaissance. Noelle Morrissette takes us back to Johnson's
upbringing alongside his brother Rosamond, who became a celebrated composer, often enlisting his brother for lyrics. She traces their engagement with
what she terms Jacksonville's "cultures of talk" in their youth, which led to
Johnson's early poetry. These poems make copious use of the tropical landscape (especially his "Ode to Florida") that informed his life for his first thirty
years (which included college in Atlanta), before a "near-lynching" drove him
to New York, where he participated in both the literary life of Harlem and
the more political racial uplift efforts of the NAACP; political appointments
in the Caribbean; and finally, a professorship at Nashville's Fisk University.
Morrissette takes us back to his early years in Florida, and his important men-
torship under the brilliant intellectual Thomas Osmond Summers, a white
surgeon who was also a poet. We see the usually overlooked cosmopolitanism of the international port of Jacksonville, especially the rich Cuban sector,
which exposed Johnson to Latino culture and language and to the resentment of Caribbean immigrants of their racial typecasting in their new home.
Morrissette shows us how Johnson's Floridian identity shaped not only *The
Autobiography* but many of his other works and activities, particularly his
approach to his consul duties in Nicaragua and Venezuela, and his experiences with the American occupation of Haiti, so fraught with racial and

economic oppression. Morrissette concludes with a focus on Johnson's concept of *badinage* and its effect on his later writings, and his late fascination with Black versions of the epic. In a link with the essay in this volume on Albery Whitman, we see Johnson's rapt reading of that work as a key example of the African American epic. Finally, we are pointed to the power and range of Johnson's actual autobiography, *Along This Way*, and his meditative *Black Manhattan*, both intent on providing the epic sweep of African American cultural and social history.

Readers here will be surprised to see Belinda Wheeler's essay on the brilliant Harlem Renaissance poet Gwendolyn Bennett (1902–1981), who was born in Texas but lived most of her life in Pennsylvania and New York. She published poems, articles, reviews, and short stories in New York, and garnered a number of fellowships. While there, she grew close to other writers of the period, and edited selections of their work in various publications. Perhaps second only to her achievement as a poet, she wrote a celebrated column for *Opportunity*, "The Ebony Flute."

However, as Wheeler reveals, Bennett moved with her new husband Alfred Jackson to Eustis, Florida, as a newlywed in 1928, after her Harlem literary life. In the couple's move to Florida, Bennett was hoping to reconnect with her Southern roots. She had every reason to be hopeful; her husband had just graduated from Howard Medical School, and she had compiled an impressive résumé. Alfred Jackson was from Florida, and they would be reunited with his mother, who adored Bennett. The move was likely encouraged by Zora Neale Hurston, who was tireless in singing the praises of her native state. And indeed, their first year was prosperous and happy. Soon, however, their income decreased, and Bennett was more aware of overt racism, especially when she learned details about the notorious Ocoee Massacre. Her dismay over the substandard segregated Black schools led her to more activist writing, the details of which emerge in Wheeler's chapter.

Wheeler shows us the mounting indignities the young couple suffered because of their race, despite their education and refinement; they learned the "new South" was still the "old." A Ku Klux Klan raid on their home terrified them and led to one of Bennett's most powerful essays. Wheeler takes us through the collateral damage of a fruit-fly infestation, which affected Jackson's practice, and the crushing effect of the Depression on Florida Blacks. We see how Bennett's traumatic Florida years generated a sea change in both her overall attitude and writing focus, one that led to an active and productive educational career once she returned north, her divorce and second marriage, and a return to poetry. These late poems were never published, but Wheeler shows us how politically and socially focused they were, far more so than her earlier work; they have an international thrust, as in the poems dealing with the Spanish Civil War. These changes, we see, can be traced to the eye-opening experiences she encountered in the Sunshine State. This essay is an ideal accompaniment to Wheeler's edited collection, *Heroine of the Harlem Renaissance and Beyond: Gwendolyn Bennett's Selected Writings*.

One of the key moments in the documentation of African American culture at every level came during the Depression, when many Black writers participated in the Federal Writers' Project. Pamela Bordelon's essay takes us through that exciting time when the national government provided unprecedented opportunities for African American participation in a well-funded effort to hold a mirror up to the myriad cultures of the United States. As Bordelon puts it, this was in effect a nation in search of its roots, and many of the writers hired to do that turned out to be Black. She takes us through the launch of the program and then turns to two key figures who played critical roles in the Florida Federal Writers' Project: the educator Mary McLeod Bethune and the anthropologist/writer Zora Neale Hurston. We learn about Bethune's burning desire to revolutionize the education of Black students in Florida, her slow but steady building of what became Bethune-Cookman Institute, and her rise to prominence, culminating in a valuable friendship with first lady Eleanor Roosevelt and a role as head of the "Black Cabinet." She and other highly placed Black leaders fought the exclusion of many qualified Black writers from the FWP, leading to the creation of the Black Writers Units. The stunning collection of oral histories these groups created became a precious archive of slavery and Reconstruction. Fanning out from Jacksonville, these Black researchers located witnesses in all the former plantation areas of the state. Their work found a receptive and appreciative supporter in their supervisor, Carita Doggett Corse, a white historian who had done research with the formerly enslaved herself. Bordelon details the interactions between Corse and the writers, and the important white folklorist John Lomax; his son Alan would establish a close relationship with Hurston.

Bordelon also shows us the work of Martin Richardson, who documented the lives and jobs of Black Floridians; he and other Florida writers provided a key element of the proposed volume on this group. Tragically, it was only published in 1993, long after most of the informants and interviewers had passed on, partly because these writers—especially Richardson—did not omit the harsh working conditions and racist atmospheres many of the workers had to endure.

Anyone who thinks of Florida's literary legacy starts with the dazzling Zora Neale Hurston, the pride of Eatonville. Folklorist, anthropologist, choreographer, actress, photographer, reporter, and above all creator of brilliant novels, stories, plays, musicals, a memoir, and essays, Hurston truly did, as her mother urged her, "jump at the sun." In the thirties, however, Hurston, like other writers, was desperate for work, and she found it in the Federal Writers' Project. Already the published author of two novels and a folklore collection, she had honed her skills as an interviewer, and relished this new work. Her contributions included her analysis of the overall nature of Black folklore and influences from the Caribbean. Unfortunately, Corse eliminated Hurston's essays from the draft, and they were not included in the version ultimately published in 1993, *The Florida Negro*. Bordelon depicts Hurston's mutually profitable work with the white folklorist Benjamin Botkin, an admirer of the FWP and its focus on Black culture. Botkin would go on to publish the seminal anthology of slave narratives, *Lay My Burden Down* (1945). He inspired Hurston's "Proposed Expedition into the Floridas." Bordelon also reveals the parallel work Paul Diggs, a tireless researcher of Black life histories who would go on to become an important social worker in Lakeland. Both of them, however, had to leave the program after eighteen months, a rule that short-circuited many other fine contributors to the effort.

Hurston's ethnography again and again returned her to Polk County, then a rural enclave that was home to multitudes of Black workers, particularly in the booming lumber industry. She made good use of the lying sessions, juke joint antics, and raucous, sometime dangerous parties and dances in her ethnographic study *Mules and Men* (1935). In 1944 she completed *Polk County*, a three-act play (ostensibly with the help of a white writer, Dorothy Waring) that was never produced in her lifetime. It has come to the fore recently, however, in Jean Lee Cole and Charles Mitchell's anthology, *Zora Neale Hurston: Collected Plays*. The production of *Polk County* in 2002 at Arena Stage in Washington, DC, received mixed reviews; two years later, productions of the play by the Berkeley (California) Repertory Company and Princeton (New Jersey)'s McCarter Theatre both garnered raves. It subsequently has been produced across the nation at a variety of regional theaters. Genevieve West's essay in this collection brings renewed attention to one of Hurston's most impressive plays, asserting that Zora reverses the perspective of her work in *Mules and Men*, where she, as anthropologist, examines backwoods culture. In *Polk County*, however, the gaze is on the ethnographer, whose methods are apparent in the new immigrant to Polk County, Leafy. In this reading, race is subservient to issues of region, class, and performance partly because, with one exception, all the characters are Black. In West's reading, Hurston is rethinking the teachings of her Columbia instructors, Franz Boas and Ruth Benedict, as she comes to a new conception of the "gaze" and agency. Building on the work of Daphne

Lamothe and Mwenda Ntarangwi's *The Reversed Gaze*, West takes us back to Benedict's *Patterns of Culture*, stating that in *Polk County* Hurston in effect is "talking back" to that study.

Turning from focused attention on key Black Floridians, Joyce Marie Jackson's "African American and West Indian Folklife in South Florida" concentrates on communal patterns and the creativity of the state's African Americans, especially after it became enriched by the influx of people of color from the wider hemisphere, particularly from the Caribbean islands. Jackson acquaints us with religious customs in the Black communities of the state, delineating the many denominations and their glorious musical traditions, particularly gospel, but encompassing many other ensemble singing units. As she notes, African American Floridians have contributed forcefully to both secular and sacred musical traditions of our nation, from field hollers to blues and jazz, generating memorable "star" singers such as Charles Wright and Alice Daye, along with stellar groups and nightclub venues. On a more mundane level, women in the various communities developed striking domestic art, particularly quilting, but also culinary traditions unique to the state and based on local produce. Soap, medical remedies, and other domestic creations receive their due from Jackson as well.

Just as valuably, Jackson goes back to the 1890s to resurrect the first large immigration from the islands, when numbers of Bahamians came to South Florida. bringing their own forms of folklore, cuisine, music, and oral histories. Jackson, a musicologist, excels in illustrating the rich musical legacy of the mixture of Black cultures in South Florida. Reggae, calypso, soca, mento, soul, funk, and steel bands receive their due, as do memorable performers of these discrete traditions. Along the way, Jackson notes the fusion in these forms of European and African elements, which found expansion and innovation in Florida after the migrations from abroad. The patterns of call and response, syncopation, and percussion, all originally emerging during slavery, are shown to have developed means for social and political commentary.

Jackson is also a leading folklorist, and she proves attuned to the strongly narrative nature of these oral cultures, where storytelling reigns as an art form. We find parallels between the Anansi/spider trickster tales of Jamaica and the moral lessons taught during slavery through animal tales involving trickster rabbits, foxes, and wolves.

A fine cook herself, Jackson takes us through the varieties of foodways in Black communities of South Florida, including the establishment of celebrated West Indian restaurants, particularly in Miami. While Jamaican eateries are the best known, Tobago and other islands have played a role in this cuisine as well.

A native and longtime resident of Louisiana, Jackson has been especially attentive to the carnival traditions of the Caribbean that were brought to South Florida in the late nineteenth century. She details in particular the heritage from Jamaica and Trinidad, and the history of annual festivals such as the Miami/Bahamas Goombay Celebration and the Junkanoo tradition from the Bahamas, all of which bear a relationship to the more famous Black traditions of Mardi Gras in South Louisiana.

We find an intriguing and original take on Florida's curious role as foundation for art in Taylor Hagood's provocative contribution, "Negotiating Kitsch and Race in Florida Writing and Art: Hurston, the Highwaymen, and Duval-Carrié," a piece that can profitably be read in conjunction with Gary Monroe's essay here on the Highwaymen. Hagood begins by reminding us that the name "Florida" conjures up images that are both beautiful and hideous, which sometimes "congeal" in what he sees as "kitsch," the preeminent manifestations of which turn up in tawdry tourist souvenirs but in other forms as well.

No one until now has related Hurston to the Highwaymen, those largely self-taught artists who hawked their homemade Florida landscapes door to door, or sometimes, from the trunks of their cars. Hagood situates kitsch as close to camp and often opposed to modernism. Kitsch is usually seen as bogus art that seeks an immediate and often superficial emotional reaction; thus, it usually involves stereotypes of various forms. But Hagood deconstructs this stance, which was created by elite white arbiters of culture, pointing to the ways in which genuine and often valuably aesthetic art created by African Americans has been all too often cast in the trashbin of "poor taste" by elite cultural referees. It was inevitable that Florida's African American culture would wind up in kitsch created by white art hustlers, in the form of grinning mammy cookie jars, dolls, and salt and pepper shakers. Those objects, however, had a function; paintings do not. The twenty-six Highwaymen artists, influenced by the success of the Florida landscape painter Albert "Beanie" Backus and his inclusion of nostalgia in his renditions, appealed to the senses, with dreamy landscapes, sunsets, flora, and vibrant color. The lack of humans in most of the paintings foreclosed any competition with the depictions of nature. The only fauna emerging in the renditions were birds. Ingeniously, Hagood links these patterns with those of Zora Neale Hurston's masterwork, *Their Eyes Were Watching God*, which he sees as flirting with kitsch but using it as a starting point for deeper presentations of existence and identity. Hagood dares to suggest that the famous significations of the novel constitute a kind of kitsch, in their appeal to basic emotions. Hagood follows this with an ingenious rereading of Hurston's most famous short story, "The Gilded Six-Bits," which features multiple examples of kitsch but winds up probing the deepest of doubts and emotions. He concludes, first by going to Hurston's study of the folk cultures—especially vodun and obeah—that are present respectively in the Haiti and Jamaica depicted in her increasingly important study, *Tell My Horse*. On both islands, cheap knockoffs of Catholic saints are tied to profound interaction with corresponding *lwas* of the African religions.[1]

The essay's final turn is to the Haitian-born but transplanted to Miami artist Edouard Duval-Carrié. Hagood employs a long quotation from this figure to illustrate a negotiation with kitsch that arguably has led to art (often paintings employing collage) that comment subversively on contemporary society and politics. These assemblages, Hagood argues, seduce with surface kitschlike appeal, but closer attention to details creates the commentary to which I have just alluded. Thus, we see how numerous African American artists have employed Florida's too often stereotyped images as a lure into "the disturbing and even frightening."

Hagood's essay makes a good starting point for Gary Monroe's chapter on the Highwaymen. The leading expert on this group of painters, Monroe provides us with a detailed history of the origin of the group, which tells us a great deal about popular art, Florida history of the fifties and sixties, and the ways in which ordinary African Americans began to accelerate their participation in American consumer production and sales. We see the shift in the kinds of tourists the state attracted, and the ways in which emerging patterns in white regional art—as in the paintings of A. E. Backus—were transformed and often, invigorated, by Black artisans. Monroe takes us through the productions of the twenty-six members of this guild, who overall created many thousands of quickly painted landscapes. We learn of the growing sales territory of the painters, their interaction with both locals and tourists, and of Monroe's early and developing interest in the Highwaymen, which grew out of his own art education and career as a photographer; he came to feel a kinship with the Highwaymen, and their stance, which he shared, as outsiders in terms of "mainstream" art. After decades of publishing about the group, Monroe has come to appreciate their relevance to environmental issues, to the civil rights movement, and to the eternal preoccupation of art with the sublime. Controversially, Monroe asserts that these paintings are not "Black Art," for they were created for a white consumer clientele. He then zeroes in on the specifics of the paintings, and in particular, on the achievement of the figure usually regarded as the leading contributor to the legacy, Alfred Hair, who was tragically gunned down at the age of twenty-nine.

Monroe closes his history by speculating on the various responses over the years to the paintings, factoring in nostalgia, romanticism, commercialism, the reaction of various critics—from the ordinary public to the Smithsonian—and the ways in which the paintings appeal by editing out "ugly features of modern life" in search of an affordable art that can "soothe, elevate, and yet also provide a transcendent concept of a very real and unusual tropical realm."

Simone A. James Alexander gifts us with an engrossing interview with one of today's most electrifying writers, the Haitian American Edwidge Danticat, who relocated to Miami in 2002. Born in Haiti, she grew up in New York, graduating from Barnard College and earning an MFA from Brown. Since 2012, however, she has mainly lived in Florida, and has taught on occasion at the University of Miami. Living there, she states, has brought her closer to her Haitian heritage, through living in "little Haiti." In one of the memorable lines in this chapter, Danticat declares "Little Haiti is what's possible when people plant new roots and try to create a community for the next generation to call home." Significantly, we learn of her adoration of Zora Neale Hurston, whose Florida/Black imaginary has now become hers as well. But the main reason for her relocation to Miami was her marriage to Fedo Boyer, a teacher who has been very involved with the immigrant Haitian community there. While Alexander certainly prompts Danticat to talk about her art, much of the conversation here focuses on the problems of income inequality, racial prejudice, and contrasting group cohesion and creative spirit. In light of this volume's title, Danticat provides a strong sense of the Florida imaginary of Black people, and she rightly equates it with the Caribbean imaginary, especially in her rapt tribute to Hurston's treatment of her native island applauding Hurston's research in Haiti for *Tell My Horse*; Danticat states, "She knew my home." An additional link between them: Hurston was the first African American woman to graduate from Barnard, also Danticat's alma mater.

One of the most moving portions of this interview comes from the writer's discussion of death—particularly that of her mother—and of the ways it intersects with Hurston's description of her mother's passing in *Dust Tracks on a Road*. But there are also reflections on the joy of the wake, so similar, Danticat notes, to the Irish form of that ritual.

Many have commented on Florida's unusual poetics of tropical space. This aspect certainly pertains to the lush foliage, many bodies of water, the surrounding sea, the climate—but all of these elements play a role in the state's urban centers as well, particularly in Miami. This emerges powerfully in the celebrated Barry Jenkins film *Moonlight* (2016), which won the Academy Award for Best Picture in 2017. Perhaps no other popular entertainment has concentrated so poignantly on the Black Florida imaginary since the glory days of the television program *Miami Vice*, which costarred the magnetic Black actor Philip Michael Thomas. Delia Malia Konzett's essay builds a foundation for her take on this film by foregrounding the racial and cultural history it represents. As she demonstrates, *Moonlight*, among other things, "articulates . . . a new global context of denationalization and deterritorialization." Her exploration of the history and present of Liberty City's projects reveals a global crossroads, where Haitians, Bahamians, and people of color from all over the hemisphere intersect. Konzett helps us appreciate Jenkins's adroit mixture of popular music, queer Blackness, and the cultural disconnects suffered by Black youth. But she is equally attentive to the aesthetic constructs and beauties of the film. While charting our perception of the innovations wrought here, she links the narrative to roots in slavery and what she calls the "culture of poverty" so often depicted in the past in "ghetto drama." She pays attention, too, to the marginal and peripheral nature of the aesthetics of the everyday found in the images. In a productive move, Konzett harnesses Heidegger's concept of "dwelling" to situate the younger Chiron, the film's central character, and to help illuminate the ways in which he seems doomed to experience what Orlando Patterson termed "social death." The construction of a new "dwelling" through the agency of the couple Joan and Teresa leads to the sublime depiction of Chiron's experience at the "Black beach" of Virginia Key with Juan. Konzett's close attention to the camera work in this crucial scene's panorama heightens our appreciation of the union of Blackness and nature as it develops in the picture.

Finally, Konzett helps us trace the reversal of the original negative view of Chiron's drug-addicted mother, which culminates in her reunion with her son in the final section that depicts him as an adult, while also delineating the ways in which Miami and Florida emerge as "a transformative and potentially oral landscape," through "lush and atmospheric cinematography." Readers will also appreciate Konzett's persuasive reading of the final diner scenes, which pull so much of the film's threads together and provide satisfying and realistic closure.

Yet another approach to the film comes in Valerie Babb's contribution, which starts with an interrogation of what it means that both Barry Jenkins and Tarell Alvin McCraney (whose unpublished play became the basis for the film script) are both native sons of Liberty City, the Miami neighborhood portrayed in the film. She relates this to the ways in which Selma, Birmingham, Topeka, and other cities are always summoned up in relation to the momentous civil rights events that occurred in each locale. In Babb's reading, however, Liberty City—which had already been a talisman in terms of Black uprisings in Florida history—now also becomes a nexus for queer civil rights. Her careful reconstruction of the original founding and development of Liberty City offers a valuable complement to the work Konzett does in her contribution to this volume.

One of the key early scenes in the film comes when the young Chiron hides out in an abandoned pastel unit of Liberty Square, the first public housing development built by whites for Black Floridians, "without frills"; yet it was also a site for Black aspiration. Babb takes us through the many ways early residents embellished the space and built community, the subsequent decline of the area through neglect and crime, and finally, the gentrification that began to drive out longtime residents. We understand how the early parts of *Moonlight* reconstruct an earlier period, when drugs were destroying the integrity of a close-knit community, thus providing a turbulent setting for a coming-of-age story, one with a queer twist. Babb, like Konzett, focuses on the scene where Juan teaches Chiron to swim at Virginia Key Beach, whose history Babb details. She then turns to the central scenes of an adolescent Chiron's immersion in a troubled segregated school, where his best friend Kevin is forced into beating Chiron before a crowd of bullies. Further scenes—including Chiron's arrest for exacting revenge—lead to Babb's meditation on the ways in which Jenkins points out how gay Black youth are doubly afflicted by such institutions, which are more like jails than schools.

As Babb reveals, the third and final portion of the film, set in the Caribbean restaurant, examines both the potential and problems of a new, global Miami, which prominently features a variety of Black identities, but in the face of enduring pressures from a still overarching bichromatic racial map that trumps ethnicity. She concludes by showing how *Moonlight* has engendered an ongoing redevelopment of Liberty Square and Liberty City, but one that has an uncertain future in terms of who will be living there, and under what conditions. *Moonlight*, Babb declares, in all these ways sheds light "on the power of Florida as cultural space," one that has continually sparked Black imagination.

John Wharton Lowe turns to Colson Whitehead's 2019 Pulitzer Prize–winning novel *The Nickel Boys*, examining the ways in which Whitehead's acknowledged sources, which come from a notorious actual reform school in North Florida, led to the artist's imaginative and powerful construction of a tropical reform school for boys—really, a prison—whose pleasing façades, set amid an exotic landscape, mask scenes of torture, embezzlement, sexual predation, and all too often death. Fortuitously, the long record of abuse at the actual Dozier "School" ceased after sensational exposures by former inmates and journalists led to its closure; Whitehead accessed many of these documents, some of them book-length and detailed. Lowe rehearses the content and nature of many of these documents, which compel shock but rarely approach eloquence or deep meditation. As Lowe demonstrates, Whitehead in this work eschewed his usual use of the magically real to provide a gripping, visceral, and ultimately transcendent narrative that uses Florida's topography and history to limn a narrative that speaks to recurrent issues of human and social identity, filling the lacunae we find in the investigative exposés that preceded the novel. Employing a varied arsenal of critical tools, Lowe concentrates on the bodies of the inmates, who are variously used as workers, entertainers, tools for embezzlement, and more seriously, targets for the basest instincts of predatory "keepers," in many ways replicating many of the more egregious excesses of slavery. The essay probes the varieties and levels of pain and endurance, the counter-rhythm of resistance and inmate comradery, and the resilience of the human spirit in the face of the basest brutality.

•   •   •

It is our hope that these essays will create an enhanced awareness of the crucial roles African Americans have played in the social, economic, political, and cultural history of one of our most tropical and unusual states, whose varied attractions, warm climate, beaches, and now booming businesses have become an ever more vital arena for a twenty-first-century nation. As the third largest state in population, one always swelled by waves of immigration, and the crucible for many key political events of our time, we need to appreciate, understand, and celebrate the roles that the state's African Americans have played in constructing the Florida imaginary.

Note

1. Several essays in Carlson and Poynor provide valuable commentaries on the long history of African religions that took on new forms and meanings in Florida over the centuries.

Bibliography

Brockell, Gillian. "Florida Set to Block Uncomfortable Themes in Schools. Its History Is Full of Them." *Washington Post*, February 9, 2023. https://www.washingtonpost.com.

Carlson, Amanda B., and Robin Poynor, eds. *Africa in Florida: Five Hundred Years of African Presence in the Sunshine State*. Gainesville: University Press of Florida, 2014.

Colburn, David R., and Jane L. Landers. *The African American Heritage of Florida*. Gainesville: University Press of Florida, 1995.

Dunn, Marvin. *The Beast in Florida: A History of Anti-Black Violence*. Gainesville: University Press of Florida, 2013.

Gannon, Michael, ed. *The New History of Florida*. Gainesville: University Press of Florida, 1996.

Glassman, Steve, and Kathryn Lee Seidel, eds. *Zora in Florida*. Orlando: University of Central Florida Press, 1991.

Hamhamovitch, Cindy. *The Fruits of Their Labors: Atlantic Coast Farmworkers and the Making of Migrant Poverty, 1870–1945*. Chapel Hill: University of North Carolina Press, 1997.

Jones, Maxine D., and Kevin M. McCarthy. *African Americans in Florida*. Sarasota, FL: Pineapple Press, 1993.

Landers, Jane G. "A Nation Divided? Blood Seminoles and Black Seminoles on the Florida Frontier." In *Coastal Encounters: The Transformation of the Gulf South in the Eighteenth Century*, edited by Richmond F. Brown, 99–116. Lincoln: University of Nebraska Press, 2005.

McDonough, Gary W., ed. *The Florida Negro: A Federal Writers' Project Legacy*. Jackson: University Press of Mississippi, 1993.

Mohl, Raymond A. "Race Relations in Miami Since the 1920s." Colburn and Landers, 326–65.

Mormino, Gary R. "Florida Slave Narratives." *Florida Historical Quarterly* 66, no. 4 (1988): 399–419.

Mormino, Gary R. *Land of Sunshine, State of Dreams: A Social History of Florida*. Gainesville: University Press of Florida, 2005.

Wilkerson, Isabel. *The Warmth of Other Suns: The Epic Story of America's Great Migration*. New York: Random House, 2010.

WPA Guide to Florida: The Federal Writers' Project Guide to 1930s Florida. New York: Pantheon, 1984.

CHAPTER ONE

Yamasee-African Ties in Carolina and Florida

Jane Landers

This essay examines the relations Yamasee Indians formed with enslaved Africans in early Carolina, their alliance in the Yamasee War that erupted in 1715, and their subsequent ties in Spanish Florida. English narratives and scholarship about the Yamasee War pay little attention, if any, to Africans in this history.[1] Africans were still relatively few in number in Carolina, and English proprietors, traders, and missionaries were naturally more focused on indigenous geopolitics. The Spanish, however, were long used to reporting on indigenous and African groups in their colonies and produced much more detailed records on each, of both a secular and religious nature. During decades of English oppression in Carolina abused Yamasee and enslaved Africans found common cause, and finally in 1715 they rose together in revolt. When their uprising ultimately failed, they fled southward to seek promised sanctuary in Florida and to become part of the Spanish community.

Spanish officials in St. Augustine considered the Yamasee returning converts and allies and allotted lands on the city's periphery on which the Yamasee chiefs formed new villages. Despite a 1693 order requiring Florida's governors to shelter runaway slaves from Carolina seeking the "True Faith," African veterans of the Yamasee War allies had a different outcome. "Heathens" among the Yamasee retained some Africans as their own slaves until Spanish officials purchased them, incorporated them into Black militia units, and deployed them alongside Indian counterparts on repeated guerrilla raids against Carolina. In 1738 the Yamasee Chief Jospo (as he was known in

Spanish records) joined in the still enslaved Africans' legal efforts to secure a long-sought freedom, which the Spanish Crown ultimately confirmed.[2]

Other scholars in this volume provide important new information on the earliest origins of the Yamasee and their amalgamated nature, the indigenous politics of the Southeast in which they were embroiled, and their initial conversion to Catholicism. Drawing on a variety of sources from colonial Carolina and Spanish Florida, I focus instead on the little-known African engagement with the Yamasee and the implications for both groups. Africans proved valuable allies to the Yamasee during their war and their southward flight to Spanish sanctuary. Once reaching Florida, wartime alliances seem to have fractured, with Christian Yamasee remaining loyal to the African warriors who aided them, and non-Christian Yamasee (infidels, in Spanish terminology) treating them as disposable property, much as the English had.

The Yamasee first begin to appear in European records in the mid-seventeenth century, and scholars theorize they were remnants of earlier groups displaced multiple times across the Southeast by Chichimeco/Westo slave raiders, armed by Virginia traders.[3] In 1670 English planter-proprietors from Barbados launched the new colony of Carolina in Yamasee lands still claimed by Spain, "but 10 days journey" from St. Augustine, further destabilizing the geopolitics of the Southeast. The region's diverse Indian nations were soon swept into a terrible international contest that would ruin most of them.[4]

Although the 1670 Treaty of Madrid recognized England's settlements in Carolina and promised peace, Spanish settlers in St. Augustine were threatened by Protestant competitors on their borders and repeatedly tried to eliminate them. In 1670 Governor Guerra y de la Vega launched the first failed attempt against Carolina, and in 1676 Florida's royal treasurer, Don Juan Menéndez Márquez, commanded a small flotilla of three ships and fourteen *piraguas* in another abortive attempt to eject the "usurpers." That expedition, which probably included both African and Indians, was undone by a storm.[5] Thereafter, more than a century of conflict ensued over the "debatable lands."[6] Anglo-Spanish hostilities trigged waves of migration, raids, and counter-raids that engulfed indigenous groups and African slaves alike in imperial contests for control of the Southeast.

Free and enslaved Africans had formed part of every Spanish exploration of the Southeast and also helped build Spain's earliest Atlantic Coast settlements of St. Augustine and Santa Elena.[7] Carolina's earliest settlers also brought small numbers of enslaved Africans with them from Barbados to begin the hard work of clearing forests and building a new settlement. Over the next years the English colonists periodically imported more "seasoned" slaves from their sugar colonies of Barbados and Jamaica. As their counterparts in

Virginia were also doing, Carolina settlers enslaved local Indians as well. But the increasing demand for labor proved greater than local indigenous supply, and in 1674 the Lords Proprietors of Carolina ordered Andrew Percival to "begin a Trade with the Spaniards for Negroes." No evidence survives that this plan was ever realized.[8]

Given their early numeric weakness, both the English and the Spaniards meanwhile used Indian and African surrogates to do much of their fighting on this unstable Atlantic frontier.[9] This, of course, was standard practice for Spanish colonizers. In 1681 Florida's governor, Juan Márquez Cabrera, followed the lead of shorthanded governors across the Spanish Atlantic and created a new *pardo* (mulatto) and *moreno* (Black) militia in St. Augustine. A 1683 roster of the forty-two men and six officers who composed this unit offer little more than names. Two members are known from other sources. The negro Juan Merino, an ironsmith from Havana sentenced to exile in Florida for some unstated crime, later became free and served as second lieutenant in the Black militia. Merino owned an iron smithing shop and repaired weaponry for the military. Christin de Tapia, a mulatto storeowner in St. Augustine involved in a trial of indigenous counterfeiters, was a corporal in the unit. They and the other Black militia members swore before God and the cross their willingness to serve the king. While their pledge may have been formulaic, it was also an effort to confirm their status as members of the religious and civil community and as vassals of a king from whom they might expect protection or patronage in exchange for armed service.[10] These Black militiamen and their successors proved an important asset for Florida's governors, who benefited from their linguistic and cultural abilities, their knowledge of the frontier, and their military skills.

In 1684 Scottish settlers established Stuart Town, closer still to St. Augustine, and shortly afterward its founder, Lord Cardross (Henry Erskine), wrote to the Lords Proprietors in London, "Wee thought fitt to acquaint you that yesterday some more of the nation of the Yamasees arrived at St. Helena to settle with those of their nation formerly settled there having come from about St. Augustine." This report speaks to the historic geopolitical mobility of the Yamasee as they attempted to navigate between contending European powers.[11]

As Amy Bushnell has noted, the newly settled Yamasee wasted no time in launching a series of attacks on the Spanish missions. In March 1685 they hit the Timucuan village of Santa Catalina de Afuyca, killing eighteen mission residents and taking twenty-five others as slaves back to Carolina. As an added insult, the former converts also sacked the mission's church.[12] [13]

The following August, Governor Juan Márquez Cabrera retaliated for the Yamasee attack on Santa Catalina de Afuyca by sending a Spanish raiding party of fifty-three unnamed Indians and members of St. Augustine's Black militia to attack Carolina settlements.[14] At Governor Joseph Morton's plantation on Edisto Island they recovered the mission ornaments stolen by the Yamasee the previous year and seized "money and plate and eleven slaves to the value of £1500" before turning southward to burn down the Scottish settlement of Stuart's Town on their way home to St. Augustine. It is tempting to wonder if some among the Black and Indian militias might actually have known the enslaved they "liberated" on Edisto.[15] As noted, the repeated cross-currents of raids and migrations past Edisto and across the Southeast acquainted many Blacks and Indians alike with the routes to St. Augustine as well as with the enmity existing between the English and Spanish colonies.[16] Africans enslaved in Carolina also learned, perhaps from St. Augustine's Black militia raiders, that Spanish religious and legal systems offered a path to freedom.

Such valuable information could also have come from the twenty-three Black and mulatto "prizes" sold in Charleston by the French pirate Sieur Nicholas Grammont following his spectacular 1683 raid on the Spanish ports of Vera Cruz and Campeche. Grammont's multiracial crew included a Black corsair, Diego, and a mulatto named Thomas who served as a translator during Diego's interrogation by Governor Juan Márquez Cabrera. Diego and Thomas were the only two from Grammont's crew to survive several days of pitched battles against the Spaniards.[17] They, too, would have understood that freedom was possible among the Spanish. Carolina's "charter generation" of slaves was thus perhaps as diverse as the confederated Yamasees. It did not take long for those Africans ensnared in English chattel slavery to attempt to reach that freedom. And their numbers were growing.

Carolina's earliest settlers brought only small numbers of enslaved Africans from Barbados to begin the hard work of clearing forests and building housing and could not afford to let this policy go unchallenged. Although the Trans-Atlantic Slave Voyages Database lists no voyages from Africa to the North American mainland for the years 1670–1720, reports from Carolina indicate a larger volume of Africans imported into Carolina than earlier supposed. Carolina planters initiated a direct trade with Africa as early as 1697, when Barbadian merchant George Peters sent slaves to Charles Town on his ship *Turtle*, but naval officials there seized them before they could be sold because the captain was a "Scots man borne."[18] In 1699 English traders established Fort James in the Gambia River as their headquarters and Captain W. Rhett brought slaves directly from Guinea to Charles Town aboard the *Providence*.[19] The same year Edward Randolph reported to the Board of Trade and Plantations that there were only 1,100 families in the province and that there were "four negroes to one white man."[20] Over the next years Carolinians also imported more "seasoned" slaves from their sugar colonies of Barbados, Jamaica, Martinique, and Guadeloupe as well as from Madeira, where the Carolinians regularly traded.[21]

Many of the newly imported Africans were destined for work in the dense pine forests and swamps of Carolina, where, encouraged by British bounties on tar, pitch, rosin, and turpentine, settlers early established critical timber and naval stores industries.[22] As Peter H. Wood has shown, early Carolina's "Black pioneers" also became "Cattle-hunters" in the Carolina forests. Africans came to know the Carolina landscape by serving as "path-finders" and linguists for Indian traders. All these occupations allowed even recently imported Africans a certain amount of autonomy and mobility as well as access to Native peoples and their knowledge of the geopolitics of the region.[23]

In 1687 eight Black men and two women, one nursing a baby girl, stole a canoe and fled southward from Carolina to St. Augustine. On reaching the Spanish capital they requested baptism into the "True Faith."[24] Given the multicultural nature of the Gambia region, early missionary reports of Portuguese-speaking slaves in Carolina, and the 1683 arrival of enslaved Blacks from Vera Cruz, it is quite possible that some of the runaways reaching Florida had already been exposed to Roman Catholicism.[25] This group then may have known of the protections and opportunities the Catholic Church offered, possibly even manipulating confessional politics to their own advantage in making a shared request for religious sanctuary.[26] As required of a good Christian ruler, Governor Diego de Quiroga y Losada saw to the African runaways' Catholic instruction, baptism, and marriage and refused to return them to Captain William Dunlop, the Indian trader who arrived from Carolina to recover them the following year.[27]

Spanish officials reported additional groups of Carolina fugitives arriving in St. Augustine in 1688, 1689, and 1690. Carolina's governor, James Colleton, complained that slaves ran "dayly to your towns." Unsure about how to handle the refugees, St. Augustine's officials repeatedly solicited Spain for guidance and finally, on November 7, 1693, Charles II issued a royal proclamation "giving liberty to all . . . the men as well as the women . . . so that by their example and by my liberality others will do the same."[28]

English colonists still trying to stabilize Carolina could not afford to allow this policy to stand unchallenged. With the outbreak of the War of Spanish Succession, or Queen Anne's War, as it is known in English records (1702–1713), Governor James Moore organized a combined force of about 1,000 men, including 600 Yamasee and Lower Creek (Uchise) warriors to wage war against the Spaniards. In September 1702 Governor Moore and Colonel Robert Daniel launched a combined naval and land attack on St. Augustine. Governor José de Zuñiga y Cerda (1699–1706) gathered his multiracial subjects into the Castillo de San Marcos during the fifty-two-day siege, and when support finally arrived from Cuba, Governor Moore burned the town and withdrew. But Moore's raid did produce results; he returned to Carolina with approximately 500 enslaved Timucuans gathered along the coast.[29] Altamaha and other Yamasee chiefs involved in Moore's raid later complained that Carolina trader John Cochran stole their plunder from St. Augustine, and the Commons House of Assembly ordered that they be given powder and shot in compensation.[30]

Although he failed to take St. Augustine, Governor Moore launched repeated raids on the Spanish colony. By 1705 Moore's forces had destroyed thirty-two Native towns, and Florida's new governor, Francisco de Córcoles y Martínez, gathered his remaining 401 indigenous subjects into six new towns: Nuestra Señora de Rosario (Apalaches), Nombre de Dios, Tolomato, Santa María, San Francisco Potano, and Costa (said to be a town of infidels).[31] Spanish accounts from the Archive of the Indies, which may have been inflated, record that thousands of Florida Indians were slaughtered and thousands more became slaves in Carolina or the Caribbean. English sources, which probably sought to minimize the carnage and the profits in their missives to the proprietors in London, put the number of killed and enslaved in the hundreds.[32]

In retaliation for these English raids, French allies joined Governor Francisco de Córcoles y Martínez's triracial forces in a counterattack on Charles Town in August 1706. An English account of the event noted: "In 1706 the Spaniards at St. Augustine joined the French from Martinico in making up a fleet of ten Sail, with eight hundred Men, Whites, Mustees and Negroes, and two hundred Indians, to invade this province." This reference to mustees again recognizes the Indian-African intermixture common in Spanish worlds. Despite some initial success, this retaliatory expedition failed, but once again Blacks and Indians in Carolina would have learned more about the multiracial military of Spanish Florida, and the Anglo-Spanish enmity that offered them an alternative alliance.[33]

Spanish accounts state that Carolina raiders had been incorporating Blacks into their largely Indian forces for some time, but during the course of the War of Spanish Succession, Carolina officials created a militia of 950 "freemen," each of whom was to present for service "one able slave armed with gun or lance."[34] By 1709 Governor Edward Randolph reported to the Board of Trade that there were "four negroes to one white man" in Carolina.[35] This points again to large numbers of enslaved men in the colony, despite their invisibility in the Trans-Atlantic Slave Voyages Database.[36] Unlike the Spanish, however, the Carolinians did not offer freedom for military service or create a militia of free Black men. The newly armed, but still enslaved, Black men Carolina officials sent into service against St. Augustine's Black and Indian militias would surely have recognized the differences between Spanish and Anglo slave systems and that Spanish Florida offered them a refuge. It is tempting to wonder if any of those men later fought in the Yamasee War and subsequently fled to Spanish Florida.

Many studies of the Yamasee War have blamed that conflict on Carolina's Indian traders who exploited the local indigenous groups, enmeshing them in ruinous debt. But the Yamasee had many other complaints as well. The *Journals of the Commissioners of the Indian Trade* reported that in 1711 a number of traders, including Thomas Jones, John Whitehead, Joseph Bryan, Robert Steale, John Palmer, and Barnaby Bull, were all settled in Yamasee lands.[37] The Yamasee filed repeated complaints against these traders with the Carolina Commissioners of Indian Trade but usually to no avail. They charged that John Wright, the Indian agent posted at the paramount Upper Yamasee village of Pocotaligo, on St. Helena Island, forced them to carry burdens, demanded that they build a house for him next to that of the council house, and debauched their young girls.[38] "Lewis King of yr Pocotalligo Town," who Alexander Sweeney theorizes may once have been baptized as Luis, also complained against traders Cornelius MacKarty (*sic*) and Samuel Hilden for "stripping and beating Wiggasay and Haclantoosa, two of his people att one of their playes."[39] The Carolina Commissioners of Indian Trade finally convicted trader John Fraser of misconduct at Pocotaligo for having violently beaten the Tomatly king, but still trader abuses continued. The "Altamahaw King" and several of his warriors complained that trader Alexander Nichols "lately beat a Woman that he kept as his wife so that she Dyed and the child within her . . . he also beat the Chasee King's Wife who is very ill & another Woman being King Altimahaw's Sister." The Yamasee threatened to leave their towns if Nichols were not punished, which led commissioners to issue a warrant for his arrest. But attempts by authorities to try to curb the worst of these abuses were largely ineffective, and the traders lived almost as rulers in their host towns.[40] In an oft-cited complaint the Huspah king reported to Governor Charles Craven: "Mr. Wright said that the white men would come and . . . [fetch] the Yamasees in one night, and that they would hang four of their head men and take all the rest of them for Slaves, and that he would send them all off the Country."[41]

While English traders were abusing and alienating the Yamasee, Governor Francisco de Córcoles y Martínez (1706–1716) was gifting delegations of Yamasee in St. Augustine and attempting to win back Spain's former allies.

Traders living in Yamasee villages noted the visits of the caciques to St. Augustine and the gifts with which they returned.[42] The same traders also lost some of their own slaves to the Spanish sanctuary of St. Augustine. Indian traders Joshua Bryan and William Bray, like William Dunlop before them, tracked their runaway slaves to St. Augustine, but Spanish officials refused to hand them over.[43]

Black slaves continued to run from Carolina, and it was possible they were treated even more brutally by these traders than were the Yamasee. After an alleged slave conspiracy in 1711, Carolinians enacted a harsh new slave code in 1712 that permitted planters to punish slaves using mutilations like castration and amputation, and also execution. Reverend Francis Le Jau, who was sent to Carolina by the Society for the Propagation of the Gospel in Foreign Parts in 1701, documented the abuse from which slaves ran, horrified at some of the tortures and mutilations he witnessed and protested. He reported that one slave from Martinique launched an abortive rebellion and was executed, while others sought divine protection and remedy. Le Jau noted that some of the slaves could read and that one had reputedly received a book from an angel's hand, had heard voices and seen fires and predicted "there would be a dismal time and the moon would be turned into blood."[44]

On April 14, 1715, that slave prophet's dire prediction seemed to come true. In an effort to resolve long simmering tensions and hostilities with their Yamasee trading partners, Carolina's Indian commissioners sent a delegation to Pocotaligo. Among them were the traders William Bray, who had tracked some of his runaway slaves to St. Augustine earlier in the year; Thomas Nairne, Samuel Warner, and John Cochran; and John Wright, against whom the Yamasee had filed numerous complaints. The Yamasee at Pocotaligo received the traders and even feasted with them the night before, but on Good Friday, they launched a well-coordinated attack against their English oppressors. Painted in red and black stripes (for war and death), the Yamasee and other Indians who joined the war killed ninety English traders over the course of the war, including traders John Wright, John Ruffy, and John Cochran, and they tortured Thomas Nairne for three days, burning lightwood splinters under his skin until he expired.[45]

Upon hearing of the massacre at Pocotaligo, Governor Craven sent Colonel John Barnwell and Captain Robert Mackey by water to retaliate. Within a week Governor Craven and a hastily raised force that included 400 Black slaves battled an estimated 500 Yamasee engaged in a "hot engagement" at Sadkehatche town. After heavy fighting Sadkehatche's war captain, Yfallaquisca, and the Yamasee dispersed into the nearby swamps.[46] Soon after, another group of Yamasee attacked a small garrison of about twenty

Carolinians, killing all but one. Captain George Chicken pursued this group and killed several. In late July 1715 the Yamasee launched another offensive, proving, as Steven Hahn argues, that this long war was not over. An estimated five hundred attacked St. Paul's parish, burning some twenty plantations. They also attacked Reverend William Treadwell Bull's parsonage, where they broke the church windows and tore the lining off the pews. These actions by the Yamasee might have been a repudiation of the evangelization efforts of the Society for the Propagation of the Gospel in Foreign Parts, one of their few advocates. But the Yamasee also killed cattle and horses they might have used, which is reminiscent of the millenarian Pueblo Revolt some years earlier, when rebels also sought to erase all evidence of the oppressors.[47] Like Reverend Francis Le Jau, Reverend Bull regarded the Yamasee War as God's punishment for the traders' abuse of the impoverished Yamasee and for the planters' equally horrific abuse of their African slaves.

Recognizing the chance for their own liberation, enslaved Africans living nearby joined in the Yamasee uprising. Unwilling to recognize such agency, Carolinians reported that their slaves had been "taken."[48] Initially it seemed they might succeed in eliminating the English colony. After military reinforcements from Virginia and North Carolina helped turn the tide for the embattled Carolinians, the Yamasees sought refuge among the very Spaniards they had once harried. Yamasee Chiefs Jospo (Huspah) and Yfallaquisca (Perro Bravo) and their African allies fled southward together to Spanish Florida, where they hoped to claim the religious sanctuary others had earlier received. The Reverend Francis Le Jau's letter of October 5, 1715, to the Society for the Propagation of the Gospel in Foreign Parts, reported that the father of the famed Yamasee Prince George, was by that time safe in St. Augustine.[49]

Apparently not recognizing the irony, the Carolinians complained, "Their refusal to Deliver up these slaves has encouraged a great many more lately to run away to that Place, and what is still more Barbrous in ye Spaniards is, that they Suffer ye Yamasees to keep Divers of our white Women & Children as Slaves amongst them of which we have certain intelligence of captive hence by Hugh Brian, confirmed by ye Master of a New York Sloop, who actually saw none but two Children whom ye Spaniards have Got, in order to make good Christians as they call their Proselytes."[50] Perhaps in retaliation for the repeated enslavement of Yamasee women and children, Chief Jospogue had captured Brian, the son of Indian Agent Joshua Bryan, but later released him in an abortive peace effort. The Carolinians reported, "At length his Master, being called the Woospau (Huspah) King, having under his command about Fifteen Men, sent him in to us, to desire a Peace with us."[51]

The Yamasee War once again shifted the indigenous geopolitics of the Southeast, and Spanish documentary sources pick up the Yamasee narrative in Florida. Only a month after the outbreak of the war, and in response to the perceived weakness of the English, Coweta's Chief Brims urged his subjects to switch their allegiance to the Spaniards. He sent a delegation of four chiefs to St. Augustine to relay this offer: Istopoyole, "heathen" cacique of Nicunapa, in the province of Apalachicola; Yfallaquisca, "heathen" war captain of Sadkehatche, in the same province of Apalachicola; Alonso, Christian *mico* and governor of Ocute in Tama; and Gabriel, "heathen" son of the Christian Yamassee, Santiago Sule. On May 28, 1715, they met with Governor Francisco de Córcoles y Martínez, the royal accountant Captain Francisco Menéndez Márquez, and the royal treasurer Don Salvador Garzía at the Nuestra Señora de Tolomato mission. Through translator Antonio Perez Campaña of the Guale nation, who was also able to speak Uchise and Yamasee, Yfallaquisca, known in Spanish records as the "heathen" Perro Bravo, related the reasons for Coweta's political realignment.[52]

Through his interpreter Perro Bravo told the Spanish officials that for more than three years the governor of San Jorge (Charles Town) had taken Yamasee children from their parents and shipped them away to be sold as slaves. Perro Bravo cast the Yamasee slaughter of the English traders at Pocotaligo as proactive self-defense, repeating an oft-cited report the Huspah king had made to Charles Craven that white settlers intended to kill their head men, enslave the rest of the Yamasee, and send them away from their homes."[53] In an interesting inversion of the story told in English narratives, Perro Bravo also stated that English trader William Bray's indigenous wife had alerted the caciques of Sadkehatche and Pocotaligo to this danger.[54] Perro Bravo's account supports William L. Ramsey's supposition that Bray's wife was indigenous, and it is possible, even probable, if Bray's wife had relatives living at Pocotaligo, she did not share Cuffy's warning with her husband. Perro Bravo's account did not mention Cuffy, but as Ramsey notes, since Cuffy or Kofi is an Akan day name for a man born on Friday, the alleged "Indian Cuffy" may well have been one of the Africans allied with the Yamasee Confederacy.[55] William Bray's account from English records stated that because of "his great love for her and her two sisters," a "Yamasee" man warned his wife that the Creeks were going to attack Charles Town, that he would return right before the event, and that "they must goe [sic] immediately to their town," probably either Pocataligo or Sadkehatche. Despite this warning, Bray left for St. Augustine "after some of his slaves." For his supposed loyalty in warning of the forthcoming attack, as Ramsey recounts, Carolina's Commons House of Assembly rewarded "the Indian Cuffy with 10 lbs of Carolina currency and a coat."[56]

Continuing his narrative, Perro Bravo told Spanish officials that, fearing for their own lives, the Yamasee decided to kill the English traders and an Englishman who arrived the next day allegedly bearing their execution orders. Perro Bravo did not name that Englishman nor the person able to read the English letters, but the Spanish reported that the Yamasee were "capaces en la idioma ynglesa por la frequencia del trafico" (capable in English for the frequency of their exchanges).[57] As Reverend Le Jau had earlier reported, some enslaved Africans were also able to read English and may have translated this letter for the Yamasee. Perro Bravo stated that the English governor's letter was also said to divulge his plans to lead troops to Pocotaligo, so the Yamasee hid their women and children inland near the Ysabel River, deployed groups of warriors to lie in wait, and were able to rout the English forces. Perro Bravo added that once the war began, Spanish prisoners "and other blacks and mulattos" as well as some Spanish women held prisoner on English plantations fled to Yamasee towns and subsequently joined their exodus to Spanish Florida.[58] Some of the "blacks and mulattos" may have been the later founders of Gracia Real de Santa Teresa de Mose in Spanish Florida, but I have found no other reference to Spanish women held prisoner by the Carolinians.[59] This reference to Blacks and mulattos confirms Chief Jospo's testimony some twenty years later, that Africans, like other indigenous groups, had been incorporated into the multicultural Yamasee confederacy prior to their removal to Florida. The reputedly warlike Yamasee must have recognized and respected the military skills of these escaped slaves, as did the Spanish, who formed them into frontier militias. In this manner the Mandinga man who became Francisco Menéndez and led the first free Black town in what is today the United States, Gracia Real de Santa Teresa de Mose, escaped enslavement in Carolina.

Governor Córcoles welcomed his new allies with gifts, firearms, and foodstuffs and also sought and received a significant increase in the annual subsidy for Indian gifts.[60] During their parlay Perro Bravo laid eight chamois cords full of knots before the Spaniards, telling them that each knot denoted a town promising to switch allegiance to the Spaniards (a total of 161 towns) and that towns of fewer than 200 persons were not even represented on the cords. Perro Bravo thus offered the Spaniards approximately 32,000 new indigenous allies, and he asked that the cords be sent to the king of Spain as a missive from Chief Brims.[61]

As was customary when Native delegations visited St. Augustine, Yfallaquisca or Perro Bravo and the others were housed among the city residents, and Perro Bravo and his subjects stayed in the house of Sergeant Juan de Ayala y Escovar. In Perro Bravo's retinue were four African "slaves," who after fighting with the Yamasee for several years surely considered that they had liberated themselves. Perro Bravo gifted Sgt. Ayala with one of his Black slaves as compensation for the food and expenses of his stay, but he stated in subsequent complaints that he expected to be paid for the three others.[62] The African Perro Bravo "gifted" to Ayala may have been the most significant of them, later to be baptized as Francisco Menéndez, and the remaining three may have been Menéndez's later subordinates at Mose, Antonio Eligio de la Puente, Francisco Escovedo, and Pedro Graxales, whose names always appear right after his on Spanish village lists.[63]

Spanish officials settled their new Indian allies in ten villages on the periphery of St. Augustine, generally grouping them by language. A census of 1717 conducted by Joseph Primo de Rivera shows that 430 Yamasee were grouped into three villages: Nuestra Señora de Candelaria de la Tamaja, Pocosapa, and Pocotalaca. Chief Jospogue was assigned to Nuestra Señora de Candelaria de la Tamaja along with other Yamasee caciques, while Perro Bravo, now don Francisco Yfallaquisca, ruled the Yamasee village of Pocotalaca (after Pocotaligo).[64]

All did not go smoothly in this resettlement. In December 1716 Chief Jospogue and other chiefs petitioned for Governor Córcoles, their old patron, who had gifted them and treated them with affection (cariño), to be returned to office. The caciques stated that Chief Brims had told them to obey Córcoles and that they did not like either don Pedro de Olivera y Fullana, who served only briefly before dying in 1716, or Juan de Ayala y Escobar, who became interim governor (1716–18). Translating for the recently arrived Chief Jospogue was the Spanish woman María Garzia de Labera (La Vera), who had been captured by unidentified Indians as a little girl and spent more than twelve years living among them. María's captors may have been Yamasee since she translated for Chief Jospogue, but she earned a soldier's plaza (salary) serving as interpreter of five or six indigenous languages.[65]

More complaints from the Yamasee followed. In the fall of 1717 Spanish officials held a hearing at the Mission of Nombre de Dios to investigate the ongoing complaints of the Yamasee cacique Perro Bravo. Present were Father Phelipe Osorio Maldonado, caciques Juan Rodríguez de Espinosa, don Joseph de Fuentes, and Francisco Navarro, and St. Augustine's public notary, Juan Solana. Cacique Bernardo de Yspolea, who headed the nearby village of Nuestra Señora de Guadalupe de Tolomato, composed of remnants of the Yamasee, Guale, Chiluque, and Uchise nations, served as translator at this session. Yspolea was said to speak Perro Bravo's language so may have been Yamasee, but he also spoke good Castilian and could sign his name. Don Bernardo reported that he had heard Perro Bravo say many times that he still had not been paid for the African slaves he had brought into Florida years earlier. Perro Bravo had also told him he had asked Governor Pedro de Olivera y Fullana many times for payment, but because the governor was a friend of Ayala's, Ayala was not made to pay. Perro Bravo threatened that if this debt were not satisfied, he would kill the slaves and that he had many other lands in which he could live. Next, Spanish officials also took the testimony of cacique don Joseph de Fuentes at Ayachin, where Perro Bravo had a *bohio* and slept although he was by then cacique of the mission town of Capuaca. Don Joseph swore on the cross and by God to tell the truth and repeated don Bernardo's account, adding that Ayala also owed Perro Bravo for an arroba and a half weight silver bar.[66] Finally, on August 31, 1718, in the presence of Father Osorio, cacique don Joseph de Fuentes, and various soldiers and residents of St. Augustine, the then acting governor of Florida, Juan de Ayala y Escovar, paid Perro Bravo the 600 pesos owed him in corn and liquor.[67]

Among the slaves whom Perro Bravo claimed and for whom the Spanish paid were Francisco Menéndez and his Mandinga wife, who had fled with him from Carolina three years earlier. Spanish slavery was not what either sought, but it would be different than the slavery they had experienced in Carolina. And although their purchase by the governor seems to have made them Crown slaves, Menéndez and his wife must have lived for some time with Ayala since Menéndez's wife took the name Ana Maria de Escovar.[68]

Thus, the soon to be Spanish governor acquired valuable intermediaries.

Meanwhile, in Carolina an ever-growing African population and the fear that slaves might ally with Spaniards in Florida led planters to obsess about slave rebellion. Carolinians discovered alleged slave plots in 1711 and 1714, leading the Colonial Assembly in that year to establish a new Act for Governing Negroes that read: "the number of negroes do extremely increase in the Province, and through the afflicting providence of God, the white persons do not proportionately multiply, by reason whereof, the safety of the said Province is greatly endangered." The new act placed duties on all slaves imported from Africa "twelve years and upward."[69] Despite their efforts at control, in 1720 the townspeople of Charles Town uncovered a major slave conspiracy in which at least some of the participants "thought to gett to Augustine." Fourteen got as far as Savannah before being captured and executed.[70] In 1724 ten more runaways reached St. Augustine, assisted again by English-speaking Yamasee Indians, and they stated they knew that the Spanish king had offered freedom for those seeking conversion and baptism.[71]

Following the precedent first set in 1687, in 1725 Florida's new governor, Antonio de Benavides (1718–1734), offered to purchase the runaways for two hundred pesos apiece, and he sent Don Francisco Menéndez Márquez and Captain Joseph Primo de Rivera to Charles Town to negotiate with their

owners, who angrily rejected the offer as insufficient.[72] Although Governor
Benavides wrote to his superiors to determine if sanctuary was still in force,
since the runaways had appeared during a time of truce between Spain and
England, as often happened, he received no reply, and after the English threatened to reclaim their lost slaves by force, Benavides sold the unlucky fugitives
at public auction to the leading creditors of the St. Augustine treasury. In this
way don Francisco Menéndez Márquez acquired the Mandinga namesake for
whom he served as godfather during Catholic baptism.[73]

Don Francisco Menéndez Márquez was sent on repeated diplomatic and
military missions to Carolina, and it seems likely he would have taken with
him the slave who had fought his way through that terrain and who also knew
so well the Yamasee and English geopolitics. In 1725 he was sent to Charleston
to demand the destruction of Fort King George and the following year
Governor Benavides named don Francisco Menéndez's slave and namesake
the captain of St. Augustine's Black militia. Thereafter the Mandinga Captain
Francisco Menéndez led important military engagements against the English
from whom he had fled, each of which would have enhanced his status in the
Spanish community.[74]

In 1728 the Spanish governor named Menéndez the captain of the slave
militia, and the same year planters near Stono "had fourteen Slaves Runaway
to St. Augustine." Governor Arthur Middleton of Carolina complained to
London that the Spaniards not only harbored their runaways but had "found
a New way of sending our own slaves against us, to Rob and Plunder us."[75]
Yamasees from St. Augustine joined the former slaves in these operations, and
Middleton reported that "Six of our Runaway slaves and the rest Indians" in
two canoes attacked near Pon Pon in the fall of 1727 and carried away white
captives. A second account of that raid added that "Ten Negroes and fourteen
Indians Commanded by those of their own Colour, without any Spaniards
in company with them" had been responsible and that they had also taken
one Black man and a mulatto boy back to St. Augustine. That year Florida's
multiracial raiders hit again at a plantation on the Edisto River, carrying away
seven more slaves.[76] In fact, Governor Antonio de Benavides had offered thirty
pieces of eight for every English scalp and one hundred pieces "for every live
Negro" the multiracial raiders brought back to St. Augustine.[77]

The repeated raids from Florida triggered an English response, and in 1728
Colonel John Palmer led a retaliatory attack against St. Augustine. By this
time the Yamasee village of Pocotalaca had moved from a location at Ayamon,
six leagues south of St. Augustine, to "the distance of a rifle-shot," and people were living in their *bohios* only during the day and sleeping within the
Castillo at night. Palmer's forces, which included approximately two hundred

Indians of unstated nation, set fire to the mission village of Nombre de Dios and "did some nasty damage to the statues" of the village church.[78] On that occasion the Black militia led by Captain Francisco Menéndez proved one of the city's most effective defense forces. By this time Governor Antonio de Benavides was so convinced of the Black militia's ability that in 1733 he proposed sending the runaways north to foment rebellion in Carolina and, once again, planned to pay them for English scalps, but the Council of the Indies rejected this design.[79] The Spanish Crown commended the enslaved forces for their bravery in the 1728 invasion and in 1733 also issued a new decree reiterating its offer of freedom to runaways from Carolina.[80]

Despite his repeated military service, Captain Francisco Menéndez, however, was still a slave and so he persisted in his efforts to achieve the freedom repeatedly promised by the Spanish king. On behalf of his community, he presented several petitions to the governor and to the auxiliary bishop of Cuba, who toured Florida in 1735, but uncertain of the legalities, these officials wrote to Spain seeking guidance, as had Governor Benavides, and Menéndez and his community remained enslaved.[81]

The Africans' fortunes changed in 1737 with the arrival of the new governor, Manuel de Montiano, and the advent of renewed hostilities with the English. Once more Captain Francisco Menéndez solicited freedom for himself and others in a petition that listed thirty-one individuals unjustly enslaved, including some who had been taken to Havana, and the names of the persons who claimed ownership over them. This time Menéndez's petition was supported by another from an indigenous ally, the Yamasee chief Jospo. Jospo claimed to be the chief who had led the Yamasee uprising against the British in 1715 and stated that he and the other Yamasee chiefs "commonly" made "treaties" with the slaves. The use of the terms *allies* and *treaties* implies Yamasee recognition of the slaves' autonomy and utility. Jospo confirmed that Menéndez and three other Africans (probably those who at baptism became Antonio Eligio de la Puente, Francisco Escovedo, and Pedro Graxales) had fought bravely with him until they were ultimately defeated and headed to St. Augustine, hoping to receive the Christian sanctuary promised by Spain. Jospo also testified that in St. Augustine Perro Bravo had betrayed the Africans by selling them into slavery, but Jospo excused Perro Bravo, saying that as a "heathen" he knew no better. Instead, Jospo blamed the Spaniards who bought the unlucky Blacks, who in his estimation had been patient and "more than loyal."[82]

Governor Montiano was expecting war with England at any moment, and the combined petitions and stated alliance of Africans and Yamasees must no doubt have made an impression on a governor in need of their services. He wisely chose to investigate. After reviewing all relevant documentation on the issue, on March 15, 1738, Governor Montiano granted unconditional freedom to all fugitives from Carolina. The powerful men, like the royal accountant don Francisco Menéndez who had received the slaves in payment for loans to the cash-strapped government, vehemently protested their emancipation, but Governor Montiano ruled that the men had ignored the royal determination expressed in repeated decrees, and therefore all deals were null and void and all the enslaved were free.[83] After reviewing Governor Montiano's actions, the Crown approved and ordered that not only all the Blacks who had come from Carolina to date "but all those who in the future come as fugitives from the English colonies" should be given prompt and full liberty in the name of the king. Further, so that there be no further pretext for selling them, the royal edict should be publicly posted so that no one could claim ignorance of the ruling.[84]

Following the preexisting model for Indian towns, Governor Montiano assigned the newly emancipated Spanish subjects lands two miles north of St. Augustine and recognized the Mandinga Captain Francisco Menéndez as leader of the new free Black town of Gracia Real de Santa Teresa de Mose. Further, in his official correspondence the governor described the almost one hundred residents of the new town, composed of nations as diverse as Mandinga, Carabalí, and Congo, as Menéndez's "subjects."[85] Menéndez was, in effect, the cacique, or natural lord, of Mose. His newly freed subjects promised to be "the most cruel enemies of the English" and to spill their "last drop of blood in defense of the Great Crown of Spain and the Holy Faith," and Captain Francisco Menéndez headed the new Mose militia that would carry through on that vow.[86]

The War of Jenkins' Ear (or the Guerra del Asiento) broke out in 1739, raged through 1742, and only concluded in 1748. Throughout this era of conflict African and Indian militias proved crucial assets to the defense of the Spanish colony. Together they patrolled the frontier, gathering information on the encroachments of hostile English and Indian attackers, rounding up cattle and horses, and herding them to the safety of Anastasia Island. Governor Montiano offered them rewards of twenty-five pesos for every Indian or English person captured. On some of the larger expeditions don Pedro Lamberto Horruitiner commanded twenty-five Spanish cavalry, an equal number of Spanish infantry, thirty Indians, and "free blacks of the fugitives from the English colonies." On others, don Romulado Ruiz del Moral commanded twenty-five Spanish cavalrymen, twenty-five Indians, and twenty-five free backs. But the Indian and Black militias also operated independently, and among the most active Indian leaders were the caciques Chislala, Juan Savina, Geronimo, and Juan Ygnacio de los Reyes, of Nuestra Señora de la Concepción de Pocotalaca.[87]

Reyes offers an example of the cultural exchanges taking place in Spanish Florida in these years. After his return from a successful mission to assess Charleston's defenses, Governor Montiano ordered Reyes to Havana to report to the captain general, but "Juan Ygnacio having declared to me that he had made a certain promise or vow, in case of happy issue, to Nuestra Señora de la Caridad de Cobre, I was unwilling to put him aboard with violence, and I let him go at his own free will to present himself to Your Excellency." La Caridad de Cobre was and still is the Black patron saint of Cuba, whose miraculous discovery was attributed to two Cuban Indians and an African who were fishing together, and was also the syncretic symbol for Ochun, the Yoruba goddess of fertility. That Reyes prayed to her on such an important issue offers tangible proof of the cultural assimilation between Africans and Yamasees on the Florida frontier.[88]

Over the next two decades, Africans and Indians reinforced their military, political, and sociocultural ties, some of which had origins stretching back to Carolina. They also formed families together. In 1745 Francisco Buenaventura y Texada, the bishop of Tricale, reviewed St. Augustine's ecclesiastical records from 1640 to 1707 for examples of racial intermarriage, both between Spaniards and Indians and between Indians and Africans. Father Pedro Lorenzo de Asevedo's notations show that Catholic marriages between men of African descent and indigenous women become more frequent after 1670. In 1690 Francisco Joseph, the drummer and Black slave of Captain Antonio de Argüelles, married Micaela, a Native of Mayaca. The following year another of Argüelles's slaves, Pedro Aponte, married María Lucia, a Native of Santa Catalina in Guale, and in 1702 Juan de los Santos, the slave of Ayudante Geronimo Rexidor, married Marta Maria, described as an "yndia ladina y natural de Guale." The priest reported many other examples, concluding approvingly that by "marrying Spaniards, blacks or mulattos, slowly their children will stop being Indians" and more easily enter into the "true knowledge of the mysteries of our Catholic faith."[89]

As newly introduced Africans or *bozales* escaped from Carolina or Georgia to claim religious sanctuary in Florida in the 1750s, Spanish officials considered then "new Christians" in need of evangelization, as Indians continued to be. In 1752 Governor Fulgencio García de Solís reestablished the free Black town of Gracia Real de Santa Teresa de Mose, near its original location, and Father Andres de Vilches, formerly assigned to the Yamasee village of Pocotalaca, now worked to evangelize these newcomers.[90]

Although Florida continued to attract runaway slaves from Carolina, its Indian populations continued to dwindle in the final years of Spanish dominion. Spanish censuses of 1752, 1759, and 1763 record this decline and the resulting amalgamation of Indian towns. To illustrate, by 1759 the Yamasee cacique Juan Sánchez, who in 1752 had headed the Yamasee village of Pocotalaca, had been relocated with his subjects to Nuestra Señora de la Leche, there joining cacique Antonio Matichaiche, who in 1752 had lived at La Punta serving as captain of Florida's Indian troops. And Miguel de los Santos, who in 1752 lived at Palica, by 1759 lived at Tolomato.[91]

When the English enemy finally acquired Florida by the Treaty of Paris in 1763, Spain relocated all its subjects, including its diverse Indian and African allies, to Cuba at royal expense. Captain Francisco Menéndez and the Black villagers of Mose received new lands to settle on the Matanzas frontier, at San Agustín de la Nueva Florida. Florida's amalgamated Indians were instead settled at Guanabacoa, a former Indian reserve across the bay from Havana. Sadly, Spanish census lists show that many of the Yamasee did not survive this final relocation, and their deaths are recorded in Spanish parish and treasury records in Cuba.[92]

Notes

1. Important accounts of the Yamasee and the 1715 War from which I draw include among others Steven J. Oatis, *A Colonial Complex: South Carolina's Frontiers in the Era of the Yamasee War, 1680–1730* (Lincoln: University of Nebraska Press, 2004); William L. Ramsey, *The Yamasee War: A Study of Culture, Economy, and Conflict in the Colonial South* (Lincoln: University of Nebraska Press, 2008); Verner W. Crane, *The Southern Frontier, 1670–1732* (New York: Norton, 1981), ch. 8.

2. Jane Landers, *Black Society in Spanish Florida* (Urbana: University of Illinois Press, 1999), ch. 2. English records use variants of Huspaw, Huspah, and Jospogue for the Yamasee village and its chief, or "king" as they sometimes called village chiefs, but I use Jospo.

3. John E. Worth, "Yamassee Origins and the Development of the Carolina-Florida Frontier," paper delivered at the Omohundro Conference, Austin, Texas, 1999.

4. Steven C. Hahn, "The Mother of Necessity: Carolina, the Creeks, and the Making of a New Order in the Southeast, 1670–1763," in *The Transformation of the Southeastern Indians, 1540–1760*, ed. Robbie Ethridge and Charles Hudson (Jackson: University Press of Mississippi, 2002); Oatis, *A Colonial Complex*; Ramsey, *The Yamasee War*; Alan Gallay, *The Indian Slave Trade: The Rise of the English Empire in the American South, 1670–1717* (New Haven, CT: Yale University Press, 2002).

5. John E. Worth, *The Struggle for the Georgia Coast: An Eighteenth-Century Spanish Retrospective on Guale and Mocama*, Anthropological Papers of the American Museum of Natural History, no. 75 (Athens: University of Georgia Press, 1995), 23, 181.

6. Herbert E. Bolton and Mary Ross, *The Debatable Land: A Sketch of the Anglo-Spanish Contest for the Georgia Country*, repr. (New York: Russell and Russell, 1968). See also Crane, *The Southern Frontier*, 6–10, and John J. TePaske, *The Governorship of Spanish Florida, 1700–1763* (Durham, NC: Duke University Press, 1964).

7. Landers, *Black Society*, ch. 1.

8. Elizabeth Donnan, *Documents Illustrative of the Slave Trade to America* (Washington, DC: Carnegie Institution of Washington, 1931), vol. 4, 242.

9. Peter H. Wood, *Black Majority: Negroes in Colonial South Carolina form 1670 through the Stono Rebellion* (New York: W. W. Norton, 1974), 95–130.

10. Roster of Black and Mulatto Militia for St. Augustine, September 20, 1683, Archivo General de Indias, Santo Domingo (hereafter cited as AGI, SD), 226, legajo 157a, John B. Stetson Collection, microfilm, P. K. Yonge Library of Florida History, University of Florida, Gainesville (hereafter cited as SC, PKY). On the history of Black military service in Florida and the Spanish circum-Caribbean, see Luis Arana, "Military Manpower in Florida, 1670–1703," *El Escribano* 8, no. 2 (1971): 40–63; Jane Landers, "Transforming Bondsmen into Vassals: Arming the Slaves in Colonial Spanish America," in *Arming Slaves in World History*, ed. Philip Morgan and Christopher Brown (New Haven, CT: Yale University Press, 2006), 120–45; and Paul Lokken, "Useful Enemies: Seventeenth-Century Piracy and the Rise of Pardo Militias in Spanish Central America," *Journal of Colonialism and Colonial History* 5, no. 2 (2004).

11. Indian trader Caleb Westbrooke reported in more detail the following month that more than one thousand Yamasee accompanied by "3 nations of the Spanish Indians that are Christians, Sapella, Soho, and Sapicbay" had also moved into Carolina's orbit. W. Noel Sainsbury, *Records in the British Public Record Office Relating to South Carolina*, Sainsbury transcripts, 36 vols. (Columbia: Historical Commission of South Carolina, 1928–47), 2: 8–9 (hereafter cited as South Carolina Records, BPRO).

12. David Hurst Thomas, "The Archaeology of Mission Santa Catalina de Guale: Our First 15 Years," in *The Spanish Missions of Florida*, ed. Bonnie G. McEwan (Gainesville: University Press of Florida, 1993), 1–34; John H. Hann, "Summary Guide to Spanish Florida Missions and Visitas," *Americas* 46, no. 4 (1990): 417–513 (repr., Oceanside, CA: Academy of American Franciscan History, 1990), 471–72.

13. William Green, Chester B. DePratter, and Bobby Southerlin, "The Yamasee in South Carolina: Native American Adaptation and Interaction along the Carolina Frontier," in *Another's Country: Archaeological and Historical Perspectives on Cultural Interactions in the Southern Colonies*, ed. J. W. Joseph and Martha Zierden (Tuscaloosa: University of Alabama Press,), 11–29; Rebecca Saunders, "Architecture of the Missions of Santa María and Santa Catalina de Amelia," in McEwan, *Spanish Missions of Florida*, 35–61; Hann, *Summary Guide to Spanish Florida Missions*, 472.

14. John Worth has gathered, translated, and published the most pertinent documents for this Spanish attack on Carolina. Worth, *Struggle for the Georgia Coast*, 146–71.

15. Morton's "stolen" slaves included Peter, Scipio, Doctor, Cushi, Arro, Emo, Caesar, and Sambo. The women were Frank, Bess, and Mammy. J. G. Dunlop, "William Dunlop's Mission to St. Augustine in 1688," *South Carolina Historical and Genealogical Magazine* 43 (January 1933): 1–30. For unknown reasons, two of the thirteen captured slaves escaped the Spaniards and returned to their English masters. Landers, *Black Society*; Crane, *Southern Frontier*, 31–33; Wood, *Black Majority*, 50; Worth, *Struggle for the Georgia Coast*, 146–71; Edward Randolph to the Board of Trade, March 16, 1699, South Carolina Records, BPRO, 88–95.

16. Helen Hornbeck Tanner, "The Land and Water Communications Systems of the Southeastern Indians," in *Powhatan's Mantle: Indians in the Colonial Southeast*, ed. Peter H. Wood, Gregory A. Waselkov, and M. Thomas Hatley (Lincoln: University of Nebraska Press, 1989), 6–20; Larry E. Ivers, "Scouting the Inland Passage, 1685–1737," *South Carolina Historical Magazine* 73, no. 3 (July 1972): 117–29.

17. Interrogation of the Black corsair, Diego, by Governor Don Juan Márques Cabrera, St. Augustine, Florida, 1686, in the John Tate Lanning papers, Thomas Jefferson Library, University of Missouri, St. Louis, 13–18. I am indebted to John H. Hann, of the San Luis Archaeological and Historical Site in Tallahassee, Florida, for this reference and his generosity. Royal Officials of Florida to the crown, St. Augustine, September 30, 1685, cited in Luis Arana, "Grammont's Landing at Little Matanzas Inlet, 1686," *El Escribano* 9, no. 3 (1972): 107–12.

18. "Case of the Turtle, 1697," in Elizabeth Donnan, *Documents Illustrative of the History of the Slave Trade to America*, vol. 4 (Washington, DC: Carnegie Institution, 1931), 245, 135.

19. Donnan, *Documents*, 4: 242–43.

20. Donnan, *Documents*, 4: 243; Edward Randolph reports to Board of Trade, 1699, Calendar of State Papers, 104. I am indebted to both Denise Bossy and Steven Hann for copies of the South Carolina Shipping Records, CO5/508, Public Record Office, London, that document additional Black slaves imported to Charles Town from the Caribbean and from Africa in the years following the Yamasee War.

21. Calendar of State Papers, Colonial, 1699, cited in Donnan, Documents, 4: 104, 243, 249; Frank J. Klingberg, *An Appraisal of the Negro in Colonial South Carolina* (Washington, DC: Associated Publishers, 1941), 13–19, 24–25.

22. Census reports for Carolina indicate a significant increase in slave imports between 1709 and 1711. By 1713 St. John's parish planter William Cantey Jr. and a crew of thirteen slaves produced two hundred barrels of pitch per year. Wood, *Black Majority*, 108–10.

23. Wood, *Black Majority*, ch. 4. Steven C. Hann in this volume describes a Yamasee Indian attack on William Stead's cowpen near the Edisto River in 1717 that resulted in Stead's death.

24. The men were named Conano, Jessie, Jacque, Gran Domingo, Cambo, Mingo, Dicque, and Robi. Dunlop did not name the women. Samuel Bordieu claimed Mingo, his wife, and daughter; John Bird claimed two of the men; Joab Howe claimed another; John Berresford claimed one woman; Christopher Smith claimed one man, and Robert Cuthbert claimed three other men. "William Dunlop's Mission," 1–30.

25. On June 13, 1710, the Reverend Francis le Jau reported, "There are 3 or 4 Portuguese slaves in this parish very desirous to receive the communion among us." Later he specified that the Portuguese-speaking slaves were from Madeira. Klingberg, *An Appraisal of the Negro*, 13–19.

26. Among the acts of charity that a good Catholic was urged to perform were to offer protection to the miserable and to shelter fugitives. Maureen Flynn, "Charitable Ritual in Late Medieval and Early Modern Spain," *Sixteenth-Century Journal* 16 (Fall 1995): 1–30; on Catholicism in Kongo, see Linda M. Heywood and John K. Thornton, *Central Africans, Atlantic Creoles, and the Making of the Foundations of the Americas, 1585–1660* (New York: Cambridge University Press, 2007).

27. The governor assigned the men to work as ironsmiths and laborers on the new stone fort, the Castillo de San Marcos, and the women became domestics in the governor's own household. He claimed to have paid all of them wages; the men earning a peso a day, the wage paid to male Indian laborers, and the women earning half as much. Royal officials to Charles II, March 3, 1699, cited in Irene Wright, "Dispatches of Spanish Officials Bearing on the Free Negro Settlement of Gracia Real de Santa Teresa de Mose," *Journal of Negro History* 9 (1924): 151–52. In April 1687 Captain Dunlop had tried to convince the Altamaha king to attack the Spanish at Amelia, but Altamahaw refused, saying the Spanish had never killed his people. Green, DePratter, and Southerlin, "The Yamasee in South Carolina."

28. Royal decree, November 7, 1693, AGI, SD 58-1-26, SC, PKY. Despite the royal decree of 1693, in 1697 Governor Laureano de Torres y Ayala returned six newly arrived Blacks and an Indian "to avoid conflicts and ruptures between the two governments." Joseph de Zúñiga to Charles II, October 10, 1699, AGI, SD 844 on microfilm reel 15, PKY.

29. TePaske, *Governorship*; John H. Hann, *A History of the Timucuan Indians and Missions*, Florida Museum of Natural History, Ripley P. Bullen Series (Gainesville: University Press of Florida, 1996).

30. Green, DePratter, and Southerlin, "The Yamasee in South Carolina."

31. TePaske, *Governorship*, 197.

32. The inability of the Spaniards to protect even the Nombre de Dios mission outside their very walls led many of their once loyal Indian allies to defect to the English. Charles W. Arnade, *The Siege of St. Augustine in 1702* (University of Florida Monographs, Social Sciences, no. 3, Summer 1959), 35; TePaske, *Governorship of Spanish Florida*, 110–16, 130–32, 196–97.

33. Kenneth R. Jones, "A 'Full and Particular Account' of the Assault on Charleston in 1706," South Carolina Historical Magazine 83, no. 1 (January 1982): 1–11; TePaske, *Governorship*, 116–22; Hahn, *Invention of the Creek Nation*, 460. "Mustee" was a term used for persons of mixed African and Indian heritage. William L. Ramsey, "A Coat for Indian Cuffy: Mapping the Boundary Between Freedom and Slavery in Colonial South Carolina," in Rosemary Brana Shute and Randy J. Sparks, *Paths to Freedom: Manumission in the Atlantic World* (Columbia: University of South Carolina Press, 2009).

34. Governor and Council to Proprietors, Board of Trade, September 17, 1708, in *The Colonial South Carolina Scene: Contemporary Views, 1697–1774*, ed. H. Roy Merrens (Columbia: University of South Carolina Press, 1977), 32.

35. Governor Edwards reported only 1,100 families (presumably white) in the province in 1709. Calendar of State Papers, 1708–1709, cited in Donnan, *Documents*, 255, 259, 444–54. A colonial census of 1719 reported the same Black-white ratio with a colonial population of "9580 souls including 1360 freemen, 900 free women, sixty white servant men, sixty white servant women, 1700 slaves, 500 Indian men slaves, 600 Indian women slaves, 1200 negro children slaves and 300 Indian children slaves." The report added that "negro men slaves [are increased in the last five years] by importation 300, negro women slaves 200 and negro children 600." Edward McCrady, *The History of South Carolina under the Proprietary Government, 1670–1719* (New York: Macmillan, 1897). McCrady cited what seem to be low slave import figures of 24 in 1706, 22 in 1707, 53 in 1708, 131 in 1709, 170 in 1710, 419 in 1711, and 81 in 1712. http://www .slavevoyages.org/tast/database/search.faces.

36. Governor and Council to Proprietors, Board of Trade, September 17, 1708, 32.

37. W. L. McDowell Jr., ed., *Journals of the Commissioners of the Indian Trade, Sept. 20, 1710–August 29, 1718*, ser. 2, The Indian Books, vol. 1 (Columbia: South Carolina Archives Department, 1955), 11; hereafter cited as JCIT.

38. Chapman J. Milling, *Red Carolinians* (Chapel Hill: University of North Carolina Press, 1940), 137.

39. On April 17, 1712, John Cochran and William Bray reported to the Commissioners of the Indian Trade that Samuel Hilden had intercepted and bought slaves from the Yamasee Indians before they got to their towns. *Journals of the Commissioners*, Indian Books, 1: 23.

40. Milling, *Red Carolinians*, 137; Hewatt on Carroll, Historical Collections, in Alexander Hewatt, *An Historical Account of the Rise and Progress of the Colonies of South Carolina and Georgia*, 2 vols. (London, 1779), 1: 192–94.

41. Huspah King to Charles Craven, 1715, quoted in William L. Ramsey, "'Something Cloudy in Their Looks': The Origins of the Yamasee War Reconsidered," *Journal of American History* 90, no. 1 (June 2003): 44–75, and Ramsey, *Yamasee War*, 228; Denise I. Bossy, "Godin & Co.: Charleston Merchants and the Indian Trade, 1674–1715," *South Carolina Historical Magazine* 114, no. 2 (April 2013): 96–131.

42. TePaske, *The Governorship of Spanish Florida*, 197–204; Hewatt, *An Historical Account*, 1: 215.

43. Ramsey, "A Coat for Indian Cuffy"; Ramsay, "'Something Cloudy in Their Looks'"; Ramsay, *Yamasee War*.

44. Klingberg, *An Appraisal of the Negro*, 16–19.

45. George Rodd, "Relation," South Carolina Records, BPRO 6: 74; Milling, *Red Carolinians*, 141–42. Also see Ramsey, "'Something Cloudy in their Looks'" and "A Coat for Indian Cuffy."

46. On the body of one of the enemy dead, a man named Smith, who may have been of mixed race, Carolinians found a letter warning Governor Craven to leave the country and boasting that all the nations on the continent were united to take it. Charles Rodd to his employer in London, May 8, 1715, *Calendar of State Papers, 1714–1715*, 28: 166–68.

47. Society for the Propagation of the Gospel in Foreign Parts, Series, vol. 4, 23, cited in Edgar Legaré Pennington, "The South Carolina Indian War of 1715, as Seen by the Clergymen," *South Carolina Historical and Genealogical Magazine* 32, no. 4 (October 1931): 251–69. On millenarian aspects of the Pueblo Revolt, see David J. Weber, ed., *What Caused the Pueblo Revolt of 1680?* (Boston: Bedford–St. Martin's, 1999).

48. Landers, *Black Society*, ch. 1.

49. A report by Commissary Johnston, however, reported that George's father and family were "taken and sold as slaves." Pennington, "The South Carolina Indian War."

50. South Carolina Records, BPRO, 6: 236–37, cited in Milling, *Red Carolinians*, 153.

51. South Carolina Records, BPRO, 6: 239, cited in Milling, *Red Carolinians*, 153.

52. Testimony of the four caciques, May 28, 1715, and subsequent report by Governor Francisco de Córcoles y Martínez to the king, January 25, 1716, AGI, SD 843 (SC 58-1-30), PKY. In Spanish records, Salkehatchie is also spelled Satiquicha, Salquicha, or Salaquiliche.

53. Testimony of the four caciques, May 28, 1715; Huspah King to Charles Craven, 1715, quoted in Ramsey, "'Something Cloudy in Their Looks'" and *The Yamasee War*, 228; Bossy, "Godin & Co."

54. Testimony of the four caciques, May 28, 1715.

55. John C. Inscoe, "Carolina Slave Names: An Index to Acculturation," *Journal of Southern History* 49, no. 4 (November 1983): 527–54.

56. George Rodd, "Relation"; Ramsey, "'Something Cloudy in their Looks'" and "A Coat for Indian Cuffy."

57. Testimony of the four caciques, May 28, 1715.

58. Testimony of the four caciques, May 28, 1715.

59. Testimony of the four caciques, May 28, 1715.

60. To secure the allegiance of their new subjects, the Spanish government almost tripled the Indian gift allotment from 2,063 pesos to 6,000 pesos annually. TePaske, *Governorship*, 198.

61. TePaske, *Governorship*, 198; Mark F. Boyd, "Diego Peña's Expedition to Apalachee and Apalachicola in 1716," *Florida Historical Quarterly* 28 (July 1949): 1–27; John H. Hann, "St. Augustine's Fallout from the Yamasee War," *Florida Historical Quarterly* 68 (October 1989): 180–200; Alejandra Dubkovsky, "One Hundred Sixty-One Knots, Two Plates and One Emperor: Creek Information Networks in the Era of the Yamasee War," *Ethnohistory* 59, no. 3 (Summer 2012): 489–513.

62. Governor Francisco de Córcoles y Martínez to the king, January 25, 1716, AGI, SD 843 (SC 58-1-30), PKY.

63. See Census of Father Ginés Sánchez, February 11, 1759, AGI, SD 2604; and Landers, *Black Society*, Appendix 5.

64. The variants of this name in English and Spanish records include Yaquisca and La Quisca. John H. Hann, "St. Augustine's Fallout"; April 1717 Census of Captain Joseph Primo de Rivera, included in Governor Juan de Ayala y Escobar to the King, April 18,1717, AGI, SD 843, SC, PKY. In the 1718 hearing regarding his African slaves, Perro Bravo is described as the cacique of the Yamasee Pueblo de Capuaca. Susan R. Parker has described the frequent relocations of these Indian villages and also of their inhabitants. She theorizes that Chief Francisco Jospogue was born on or near St. Catherine's. In 1702 he was chief of Nombre de Dios Chiquito. His loyalty to Spain and Christianity cost him dearly when the English attacked and enslaved his family in 1715. He was then assigned to "shepherd" the Yamasee refugees at Nuestra

Señora de Candelaria. Don Francisco Yospogue, Cacique del Pueblo de el Nombre de Dios Chiquito, October 18, 1728, AGI, SD 2584; Susan R. Parker, "The Second Century of Settlement in Spanish St. Augustine, 1670–1763," PhD diss., University of Florida, 1999, ch. 3.

65. Testimony of Cacique Jospo de los Yamasees, December 12, 1716, included in Governor Juan de Ayala y Escobar to the King, January 18, 1717, AGI, SD 843, SC, PKY.

66. Governor Antonio de Benavides to the King, August 25, 1718, Buckingham Smith Papers, Reel 1, frames 747–66, PKY. I am indebted to James Cusick for a copy of this material. Franciscan census and copy by Gelabert, January 10, Havana, AGI, SD 2604.

67. Franciscan census and copy by Gelabert, January 10. Domingo, of the Chachis nation, also held a Black woman in slavery for whom he demanded 200 pesos.

68. Crown slaves in Cuba were primarily single males assigned to public works who lived in communal barracks. Evelyn Powell Jennings, "War as the 'Forcing House of Change': State Slavery in Late-Eighteenth-Century Cuba," *William and Mary Quarterly*, 3rd ser., vol. 62, no. 3, The Atlantic Economy in an Era of Revolutions (July 2005): 411–40. This couple, however, were always listed together, and the Spanish seem to have recognized their union. They later lived together in Cuba. List of individuals from the presidio of St. Augustine housed in Regla in the house of Don Gonzalo de Oquendo; AGI, Cuba 1076, f. 395.

69. Donnan, *Documents*, 257.

70. The following year Carolina enacted a new and harsher slave code. Wood, *Black Majority*, 298–99, 304.

71. Memorial of the fugitives, 1724, AGI, SD 844, on microfilm reel 15, PKY.

72. For the exchange on this mission, see the letters of Governors Arthur Middleton (Carolina) and Antonio de Benavides (Florida) in *Documentos históricos de la Florida y la Luisiana, Siglos xvi al xvii* (Madrid, 1912), 252–60.

73. The governor gave the proceeds to the envoy from Carolina who would have preferred to reclaim the former slaves. Other buyers included several military officers and even some religious officials. Governor Antonio de Benavides to Philip V, November 11, 1725, cited in *Documentos históricos*, 164–66. Carolinians charged that the Spanish governor "Makes Merchandize of all our slaves, and ships them off to Havanah for his own Profit," and they were at least partially correct. Accord, June 27, 1730, AGI, SD 844, on microfilm reel 15, PKY; Wood, *Black Majority*, 305. Some of the slaves sold at the 1729 auction were taken to Havana by their new owners. Nine years later Governor Manuel de Montiano would try to retrieve them. Decree of Manuel de Montiano, March 3, 1738, AGI, SD 844, on microfilm reel 15, PKY.

74. Francisco Menéndez to the king, January 1, 1740, AGI, SD 2658.

75. June 13, 1728, South Carolina Records, BPRO, 12: 61–67, cited in Wood, *Black Majority*, 305.

76. Four slaves who fled or were taken from a plantation near Port Royal in 1726 were later spotted in St. Augustine. Governor Arthur Middleton, June 13, 1728, South Carolina Records, BPRO, 13: 61–67, and John Pearson, October 20, 1727, South Carolina Records, BPRO, 19: 127–28, cited in Wood, *Black Majority*, 305.

77. Wood, *Black Majority*, 305.

78. Fray Joseph de Bullones to the King, October 5, 1728, AGI, SD 865 (58-2-16/8), SC, PKY.

79. Governor Antonio de Benavides to King Philip V, April 27, 1733, AGI, SD 833.

80. The crown actually issued two separate edicts in 1733. The first, on October 4, 1733, forbade any future compensation to the British, reiterated the royal offer of freedom, and specifically prohibited the sale of fugitives to private citizens, no doubt in response to the auction of 1729. The second, on October 29, 1733, commended the Blacks for their bravery against the British in the invasion of 1728 but also stipulated that the enslaved would be required to complete four years of royal service as an indenture prior to being freed. Royal decree, October 4, 1733, AGI, SD 843 (58-1-24), SC, PKY; Royal decree, October 29, 1733, AGI, SD 843 (58-1-24), SC, PKY.

81. Report of the Visita of Bishop Francisco de San Buenaventura, April 29, 1736, AGI, SC 5543, PKY; TePaske, *Governorship*, 167–69. Memorial of the Fugitives, included in Governor Manuel de Montiano to King Philip V, March 3, 1738, AGI, SD 844, on microfilm reel 15, PKY.

82. Memorial of Chief Jospo, included in Governor Manuel de Montiano to Philip V, March 3, 1738, AGI, SD 844, on microfilm reel 15, PKY. In earlier works I misread this very blackened microfilm to read Jorge. Jospo is also spelled Jospe and Jospogue in other Spanish documents. Since Chief Francisco Jospo was already deceased by 1737, this is a different Chief Jospo. It is still possible, however, that this Jospo was father of the Yamasee youth educated in England to be a native missionary for the Society for the Gospel in Foreign Parts who returned to Carolina with Commissary Gideon Johnston in 1715 in the midst of the Yamasee War. The young Prince George returned and later wrote, "I have had noos that my Father as gone in Santaugustena and all my Friends." A later account reporting that the father had been killed proved untrue, and another report that he had been captured, returned to Charles Town, and then sold with the rest of his family as slaves was unconfirmed. There are no further reports about the young Prince George after Commissary Johnston's death in 1716. Frank J. Klingberg, "The Mystery of the Lost Yamasee Prince," *South Carolina Historical and Genealogical Magazine* 63 (1962): 18–32. Also see Denis I. Bossy, "Spiritual Diplomacy, the Yamasees and the Society for the Propagation of the Gospel: Reinterpreting Prince George's Eighteenth-Century Voyage to England," *Early American Studies: An Interdisciplinary Journal* 12, no. 2 (2014): 336–401.

83. Petition of Diego Espinosa and reply by Governor Manuel de Montiano, May 5, 1738, AGI, SD 845, on microfilm reel 16, PKY. Diego de Espinosa was a successful mulatto cattle rancher whose fortified ranch twenty miles north of St. Augustine on the Diego Plains served as an important outpost guarding the Spanish city.

84. King Philip V to Governor Manuel de Montiano, July 15, 1741, AGI 58-1-25, SC 5943, PKY.

85. Scholars hotly debate the origins and meaning of these African ethnonyms. I have used them throughout as they appear in Spanish documents. See for example, Paul E. Lovejoy, "Identifying Enslaved Africans in the African Diaspora," in *Identity in the Shadow of Slavery*, ed. Paul E. Lovejoy (London: Continuum, 2000); Gwendolyn Midlo Hall, *Slavery and African Ethnicities in the Americas: Restoring the Links* (Chapel Hill: University of North Carolina Press, 2005); Philip D. Morgan, "The Cultural Implications of the Atlantic Slave Trade: African Regional Origins, American Destinations and New World Developments," *Slavery and Abolition* 18, no. 1 (1997): 122–45.

86. Fugitive Slaves to the King, 1738. Memorial of the Fugitives, included in Governor Manuel de Montiano to King Philip V, March 3, 1738, AGI, SD 844, on microfilm reel 15, PKY.

87. Governor Manuel de Montiano to the King, January 31, 1740, AGI, SD 2658. Montiano counted only 366 Indian subjects (men, women, and children) at the eight nearby and allied Indian towns of Nombre de Dios (43), San Antonio de la Costa (22), Nuestra Señora de Guadalupe de Tolomato (29), San Juan del Puerto de Palica (52), Nuestra Señora de la Concepción de Pocotalaca (44), Nuestra Señora del Rosario de la Punta (51), Santo Domingo de Chiquito (55), and San Nicolás de Cacepullas (70). Governor Manuel de Montiano to the King, May 9, 1740, AGI, SD 2658.

88. Jane Landers, "An Eighteenth-Century Community in Exile: The Floridanos in Cuba," *New West Indian Guide* 70, nos. 1 & 2 (Spring 1996): 39–58.

89. Letters and reports of ecclesiastics, January 8, 1642–July 23, 1759, AGI, SD 864.

90. Father Andres de Vilches recounts his services, December 8, 1757, AGI, SD 864. For examples of continuing intermarriage, see Landers, *Black Society*, 47–53.

91. Censuses of Gelabert, 1752, AGI, SD 2604; Ginés Sánchez, 1759, AGI, SD 2595; and 1763 Exit Census AGI, Cuba 416.

92. Lista de las familias de Indios venidos de Florida que se hallan alojados en Guanabacoa, AGI, Cuba 416, f. 728–63. Cacique Juan Sánchez died at age forty, one of many. The many orphaned children became part of amalgamated Indian families in Guanabacoa.

CHAPTER TWO

The Rape of Florida and Albery Whitman's Poetic-Political Theory of a Reparative Ontology

José Felipe Alvergue

Behind them were their homes, wives, children—all!
Forth in the breach, sons, husbands, fathers stood
To meet what came if e'en the heav'ns must fall!
Thro' unpolluted fields by Waxe's flood,
O'er meadows sweet and in the palmy wood,
The armor of the foe gleamed in the sun:
Proud was the aged maroon's incensed mood,
As forth to meet them in a feeble run,
He waved his servants back, and thus his speech begun:
    (WHITMAN, Canto II, XXXIV, 21)[1]

In its content, Albery Whitman's long poem *The Rape of Florida*, first published in 1882, recounts a betrayal of key American ideals played out in the forceful invasion and removal of the Seminoles from the territories of current-day Florida. Dramatizing the first two Seminole Wars (1817–18 and 1835–42) allows Whitman to disclose a long historical perspective, roughly a thirty-year span, and condense multiple historical instances of the "breach"— sites and instances where the muster of American exceptionalism, as witnessed by those subjugated by its logics, discloses an ontological struggle. The blatant white supremacy that deploys settler-colonial tactics in the acquisition of territory and the violent homogenization of nonwhite people during that process of accumulation reveals fractures to the exceptionalist veneer of a singular national, liberal worldview, which decolonial researchers readily cite in their critiques.

"Forth in the breach," however, provides another dimension to decolonial critique. Witnessing the hypocrisy of exceptionalism, those made vulnerable by its violence are in a position to feel the immediate indignity of, simultaneously, being put at risk of death as well as being subjected politically as ciphers in the various historical narratives that sustain the exceptionalist identity of nation. When these witnesses speak poetically in Whitman's work, their language, the poetic speech act, goes beyond direct critiques of the juridical, epistemic, and moral institutions exceptionalist violence creates in its attempt to homogenize. These witnesses, their emotional and historical reflections, initiate a reorientation toward Other ontologies whose sensory archives of events often go ignored in dominant historical discourses.[2] Our coming to these sensory-rich ontological reflections signals what I refer to as a reparative historical moment.

These archives of witnessed emotional and historical memory find their way into aesthetics, and it is in this simultaneously aesthetic and decolonial strategy that I locate Whitman's poetics, as well as what I refer to as the poetic-political theory of his work. The latter describes how Whitman's approach to emotional and epistemic realizations, which his poetic speakers address and articulate at the sites of witnessing settler-colonial violence, returns the audience and the speakers themselves to the sensory. Whitman's speakers portray a historically sentient orientation to "rights," away from the dominant and exceptionalist narrative of American expansion, toward a knowledge of "America" as a spatiotemporal reality that verifies a Black ontology of liberal democratic experience, as one experienced in Black feelings, Black speech, and Black metaphysical reflection.

Whitman's focus on the Black Seminoles is a decolonial history lesson as well as a collaborative emotional and sensory song meant to heal the wounds of endurance, both personal and geographic. It's also an epic parsed in the meter provided in the commune of ontological worldview and Nature. The breach is a physical location, a metaphorical rupture scripted over some horizon, or thin reminder of human-made laws imposed over natural phenomena.[3] "[U]npolluted fields" and "meadows sweet," one side of the breach is an idyllic land, a desirable land. On the other, an invading horde of murderous troops wants it. But throughout the work, Whitman reminds the reader of something elemental in the relationship the Black Seminoles have established with the land they occupy. The land provides their freedom in the form of holding their substance. The land is a space-time for Being, and is experienced in the ontic struggles over being free. For the Creek migrants and Black exiles that comprise the Black Seminoles, land and liberty experienced on the other side of a thin, even if permeable, wall to the American slave state inspires the true liberal ideals. Their survival of indignity and genocide authenticate their moral compass in regard to "right." From their side of the breach, the Black Seminoles, and the reader, see American exceptionalism as the brutish force of power so many feel it to be.

> Plebian, Savage, Sage, or lord or fiend,
> Man hath of justice and of right a cause.
> Prior to all that e'er has contravened,
> Or e'en to man's existence, justice was.
> Right would be right amid the wreck of laws:
> 'Tis so, and all ordaining Nature gives
> Somewhere to live, to every child she has;
> She gives, and to her bosom each receives,
> Inducing it to love the spot whereon it lives.
> (Whitman, Canto I, IX, 12)

In the same breath of address Whitman's poetic speaker simultaneously deconstructs the exceptionalist premise of a gifted group, civilization, class, or generation, or exceptionalism, while providing in its place an alternative concept of law. "Prior to all that e'er has contravened, / Or e'en man's existence, justice was," is a difficult ontological horizon for many to imagine, given the sheer temporal breadth. It is, one might argue, an impossibility.

The witnessing of invasion, and the witnessing of reneged truce: these result in a kind of assembly that can be extrapolated as a sort of poetic-political theory, as I mention above—one that undermines the racial exceptionalism upon which dominant characteristics of nation, as assembly, are maintained. But the creative premise of this impossibility is what makes *The Rape of Florida* so utterly timeless. It foregrounds the Black ontological horizon in metaphysical and historical terms that America must grapple with. For Black life to "love the spot whereon it lives" requires knowing and being conscious of slavery and anti-Blackness, while also acknowledging how assembly emerges from the emotional and psychological event of witness. In other words, America's Black ontology is a knowledge of Being within the spatiotemporal history and contemporary reality of anti-Blackness as the disavowal of Black beings. It involves feeling something about what we know about our national past. This requires a precariousness or vulnerability that exceptionalism, as a vain chauvinism, refuses to acknowledge. Recognition, as a complementary disposition to address, as speech, is a vital role we, as the reader, are placed in amidst a poetic work comprised almost entirely in a continuous speech act.

Speech acts of witness, moreover, manifest history as events in time given linguistic evidence, and in this attention to speech acts Whitman devises a historical logic, an unfolding of democratic *Dasein*, so to speak, which substantiates what settler-colonial ontology disavows. When we include the poetic narrator's disclosures of American institutional failure and anti-Blackness, which Whitman deploys in addressing the reader directly, to the Native-Black speech acts that give voice to the witnessed events of settler-colonial violence undergirding American expansion, the thirty-year view of Floridian history swells to include earlier, later, and national forms of accumulation and dispossession: chattel slavery, Reconstruction-era failures to deliver on Civil War Amendments, new forms of finance and bondage, and impending twentieth-century disillusionments in housing, education, and so on. As I will repeat throughout this essay, it is not about how settler-colonialism expels the subject but how it incorporates the subjected into its historical world view, how subjection and subjugation, in various and practiced forms, become spatialized along a temporal record of what we are.

spatial | aural | form

The postnational geography of Whitman's *The Rape of Florida* is an ontological totality verifying the existence of an America, but the history of this America is comprised of criminal acts perpetrated in the name of white supremacy. In fact, I would argue that the postnational premises of assembly that Whitman's Black Seminoles embody in their deeds and speech continue, in this moment, to provide the spatiotemporal reality many poets, activists, educators, politicians, scholars, and scientists reiterate as the foundation of anti-exceptionalism. And the decolonial work of poetic empathy lives in what we now refer to as antiracist consciousness.

There is something specific I'd like to draw a circle around when it comes to Whitman's poetic setting, the territory of current-day Florida, and why I use the term *postnational*.

Postnationalism "indicates a movement away from a simplistic dichotomy of colonizer and colonized," argues Ellie D. Hernández.[4] The work inherent to the term "correctly labels identities and institutions that cannot be said to have just one national identity." However, in so describing a more nuanced relationship between individual and assembly, postnationalism also points to the gap created by the material effects of capitalism, which aestheticizes a parallax through which all of us living in the shared national geography do not see or experience the ontological terror of "national identity" positioned upon the subjugated. Those who do, those who experience the disavowal of anti-Blackness or Native genocide, for instance, are charged with the task of giving evidence of the fact of their own status. This parallax view of the spatiotemporal world we share and call "nation" functions in communication with the "power differential," as Lisa Lowe has pointed out.[5] The power differential outlines where ontologies meet, how they are felt, and in what ways lasting effects of power are carried over into the next generation.

The relationship between postnationalism and the speech act in Whitman is fundamental to locating his poetic work at the intersection of race and geography, of documenting the spatiotemporal reality of the Black experience, but not for the project of "African American identity" as a national identity, but Black identity as an impossible linguistic act in any and every facet of American liberal discourse, as this discourse operates. While the latter, in its exceptionalist form, induces blind love, or patriotism without study, Whitman's postnational identity induces us to "love the spot" where we live. But not without the difficult historical work of listening to the archive of witnesses who have experienced and endured the events of its formation and present assembly; not without feeling the brunt of America's power differential; and not without repairing the psychological trauma of negating the truth of what generations of witnesses have been telling the rest of us from the last centuries in regard to state-sanctioned genocide, removal, dispossession, and moral illegitimacy.

If in its content the poem depicts a betrayal and breach of sovereign agreement between America and the Seminole nation, in its demonstration *The Rape of Florida* presents an interesting impossibility in the political potential of the Black record, the Black archive of experienced liberal democratic modernity, of failure in the form of poetic song. America is the ontological evidence that Black people exist. But American history remains a contested and manipulated narrative over how, exactly.[6]

"The subtle evolutions of thought must yet be expressed in song," writes Whitman in the dedicatory address. We have to understand the archival and social justice elements at work in the high form of Whitman's Spenserian stanzas in order to fully appreciate the insistence of Black life as the insistence of an Other ontology to the world construed through settler-colonial exceptionalism. The poem's insistence as form is the insistence of the spatiotemporal reality of voice, Black and Native voice.[7] The insistence of voice demonstrates the presence of sentience in the speakers, who in their presence, their availability to witness and give speech to the breach, demonstrate the epic progress that is the whole work: the poetic work, and the work of assembly.

. . . poetry is the language of universal sentiment. Torch of the unresting mind, she kindles in advance of all progress. Her waitings are on the threshold of the infinite, where beckoning man to listen, she interprets the leaves of immortality. Her voice is the voice of Eternity dwelling all great souls . . . In her language there is no mistaking of that liberal thought which is the health of mind. A secret interpreter, she waits not for data, phenomena, and manifestations, but anticipates and spells the wishes of Heaven. (Whitman, 5)

There is a sense of moral arc in Whitman's poetic attention to "Eternity." But I also don't think "Eternity" can only mean a speculative optimism. "She waits not for data, phenomena, and manifestations," poetry's idiomatic situatedness, the premise of its aural authenticity, is not a science, meaning a scientific kind of epistemology through which the truth of identity is to be verified (or verified in its positional status to superiority). Scientific truth is binary. There is the known and unknown. Given the colonial history regarding epistemology, the true path for Whitman was a harmony that only music could accord. Ivy G. Wilson refers to this ambition as a sort of "sound system" (Wilson 2009, 7). Though Wilson is referring to harmony, "sound system" also makes one think of more situated technologies of sound as they have evolved over time, and I think of specters of sound recorded in otherwise silenced archives, including geological and oceanic archives. Ghosts, in other words, whose screams and eloquence exist in time but not knowledge.[8] Sound systems belie the power differential with an aesthetic proposition, which audience can approach and yet still feel. "Eternity" is also an aesthetic panic that translates into an epistemic refiguration of the power differential's parallax into our spatiotemporal assemblies—a disorientation, if you will, of sensory knowledge toward repossessing what the senses have witnessed and recorded but our historical minds have been told not to authenticate. We lose the known amidst the unknown; what is felt guides us through what we have been told does not exist to feel.

There are tensions that form alleviates: temporality, history, progress, the soul of civilization, liberalism, moral right. Whitman's ambition in aurality confronts the tension arisen in the pregnant pause prior to redemption, which could describe the unique historicity experienced in those positioned by American racialization. Whitman was born into slavery prior to the Civil War. Becoming emancipated in his teens, Whitman had at that point already become orphaned, and migrated between Kentucky and Ohio before settling into a prominent role at Wilberforce University. Living through Reconstruction, Whitman also became a prominent figure in the AME

Church, and publicly renowned as a speaker in the African American national community. In his later life he would be criticized for not espousing a militant enough attitude toward racial politics in America.

> Prior to all that e'er has contravened,
> Or e'en to man's existence, justice was.
> Right would be right amid the wreck of laws:
>> (Whitman, Canto I, IX, 12)

Prior to society, prior to its record, after its assembly's dissolution amidst the "wreck" of liberalism: no matter the form through which we come to know or experience it, Whitman argues that there is already an ethical demonstration of assembly within which we must think of performances of address and recognition. Though Whitman's conceptualization encompasses a Judeo-Christian worldview, it remains nihilistic with regard to the structures of assembly sustained by an exceptionalist nation-state. The latter survives by citing a religio-secular moral right, but more importantly by installing that ontology into a static and bounded, or governed territory.

> If earth were freed from those who buy and sell,
> It soon were free from most, or *all* its ills;

And

> What meant the actions of the great and good—
> The Christ and his Apostles—holy men!
> Why wandered they about in solitude,
> Despising what the world called greatness then?
> Why shun the num'rous city's places, when
> Eternal themes in their wandering tongues inspired—
> Why, but to reach Edenic sources again
> In nature?
>> (Whitman, Canto I, XIII, 14)

The settler-colonial desire professes to control and harness what governs itself, Nature, and indeed uses the rhetoric of the "good," borrowed from the natural to compose metaphors for world order based on ownership and governance—specifically, governing others. Against this construct Whitman's nihilism does away with a sense of governance as "good" ownership altogether. Time occupies the place of the owner. Time becomes a measure of freedom, not governance.

Thus, on a strand dividing worlds I've stood,
Till, touched by the dark wand of mystery,
I felt the brow of night, and earth imbued
With dread emotions of a great eternal Good!
    (Whitman, Canto I, XVII, 15)

Others translate this power-powerlessness in more direct terms. Calvin Warren's "ontological terror" describes the interstice or "strand" Whitman might have lived in terms of an impossibility in the democratic politics of freedom to fully dismantle structures premised on the ontology, or worldview, of anti-Blackness. This, we must understand, and indeed I will argue, comes to not only encompass our historical vision, but indeed serves to maintain the spatiotemporal realities that reaffirm its many forms of norming violence as morally legitimate and legally exigent. "Freedom exists *for* Being," Warren underscores, "it enables the manifestation of Being through Dasein":

> Our metaphysical notions of freedom also reduce antiblackness to social, political, and legal understandings, and we miss the ontological *function* of antiblackness—to deny the ontological ground of freedom by severing the (non)relation between blackness and Being. What I am suggesting is that our metaphysical conceptions of freedom neglect the ontological horrors of antiblackness by assuming freedom can be attained through political, social, or legal action. This is a humanist fantasy, one that masks subjection in emancipatory rhetoric.[9]

In its poetic demonstration, its performativity, Whitman seeks out alternative ontological events of this metaphysical freedom, which he finds in the alternative sovereignty nourished in the Black Seminole nation. The assemblies, which have and do witness the breach, authenticate different heroes and criminals to the historical narratives curated by perpetrators of settler-colonial exceptionalisms. But he also finds that in the spatiotemporal form of the very territory, as a natural scene.

Upon the shells by Carribea's wave
I've heard the anthems of the mighty sea;
Heard there the dark pines that their voices gave,
And heard a stream denote its minstrelsy—
How sweet, *all* lonely, was it there to be!
The stars were bright, the moon was up and clear;
But, when I thought of those who once were free,

And came at wonted times to worship there;
The sea's deep voice grew sad and claimed of me a tear!
    (Whitman, Canto I, XVII, 15)

The Caribbean as an archipelago of strands, and breaches, carries an archive of voices: Africans, Maroon communities, uprisings, liberties—all "anthems of the mighty sea," all a "sound system."[10] The simultaneity of multiple assemblies reiterates the postnational claim to liberalism. This speech act ends in lamentation, in a loneliness. From that loneliness we sense a call as readers to join the speaker in the affective conclusion regarding history as it is stored in nature, and its evocative scenery. It is vital that we approach the lament conscientiously, however. That we approach the breach for what it is, an ontic and real horizon between a reparative ontology, and the violent ontology that maintains the ontic trauma, or anti-Blackness. The purpose in approaching the breach is not so as to maintain our gaze on it, or fetishize lamentation—to keep Black ontology at a media distance in the parallax. The act of recognition requires a restoration of *an* ontology, a space-time within which what is happening to us happens to us. Black ontology is the reparative ontology to the damage of anti-Blackness.

The experience of settler-colonialism, which includes tightly braided methodologies for carrying out anti-Blackness,[11] by those whose assembly and ontologies are breached, are also being recorded and thus written: given aesthetic dimension, affective register, put into genre, invented upon, archived, passed down, and so on. Their record of events travels with them when they are displaced, are shared with others in exile, are retold in the carceral nightmares that surrounds them and others who are similarly divorced from the liberal ontologies under which assembled life in the Americas has produced positional subjectivity. "Forth in the breach," we not only find the speaker, addressing us directly, but also the poetic heroes who are mid-rehearsal of these "anthems."

Whitman locates the creators of a democratically sovereign identity, and it is one based on acts of interlocution between individuals recognized for their difference, not homogenized into a singular narrative, and not based on the racial fiction of purity, superiority, or an exceptionalist supremacy devised for the purposes of property monopoly.

The poorest black that came upon their shore,
To them was brother—their own flesh and blood,—
They fought his wretched manhood to restore,—
They sound his hidings in the swampy wood,

And brought him forth—in arms before him stood,—
The citizens of God and sovran earth,—
They shot straight forward looks with flame imbued,
Till in him manhood sprang, a noble birth,
And warrior-armed he rose tall that manhood's worth.
    (Whitman, Canto I, XXVIII, 19)

There is a strong sense of solidarity from this witnessing, "The poorest black that came upon their shore, / To them was brother—their own flesh and blood." Ethnic and racial heterogeneity is not only a marker of assembly, but moreover there is a strong theoretical claim made on liberal politics when difference, not homogeneity, is the premise for citizenship.

In a poetic twist of focus and historical consciousness, the indigenous and Black interlocutors of the poem demonstrate the very Americaneity dominant American narratives of displacement, slavery, and violence seek to erase or de-authenticate. This spatiotemporal rewriting of the historical subject's emergence from a liberal democratic "place" via Whitman's geographic lyricization of Florida, and the various demonstrations of Black-Native speech acts, reveal the very legitimacy of an American moral ground to be a falsified ontology aligned to settler-colonial violence and forceful white supremacist ideology that had evolved, in Whitman's own time, into Jim Crow, Black Codes, policing born out of fugitive slave law, convict leasing and the privatization of carceral logistics, and so on. In the heroic characteristics attributed to Atlassa, the executive character granted Palmecho, the virtue and courage given Palmecho, and the service and sacrifice of Abraham, a sovereign runaway, Whitman crafts an epic story of freedom as the longevity of an identity forged and "self-restrained" in the face of outright and authentic criminality. Almost as if to say: the despotism American historical narratives position as the rhetorical situation of democratism, as the speech act of liberalism (the establishing and promoting of rights via discourse and debate), is in practice not the revolutionary antagonist, nor empire, nor the establishment of nation as *the* revolutionary act against despotism, but its own genocidal disorder, its own crimes perpetrated under cover of lawfulness, morality, and exceptionalism.

My substance—what of that?

If e'er the muse of history sits to write,
And Florida appear upon her page,

This nation's crimes will blush the noonday light,
And ******'s name will lead her criminal age!
  (Whitman, LXXIII, 51)[12]

"Extermination was his highest creed," declares Whitman's poetic speaker of Zachary Taylor specifically, "Bondage the *one* provision of his will" (LXXIV, 52). Absence through genocide, or slavery as social death—these are the coordinates of nonbeing. "I never was a slave—a robber took / My substance—what of that?" is the poetic speaker's response to this ontology (XI, 31). This is what I refer to as Whitman's demonstrative speech act. They identify the ontological terror of settler-colonial violence, while confronting the social death of settler-colonial subjugation, remembering that the real terror of this ontological "breach" is not in how the subject is cast out of Nation, but rather how the subjugated is included in national history, and memory. Speakers address each other, address an audience, and address history itself throughout the epic. In each instance the speaker is verifying and documenting what is witnessed, but also what is felt about the event itself.

Throughout this essay I've been situating Black ontology on the other side of the "breach," which might lead one to believe that the settler-colonial worldview, and indeed the ontology it posits, are of equal legitimacy. That it's merely a matter of circumstance and choice which ontological horizon one chooses. This is not the case, as I argue above. Power is at stake, and power needs to be delinked from the settler-colonial worldview its ontology organizes and maintains.

• • •

In the latter decades of the nineteenth century, particularly following the Civil War Amendments and the reshaping of voting rights, the "extermination" and the ethical question of "substance" disavowed are contextualized in a new rhetorical impossibility, which I explore below through the idea of *stasis*. However, even during liberal periods of progress, anti-Blackness has manifested in violent and murderous forms, particularly in relation and as a response to juridical evolution and civic decolonization.

I'm building toward a contemporary emergency along a historical track that has recently been made visible, audible, material, and otherwise real for many outside the communities of direct, sensory witness. The unique role of governance in crafting, amplifying, and manipulating history has disrupted normed beliefs in history itself, to a point of dramatizing governance as property that has belonged to an exceptional group. It is not property readily shared, or truly deemed public. This manipulated narrative, moreover, reminds the public that persons whose ancestors were themselves property cannot, should not, be allowed in turn to own property, and particularly a kind of property that seemingly requires a strict regulation of feelings or emotions. This has also focused our collective attention on electoral politics and how they have been organized around monopolizing representation.

It has been discovered that during the 2016 presidential election, big data was used to dissuade African American voters in Floridian counties along the I-95 corridor. Whether or not it can be proven that isolating and mobilizing (or dissuading) these "deterrents"—voters who could be turned away from voting—during that election worked, what is important is how data was used to include African Americans into a national construct, and the exercise of this right, a property of the individual to vote. Remembering that one of the lasting modes of violence through which settler-colonialism consolidated power is not how subjects were cast out of nation, but rather how the subjected were made part of nation. The use of demographic data in this way—counting bodies so as to dispossess subjects—falls within a problematic continuum that Whitman himself spoke against in the 1880s, including how African American voters might either be manipulated by politicians that cite freedom, but mean freedom, in attracting their vote, or how politicians and government clerks might purposefully violate access to voting as a way of disenfranchising Black voters all together.[13] These strategies contributed to the ways in which African Americans became included in the national ontology of liberalism following the Civil War.

In the early 1880s, Florida census data was being used to weaponize districting and representation, intimidation and dispossession, against Black voice. Its "Black Belt," comprised of nine northern counties, posed an electoral opportunity to deliver on the very promises of Emancipation. For many white Floridians the population of Black voters in these counties was considered a threat to the ontological order white supremacy and settler-colonialism had long established. While in *The Rape of Florida*, Whitman spends ample poetic space in describing a rich landscape already prepared for farming and residence as a manner of mapping the desire of American occupation, at the end of the nineteenth century it is the political possibility of the vote and representation that motivates new mechanisms of displacement, voting restrictions, carceral enterprise, and the Black Codes.

In a letter to the editor of the *Weekly Floridian* dated July 4, 1882, one James T. Magbee of Tampa writes, in the hopes of inducing farmers to move to Florida, "One great advantage the farmer has here is that he need never fail to raise a crop; for if one thing fails he can raise others, as he can plant a marketable crop the year round. He need never be idle, and will always find the soil returning a rich reward for his labor." There are three threads I would like to pull at here: first, the imaginary of Florida, an anachronistic and romanticized portrayal of a fecund and untouched land full of simultaneously untapped yet underwritten "reward"; second, a new demographic that emerges from the destabilizations in post–Civil War agriculture, in terms of itinerant white farmers, migration, and land; and third, an exigent fear of the Black vote in Florida's northern counties where Black men outnumbered white voters in drastic proportion.

In terms of the first thread, this kind of rhetoric exists in a hemispheric continuum of colonization that involves dispossessing ownership and accumulating resources.[14] Recent forms of terrorism like threatening emails sent to Democratic voters in Florida[15] weaponize the same passive forms of abuse as previous examples of violent white supremacy, like hanging effigies of Black voters in Miami in the 1940s.[16]

In regard to the second, the exploitation of poor whites, including communities that align themselves with whiteness, is a long-practiced strategy toward maintaining capitalism through social vocationalism. The third strategy alluded to is more revealing in relation to the 2016 tactics described above.

In the same issue of the *Weekly Floridian*, in its coverage of an impending Democratic Mass Meeting to be held on the 8th of July, the editors illuminate their readers on the situation of the "Black Belt," a portion of the state made up of the nine counties: Alachua, Duval, Gadsden, Jackson, Jefferson, Leon, Madison, Marion, and Nassau. In the 1880 census the population of Florida numbered 269,493. According the the *Weekly Floridian*, 133,798 were living in those nine counties. Of that number, 90,132 were Black Floridians, 43,563 white. In the rest of the state, roughly 37,000 were Black, almost 98,000 white. "It is in the black belt," affirms the editorial piece, "that strength of the Radical party is to be found," the "Radical party" being the Republican party. "Their possession of the election machinery," it continues, "gave them opportunities for swelling their vote at pleasure and furnished the means for perpetuating their power." Much of the rhetoric used in illustrating electoral politics hasn't changed, including the reduction of voting behaviors and intentions to the machinistic function of parts in a system, or the sum of ciphers, in other words the transliteration of human voice and ideas, desires and representative acts into logistics and the accounting of population, rather than its consideration.

Then comes this:

To sum up: the "black belt" contains within a fraction of one-half the population of the State, has nearly 45 per cent of all the taxable resources, pays about the same per cent of all the taxes, and gives in the neighborhood of 38 per cent of the Democratic vote cast in the whole State. Its drawbacks are the presence of nearly 75 per cent of all the negroes within the commonwealth, which deprives the tax-paying people in the belt, except in exceptional cases, of any voice in shaping legislation or in controlling questions vital to the whole State and especially so of themselves.[17]

Driving home the point in terms of liberal "progress" and debate, in other words citing America's democratic ontology,[18] the editorial makes its call to the settler-colonial strategy of forming an "invading horde," and approach the vote as it would the "breach." "Being thus powerless, the people of these counties have necessarily to look for protection against vicious legislation to their brethren of the white counties."

Just like that, 90,132 bodies counted in the 1880 census are erased from humanity, from being considered "people," and rhetorically situated as "legislation," as merely politics. But more than this, what strikes me is how the editorial invokes power in feeling "powerless." Blackness here is literally treated as a form of power, not the identity of persons within a nation. Blackness, in other words (a specific idiom of Blackness, I should add), is revealed to be an invention. As such, the invention is a fabrication within the fabrication of the ontology that establishes rule of law in relation to it, as a power against which governance must direct its power—the will of the people, no matter how fictional. Invoking Blackness this way, as anti-Blackness, calls to white supremacy and situates images like the effigy of a Black Florida voter above. The image resonates with sensory trauma, and sensory language—I think about, literally, the "sound systems" of people gathered together, the vibrating cords to cochlea, the feeling in children of their caregivers' chests rising and falling quickly as they speak, their hands becoming warm and sweat-covered from the adrenaline as they remember.

a postnational poetics of the impossible

Witnessing the breach is a contemporary measure of the spatiotemporal experience in America, and for many whose national identity is transformed into a fear, made into targets.

Thus, San Augustine's church and prison joined,
Fitly portrayed crimes' eminent success;
When hounds and murderous troops were loosed to find

The unsuspecting exile, and to press
The wretched Seminole from his recess
In hommock far, or by the dark bayou:
To burn his corn-fields in the wilderness,
An drag the helpless child and mother, thro
Infested swamps to die in chains as felons do.
    (Whitman, Canto II, LXXI, 51)

Black Seminole dispossession played a central role in Florida's ratification, as did America's anti-Blackness in building consensus among divided delegates.[19] Statehood would come to encompass not only land acquired through a number of contractual breaches, but also the legislative monopoly over the narrative authenticity of its constitutional history, and the state's carceral relationship to Black denizens in the history of Black exiles, runaways from Southern plantations and therefore "criminals" prior to Emancipation.

"I regret to hear of the recent murders committed near Fort Lauderdale," writes Zachary Taylor to Thomas Jesup in 1838. "& am satisfied you have fixed the real perpetrators, the Seminoles, which shows conclusively that no reliance can be placed on their promises or engagements, could the perpetrators of the act be gotten hold of, they ought to be put to death in some way as a terror to others of their nation."[20]

Two years prior, in addressing the legislative session of 1836, Jesup argued before legislators that "This," referring to the Seminole wars and the Black Seminoles in particular, "is a negro, not an Indian war; and if it be not speedily put down, the south will feel the effects of it on their slave population before the end of next season."

This sort of anti-Blackness survives in how the Black Seminoles were cast in public opinion, and I think of it in the rhetorical terms Amber Kelsie outlines when arguing how "Polite discussions that acknowledge racial terror only so as to explain away racial violence as the unique domain of extremists maintain a sense of white innocence that not only individuates a structural condition, but also pathologizes and prohibits black utterance (especially when that utterance might take on the form of rage) by adjusting the impossible demands of blackness back to the acceptable terms of debate" (2019, 65). "Raciality," she continues, "is intrinsic to modernity because it is necessary for the construction of the Subject—it names the materialization of the spatiotemporal forms that make the modern grammar." The grammar of liberalism, Kelsie establishes, is stasis, civic equilibrium via debate. But Blackness presents itself as an impossibility. It is an invention evoked in certain manifestations of an ungovernable power that must be extinguished by law. Blackness describes criminality; Blackness is an influence; Blackness is readily made effigy. Black life does not matter, and yet Blackness is the only thing that matters to law and order, and to the progress of the liberal democratic nation-state as it exists and operates ontologically as what is "good."

The contradiction of the American democratic context is that, as a rhetorical exhibition of progress via debate and thus an archive of speech acts meant to overcome institutional challenges, it can only premise the human liberal project, a consciousness capable of envisioning a historical continuum of stasis, while maintaining, often through some understanding of violence, a complete disavowal of Black life as part of that stasis, that civic equilibrium maintained by continuous speech. What I wish to highlight here is the spatiotemporal role in maintaining, perhaps not civic stasis, but a collective aesthetic imagination of a place wherein civic stasis needs to be, somehow, repaired and restored.

The premise of debate, itself a speech act, illustrates the inescapable and impossible ontological breach Whitman directly confronts when he writes in the dedicatory address: "I was in bondage—*I never was a slave*;—the infamous laws of a savage despotism took my substance—what of that?" (Whitman, 4). This same ontological challenge would be posed nearly one hundred years later in 1963, and on broadcast television, by James Baldwin. "What white people have to do, is they have to find out in their own hearts why it was necessary to have ******* in the first place, because I'm not a ******, I'm a man, but if you think I'm a ******, it means you need it."[21]

I think this is what Whitman also asks of America. To reflect on why it needs for him to only have been a *slave*.

> Thus ends my lay: Reluctantly I leave
> Atlassa and his sweet-eyed Southern maid;
> Palmecho, too, with whom I much did grieve,
> I turn from sadly! Could they but have stayed
> Beneath their "vines and fig trees," not afraid!
> Yet, by their Santa Rosa, let them dwell,
> Rejoicing in their freedom, long delayed!
> And while my heart's untrained emotions swell,
> Once more I turn to gaze and sigh: farewell! farewell!
>   (Whitman, Canto IV, LI, 95)

I've always had something of a problem with Whitman's ending. Palmecho and the Black Seminoles embrace their roles as farmers in their new Mexican home. But I understand the humanity in the ending when read rewatching

Baldwin's interview. The poetic speaker's "sigh" to me is devastating. It's a long and seemingly eternal exhale. It is the weight of returning to the impossible "love" of being born American, being made American.

Notes

1. Albery Whitman, *The Rape of Florida* (Miami, FL: Mnemosyne Publishing, 1969; reprint of an 1882 edition from the Fisk University Library Special Collections).

2. Walter Mignolo argues that artists working within the context of decolonial thinking and study recover the knowledge and information of felt experiences of contact and subjection/subjugation. The aesthetics created from the sentient/sensory project he calls aestheSis. Mignolo uses this term to elaborate on connotations of senses in aesthetics, to include emotional dimensions, which promote ways for healing. See "Decolonial options and artistic/ aestheSic entanglements: An Interview with Walter Mignolo," *Decolonialization: Indigeneity, Education & Society* 3, no. 1 (2014): 196–212.

3. This sort of poetic construct puts Whitman's "breach," and indeed the territorial setting, in conversation with more contemporary works like Gloria Anzaldúa's decolonial rewriting of the Mexico-US border (1987). Specifically the concept of "raja," and the "thin" barbed wire her poetic speaker in *Borderlands/La Frontera* "calls home."

4. Ellie D. Hernández, *Postnationalism in Chicana/o Literature and Culture* (Austin: University of Texas Press, 2009), 18.

5. See Lisa Lowe, "History Hesitant," *Social Text* 33, no. 4(125) (2015): 85–107. How persons throughout the world have survived, and indeed live out the spatiotemporal effects of this "power differential" is the premise of what Lowe terms an "intimacy," which in turn we can use here to illustrate the Native Black relationship to the Black Seminole nation.

6. One only need read the section on slavery in the President's Advisory Commission *1776* report (2021), which explains away American slavery as a matter of historical necessity, and hemispheric coincidence, and not as the egregious historical fact of violence responsible for, among other forms of genocide, a continuum structuring and norming contemporary forms of anti-Blackness (10–12). The report, which was taken down by the Biden administration, can be found here: https://trumpwhitehouse.archives.gov/wp-content/uploads/2021/01/The-Presidents-Advisory-1776-Commission-Final-Report.pdf.

7. This is not meant to propose a Eurocentrism regarding voice, especially Black and Native voice, but rather to present Whitman's formal approaches to his awareness of canonical archive. Form ensures the longevity and existence of the work into the future. It would be preserved as a vehicle for his poetic-political theory.

8. I think specifically here of how Whitman's poetics might offer insight on how to read contemporary Black poetry, from M. NourbeSe Philip's *Zong!* to Douglas Kearney's various "sound systems." See Ivy G. Wilson, ed., *At the Dusk of Dawn: Selected Poetry and Prose of Albery Alison Whitman* (Boston: Northeastern University Press, 2009).

9. Calvin Warren, *Ontological Terror* (Durham, NC: Duke University Press, 2018), 15. Accessed through openmonograph.org.

10. In this context I am also reminded of Kamau Brathwaite's "nation language," and the idea of the experience of the speakers of a language who are responsible for revolutionary actions in poetry. His descriptive foundation behind this term engages with a "sound system," or what he calls "software," of the Caribbean through observations of calypso and oral traditions and an extended observation of tides and people. Coincidentally, Brathwaite also invested heavily in "sound" in terms of real sonic networks like radio, recording equipment, his

computer, and cameras. See Kamau Brathwaite, *History of the Voice: The Development of Nation Language in Anglophone Caribbean Poetry* (New Beacon, 1984), 309–13.

11. The question here is not of ranking which is worse, settler-colonialism or anti-Blackness. They are the same "weather," so to speak, citing Christina Sharpe. Moreover, during the nineteenth century the terminology of anti-Blackness often inflected how Native and indigenous identity was constructed, with many Native men often referred to as "******" in newspapers and legal documents, particularly in advertisements seeking the "capture" of runaway slaves. This reveals how criminality narratives are often used to underscore racialization by deprioritizing mentions of race to law and order, but in so doing actually racialize the commons as the site of stasis.

12. The 1882 edition of the poem redacts specific mention of Zachary Taylor, America's twelfth president who was in office during the second Seminole War, using instead asterisks: "******'s."

13. *Newton Kansan*, May 24, 1888, 4.

14. Joan Bleau, *Atlas Maiora*, 1665. I would also include as a sort of triptych here Winslow Homer's "Florida Jungle" paintings, which portray an unpopulated, almost impenetrable scene of palmettos in soft hues. Homer's "vacation" paintings, moreover, played an indirect role in promoting tourism and its networks, and the narratives of "wildness" that attracted many Northeasterners to the area.

15. See, for instance, "FBI Investigating Threatening Emails Sent to Democrats in Florida," WLRN, https://www.wlrn.org/2020-10-20/fbi-investigating-threatening-emails-sent-to -democrats-in-florida.

16. See, for instance, "Effigy strung up by the Ku Klux Klan, Miami, Florida, 1940," Georgia State University Archives, https://digitalcollections.library.gsu.edu/digital/collection /SKennedy/id/13383/.

17. *Weekly Floridian*, July 4, 1882. *Chronicling America: Historic American Newspapers*. Library of Congress.

18. In another interesting echo, calls to reopen the economy during the height of the COVID-19 pandemic by then White House advisor Kevin Hassett (May 25, 2020, briefing). Hassett similarly appeals to the liberal democratic ontology, this time in the form of the economy as a living organism, while simultaneously referring to working people as "human stock." The perverse relationship to life and death in that ontology is historical, wherein life and whiteness are conflated beyond corporeal limits, which are in turn de-amplified in Black life. The result is what many have since called the "Death Cult" behind many of Trump's anti-life appeals to the confluence of matters: protests regarding anti-Blackness, and a call for the health of a universal civic body (which includes Black beings).

19. During debates, delegates from the "nucleus" (central, pro-bank cotton growers) argued against *ex post facto* laws the "loco focos" (anti-bank delegates) saw as a way out of faith bonds. In what seemed like an impasse, the nucleus appealed to the other delegates by arguing that making something that had been legal—faith bonds, as contracts—illegal, was similar to abolitionists' arguments that slavery should from henceforth be illegal. See Stephanie Moussalli, "Florida's Frontier Constitution: The Statehood, Banking, and Slavery Controversies," *Florida Historical Quarterly* 74, no. 4 (1996): 423–39.

20. *New York Times*, August 1, 1865.

21. "A Conversation with James Baldwin," from the series *Negro: An American Promise*, aired June 24, 1963. WGBH Educational Foundation, WGBH Boston, MA.

CHAPTER THREE

Grappling with an "Omen of Doom"

Learning from the Ocoee Election Day Massacre

Paul Ortiz

Good evening. First, I want to thank Bill Maxwell and the City of Ocoee's Human Relations Diversity Board for inviting me to speak at this amazing event. The *100 Year Remembrance Ceremony* commemorating the Ocoee Election Day Massacre of 1920 is essential to understanding how the history of Florida intersects with US history. What you are doing today, what you have been doing during this week of remembering, is a critical part of moving this nation toward a sense of equality before the laws, the idea that we should all have equal citizenship rights. No exceptions.

One century ago, white terrorism against African Americans was the greatest enemy of liberty in the United States. In 1920, African Americans in Ocoee were endeavoring to exercise the right to vote on Election Day.[1] The men who mobilized to stop Black people from voting did so to defend the prerogatives of one-party rule and the culture of corruption and graft that one-party states inevitably foster. And Ocoee was only one of many places where white people came together to ensure Black voter suppression in 1920. That year, promising African American voter registration drives in states like Georgia, Virginia, and North Carolina were decimated by the resurgent Ku Klux Klan and venal state officials.[2] Imagine the better world we would live in today had African Americans been able to enjoy access to the ballot box in 1920. As educators, parents, and concerned citizens, the African American struggle for dignity against devastating obstacles over four centuries gives us an unparalleled civics lesson. In contrast, the whitewashing of the history of anti-Black violence is a fatal impediment to democracy. In organizing this week of remembrance, the people of Ocoee and of Orange County, Florida, personify the words of the great Czech novelist Milan Kundera who wrote, "The struggle of man against power is the struggle of memory against forgetting."[3] Thank you for asking us to remember!

This evening I propose to do three things. I will situate the Ocoee Election Day Massacre and its legacies in regional, national, and international contexts. This will help us understand why the massacre occurred and how it continues to affect our society in ways we may not be aware of. I will also discuss what I call "the Ocoee truth-telling story" and why continuing dialog and historical work on the events of 1920 is so important today. Finally, I would like to share some thoughts on possible next steps in this dialog as we think about school curriculum, museum exhibits, public programs, and other venues for sharing the stories that you have been promoting during this inspiring week of events. My major goal this evening is to say: please keep engaging in these vital forums about racism and racial reconciliation.

We cannot allow ourselves to revert to the dishonest decades when events like the Ocoee, Tulsa, and Elaine massacres—and other anti-Black pogroms— were swept under the rug. Coverups breed distrust, poisoned social relations, and a corrosive cynicism that destroys the very fabric of society. Lester Dabbs, a retired school administrator and former mayor of Ocoee, stated in 1969, "The race riot of November, 1920, hangs over the area like an omen of doom which blights everything it touches."[4] What you have collectively achieved over the past two decades of oft-heartbreaking dialogues, disputes, and discussions, proves that historical traumas can only be treated when we open our hearts and minds to honoring the victims, acknowledging the guilt of the perpetrators, and reckoning with the legacies of racism. This is what I mean by the Ocoee truth-telling story, and it is worthy of study, refinement, and emulation.

The Black Lives Matter movement has brought us into a national moment of critical reflection on this nation's struggles to address systemic racism. The 2020 protests, which rapidly went global, were initially sparked by the police murders of Breonna Taylor and George Floyd.[5] This popular insurgency has created new spaces to talk about the troubled relationship between past and present in the United States. Black Lives Matter has demanded greater candor on all our parts as we discuss the vexing social problems of our time, especially racial and class inequalities. With renewed energy and a revived spirit of hope, we are rethinking our history, our cultures, and the ways that racism has prevented our nation from being a good place for all to live. As a historian involved with K–12 education across the country, I have had the privilege of seeing high school students, their parents, and teachers demand more rigorous social studies curricula that include the contributions of *all the citizenry* and not just a few elites in powdered wigs and silk stockings. I wrote *An African American and Latinx History of the United States* with the goal of centering the experiences of African Americans, Haitians, Cubans, Mexicans, and other groups from Latin America, the Caribbean, and Africa who built this nation from the very beginning of its existence.[6]

This past year, the citizens of Ocoee and Orange County have played a crucial role in our national truth-telling moment on racism by supporting Florida House Bill 1213, which now requires that every school district in the state teaches about the events surrounding the Ocoee Massacre.[7] I will conclude my address this evening with a reflection on this critical piece of legislation as well as a call for action on its implementation.

In my capacity as director of the Samuel Proctor Oral History Program at the University of Florida, I work with racial truth and reconciliation initiatives in different states.[8] Each of these initiatives, from the Elaine Legacy Center in Phillips County, Arkansas, to the Alachua County Florida Community Remembrance Project, has faced unique challenges in ensuring that the victims of racial terrorism are memorialized and that their stories are taught in schools. Inevitably, remembrance initiatives experience false starts, frustrating controversies, and logistical problems. The pathway to commemorating the Ocoee Election Day Massacre has not always been an easy road.[9] Tensions within organizations, conflicts between "town and gown" collaborations, and sharp disagreements over the historical narrative have arisen. That is inevitable.[10] Please do not blame each other for these disputes. Blame the local, state, and federal officials who colluded to cover up mass murder and voter suppression in Orange County! The lack of records, missing voter registration lists, selective memories of law enforcement—this has made reconstructing this horrific event stressful and at times excruciating.

Given these difficulties, I ask you to think about how far you *have* come in addressing a grave injustice that festered in this region for generations. I argue that *all* the organizations that have taken part in this process have contributed mightily to bringing the once hidden atrocities of the massacre to light. I am a great fan and admirer of the work that you are doing today in Ocoee. This remembrance ceremony, this round of vigils, marches, testimonials, and museum exhibits is not the end point but part of a journey of candid reconciliation.

We are going to use the *100 Year Remembrance Ceremony* as a springboard to building what Dr. Martin Luther King Jr. called "The Beloved Community." The creation of this community is hard work. A candid relationship to our mutual histories of tragedy and overcoming adversities is an essential part of living together honestly. August Wilson, one of our nation's greatest storytellers, used his play *Piano Lesson* to pose the following question: "Can you acquire a sense of self-worth by denying your past?" Too often, in our nation's history, we have answered this question in the affirmative. Like children, we are inclined to sweep our flaws and misdeeds under the carpet. Dr. King believed that the teaching of African American history was a mandatory part of this nation's chance at redemption. At a meeting of the Southern Christian Leadership Conference, King observed: "The tendency to ignore the Negro's contribution to American life and to strip him of his personhood is as old as the earliest history books and as contemporary as the morning's newspaper. To upset this cultural homicide, the Negro must rise up with an affirmation of his own Olympian manhood. Any movement for the Negro's freedom that overlooks this necessity is only waiting to be buried."[11]

Martin Luther King Jr. believed that African American history must be a centerpiece of the American educational system. However, just learning Black history was not enough. Rev. King eschewed the fad of knowledge for knowledge's sake. To the contrary, he stated in his final book, *Chaos or Community*: "Education without social action is a one-sided value because it has no true power potential. Social action without education is a weak expression of pure energy. Deeds uninformed by educated thought can take false directions. When we go into action and confront our adversaries, we must be as armed with knowledge as they. Our policies should have the strength of deep analysis beneath them to be able to challenge the clever sophistries of our opponents."[12]

How do Dr. King's teachings on history apply to our memorial activities this week? The white people who carried out the Ocoee Massacre in 1920 viewed citizenship as a zero-sum game. They assumed that if Black people gained more rights then white people would lose some of *their* rights. Today, racism grows from the same set of nihilistic assumptions. The reality is so much more edifying, as you have proven with the *100 Year Remembrance Ceremony*. The fact of the matter is that my security and happiness in large part depends on the security and happiness of my neighbor. An integral part of the Ocoee truth-telling story is about using education to become better citizens and better neighbors in the twenty-first century.

I owe my first visit to your city to a man who has become a good friend, Curtis Michelson. Curtis first invited me to Ocoee when I was a graduate student at Duke University in the summer of 1999. I was doing research on my dissertation, which centered on the Black freedom struggle in Florida between Reconstruction to the eve of the Great Depression.[13] Mr. Michelson was a part of a community organization called the Democracy Forum, whose members worked to bring what was then known as the "Ocoee Race Riot" to public attention.[14] I will never forget how Curtis, Francina Boykin, and other members of the Democracy Forum took me—a stranger—to key sites in the story of the 1920 election-day catastrophe.

We came to a location that had once been the neighborhood of African Americans forced to flee the town because they had registered to vote. A place where families with aspirations once lived. All one had to do was to scratch beneath the surface dirt to see the outlines of the doomed settlement. Now, it was an abandoned orange grove. Rioting whites had burned this community's churches and lodge building to the ground. Racial terrorism exiled African Americans from the soil where they had set down roots. Former Ocoee Mayor Lester Dabbs noted that four decades after whites drove African Americans out of the town, ". . . a sign admonished the Ocoee visitor as he approached the city limits that Negroes and dogs were unwelcome."[15] I had served in combat zones in Central America and had seen much destruction. However, nothing had prepared me for this moment. I wept. Afterwards, members of Democracy Forum invited me to share a meal and my thoughts. I promised to include the struggles of African Americans in Ocoee in my dissertation. Curtis, Francina, and the Democracy Forum persevered in holding public history programs despite opposition from the entrenched elite in Orange County, who did not want the story about the "Race Riot" told.[16]

In 2005, I published *Emancipation Betrayed: The Hidden History of Black Organizing and White Violence in Florida from Reconstruction to the Bloody Election of 1920.* The final chapters of the book cover the organizing efforts that Black Floridians took to regain the right to vote and to smash Jim Crow in the wake of World War I. African American women leaders in Florida including Mary McCleod Bethune, Eartha White of Jacksonville, and Emma J. Colyer in Orlando—all members of the powerful State Federation of Colored Women—vowed that African American military service and support of the Allied war effort should result in equal citizenship at the end of that great conflict. After the Armistice, community organizers from Pensacola to Miami and in between—including July Perry and Moses Norman in Ocoee—began registering African Americans to vote. Black women were the most effective voter registration organizers statewide. On the eve of Election Day, the *Orlando Reporter-Star* warned, "The suffrage victory, according to Miss [Alice] Paul is 'won but not paid for.' We should worry! But we do. The struggle for white supremacy in the South now confronts us."[17]

The first years of my academic career took me far away from my research in Florida, all the way to the West Coast. In 2008, I left my position at the University of California, Santa Cruz to become the director of the Proctor Program at the University of Florida. One evening around midnight in the fall of 2009, my phone rang. (This was back in the day when most of us still had landlines.) I am a night person; I do most of my writing, grading, and so forth well into the early morning hours. And I engage in the kind of scholarship—you may have guessed—that sometimes elicits anger and animosity. I am not unused to getting prank calls or angry emails from white nationalists. I wondered whether I should answer the late-night call. However, something moved me to pick up the phone. The man calling introduced himself as Bill Maxwell. Before I could respond, Mr. Maxwell said, "Professor Ortiz, the City of Ocoee, the Human Relations Diversity Board, would like to invite you to give the keynote lecture about the ninetieth anniversary of the events in Ocoee for our annual MLK Day Unity Parade and Celebration." Honestly, I almost hung up the phone, because I thought incredulously, "This has got to be a hoax. The City of Ocoee inviting me to come down and give a talk about the Ocoee Massacre?"

I am glad I did not hang up the phone. Mr. Maxwell explained where he was coming from. He expressed the need to candidly acknowledge the Election Day catastrophe as well as his plans to use discussions of this shocking event to bring people together. Bill sold me on his vision. I travelled to Ocoee and gave the keynote address for the Martin Luther King Jr. Unity Parade and Celebration in 2010. My wife Sheila Payne travelled with me. It was a memorable experience. The city welcomed us with open arms. We engaged in intensive discussions on Florida history during a book signing for *Emancipation Betrayed* and at other events. During a wide-ranging conversation at the Ocoee Cafe, Mayor Scott Vandergrift took exception to my description of the events of November 2–3 as a "massacre." We went back and forth on the topic. Sheila ended the discussion by saying: "Mayor Vandergrift. Paul is a scholar. He spent years on this research. He has one hundred pages of footnotes in *Emancipation Betrayed*. If he says what happened was a massacre, it was a massacre." That clinched it.

In the two event-filled days leading up to my lecture, we talked with numerous area residents who were trying in their own ways to bring the history of the massacre to public attention. I especially remember talking at length with Lester Dabbs, a retired school principal and former mayor of the city. I know that many people gathered here this evening remember Mr. Dabbs with great fondness. In 1969, while enrolled at nearby Stetson University, Lester wrote his master's thesis on the Election Day massacre. This was an act of courage.[18] In the introduction to his thesis, Mr. Dabbs wrote, "The race riot of November, 1920, hangs over the area like an omen of doom which blights everything it touches."[19] Lester used his research as a call for action. Unfortunately, three decades would elapse before the Democracy Forum pierced the veil of official denial regarding what had happened on Election Day 1920. In an early passage in his thesis, Mr. Dabbs discussed law enforcement's denial of the massacre, and he evaluated the costs of the whitewashing of history in his town:

> At present, the Ocoee Junior-Senior High School is the only secondary school in the county without at least token integration, even though the principal and the researcher [Lester Dabbs] have attended desegregation institutes at Stetson University at one time or another. Many adults and students of the community are proud of the fact that the local Klan unit was the third one formed in the state. They are proud of the local resident cited by Congress in its recent hearings and they are proud of the two area units of the United Klans of America.[20]

In our discussions four decades after he had written these words, Lester Dabbs expressed a sense of relief that so many people were working to set the record straight about Ocoee.

Shortly after I returned to Gainesville, I received a call from an African American man in Ocoee who had attended the MLK program. He was a Vietnam War veteran and a retired military service member. He had moved to Ocoee without knowing about the history of the massacre. Something about the town had not felt right to him. He wanted to let me know about the power of history: "Dr. Ortiz, I just wanted to let you know how much of an impact your lecture has made on this town. For the first time in the several years I have lived here, white people actually *look me in the eyes*." This was a profoundly humbling moment in my life. I share it with you publicly because it is a testament to *your* collective efforts to break free of what Lester Dabbs called "this omen of doom" that for too long has undermined our capacity to treat each other with the dignity and respect that all of us deserve.

Let me move now to discuss the actual events of Election Day 1920. It is important to understand that the Ocoee Massacre was not an isolated event. White Americans have carried out ethnic cleansing against African American communities from the inception of this nation's history. However, historians have noted that the period between 1917 and 1923 witnessed a virulent upswing of anti-Black mass murders across the nation.[21] A partial list of these conflagrations would include the 1917 anti-Black assaults that took place in East St. Louis; the "Philadelphia Race Riot" of 1918; 1919's "Red Summer" with organized mass murders of African Americans in Elaine, Chicago, Charleston, and elsewhere; Ocoee in 1920; Tulsa, 1921; the Perry, Florida, "Civil War" of 1922; and of course, the Rosewood Massacre in 1923.[22]

Why was there an upsurge of anti-Black violence between 1917 and 1923? We can turn to the great scholar W. E. B. Du Bois for answers. In a series of sociological studies conducted between 1900 and World War I, Dr. Du Bois highlighted the fact that despite the Jim Crow system of white supremacy, African Americans were making tremendous economic, political, and social progress.[23] In the early twentieth century, African Americans who moved up north to cities like Detroit, New York, and Pittsburgh were making political strides. They were registering to vote, they were participating in ward politics, and they were beginning to exert a swing vote impact in statewide as well as national elections.[24]

Like their counterparts across the South, Black Floridians were making headway in land ownership, in farm ownership especially. In fact, by the eve of the Great Depression nearly 40 percent of African American farmers in Florida owned their own farms.[25] During the months leading up to the 1920 presidential election, African American activists who urged Black men and women to register to vote connected economic security with political power. For example, Florida Negro Uplift Association leader Rev. S. H. Betts exhorted African Americans to ". . . settle down, save their money, buy land, qualify and vote, just as all other races do, before they count for much." Rev. Betts told African Americans to "quit supporting false leaders, men who will not stand by a righteous cause, but will sell their birthrights for a mess of pottage." Betts praised African American endeavors in land ownership: "Why, in our little state of Florida, we own nearly half the land which we are now cultivating. Oh yes, it is best for us to go to the country."[26]

Rev. Betts's admonitions to African Americans may sound rather conservative to our modern ears; to the thinking of the white power structure in 1920, however, Rev. Betts might as well have been a Marxist revolutionary. Dr. Du Bois noted that white business leaders and politicians had built the edifice of the Jim Crow system on the assumption of permanent, cheap labor. Hence, they countered rising Black aspirations in the early twentieth century by vowing "To break the political power of the Black labourers in the South."[27] In addition to voter suppression, this meant mobilizing white society to engage in extreme violence to crush African American efforts to achieve independence. As historians Michael Newton and Jerrell Shofner have revealed, the Ku Klux Klan in Florida was often directed by the state's large employers as antilabor shock troops to keep working-class people poor and businesspersons rich.[28] Dr. Du Bois noted that the propertied elite in the South manipulated poor whites to do their bidding ". . . under the cry of race prejudice. No method of inflaming the darkest passions of men was unused. The lynching mob was given its glut of blood, and egged on by purposely exaggerated and often wholly invented tales of crime on the part of perhaps the most peaceful and sweet-tempered race the world has ever known."[29]

The Ocoee Massacre and other acts of white violence were designed to thwart African American political, economic, and social progress. The loss of Black property and wealth in these incidents of mass murder—all of which went unpunished—is incalculable. And let me be clear. These were not the actions of unthinking "mobs." These were planned paramilitary operations carried out to impoverish Black people. For example, when white furniture merchants in Orlando discovered that African Americans in Ocoee were registering to vote ahead of the presidential election, many of these merchants drove out to the town to repossess items purchased by African Americans on credit. According to a report published in the *National Republican*, "... trucks were backed up to a number of homes and pianos and furniture removed by white people who had sold these on the installment plan, in order that they might not suffer loss."[30] What happened in Ocoee was a premeditated assault aided and abetted by the media, law enforcement, and elected officials. On the eve of the Ocoee, Tulsa, or Elaine attacks, one could point to groups of successful Black farmers, businesspeople, and landowners in each town. In the aftermath of the terror, African Americans were reduced to poverty and driven out of their homes—literally stateless individuals or refugees. Any effort today to address the issue of the racial wealth gap must begin with a reckoning with the history of America's anti-Black violence.[31]

Let me now suggest a framework for how we might teach about Ocoee as both a tragedy as well as a lesson in civic engagement for Florida's K–12 students. To reiterate: African Americans launched a statewide voter registration movement in the weeks after the end of the end of World War I. Organizers in thirty-five counties including Orange County, including Western Orange County, hatched this movement in their churches, fraternal lodges, labor unions, and other organizations. Secret societies raised subscriptions so that poorer members could pay their poll taxes. By September 1920, tens of thousands of African Americans had paid their poll taxes, were registering to vote, and were urging each other to march to the polls on Election Day.

In the weeks leading up to the 1920 election, Black Floridians developed a stunning vision of creating a new democratic society to replace the rotten edifice of white business supremacy. Hundreds of Black institutions—women's clubs, military veterans' organizations, business groups—came together, and said "We've had it with white supremacy. We are going to break down one-party rule in Florida. We are going to regain the right to vote. We are going to create decent educational opportunities for our children. We are going to create dignified employment opportunities for our sisters, daughters, and mothers. We are going to demand equal pay opportunities for Black teachers. We're going to achieve equality for all."

The Florida Movement of 1920 seems to belong to the 1960s. I must admit that when I first started researching this, I was stunned at the depth and history of African American organizing in Florida. I had never heard of this movement and when I began to unearth it, and it challenged a lot of my preconceived notions about American history. I was taught that the civil rights movement began in the 1950s, with either the *Brown v. Board of Education* ruling by the Supreme Court, or the Montgomery Bus Boycott, or both. To see that Black Floridians had organized this incredible civil rights movement over three decades earlier, in 1920, was a wake-up call for how I understood the broader story of American democracy. It was revelatory.

When I began to look deeper, I realized something very important about Black history in Florida. The African American freedom struggle has been a continuous theme in the Gulf South. It is not a sidebar to a larger national narrative; it is the key to the entire story of American liberty. In truth, the Florida Movement of 1920 was rooted in three centuries of African American struggles for freedom in the Deep South. Consider that the first free Black community on this continent existed just a two-hour drive north of where we are holding this event now. Escaped slaves built and fortified Fort Mose, just outside of the Spanish colony in St. Augustine. The Spanish Crown granted provisional freedom to African American slaves who escaped from the British Colonies beginning in the 1680s if they agreed to bear arms to defend the colony. Fort Mose endured numerous Anglo settler attacks and became a redoubt of liberty purchased with African American blood, sweat, and tears.[32]

The Africans of Spanish Florida were forced to evacuate to Cuba once the British took control of the colony in 1763. Barely two decades later, in a breathtaking prelude to the Underground Railroad, first dozens and then hundreds of escaped African American slaves found sanctuary with Native Americans in what is now the Panhandle. With some assistance from the British, this Black-Native alliance established "Negro Fort" on the Apalachicola River to defend a maroon community of self-emancipated slaves at Prospect Bluff.[33] Secretary of State John Quincy Adams dispatched Andrew Jackson to suppress this security threat to slavery in the Southeast. After suffering a devastating defeat, the survivors of Negro Fort moved deeper into Florida and hundreds built a new maroon community along the Manatee River in present-day Bradenton between 1812 and 1821.[34]

At the outset of the Second Seminole War (1835–42) hundreds of African American slaves in Florida rose in the Alachua and St. Johns River plantation districts. They joined the battle to drive slavery out of Florida and to strike for liberation. Many historians now consider this to be the largest slave revolt in North American history.[35] Commanding General Thomas Sidney

Jessup observed that the Second Seminole War was "a [N]egro, not an Indian war."[36] After the final defeat of the Seminole–ex-slave alliance, a candid white observer revealed the scope of the tragedy: "The Seminole made a desperate stand for his Florida home. He was exacting from the whites a terrible price for the acres they coveted. And even more desperately than the Indian, fought the [N]egro fugitive. Defeat for him was not the loss of land, but of liberty; to yield meant not exile, but bondage."

Let's use the history of the Black struggle against slavery in Florida to jump forward in time to the civil rights movement in the 1950s. No narrative of the freedom struggle is complete without the name of Howard Thurman. Reverend Thurman is one of the greatest Christian theologians in this country's history, a man known as a mentor for Dr. Martin Luther King Jr., who always carried a copy of Thurman's *Jesus and the Disinherited* with him during his travels. Rev. Thurman was also a Floridian. And Howard Thurman tells us that he gained his insights into transforming Christianity into a religion of liberation through his grandmother, who had been a slave in Madison County, Florida. "The fact that the first twenty-three years of my life were spent in Florida and in Georgia," the Reverend Dr. Howard Thurman later recalled, "left its scars deep in my spirit and has rendered me terribly sensitive to the churning abyss separating white from black."[37]

African American history in Florida is the epitome of the battle for freedom in American history. Let us keep going. James Weldon Johnson, a brilliant poet, national leader of the NAACP, and key organizer of the Florida Voter Registration Movement in 1920, was reared in Jacksonville. Mary McCleod Bethune arrived to Daytona in 1904 and founded a Black educational institution for young African American women that we know today as Bethune-Cookman University. A. Philip Randolph, originally from Crescent City, is the founder of the Brotherhood of Sleeping Car Porters and Maids and is the organizer of the 1963 March on Washington for Jobs and Freedom.[38]

All these individuals are from Florida. (One could name many more!) And it begs the question: Why Florida? Well, it is because of the strength and resilience of Black communities. From slavery to Emancipation and the modern civil rights movement, families, elders, and neighborhoods— under siege by white supremacy—nurtured generations of some of the most superb freedom fighters in the history of this nation. Mrs. Bethune was a brilliant educator and organizer; however, she relied upon the Black community in Volusia County and surrounding areas to sustain and to protect the Daytona Industrial School for Girls because it was the target of numerous Ku Klux Klan attacks.

Black Floridians wove centuries of hopes for liberty and emancipation together in the weeks leading up to the election of 1920. The stakes of this election were incredibly high. The epicenter of sustained anti-Black violence was in western Orange County. However, the Ku Klux Klan, police, and other whites targeted Black Floridians all across the state for simply trying to vote. Because the phrase "simply trying to vote" hides the fact that if African Americans got the vote back, got the ballot back, in 1920, it would have turned this society upside down. It would have brought democracy to a state in the throes of one-party rule.

I want to say a few words about Mr. Perry and Mr. Norman, martyrs in the voter registration movement in Ocoee, because it's very important that we remember their example today. We know that July Perry and Moses Norman were lodge members, and that lodges played pivotal roles in the 1920 election. As I mentioned earlier, lodges, secret societies, and fraternal orders pooled resources to pay members' poll taxes. African American lodges like the Knights of Pythias, the Masons, and the Daughters of the Eastern Star were the outstanding practitioners of mutual aid and community building in rural areas and cities alike in the Gulf South.

Moses Norman and July Perry were part of an extraordinary cohort of organizers in Florida who successfully urged their fellow Black citizens to register to vote. It took incredible courage for an African American to become a qualified voter in Florida. When you asked a Black person to register to vote in Florida in 1920, you were asking them to risk their life and their livelihood. Florida had the highest per capita lynching rate in the entire nation—higher than Georgia, higher than Alabama, higher than Mississippi! Black Floridians were assassinated in the years leading up to 1920 simply for talking assertively to a white person.

What African Americans in Ocoee did in attempting to register to vote in 1920 is an incredible example of civic engagement. No student will ever take the responsibilities of citizenship lightly after a deep dive into the history of Moses Norman, July Perry, and the Florida Voter Registration Movement. The fact that Mr. Norman and Mr. Perry were able to encourage so many people to become qualified voters—and one day I hope we are able to find out exactly how many there were—speaks volumes. It speaks about the trust that they had earned from their neighbors. But, above all, it speaks about the faith and hope that African Americans in western Orange County had that they were willing to risk their lives to build a better day.

Infuriated by the persistence of African Americans in Ocoee, the Ku Klux Klan mobilized. A month before Election Day, the KKK began warning the African American community at Ocoee that "not a single Negro would be permitted to vote." Local Democrats in Ocoee claimed that the Black voter registration campaign had made African Americans too assertive in their interactions with whites and they plotted to rig the election. Lester Dabbs noted:

In preparation for the expected attempts by the Negroes to vote on election day, the political leaders of the community had taken the necessary precautions to preclude the possibility of a Negro's being able to vote. These leaders had, for instance, stationed persons at the polls whose job it was to challenge the vote of any Negro making an effort to exercise the franchise. This challenge would then necessitate the Negroes appearing before a notary public, in this case Justice of the Peace R. C. Bigelow. The concluding preparation of the whites was to arrange for the Honorable Mr. Bigelow to vote early and then conveniently go fishing, thus making it necessary for any Negro desirous of voting to make the long trip into Orlando.[39]

Toward a Conclusion

It has been a privilege and an honor to be able to witness over two decades' time how you have used the history of this very tragic event to reimagine what the beloved community might look like in the twenty-first century. Again, it has not been easy. At the truth-telling forums, there has been tears, there has been anger. Sometimes people get up and walk out of the room and shake their heads—and they should. History should *never* be boring, friends, it should always be passionate. American history, especially, should make you cry, it should make you laugh, it should make you get up and shake your head, you know? It should give you joy; it should give you great anger—that is the history of this country. It is a history of striving for equality, but it is also the history of coming up short time and time and time again. And that's why I'm so proud about the events that you've been organizing for the hundred-year remembrance ceremony.

Let me suggest where we might go next. As you know, the State of Florida has passed a law requiring all school districts to teach the story of the Ocoee Election Day Massacre. So, my charge to all of us today is to bring that law—which, we must remember, is an unfunded mandate—into reality. And we all can play a role as parents, as students, as concerned citizens, to make sure we go to our respective school boards and say, "What types of resources do you need to implement a curriculum which will have lesson plans about African American history, civic engagement, and the Ocoee Election Day Massacre? How can we work in tandem with existing institutions, like the Commissioner of Education's African American Task Force, the Florida Humanities Council, the Florida Historical Society, as well as our regional and national universities and colleges to share the Ocoee story and its legacies? How can we help K–12 teachers to develop curriculum around the Ocoee Election Day Massacre?"

I am excited to report that this work is well underway in many areas of our state; however, we need more help! I pledge the continuing support of the Samuel Proctor Oral History Program in all these endeavors. It is more important than ever because the Ocoee Massacre highlights great and perennial themes in American history: the struggle for equality and the unfulfilled promise of democracy. This is the story of Ocoee writ large. In conclusion, thank you for inviting me and my students to be a part of this endeavor. I wish I could be with you in person for the historical marker ceremony. Finally, let us build on this week's remembrance events to keep working for the historical pursuit of truth and justice. Thank you again for inviting me and have a wonderful, wonderful day.

Notes

This essay is a revised version of the address I gave for the City of Ocoee, Florida's 100 Year Remembrance Ceremony of the 1920 Election Day Massacre on November 8, 2020.

1. I discuss the origins of the Ocoee Massacre in *Emancipation Betrayed: The Hidden History of Black Organizing and White Violence in Florida from Reconstruction to the Bloody Election of 1920* (Berkeley: University of California Press, 2005). Zora Neale Hurston wrote about the incident during her work with the Works Progress Administration in the 1930s. See Zora Neale Hurston, "The Ocoee Riot," Box 2, Folder, "Atrocities Perpetrated Upon June 1938" (WPA Papers), The Florida Negro Papers, Special Collections Library, University of South Florida. See also: "Notes Taken by Stetson Kennedy on Dialogue between Zora Neale Hurston and Dr. Carita Dogget Course [sic]," n.d. Box 1, Folder 13, Stetson Kennedy Papers, Federal Writers Project, 1936–1940, Southern Historical Collection, University of North Carolina, Chapel Hill. In 2019, the Florida State Legislature commissioned a report of the "1920 Election Day violence in Ocoee, Florida to provide information on the scope and effects of the incident." "Ocoee Election Day Violence—November 1920," *Office of Program Policy Analysis and Government Accountability*, Report No. 19–15 (Tallahassee: November 1, 2019).

2. *Emancipation Betrayed*, 224–25.

3. Milan Kundera, *The Book of Laughter and Forgetting* (1979; New York: Harper Perennial Modern Classics, 1999), 4.

4. Lester Dabbs, "A Report of the Circumstances and Events of the Race Riot on November 2, 1920, in Ocoee, Florida" (MA thesis, Stetson University, 1969).

5. For the origins of the Black Lives Matter movement, see Patrisse Cullors and Asha Bandele, *When They Call You a Terrorist: A Black Lives Matter Memoir* (2017; New York: St. Martin's Griffen, 2020).

6. Paul Ortiz, *An African American and Latinx History of the United States* (Boston: Beacon Press, 2018).

7. Kirby Wilson, "Florida Schools Must Now Teach the Ocoee Election Day Massacre," *Tampa Bay Times*, June 25, 2020, https://www.tampabay.com/florida-politics/buzz/2020/06/25 /florida-schools-now-have-to-teach-the-ocoee-election-day-massacre-heres-why-that-matters/.

8. For information on the Samuel Proctor Oral History Program, see the program's website: https://oral.history.ufl.edu/. Our program's "Resources on African American History, Anti-Racism & Racial Justice" may be viewed here: https://oral.history.ufl.edu/research/anti-racist-resources/.

9. After being invited to give the keynote address for the City of Ocoee's 2010 Martin Luther King Jr. celebration, titled "90 Years After the Ocoee Election Day Race Riot," I wrote the following essay as a reflection on my experiences working with local community members to excavate the massacre's multiple legacies: "Ocoee, Florida: Remembering 'The Single Bloodiest Day in Modern U.S. Political History,'" *Facing South*, May 14, 2010, https://www.facingsouth.org/2010/05/ocoee-florida-remembering-the-single-bloodiest-day-in-modern-us-political-history.html. I was also invited by the City of Ocoee to deliver an address on the Ocoee Massacre for Ocoee's Martin Luther King Jr. Unity Parade and Celebration in 2020.

10. Works that examine controversies in public history and historical memory include Michel-Rolph Trouillot, *Silencing the Past: Power and the Production of History* (Boston: Beacon Press, 1995); Alessandro Portelli, *The Order Has Been Carried Out: History, Memory, and Meaning of a Nazi Massacre in Rome* (New York: Palgrave Macmillan, 2007); Raul Hilberg, *Politics of Memory: The Journey of a Holocaust Historian* (Chicago: Ivan R. Dee Publishers, 2002).

11. Martin Luther King Jr., "The Southern Christian Leadership Address, 16 August, 1967," *World History Archives: Documents by Rev. Martin Luther King, Hartford Web Publishing.* Accessed May 20, 2021, http://www.hartford-hwp.com/archives/45a/index-bca.html.

12. Martin Luther King Jr., *Where Do We Go from Here: Chaos or Community?* (Boston: Beacon Press, 1967), 155.

13. My dissertation was titled *"Like Water Covered the Sea": The African American Freedom Struggle in Florida, 1877–1920* (PhD diss., Duke University, 2000).

14. For an overview of the work of the Democracy Forum, see Curtis Michelson and Julian Chambliss oral history interview, June 28, 2017, Joel Buchanan Archive of African American Oral History, University of Florida Digital Collections, University of Florida, https://ufdc.ufl.edu/AA00066245/00001; Katherine Perry, "Constructing African American Histories in Central Florida" (MA thesis, University of Central Florida, 2008).

15. Dabbs, "A Report of the Circumstances and Events of the Race Riot on November 2, 1920," 41.

16. Craig Quintana, "Riot Still Painful for Ocoee," *Orlando Sentinel*, November 2, 1998, https://www.orlandosentinel.com/news/os-xpm-1998-11-02-9811020046-story.html.

17. *Emancipation Betrayed*, 205.

18. Dabbs, "A Report of the Circumstances and Events of the Race Riot on November 2, 1920."

19. Dabbs, "A Report of the Circumstances and Events of the Race Riot on November 2, 1920," 4.

20. Dabbs, "A Report of the Circumstances and Events of the Race Riot on November 2, 1920," 4–5. Emphasis in the original.

21. Paul Ortiz, "U.S. Race Riots, 1917–1923," in *The Encyclopedia of Race and Racism*, ed. Nicole Watkins (New York: Gale Group/Macmillan Reference USA, 2007), 435–43.

22. For an overview of the anti-Black riots of the era, see Nan Elizabeth Woodruff, *American Congo: The African American Freedom Struggle in the Delta* (Cambridge, MA: Harvard University Press, 2003); Leon Litwack, *Trouble in Mind: Black Southerners in the Age of Jim Crow* (New York: Knopf, 1998); Elliot Rudwick, *Race Riot at East St. Louis, July 2, 1917* (Carbondale: Southern Illinois University Press, 1964); James R. Grossman, *Land of Hope: Chicago, Black Southerners and the Great Migration* (Chicago: University of Chicago Press, 1989).

23. W. E. B. Du Bois, "The Economics of Negro Emancipation in the United States," *Sociological Review* 4, no. 3 (October 1911): 303–13; Joe P. L. Davidson, "Ugly Progress: W. E. B. Du Bois's Sociology of the Future," *Sociological Review* 62, no. 2 (March 2021): 382–95.

24. Michael Brandon, "Black Chicago's New Deal Congressmen: Migration, Ghettoization, and the Origins of Civil Rights Politics" (PhD thesis, University of Florida, 2015).

25. For statistics on farm ownership, see Charles S. Johnson et al., *Statistical Atlas of Southern Counties* (Chapel Hill: University of North Carolina Press, 1941), 73.

26. *Emancipation Betrayed*, 197.

27. Du Bois, "The Economics of Negro Emancipation," 311.

28. Michael Newton, *The Invisible Empire: The Ku Klux Klan in Florida*, Foreword by Raymond Arsenault and Gary R. Mormino (Gainesville: University Press of Florida, 2001). Jerrell H. Shofner, "Communists, Klansmen and the CIO in the Florida Citrus Industry," *Florida Historical Quarterly* 71, no. 3 (January 1993): 300–309.

29. Du Bois, "The Economics of Negro Emancipation," 311.

30. "Election Crookedness," *National Republican*, January 1, 1921.

31. For examinations of the racial wealth gap, see William A. Darity and A. Kirsten Mullen, *From Here to Equality: Reparations for Black Americans in the Twenty-First Century* (Chapel Hill: University of North Carolina Press, 2020); Melvin Oliver and Thomas Shapiro, *Black Wealth/White Wealth: A New Perspective on Racial Inequality* (New York: Routledge, 1995); Mehrsa Baradaran, *The Color of Money: Black Banks and the Racial Wealth Gap* (Cambridge, MA: Belknap Press, 2019).

32. Jane Landers, *Black Society in Spanish Florida* (Urbana: University of Illinois Press, 1999); Jane Landers, "Gracia Real de Santa Teresa de Mose: A Free Black Town in Spanish Colonial Florida," *American Historical Review* 95 (February 1990): 9–30; Peter H. Wood, *Black Majority: Negroes in Colonial South Carolina From 1670 Through the Stono Rebellion* (New York: Norton, 1974), 23.

33. Nathaniel Millett, *The Maroons of Prospect Bluff and Their Quest for Freedom in the Atlantic World* (Gainesville: University Press of Florida, 2015); Terrance M. Weik, *The Archeology of Antislavery Resistance* (Gainesville: University Press of Florida, 2012).

34. Canter Brown Jr., "The Sarrazota, or Runaway Negro Plantations: Tampa Bay's First Black Community, 1812–1821," *Tampa Bay History* 12 (1990): 5–19.

35. Larry Rivers, *Slavery in Florida: Territorial Days to Emancipation* (Gainesville: University Press of Florida, 2000), 219; Cantor Brown, "Race Relations in Territorial Florida, 1821–1845," *Florida Historical Quarterly* 73 (1995): 287–307.

36. Kenneth Porter Wiggins, *The Black Seminoles: History of a Freedom-Seeking People*, rev. and ed. Alcione M. Amos and Thomas P. Senter (Gainesville: University Press of Florida, 1996), 66; Kevin Mulroy, *Freedom on the Border: The Seminole Maroons in Florida, the Indian Territory, Coahuila, and Texas* (Lubbock, TX: Texas Tech University Press, 1993).

37. Howard Thurman, *The Luminous Darkness: A Personal Interpretation of the Anatomy of Segregation and the Ground of Hope* (1965; Richmond, IN: Friends United Press, 1999), x. See also, Howard Thurman, *With Head and Heart: The Autobiography of Howard Thurman* (New York: Harcourt Brace, 1979), 20–21.

38. William P. Jones, *The March on Washington: Jobs, Freedom, and the Forgotten History of Civil Rights* (New York: W. W. Norton, 2014).

39. Dabbs, "A Report of the Circumstances and Events of the Race Riot on November 2, 1920," 24.

CHAPTER FOUR

From Floridian Ode to National Epic
James Weldon Johnson's Digressive Quest
for a Modern African American Poetics

Noelle Morrissette

A white cockatoo they owned outlived both James Weldon (1871–1938) and Grace Nail Johnson (1885–1976). A gift from an admiral during Johnson's final diplomatic post to Nicaragua (1909–1912), Lorita was a beloved presence in their childless household. Ollie Jewell Sims, Johnson's nurse from 1934 until his tragic death four years later and Grace Nail's companion until the end of her life, inherited the bird. One wishes for a Flaubertian parrot who could speak. Even by her name, however, Lorita tells us something about the Johnsons' cultural and hemispheric travels between Latin and Black cultures: gifted as "Lorita," by the 1930s they had altered her name to "Loretta."

In this essay, I present Johnson's innovative, formative ideas about a Black culture that reached beyond national boundaries to resituate his culture-building, national commitments. From 1901 to 1912, the years of his first endeavors as a national artist and author, Johnson engaged in linguistic, geographic, and musical digressions that, through their movements outward, reshaped American discourses and reconceptualized Black citizenship within the United States. What I call Johnson's engagement with "cultures of talk" in Jacksonville, Florida, through his exposure to Spanish-speaking and Cuban culture became, in the early years of the twentieth century, a formal practice of what Johnson called *badinage* and Brent Edwards refers to as *décalage*: shifting cultural gaps that defy location and are defined by this defiant movement.[1]

• • •

In 1901, James Weldon Johnson's life divided into two halves: the first thirty years of his life in Florida; the remainder of his life in New York and the nation at large. The geographic and psychic break was occasioned, he wrote in his autobiography *Along This Way,* by "a near-lynching" by a militia in his home-town of Jacksonville in the weeks after what became known as the "Great Fire."[2] The experience left him traumatized for decades, and he did not write or speak about it for almost thirty years.[3] Neither of his parents, pillars of Jacksonville's Black community, would know what had happened to him before they died. Only Johnson's brother John Rosamond, who kept the secret, knew.

Shortly after this pivotal experience, Johnson submitted his resignation as principal of Stanton School and went north, to New York City's Tenderloin District, with his brother, and made music like his life depended upon it. While the Johnson brothers and their partner Bob Cole were aware of the limitations of the genre of musical comedy from the start of this endeavor, they aspired to create something freer and more elevated out of a form that often advanced the worst stereotypes of the minstrel stage. The trio's songs aspired to elegant love lyrics—a pathbreaking treatment of Black mate-rial—that emphasized universal appeal. The songwriting team worked from Rosamond's project of creating "art songs," or lieder, with popular appeal for the masses. While Rosamond continued this project with partner Bob Cole until the latter's death in 1911, Johnson moved into a diplomatic post in 1906 that advanced his lifelong engagement with American politics, with Johnson walking the line between advocacy for Black civic equality and defense of American interests abroad.

In his formative years in Florida, Johnson had aspired to the kinds of writings that typified the late nineteenth century: minstrel ditties and loft-ier poems of praise, these latter works endeavors to align a much younger speaker with prominent individuals and elevated subjects. His elegy for Frederick Douglass, a speech delivered by Johnson to his fraternity at Atlanta University where he would receive a masters, was one such work. To write to Frederick Douglass was as much about honoring a man of esteem as it was about announcing a younger generation's aspirations to greatness. Among these early works of speech and poetry one finds direct addresses to local elements   to landscapes and personae. These college-era works demonstrate Johnson's ambition to be known as a writer well before he would become known as the author of *Fifty Years and Other Poems* (1915), *The Autobiography of an Ex-Colored Man* (1912, 1915, 1927), and subsequent works.

Among these college works, Johnson's "Ode to Florida," a trite if deeply felt praise poem to his birthplace, stands out as an example of the young man Johnson's effort to assume poetic greatness through the form of the praise poem. Emphasizing the natural wonders of the state, this ode invokes "plains . . . rivers and lakes . . . / forests . . . marshes and brakes," and the Everglades. The poem traces "a path to the rivers and thence to the sea" in the grand scale appropriate to the ode form, while finding a place for the speaker, who woos his homeland as if it were a lover. "Ode to Florida" represents an early phase of Johnson's writing that has relevance to his subsequent works. We find the author, in his "Ode," asserting an individual lyricism tied to region; while in his later poetry, written after 1901, we find the poet's view of the world has altered to take region into account in a larger cultural perspective. His work from 1901 forward represents a modern poetic discourse in the making.

For Johnson, two works wedded in this discourse of emancipation as harbingers of a new century of poetry, and also of poetic form, centered on the gaps in modern Black experience. The lyrical song "Lift Every Voice and Sing" and the poem "Fifty Years" were conceived by the same occasion: Johnson was asked to write a speech as part of a celebration of Lincoln's birthday, scheduled to take place in the city of Jacksonville in 1900. Together, these lyrical works represent the epochal shift of Johnson's life before and after his harrowing experience at the hands of the roving militia. Although begun out of the same celebratory event for Lincoln, "Fifty Years" was shelved for several years following the composition and performance of "Lift Every Voice and Sing."

Johnson's engagement with print culture in Jacksonville from the 1890s through to his departure for the North in 1901 can be attributed, in part, to the intense relationship he had with Thomas Osmond Summers (1948–1899), a brilliant and dissipated surgeon who established himself in Jacksonville after burning through his, and his wife's, inheritances and livelihoods in Nashville. Summers, born in South Carolina, studied in Alabama, London, Berlin, and Edinburgh; he became an ether addict while teaching at Vanderbilt University in Nashville. The US government appointed Summers to study yellow fever in South America in 1879, during which time he also served in the US South, including Jacksonville, studying the epidemics of 1878, 1888, and 1897. In 1898, during the Spanish-American War, he served in Cuba as a yellow fever expert and brigade surgeon.[4]

Dr. Summers published prolifically in medical professional journals,[5] and also wrote poetry that on occasion was published in the *Times-Union*.[6] He founded and served as editor of the *Florida Medical and Surgical Journal*, first published November 1, 1886. His extensive library, to which Johnson was introduced in 1888 when he was hired as Summers's receptionist, matched Summers's cosmopolitan travels: an extensive library of Latin and Greek classics, essays by Montaigne, works by French and American Enlightenment-era authors, and "forbidden works," including Bocaccio's

Decameron and other erotica, including *School Life in Paris*, a limited edition, privately printed work.[7]

Summers, his library, and Jacksonville in this period represented to the seventeen-year-old Johnson an expansive, uncensored realm of possibility. Of Summers, Johnson wrote in his autobiography, "what was unprecedented for me was that in him I came in close touch with a man of great culture. He was, moreover, a cosmopolite. He had traveled a good part of the world over . . . the relation between us was on a high level. It was not that of employer to employee. Less still was it that of white employer to Negro employee. Between the two of us, as individuals, 'race' never showed its ugly head. He neither condescended nor patronized; in fact, he treated me as an intellectual equal."[8] Johnson describes him as a "kindred spirit."[9]

Yet Johnson advanced an authorial persona and a lifetime of reportage that went beyond Summers's self-indulgent and tragic cosmopolitanism. Even as the young Johnson admired the manic productivity of this high-functioning ether addict, he understood Summers's profound limitations. Joseph Skerrett aptly observed Johnson's rejection of the older man's "leap into eternity" as an aesthete and the younger man's prioritizing of the role of man of letters, as author, as a political act.[10] Belonging nowhere, with no allegiance, Summers was freed from America's default position of race prejudice against Blacks. Yet he could not see himself aligned with Black culture, and indeed he lacked a vision of the world beyond himself. In contrast, Johnson would align himself with Caribbean migrant populations in his prose writing, from his mother Hellen Louise Dillet's Bahamian and Haitian heritage to the Cuban community of Jacksonville. He remained committed to an inner life that was represented best by an expansive cultural and physical geography, one that diverged from the nation's imperialist and patriotic imperatives.

A port city strategic to US imperialism during the time of their meeting and friendship, Jacksonville also demonstrated the highly permeable boundaries of the nation. Summers, who had just returned from his assignment in Cuba when he hired Johnson as his receptionist, represented a cosmopolitanism that included both American expansionism and Caribbean migration. Jacksonville in these years was less a Northern Florida city than a hub of hemispheric Black politics. As Cartwright observes, "complex blood, sweat, and milk bonds of Haiti, England, Africa, France, Virginia, and New York cross in Nassau and Jacksonville along routes linking Atlantic plantation economies and an emerging tourist trade."[11] Johnson's very existence, which he narrates in his autobiography *Along This Way* (1933), describes this complex flow of cultures, an "Afro-creole backstory of globalizing hegemonies and their accompanying forces of displacement that have shaped trade and travel in the Atlantic world."¹² From his mother's matrilineal line, which reached back to Haiti and the Bahamas and included her travel to and from New York and the Bahamas prior to and after the Civil War, to his father's migrating travels from Richmond, Virginia, to New York, to Nassau and to Jacksonville to settle his family while laboring in a growing market for tourism and vacationers, Johnson's autobiography charts a cultural reach that includes a diverse African diaspora in the New World setting of the circum-Caribbean. Its displacements are also its points of transference: Black culture exceeds its bounds, as when his father acquires "working knowledge of the Spanish language" in Jacksonville. The acquisition, "to increase his value as a hotel employee" (*ATW* 17), also served to bridge the Cuban and Black communities of Johnson's Jacksonville boyhood. La Villa, as the neighborhood was known, formerly an independent city, was incorporated into Jacksonville in 1887. Haiti's "revolutionary agency" and exiles will join with subsequent revolutionary movements, as Cuban exiles shape the Jacksonville of Johnson's boyhood. Johnson's birth, and also the region as a whole, "flows between the Bahamas and ports in Key West, Miami, Jacksonville, Savannah, and Charleston," which ". . . have continued to circulate new Creolizations via the routes of tourism and commodity culture[.]"¹³

That "creolizing" flow, which Johnson noted in his preferred term "Aframerican," found expression in his co-compositions with his brother and Bob Cole in the new century. Johnson, Rosamond, and co-collaborator Bob Cole composed and copyrighted *The Evolution of Rag-Time: A Musical Suite* in 1903. It represents an early effort on Johnson's part to create a story of Black expressive practices, and anticipates the work of *The Autobiography of an Ex-Colored Man* in presenting a linguistic and musical heterogeneity that advances a Black cultural framework of existence beyond the nation. The productive differences of its three composers represented their visions of a Black past and future through cultural transference: Cole's, of Black US culture's fusion with Latin America; Johnson's, of interpolated Blackness; and Rosamond's, of the art song as a Black form. It was not an ambivalent portrait of Black culture, but rather an early example of the experiments in digression that Johnson would place at the center of his writing from *The Autobiography* forward, presenting Florida itself as a culturally shifting location between the US and Latin America, between Black and white, and between Spanish and English.

In this 1903 work, the suite's final song, "Sounds of the Times. Lindy" "was the high point of the theatrical production, presented with the most lavish costumes and the grand cakewalk finale." It was "the musical climax": "the final song is built on motives introduced in the preceding songs and brings these motives to fullest fruition."¹⁴ The song had an atypical, and compelling, structure: "After reprises of verse and chorus, the formal extensions begin, first with a variant of the chorus, now in a new key and with a habanera-like accompaniment . . . This accompaniment is retained for a 16-measure modulatory 'development' of the chorus . . . leading finally to a 'recapitulation' of the original chorus, in the original key, and an 8-measure coda" (27).[15] As Berlin notes, the use of a "Hispanic rhythm" interwoven with the syncopation of ragtime made the composition distinct. It emphasizes a musical and compositional culmination, one that advances the nineteenth-century Cuban rhythmic structure of habanera as central to the overall "world conquering influence" of "Rag-Time music" that Johnson's narrator of *The Autobiography* will both marvel at and perform. The Cole and Johnson trio's use of the habanera in *The Evolution of Ragtime* advances the thesis of the shifting frameworks of Black expression, which cannot be limited to page or notation but must be put into practice and into motion.

In his 1912 novel, Johnson presented a series of digressions from a culturally limited, nationally bounded sense of the American nation. At the same time, he marked a pointed reference to the American expansionist projects with which he was intimately familiar because of his work as American consul to Venezuela and Nicaragua from 1906–1912, during which he wrote the novel. His digressive work in *The Autobiography* creates a thesis of cultural transference that takes place as the narrator encounters diasporic Blackness in Cuba and beyond. Cultural *translation* preserves the boundaries of power and difference; cultural *transference* provides opportunities for transformation through embodied expressive practice.[16]

The novel's digressions introduce a "culture of talk" through the narrator's encounter with Spanish-speaking Cuban culture in Jacksonville.[17] Here, seemingly trivial conversation—"purely ordinary affairs" and "mere trifles" (*AECM* 43) is interwoven with profoundly political subjects "nearest . . . [the] heart": "the independence of Cuba" (*AECM* 45). Expressive practice, here, transforms talk ("spirited chatter") to eloquence, as a speaker becomes "positively eloquent" (*AECM* 45) in addressing political matters that are also matters of the heart. Although he is not Cuban, the narrator himself practices this form of eloquence as he rises through various positions in the Cuban cigar factory to the role of "reader." He explains:

The "reader" is quite an institution in all cigar factories which employ Spanish-speaking workmen. He sits in the center of the large room in which the cigar makers work and reads to them for a certain number of hours each day all the important news from the papers and whatever else he may consider would be interesting. He often selects a novel, and reads it in daily installments. He must, of course, have a good voice, but he must also have a reputation among the men for intelligence, for being well posted and having in his head a stock of varied information. He is generally the final authority on all arguments which arise; and, in a cigar factory, these arguments are many and frequent. (*AECM* 46)

The reader's role emphasizes the processes of selection, relation, cultural store, and interpretation, underscoring the power of cultural transference. Facilitating this transference, the reader serves as an interlocutor of audible, voluble, politicized talk.

In this role, the reader acknowledges the way in which Cuba's struggle for independence represented the entire region's efforts to obtain self-government, resisting dictatorship, colonialism, and expansionism. The "small wars" of Cuba and the Philippines, later Puerto Rico, the Dominican Republic (1914), and Haiti (1915), among others, were the testing ground for the recently expanded power of the American navy, which was intended to rival England's Royal Navy and secure the United States' "national interests." As a result, "intervention" in Latin American and Caribbean nations was often justified by the American government as the defense of political and economic security but was often justified by claims to a moral superiority. These "moral rights," as Woodrow Wilson called them, were often militarily enforced.

As diplomat to Venezuela (1906–9) and Nicaragua (1909–1912), Johnson found himself at the center of this morally murky moment, a representative of the United States as its diplomat and a skeptic of its practices, which he viewed as economically motivated and exploitative. Spain's brutal reaction to the nascent Cuban rebellion included the forced relocation of 400,000 Cubans to concentration camps, reported the *New York Journal*, an act that earned the outrage of Americans. But American interests in Cuba as a key strategic point meant that William McKinley did not intend to grant the island independence, but rather wished to control its fate. The Monroe Doctrine had provided hemispheric protection of American interests in the Americas from European presence; the Platt Amendment gave the United States the right to intervene in these same regions.

The narrator's landlord in *The Autobiography* "was in exile from the island [of Cuba], and a prominent member of the Jacksonville *Junta*. Every week sums of money were collected from *juntas* all over the country. This money went to buy arms and ammunition for the insurgents" (*AECM* 45). Much like the culturally authoritative status of the "reader," that the narrator later achieves in the Spanish language, this Cuban exile "also showed . . . that he was a man of considerable education and reading. He spoke English excellently, and frequently surprised . . . [the narrator] by using words that one would hardly expect from a foreigner. The first one of this class of words he employed almost shocked me, and I never forgot it, 'twas 'ramify.' We sat on the piazza until ten o'clock" (*AECM* 45).

A few weeks after leaving the consulate, Johnson delivered an address in New York, "Why Latin America Dislikes the U.S."[18] He remarked upon the region's "smouldering dislike for the United States," which "stands lower in the affections of the Latin-American people than Spain, France, Italy, Germany, or England." Johnson provocatively argued that "the deep-seated cause of this feeling of hostility does not spring from the actions of Americans who go to Latin America but from the treatment accorded to Latin Americans who come to the United States. In truth, the whole question is involved in our own national and local Negro problem."[19]

Latin Americans, Johnson observed, who, "by an overwhelming majority are not white people," noted their treatment "'like n----rs'" in the United States. Moreover, "these travelers have returned home and facts concerning the treatment accorded in the United States to a dark skin have been disseminated with something of a Masonic secrecy[.]"[20] Because Latin Americans are "citizens of sovereign and independent nations," they are reluctant to associate themselves directly with the experience of "the Negro in the United States" and, by association, be attached to "the stigma of inferiority" of its second-class citizens. However, Johnson found that the similarity of circumstance was addressed tacitly in the Latin American newspapers:

Any observation of the newspapers of the capitals of Central and South America will show that these publications make a point of giving space and prominence to lynchings and other outrages perpetrated against Negroes in the United States, even though these outrages may be committed in most obscure communities; and this is often done to the exclusion of other and more important world news. It appears that they cull the American newspapers for these items; the writer [Johnson himself] has seen as many as three in a single issue of a Latin American paper. No comment on them is every published, but they always carry a silent warning.[21]

As in *The Autobiography of an Ex-Colored Man*, the great shame of lynching is a national shame, borne by the United States: "the great example of democracy to the world" is "the only civilized, if not the only state on earth, where a human being would be burned alive" (*AECM* 111). Countering this savage reduction of human life is the vibrant culture of dynamic, and dissenting, voices that comprise culture beyond the limits of nation.

For Johnson, the "talk" of many, embodied by dynamic, politicized language, directly opposes the uniformity of a national doctrine that cannot see beyond itself. Voluble Cuban talk opposed the uniform imperative of American expansionism, where the US defense of interests abroad, predicated on the presumed moral superiority of the United States, also advanced the idea that its human lives possessed greater value. This advancement represented practices that more closely resembled the dictatorial regime that Johnson observed in Venezuela, where the "efflorescent," distorted (and autocratic) propaganda of *El Constitucional*, the state-sponsored newspaper, asserted the authority of its dictator Cipriano Castro while silencing and diminishing the voices of Venezuelan citizens.

As Johnson describes it, "the fear that lies closest to . . . [the Latin American's] heart is not that the southern republics will lose their independence to the United States, but that they will fall under the bane of American race prejudice, a process which he has without doubt, observed going on slowly but surely in Cuba, Puerto Rico and Panama."[22] "Enslavement by military tyranny" is what Johnson called it in his exposé on the US occupation of Haiti. In this case, censorship of the Haitian press controlled the discourse about American military intervention. Johnson wrote that Haitian newspapers received orders not to print criticism of the occupation, and, he emphasized, *the same order carried the injunction not to print the order.*"[23] Instead, Johnson relied on local informants to provide him with reports of the occupation forces' atrocities throughout the districts. He used back issues of the Haitian newspaper and secured copies of the new constitution of Haiti, which had been written by the American military occupation and passed through the Haitian legislature in 1918.

The news was sobering. Johnson observed that "marines talk freely of what they 'did' to some Haitians in the outlying districts," stories that Johnson frequently learned "from the lips of the American marines themselves." It was an atmosphere of terror and brutality: Johnson witnessed a child, caught stealing sugar, have his brains battered out. Women were raped; men were forced into work camps where they were beaten. The major factor of this reign of American imperialist terror was down-home American racism, Johnson believed. The type of soldier who found himself in Haiti at this time was one who had been passed over for service in World War I and who had since remained in Haiti. Johnson observed that, officered "entirely by marines," "many of these men are rough, uncouth, and uneducated, and a great number from the South, are violently steeped in color prejudice . . . [I]t falls to them, ignorant of the Haitian ways and language, to enforce every minor police regulation." Therefore, he wrote, "brutalities and atrocities on the part of American marines have occurred with sufficient frequency to be the source of deep resentment and terror" (211, 216–17). American-bounded identity instills and enforces terror and subjugation.

Badinage, the term used in *The Autobiography* to describe the lively conversation of Cubans in Jacksonville, marks Johnson's intentional transference of a French word to a Spanish-speaking, Latin-American context. Talk gains gravity through this term, which advances referents both within and outside the bounded nation, using the margin to articulate what cannot be said about the Negro question in America. Transference preserves the instability of expression, beyond notation. *Badinage* as a cultural practice of talk allows Johnson to explore Black expressive practices beyond the nation, and to draw on his prior conversations in musical composition, to propel Black cultures toward an artistically and politically productive modernism formed from its transferences and the speech and citizenship rights they affirmed. *The Evolution of Ragtime* carries forward a digressive aesthetic that centers the continuous motion of Black cultural expression and production beyond the nation state, developing an aesthetic that affirms the movement of Black cultures through the circum-Caribbean, with Jacksonville, Florida a site of its transference.

The expansive nineteenth century that Johnson perceived in part through Summers's travels and writings died with his experience with the "bloodthirsty" militia he encountered in 1901. Summers, too, was dead. The Floridian region had begun its shift from circum-Caribbean port city to yet another town of the national South, run by white racists. In his autobiography, Johnson describes the transformation's result: Jacksonville, by 1933, is a "one hundred percent Cracker town" (*Along This Way,* 45). Jacksonville as part of the national South sent its most provincial and undesirable men to Haiti during American occupation, Johnson later wrote in his investigatory journalism. He personally identified with the Haitians during the occupation he investigated on behalf of the NAACP in 1919. Birth and death: his matrilineal Haitian heritage, and the moment where he "face[s] death" in his confrontation with the roving militia in Jacksonville in 1901, orient his alignment with the Haitians.

Johnson's poetic form, developed in his writing after 1900, recognized this different potential for lyric in the modern century. In these deaths and transitions we find Johnson's shift in emphasis from a regionalism that aspired to universal aesthetics, such as one finds in "Ode to Florida," to an expansive Black cultural identity that preempts region as provincialism within the bounded nation. Edwards discusses Johnson's preface-writing to *The Book of American Negro Poetry* (1922, Rev. Ed. 1931) as a work in which the author-editor begins to conceive of a breathing line of poetry, and a more expansive idea of Black poetic voice, as he includes the Cuban poet Placido and continues to expand past the structures of difference defining American and Black writing in the period of American imperialism. Johnson's digressive expansions of Blackness, such as the inclusion of Placido's poetry in his own translation, defy the prescribed national bounds. While the decades of African American poetry following Johnson's death in 1938 will see a returning emphasis on a narrow, nationally defined regionalism as a form social protest, Johnson's poetry rejected this engagement. Even in a work like *God's Trombones* (1927), which focused on African American vernacular and Black preaching, we find Johnson advancing a thesis of Black cultural and political engagement. Lyric becomes tied to the epic sweep of Black experiences, and the new century advances a new potential for a Black epic as cultural leaps back and forth in circum-Caribbean time and space.

The epic, although widely viewed as a dated form in the early twentieth century, nevertheless offered a form of poetry that was also public discourse. In his original preface to *The Book of American Negro Poetry* (1922), Johnson acknowledged the "sustained work" of the epic in the previous century by African American authors Frances Ellen Watkins Harper, James M. Bell, and Albery Whitman.[24] These epic poems, particularly Harper's *Moses: A Story of the Nile* (1869) and Whitman's *Not a Man, and Yet a Man* (1877) and *The Rape of Florida* (1884) express "a sense of wrong and injustice," he wrote. Johnson acknowledged Whitman's *The Rape of Florida*, which revisits "the taking of Florida from the Seminoles," paused to discuss "the race question."[25] "He discusses it in many other poems; and he discusses it from many different angles," Johnson approvingly observed.[26] The subject gained dimension through multiplicity—something Johnson had done (and would continue to do) with his *The Autobiography of an Ex-Colored Man* by referencing it in all of his subsequent works. By 1922 Johnson, a seasoned poet and author, recognized Whitman's "note of faith and a note also of defiance"[27] as a repeating pattern of questioning that could take place within the national epic without being limited by the form. In his modern century, Johnson recognized the potential of the epic of Black modernity that exceeded the boundaries of epic and nation, reaching beyond his youthful aspiration in "Ode to Florida."

The tension between the lyrical individualism found in Johnson's "Ode" and the expansive framing of Black culture and experience found in his preface to *The Book of American Negro Poetry* demonstrates the author's discursive shaping of a hemispheric Black modernity in the midst of national expansion. The Black poet's national, collective engagement with racial conflict, which emerged as *the* story of African American modernity by 1931, represented something other than uniformity. By 1931, in the preface to the revised edition of his anthology, Johnson remarked on "the power and artistic finality found in the best poems arising out of racial conflict."[28] The New Negro Renaissance had seen its heyday, and the Depression was in full swing, felt acutely by working-class African Americans and other marginalized groups throughout the nation. Evaluating the African American poetic project past and future, Johnson observed,

> Up to this time, at least, "race" is perforce the thing the American Negro poet knows best. Assuredly, the time will come when he will know other things as well as he now knows "race," and will, perhaps, feel them as deeply; or, to state this in another way, the time should come when he will not have to know "race" so well and feel it so deeply. But even now he can escape the sense of being hampered if, standing on his racial foundation, he strives to fashion something that rises above mere race and reaches out to the universal in truth and beauty.[29]

Johnson's revised preface frames the question of epic's potential in the era of modernity and modernism. It is a form through which to assert the individual subjectivity of lyric expression; *and* it is a form through which to acknowledge Black citizens as they move through the hemisphere and the globe.

Just three years after Johnson's death, Sterling Brown, Arthur P. Davis, and Ulysses Lee in their 1941 anthology, *The Negro Caravan*, repeated Johnson's evaluation of the preceding decade: "it is likely that Negro poets will for a long time write of what they know best, and that is, what it means to be a Negro in America."[30] But the editors observed the potential for poetry to move beyond "escapist" individual lyricism to "a poet's view of his world":

> Far more books of poetry have been published by Negroes than of any other type of literature. Writing poetry is still popular among Negroes, but it is largely occasional verse, derivative, and escapist. Part of a large company of readers who believe that poetry should be divorced from reality, many Negroes resent what they consider the Negro poet's preoccupation with Negro subject matter. But *poetry is not simply lyrical subjectivity; it can also give a poet's view of his world in dramatic, narrative, and philosophical poetry.*[31]

With this observation, the editors suggest a renewed place for epic in African American poetry, while also acknowledging the power and renewed political thrust of a narrow regionalism in the articulation of Black nationality. Johnson's epic was more expansive, incorporating his tropical experience of the United States as he moved from his youthful poetry for the self to a poetry that could chart Black cultures in the world. Acknowledging the great social changes produced by and through the New Negro Renaissance, in which "a more vigorous, socially aware poetry was produced,"[32] the editors of the *Negro Caravan* suggested that the twentieth century could advance a nationally bounded regionalism tied to social protest.[33] In the years prior to their evaluation, Johnson's prose works—the anonymous *The Autobiography of an Ex-Colored Man* (1912), *Black Manhattan* (1930), and *Along This Way* (1933)—provide an epic sweep of Black life through centuries, modes of expression, cultures and geographies. From Johnson's "Ode to Florida" to the epic represented by his many prose works, we appreciate the swing of a national epic of African Americanness that shifts between circum-Caribbean locations, destabilizing nationally bounded alignments of Black culture and resisting narrowly defined ideas of region.

In the perspective of the twentieth century, and in the aftermath of Johnson's migration from Jacksonville to New York City, the final stanza of Johnson's "Ode to Florida" becomes a more complex expression of the tropics in the author's life:

> O, land of my birth, be the land of my death.
> May I draw 'neath thy skies my last fleeting breath,
> May my grave be beneath the moss-covered trees,
> My requiem sounded by thy tropic seas[34]

We might take the sounding of the tropic seas as a metaphor that extends Johnson's Afro-creolizing flows from the port of Jacksonville to the American nation overall, as the tropics offer multiple gateways to cultural transference.

The "loud . . . rolling sea" of the tropics finds expression in the poignant "Lift Every Voice and Sing," from the occasion of the song's writing through to the continuation of the song in Jacksonville beyond the Johnson brothers' departure.

> Let our rejoicing rise
> High as the listening skies,
> Let it resound loud as the rolling sea.
> Sing a song full of the faith that the dark past has taught us
> Sing a song full of the hope that the present has brought us"[35]

Although Johnson was careful never to refer to "Lift Every Voice and Sing" as a national anthem—"Negro" or not—he advanced the song *as a modern-day spiritual*, a breathing collective of Black Americans in a modern century a generation past Emancipation. The song takes on new meaning not so much from the occasion of its writing—Lincoln, the Emancipator—as from Johnson's emphasis on the voices of the emancipated and the experiential dynamic of the Great Fire of Jacksonville, which displaced thousands of Black Jacksonville families and led to Johnson's near-lynching. But Johnson's care in sidestepping "anthem" quite possibly reflected his conviction that the "loud" "resound[ing]" song was most powerfully and continually voiced through the circum-Caribbean, not the bounded nation. Thus, this "anthem" as a spiritual or hymn participates in the formal practice of linguistic, geographic, and musical digressions that, through their movements outward, defy location and reconfigure American discourse. A Black anthem of the circum-Caribbean flows through these spaces.

Notes

1. Brent Edwards's idea of *décalage* appears in his *The Practice of Diaspora: Literature, Translation, and the Rise of Black Internationalism*, a transformative study of Black cultures in translation during the New Negro era (Cambridge, MA: Harvard University Press, 2003). See also Jean-Christophe Cloutier, *Shadow Archives: The Lifecycles of African American Literature*. New York: Columbia, 2021. Cloutier discusses the connotative, varied meanings of *décalage*, emphasizing the critical power of the term as Edwards uses it.

2. James Weldon Johnson, *Along This Way: The Autobiography of James Weldon Johnson* (New York: Viking Press, 1933).

3. Johnson, *ATW*, 143.

4. "Thomas Osmond Summers, A.M., M.D." Summers was Brigade Surgeon of the Second Tennessee Volunteers, according to an obituary published in *Transactions of the Annual Meeting of the Missouri State Medical Association*, Vol. 43 (St. Louis: Hobart & Company, 1901), 332.

5. Dr. Summers published pieces in, among other journals, the *London Medical Record* (1875), *Galliard's Medical Journal* (1885), the *St. Louis Medical Journal* (1886), the *Maryland Medical Journal* (1886), the *New England Journal of Medicine* (1895), *Hot Springs Medical Journal* (1895), the *New York Medical Journal* (1898), the *New Charlotte Medical Journal* (1898), the *Philadelphia Medical Journal* (1899), the *American Medical Journalist* (1899), and the *Journal of the American Medical Association* (1895, 1899).

6. Johnson, *ATW*, 95.

7. I discuss this book in my *James Weldon Johnson's Modern Soundscapes* (Iowa City: University of Iowa Press, 2013), 91. Johnson vaguely refers to this work in *Along This Way*, 96.

8. Johnson, *Along This Way*, 95.

9. Johnson, *Along This Way*, 97.

10. Joseph T. Skerrett Jr., "Irony and Symbolic Action in *The Autobiography of an Ex-Colored Man*," in *Critical Essays on James Weldon Johnson*, ed. Kenneth M. Price and Lawrence J. Oliver (New York: G. K. Hall, 1997), 70–87. Summers's suicide note left for his wife declared that he put the bullet through his brain so that she might know that the last beats of his heart were for her.

11. Keith Cartwright, *Sacral Grooves, Limbo Gateways: Travels in Deep Southern Time, Circum-Caribbean Space, Afro-creole Authority* (Athens: University of Georgia Press, 2013), 72.

12. Cartwright, *Sacral Grooves, Limbo Gateways*, 72.

13. Cartwright, *Sacral Grooves, Limbo Gateways*, 73.

14. "New Spectacular Show," *New York Times*, December 3, 1903, 6, qtd. in Edward Berlin, "Cole and Johnson Brothers' The Evolution of 'Ragtime,'" *Current Musicology* 36 (1981): 21–39, 23.

15. A more extensive discussion of this work of the Cole and Johnson Trio can be found in my *James Weldon Johnson's Modern Soundscapes*, 66–68.

16. I am indebted to Edwards, *The Practice of Diaspora*, for this idea.

17. I am indebted to Stansell for the use of this phrase. See Christine Stansell, *American Moderns: Bohemian New York and the Creation of a New Century* (Princeton, NJ: Princeton University Press, 2010), 21–26.

18. James Weldon Johnson, "Why Latin America Dislikes the U.S." (1913), in *Selected Writings of James Weldon Johnson*, 2 vols., ed. Sondra Kathryn Wilson (New York: Oxford University Press, 1999), vol. 2, 195–97.

19. Johnson, "Why Latin America Dislikes the U.S.," 195.

20. Johnson, "Why Latin America Dislikes the U.S.," 196.

21. Johnson, "Why Latin America Dislikes the U.S.," 196–97.

22. Johnson, "Why Latin America Dislikes the U.S.," 197.

23. James Weldon Johnson, "Self-Determining Haiti," *The Nation* (1920), in *Selected Writings of James Weldon Johnson*, vol. 2.

24. Johnson, Preface, *The Book of American Negro Poetry*, 26–27.

25. Johnson, Preface, 32, 33.

26. Johnson, Preface, 33.

27. Johnson, Preface, 31.

28. Johnson, Preface, revised edition, 1931, 7.

29. Johnson, Preface, revised edition, 1931, 7.

30. "Poetry," in *The Negro Caravan*, ed. Sterling Brown, Arthur P. Davis, and Ulysses Lee (1941; Rpt., Ayer, 1969), 282.

31. *The Negro Caravan*, 282. My emphasis.

32. *The Negro Caravan*, 279.

33. "[Sterling] Brown's work belongs to the new regionalism in American literature; regionalism and social protest characterize his later poems," the authors wrote. *The Negro Caravan*, 282.

34. James Johnson, "Ode to Florida," in *James Weldon Johnson: Complete Poems*, ed. Sondra Kathryn Wilson (New York: Viking Press, 2000), 188–89.

35. James Johnson, "Lift Every Voice and Sing," in *James Weldon Johnson: Complete Poems*, 109–10.

CHAPTER FIVE

Gwendolyn Bennett's Florida Renaissance

Belinda Wheeler

Because the African American writer Gwendolyn Bennett (1902–1981) was born in Giddings, Texas, one might assume that she was quite at home in the Deep South. For much of her life, however, Bennett lived in New York and Pennsylvania, so when she moved to Florida as a newlywed in 1928, after a brief but celebrated literary life in Harlem, nothing could have prepared her for the shocking reality she would soon face. For someone who aspired to reconnect with her Southern roots, Bennett and her husband, Alfred Jackson, quickly learned that the social standing and freedoms they enjoyed in the North as a successful writer, editor, artist, and teacher (Bennett) and doctor (Jackson) meant little in the Jim Crow South. Bennett's traumatic experiences in the state had a dramatic impact on her personally, shaking this once confident young Black woman to her core and destabilizing her marriage in ways that she had never imagined. Bennett's writing was also heavily influenced during this period. Bennett used this time to reflect on her own journey thus far, and became more engaged with social justice issues in ways she had not previously. Bennett's ability to recognize and resist oppression with sharper clarity than she previously had would become a valuable resource in the second phase of her artistic voyage after leaving Florida a few short years later.

In order to fully comprehend how dramatic a shift Bennett made in her literary output during and after her time in Florida, it is important to briefly meditate on her earlier, lauded work. Although Bennett's legacy has yet to be as celebrated as highly as many of her good friends, including Langston Hughes, Claude McKay, Jessie Redmon Fauset, Countee Cullen, and Zora Neale Hurston, it was clear that her trajectory between 1923 and 1928 had her on pace to become an important member of the canon. During those five years, Bennett published over forty poems, articles, reviews, short stories, and cover art in leading African American magazines, most notably the NAACP's *Crisis: A Record of the Darker Races* and the National Urban League's *Opportunity: A Journal of Negro Life*. She regularly attended literary soirees at Alice Dunbar Nelson's house; she traveled to Paris, France, on scholarship to study art at several institutions, including the Sorbonne; she completed a fellowship alongside Aaron Douglas with Dr. Albert C. Barnes at the Barnes Foundation in Pennsylvania; and until her relationship with Jackson became known and she was forced to resign, she had held a coveted faculty position in the art department at Howard University in Washington, DC.[1]

One artistic medium that saw Bennett's work anthologized early in her career was her poetry. Countee Cullen, William Stanley Braithwaite, James Weldon Johnson, and Alain Locke, among others, all hailed her artistic talent. In his critique of Bennett's lyric poems, including "Sonnet II," Johnson noted, "Miss Bennett is the author of a number of fine poems, some of them in the freer forms, but she is her best in the delicate, poignant lyrics that she has written" (243). Locke and Cullen were unrelenting in ensuring Bennett's poems were featured in their now canonical anthologies. In the music section of Locke's *The New Negro: Voices of the Harlem Renaissance* (1925), Bennett's poem "Song" was placed alongside Cullen's "Negro Dancers" and Hughes's "Jazzonia" and "Nude Young Dancer." Cullen's *Caroling Dusk* (1927) featured ten of Bennett's poems that were nestled between two great writers of the period, Hughes and Arna Bontemps. According to Sandra Govan, the first scholar to complete a full-length work on Bennett's artistic output, Bennett's early poetry can be divided into two categories: the "race-conscious public poetry responding to the challenge of the New Negro arts movement and the private poetry motivated by mood or appropriate inspiration" (143).

Another medium where Bennett shone was her editorial work. Bennett's editorial skill was much in demand prior to her departure to Florida. In 1926 Bennett, alongside Hughes, Cullen, Wallace Thurman, Hurston, Aaron Douglas, John P. Davis, Richard Bruce Nugent, and Lewis Grandison Alexander, created the short-lived yet since canonical journal *Fire!!* Though a fire ironically burned a large portion of the magazine's inventory and would ultimately force the venture's closure, scholars have long regarded the collection as a bold portrait of New Negroes claiming their space within the blossoming artistic renaissance. Between 1926 and 1928 Bennett also published a much-praised column, "The Ebony Flute," in *Opportunity*. Introducing Bennett to readers, editor Charles S. Johnson wrote in the August 1926 issue: "The growth of Negro literature groups throughout the country and their manifest concern about the activities of other writers prompts the introduction this month of a column carrying informal literary intelligence. It begins under the hand of Gwendolyn Bennett, one of the most versatile and accomplished of our younger writers" (241). The monthly column "was a delicate blend of communal literary society and outspoken critique of important literary and artistic events taking place inside and outside Harlem" (Wheeler and Parascandola 13). "The Ebony Flute" was such a success that leading writers from around the country, both Black and white, often wrote to Bennett praising her important column. Bennett's column arguably laid the foundation for the introduction of Cullen's own monthly column "From the Dark Tower," which debuted just prior to Bennett's departure. Cullen's column had great merit and Johnson planned this new addition well so that Bennett's departure would not create an artistic desert for *Opportunity*'s readers.

The continuing praise Bennett received for her artistic work and her editorship highlighted her centrality within the Harlem Renaissance at a pivotal time.[2] Although her impending departure to Florida would most certainly disrupt her place within the Renaissance, Bennett was, as newlyweds are, enthusiastic about beginning the next phase of her life. As Bennett reflected years later: "The beginnings of our life together had been so bright with promise. Fresh from his internship after graduation from medical school with highest honors he had married me as I stood on the threshold of my own career. Together we would conquer the world—the bright hope of every young couple" ("Last Night," 167). In moving to Florida to join her husband, who was opening his own practice in the area where he was raised, Bennett believed that his career was indeed on the "threshold" of something great. It is unclear just how much Bennett understood the move to Florida would have on her career, but her writings from this period let readers know that she initially appeared willing to push aside any potential complications her marriage and move would have on her career.

Bennett's unpublished writings reveal how exciting the prospect of moving to the Deep South was for her. In Bennett's unpublished essay "I Have Seen" (1929), which she tried unsuccessfully to publish in at least one location (*The Nation*), she wrote "I, who am black, have just returned from my first visitation to the southland. As the poet might say, having my roots in the warm earth of the south, I returned—there to re-know my homeland. With the clear sophistication of eyes trained to the larger, busier canvas of Gotham. I have seen . . ."[3] Bennett's acknowledgment of "having my roots in the warm earth of the south" and her eagerness to "re-know" her "homeland" suggests her willingness to reconnect with her heritage and forge a new path of personal happiness as a newlywed. Prior to meeting Jackson, Bennett's personal life had been filled with many upheavals, largely at the hands of her father. Had it not been for her father's kidnapping her from her mother when she was approximately three years old and living "on the run" for almost a decade, Bennett might have had a sense of home and her "roots" in the South. Even after her father remarried in 1914 and Bennett began a somewhat stable academic journey in Brooklyn, New York, her father's extramarital affair with a former friend of hers, his financial trouble, and in 1926 his suspected suicide in front of a train, reportedly witnessed by Bennett and her stepmother, continued to leave a gaping hole in the young woman two short years later ("Eastern"). Indeed, considering the forced removal from her roots, the shame of her father's legacy, and the humiliation of having to resign from her position at Howard because of her engagement to Jackson, it is little wonder that Bennett was eager to start a new adventure as a doctor's wife in the rural South.

In addition to her own life thus far, Bennett likely would have heard some positive things about the South from her husband and literary friends. Not a great deal is known about Bennett's first husband, most of it coming from Bennett's own writing, but we do know that he was born in Florida and at the time that he and his bride had moved to his home state his mother was living close by in a neighboring town. Bennett likely heard glowing praise about the area from her husband, given his desire to return to his home state, establish his own practice, and start his new marriage with his bride; the positive relationship Bennett reports that he had with his mother; and his burial back in Florida after his early death. In addition to Jackson's reports, Bennett no doubt heard beautiful homages to Florida from her friend and former coeditor at *Fire!!*, Zora Neale Hurston. Although Hurston was born in Alabama, at the age of three she moved to Eatonville, Florida, one of the country's first incorporated all-Black towns. Hearing Hurston's immense love for the town that she would always call "home," and given its close proximity to the township to which she would be moving, Eustis, Bennett could be forgiven for thinking that the community would welcome her and her husband, a socially elite couple, with open arms. Bennett's friendship with NAACP founder James Weldon Johnson also provided her with the opportunity to discuss her impending move to Florida and hear about what opportunity Jacksonville, Florida, afforded him and his family after his grandparents had fled Haiti in early 1800s. Although Johnson's time in Florida was likely not framed as lovingly as Jackson's or Hurston's, he would have been another touchstone for Bennett as she prepared for her departure. If there were any lingering doubts for Bennett about moving to Florida, her husband's departure ahead of her arrival, so he could establish his practice, secure a home of their own, and so on, would have assured her that everything would be in place by the time she arrived. As Jackson established new roots for himself and his wife, Bennett finished up her role at *Opportunity* and a teaching appointment at Tennessee Agricultural and Industrial State College during the summer of 1928 before reuniting with her husband in Eustis.[4]

From all accounts, the first eight months of Bennett's new life in Florida were wedded bliss. It appeared, as Bernice Dutrieuille predicted after their wedding, to be the perfect merger between art (Bennett) and science (Jackson) (Dutrieuille 6). As Bennett later recalled, "We caught the tail-end of the 'boom' in Florida where he [Jackson] started his practice of medicine. He made quick money for about eight months" ("Last Night" 167). This influx of cash, noted Bennett, "allowed us to enjoy moderate good living" with Bennett not having to work (167). We "kept a maid, had a laundress come in two days a week, dress[ed] well and deposit[ed] a neat sum of money in the bank" (167). In addition to the financial freedom Bennett enjoyed at the beginning of her sojourn in the South, she was also clearly taken with the immense beauty she found within the South and Florida's African American community. In "I Have Seen" Bennett writes: "The legend of the beauty of the South is no false one. Here I mean the Negro's South. I have seen gnarled black men and women sitting with intriguing laziness in a half-rotten row-bed, surrounded by multi-colored water-lilies. It was a lovely pleasure!" She continues, "I have heard hymns, sung in 'common meter' wailed out across the torpid Florida night" ("I Have Seen"). It is this portrait of American life in the Negro South that is reminiscent of several of Bennett's earlier poems including the earlier mentioned "Song," which Alain Locke published in his 1925 anthology *The New Negro: Voices of the Harlem Renaissance*. With a sense of deep appreciation for Southern Negroes, Bennett's joyfully writes, "I have seen Negroes, happy Negroes, laughing and joking at their work . . . black fingers picking oranges, melting together in tints of bronze and gold. Oh yes, the Negroes are an integral part of the southern picture" ("I Have Seen"). It is in these moments that readers recognize how happy Bennett originally was with her and her husband's place in the Southern mosaic.

As with any situation, however, one must view it from all sides, not just the rosy one. Before long, Bennett's essay moves from immense admiration of her fellow Southern brethren to a sense of hopelessness: "Those who are born and bred there are happy and have no desire to be elsewhere under else-conditions. That is the essential sadness of the situation" ("I Have Seen"). It could be that the sad reality Bennett cites in the essay are reserved for the townspeople among whom Bennett and Jackson live. After all, Bennett recalls later that her "husband's practice was largely among the poorer people who made their living picking oranges and working in the packing houses" ("Last

Night," 167–68). Given, however, that her husband was born in this area and has since returned, one might justifiably wonder if Bennett might also be suggesting that his lack of "desire to be elsewhere" and "under else-conditions" might have also saddened or frustrated her. The image of a doctor's wife that Bennett might have conjured with all the rights and privileges that a woman like Bennett would have seen in the North was likely in stark contrast to the one she started to witness after their initial honeymoon period. Given the economic base that supported her husband's practice and given the ongoing racial climate, Bennett and her husband soon realized that the foundation they had built was not as sustainable as they had originally assumed. Realizing that the career she had envisioned for her husband was not going to materialize, Bennett turned her gaze back toward Harlem and the blossoming career she left. It was at this time that Bennett and Jackson started quarrelling about money and their respective careers. Jackson refused to return to Harlem and pressured his wife to begin working as a local schoolteacher.

As Bennett's essay continues, readers see that the situation in Florida, and likely her increased interaction with it as a teacher, pushes Bennett to reexamine her initial portrait of the region. Bennett states, "Florida was the scene of my reawakening" before asking her audience: "Am I wrong to suppose that this part was an indication of the stuff of which the whole to a larger or lesser degree was woven? Rumors here and there have convinced me that with but few alterations my story might stand as the story of all southern states—wedded to the theory of 'this land for these white people'" (167). As someone who was raised in the North and lived in a financially stable environment until her father's demise, Bennett had been somewhat sheltered from the level of financial and racial bias African Americans in the South regularly endured. When Bennett first arrived in Florida, she noted that while she "was a northern outsider," she had wrongly assumed that because their "car was new; we were well-dressed" that the local whites would see the couple's class as an equalizing factor ("Ku Klux" 164). Bennett, of course, was wrong. With exasperated breath Bennett exclaims from the same time period, "how much sadder to have seen myself and other Negroes catapulted into the noxious ambiguity of being neither man nor beast. True, one buys and sells at the marts of the white man; true, one's back does not ring beneath the whip of slavery; true, that to all appearances this bugaboo of Jim-Crow-ism is curbed, restricted and minimized" ("I Have Seen"). It appears that at around this period Bennett appears to almost accept defeat: "The trade winds and the Gulf Steam caress the shores of Florida. White northerners with advanced and liberal opinions bathe in this contaminated water. Somehow, it must rub off. It frightens me. The warm winds touch the ocean and the ocean touches the world . . ." She continues: "I am no pessimist and yet there is little hope for Florida. Florida is a sample of what other southern places are to a greater or lesser degree. One year in the south makes me quake for fear ten or twenty years from now the new south will become newer and the old north will become the 'new north' just as southerners and hopeful liberals have prattled about the 'new south'" ("I Have Seen").

Bennett's shock at the South's racist actions toward African Americans highlights her naivety about life in the South before relocating there. In "I Have Seen" Bennett notes the stark reality she faces and how blithely unaware she has been until moving to the South: "I have ridden, full of wonderment, through the town of Ocoee where today there are no Negroes. Some nine or ten years ago thirty-odd were killed because of an attempt to vote. The tropic palms and palmettos thereabouts carry no whisper of that forgotten tragedy . . . only the total absence of black faces tells the story." The historic event Bennett is referring to was one of the South's worst massacres. On election day November 2, 1920, more than thirty African Americans were slaughtered in Orange County, Florida, and their businesses and residences burned to the ground. The Ocoee Massacre, as it was later known, reportedly happened, as Bennett noted, because African Americans dared to exercise their right to vote in the federal election. In "The Truth Laid Bare," Robert Stephens provides readers with some historical context about why many African Americans originally moved to the small town. After Emancipation, states Stephens, many African Americans moved "from the Carolinas, Georgia and Alabama" finding "opportunity in the fruit-bearing land of Orange County," buying "parcels of citrus groves" and flourishing. At the time of the 1920 census, Stephens reports that there were "255 Black residents and 560 white residents" living in Ocoee. With the NAACP actively enrolling residents throughout the state to vote in the upcoming election, the Ku Klux Klan, which had a documented stronghold in the area, warned African Americans of reprisals should they vote. Newspaper reports and personal testimonies from that day differ considerably, but Paul Ortiz's comprehensive examination of African Americans' long history of organizing throughout Florida from the Civil War until that fateful day shows that a large proportion of African Americans were set to "storm the walls of segregation [. . . by] cast[ing] their ballots" (Ortiz, xv). Before that day would end, however, Black communities were massacred or run out of town and their belongings were burned. "Within months of the Election Day massacre," note Stephens, Ocoee's 255 Black residents dwindled to two. No members of the white community were ever convicted of murder or arson and newspapers soon after the event reported that order had been restored and that life should go back to normal, but it was clear that that town, the community, and the state had forever changed.

It appears that it was not until Bennett emersed herself within the local Florida community that she realized the continued stranglehold white nationalists had within the region and how "the total absence of black faces" in the area is all that "tells the story" of the "forgotten tragedy" ("I Have Seen"). It is unclear whether Bennett spoke with Hurston about this historic event, given that it occurred less than twenty miles away from her beloved Eatonville, but Hurston did not write her story about the event, "The Ocoee Riot," until 1939 as part of her Works Progress Administration work. In this essay Hurston labels the event a riot and not the massacre as other African Americans viewed it; she never mentions the Ku Klux Klan's participation in the event; and she claims that the death toll was considerably lower than the reported thirty-five. Perhaps because of the controversy Hurston's story could have received from her African American counterparts, it remained unpublished for fifty years. In 1989, Hurston's essay was released from the archive and published in *Essence* magazine. Given all that Bennett reveals about the region in her Florida reflections from this pivotal period, one might well wonder when they will be afforded the reverence they deserve.

Another area of Southern life that Bennett rails against in her writing is how white "philanthropists" take great pains to celebrate their philanthropic efforts that, according to Bennett, simply keep the Black man in his place. As Bennett notes in "I Have Seen": "One daily encounters philanthropists who pat each other on the back at having donated fabulous sums to the building of southern schools for Negroes. One hourly meets the successful Negro fruit-grower or barber." According to Bennett, however, "These all go into the mixture that places the southern Negro in a position that is to my way of thinking worse than these kindly though agonized days of slavery." Bennett's position is clearly in line with her friend W. E. B. Du Bois who staunchly disagreed with Booker T. Washington's view of trades (blue-collar professions) being more important than degrees (white-collar professions) and his notion of the "Talented Tenth." Bennett continues her assessment of Florida's education system by stating, "Negro education in Florida is a 'white sepulcher'" ("I Have Seen"). Not listing the town and removing herself directly from almost all her testimony, Bennett writes, "One small city with which I was familiar presents a fair example of what is true throughout the state. There is a splendid schoolhouse, built in the Spanish mission style, large, sunny and comfortable. With a possible five thousand children of school age from which to draw only two hundred and sixty-odd were enrolled at the beginning of last year's school term." Bennett expounds upon this situation by providing important context for readers regarding the failing town's and state's educational infrastructure. She continues, "Nor was there any effort made to get the other two-fifths into school since there is no system by which truancy may be checked in the colored schools of this community.... The entire four years of the high school only has enrolled for 1928–29 twelve students and there was no way to check up on their attendance because all except two of them were beyond the age limit and for that reason only came to school when they felt so inclined." Bennett explains how the school, which "included [students] from the kindergarten through the twelfth grade or senior high school" had but "One teacher [who] had charge of all the high school work except two subjects. This one high school teacher," explains Bennett, "taught the following subjects: Spanish, Latin, General Sciences, Chemistry, Ancient History, Early European History for the High school groups; 8th grade English; and Physical Education and Art for the entire twelve grades and the kindergarten of the school." Still not revealing her name, Bennett provides further background about this "teacher," while mentioning the measly sum the teacher receives for her incredibly hard work, "Although trained in Northern schools that were A class she received for this work seventy dollars a month" ("I Have Seen").

Bennett continues to detail the range of duties teachers have in the school before then turning her attention to the substandard level of education available to Negro children:

School opened September seventeenth. The classes ran smoothly until near the end of January. At that time word went out to all the teachers that they were to bring their work to a close since there would no more school after the fifth school month ended. The county had refused to carry on the _colored_ schools any longer than that because of lack of funds, but the local city board had taken the responsibility of carrying on this particular school through another month. After much agitation and many conferences school was extended to an eight month term which is the regulation length for _colored_ schools in Florida, the white term being nine months. All the teachers' salaries were cut twenty-five per cent. The mere fact this school remained open made it the envy and talk of the whole state since there was wide-spread closing of Negro schools in January 1929. It may be noted that in the county wherein this school was situated all the rest of the colored schools, and there were at least five, were closed as soon as the Christmas holidays were over. So much for the happenings in a colored school for _one_ year. ("I Have Seen")

Bennett also critiqued the unequitable resources between schools:

the lack of equipment was appalling. In the whole twelve grades of the school there was not a single wall map or large sized globe. Chemistry and General Science was taught without so much as a test-tube for demonstration. The library was limited to second-hand copies of mediocre fiction cast off by the white library of the city and two very inadequate sets of reference books. The children had to buy their own books and in many instances where there was a shortage of many children studied the whole year without having a textbook. There was not even a bottle of school ink with which to fill the inkwells in the children's desks. Small wonder there are only 5 A class grammar schools in the whole of Florida. And yet I saw these same handicapped children drinking in the words of the D.A.R. ladies who upon presentation of a flag to the school made long, elaborate speeches about the equal chances of both black and white under its red, white and blue folds. ("I Have Seen")

Bennett's critique of the unequitable situation clearly resonated for the young woman years after she left Florida. Up until her time in Florida, Bennett had devoted herself to educating college-level students, most notably at Howard University and Tennessee Agricultural and Industrial State College, two of the nation's premier Historically Black Colleges and Universities (HBCUs). Years later, however, Bennett would expand her educational expertise as a teacher and administrator to multiple schools and districts in New York, including the School for Democracy and George Washington Carver School. In fact, between her work at those two institutions and her time at the Harlem Artists Guild and the Harlem Community Art Center, most of Bennett's post-Florida career was devoted to making education available to all students regardless of their academic level or financial situation. Bennett's philosophy of making educational opportunities open to all, regardless of race or class, would later earn her the ire of the FBI, who hounded her for decades alleging, but never proving, she was a Communist sympathizer.

Just as Bennett was horrified of the color line within Florida schools and how African Americans were treated unfairly, she was also shocked how she—a woman with means, education, and position within the community (teacher and doctor's wife)—would be restricted from a basic community right, borrowing books from the town's local library. Unlike other examples in the essay where Bennett does not use the word "I" to connote her position within the story, in discussing what occurred in her local library Bennett personalizes it by directly using the word "I." The story recounts Bennett's library card "number 967." Bennett begins by stating, "Let me relate this story of myself. I was informed by the Principal of the local high school in which I taught that the library would permit teachers in the colored school to have a library card and to take books from the library." Bennett continues, "Thus, fortified and reassured, I ventured forth to procure a card. I so chanced to arrive at the library when only the head librarian was present. She was a northern woman who gladly gave me a card writing thereon my name with the appropriate 'Miss' before it" ("I Have Seen").

Bennett notes that for months afterward there were no problems checking out books: "For two months I came and went, getting books and reading and in my mind's inner recesses I felt that I was proving to myself that all this talk about prejudices in the South, were not so far-reaching after all. A southern lady, who was a librarian there, . . . waited on me when I brought my books. She had that gracious courtesy that is so disarming to a person who is used to the subway manners of New York City" ("I Have Seen"). Though Bennett was content believing that she was able to successfully ascend above "prejudices in the South," before long she was unceremoniously brought back to reality. Bennett writes, "One day when I returned some books, she took them and in what at the time seemed to me an undue hurry she fled to the basement" to recall the head librarian, who swiftly removed Bennett's direct borrowing privileges and right to be registered:

"Are you Miss Bennett?"
   "Yes."
   "Well, Miss Bennett, you and I are going to have a talk. I suppose you know what about."
   And by that swift telegraphy that all Negroes know I realized what was coming and said,
   "Has someone objected to my coming here?"
   Then followed a declaration of her sympathy and an explanation of how the library staff and board did not object to my reading and using the books, but they resented my being registered. So that is I would please return these books I was taking to the rector of the white Episcopal Church and then on he would get whatever books I wanted. Her slender white hand pushed the books toward me and turned itself up and her thin voice said,
   "Your card, please."
   So it was that card number "967" went into oblivion. ("I Have Seen")

True to Bennett's word, there is no evidence of Bennett's library card ever existing. The discrimination Bennett encountered at the local library was personal for the author. A longtime supporter of local libraries, including New

York Library's 135th Street Library (later known as Schomburg Center for
Research in Black Culture) prior to leaving for Florida, Bennett regularly gave
talks and readings alongside Countee Cullen, Langston Hughes, and other
New Negroes from the period. Upon her return from the South, the 135th
Street Library was one of the first locations she sought out to reconnect with
her beloved Harlem, and it remained an important place for her throughout
her life ("Harlem Reflection").

   Another focus for Bennett in her writing from this period was the overt
racism even accomplished doctors like her husband faced and how the
threat of the Ku Klux Klan remained long after the 1920 Ocoee Massacre.
Although Bennett's story details her husband's experience, perhaps because
of the threat of the Klan's retaliation, she does not list him explicitly. Bennett
opens by stating,

> There are countless tiny things here and there that make one know that
> the "new south" is still the old. . . . I have heard firsthand how a col-
> ored physician in Orlando was told, "N----r, take your hat off," when he
> walked into a police station where other men had their hats on. When
> the physician apologized and explained why he did not remove his hat,
> after the clerk had delved into his origins and was surprised to find that
> he was born and raised right there in Florida, remarked, "Well, n----r, I
> sure wish I had you up in Georgia where I come from." ("I Have Seen")

Bennett then continues with two other scenarios her husband encountered:
"There is the druggist in Leesburg who told a colored man that the 'n----r doctor' was trying to poison him because he had prescribed tincture of belladonna
when ulcer of the stomach was indicated. There is the druggist in Umatilla
who refused to fill a prescription written by a colored doctor" ("I Have Seen").

   It was the last example featuring the doctor that Bennett expounded upon
in her essay "Ku Klux Klan Rides," in which she details a terrifying night at her
Florida home when a group of thirteen Klan members came to their house
with the intent of terrorizing them. The week before Jackson had had "heated
words" with a "druggist in Tavares" because he had substituted one drug for
another (163). "Just the day before," Bennett continued, one of her husband's
patients "had told how the pharmacists, after questioning him about the 'new
doctor' [said] 'We don't fill n----r prescriptions in this town'" ("Ku Klux Klan
Rides," 163–64). Earlier in the week, Bennett reported that her "husband had
come home excitedly telling of an announcement he had seen in the town
Post Office. Hanging around the other regular Post Office notices a large
printed poster had borne this message: Ku Klux Klan Rides Tuesday, March

30th 1929" (161–62). Although Bennett reveals that her "husband had seen the Klan ride on horses with padded hooves in Atlanta, Georgia, when he was a student at the university," she confesses, "I had never really believed it actually happened except in the far days following the Civil War, in distasteful moving pictures, and in books about the 'Romantic South'" (163). In eerie detail, Bennett recounts the harrowing March 30 scene as the men march toward her home: "Almost they didn't move, so slowly they came. Only a Negro who has watched such a procession come nearer can understand the prickled awareness with which one stands rooted to the spot that is somewhere in the eyes and deep in the heart" (164). Bennett continues, "Their white robes were grotesque as they come across the wide street to our front yard. There must have been a dozen hooded Klansman stepping onto the little rise of ground that served as a pavement before one entered our front yard" (164). The Klan were poised to attack Bennett's house when the men unexpectedly noticed a rare nonnative Cottonwood Rose in the yard and without a word started turning back to their cars. Bennett recalls that while the rare tree that a former owner had brought from Georgia appeared to have save their lives that night, the Klan continued on a rampage including giving "an 'uppity n----r' . . . a severe beating from which he had never full recovered" and "tarred and feathered a well-to-do white man, a northerner, whom they had surprised in the bed of a much sought-after Negro prostitute whose name was Lily" (165). These eye-opening experiences Bennett has within a short period time in Florida are a stark reminder to the young wife that despite their socioeconomic status and professional positions (or perhaps because of it), they would never be able to rise above their station in the South (164).

If her Southern community's racial history and current racial climate were not enough, Bennett reveals the even tougher times she faced in Florida during the second year of her marriage when a Mediterranean fruit fly infestation quickly decimated the community. "Only people who lived in Florida during the last part of 1928 and early 1929," states Bennett, can "realize the part this lusty little beast played in what proved to be the forerunner of the holocaust which was to consume the nation's finances in less than a year" ("Last Night," 166). The fly, "Having destroyed vast acres of oranges, . . . began nibbling daintily at unsuspecting vegetables" (167). With no end in sight, "The order went out to destroy all fruit and vegetable crops. There was no discrimination between large farms comprising wide acreage and the tiny truck gardens in which the poorer people raised their daily food" (167). As a short-term solution, "More money was borrowed," but "there were runs on banks—the story of Florida's bank failures and financial collapse was front-page news all over the country" (167). Bennett reports that she and her husband were not immune from the financial devastation: "That a large bank closed with our modest thousand dollars in it was just a minor tragedy. My husband's practice was largely among the poorer people who made their living picking oranges and working in the packing houses. They not only had no money to pay their bills; their very food they needed for subsistence had been destroyed by state order" (167). Bennett recalls, "As yet, Washington was not aware that thousands of people were on the verge of starvation. Belief had not become the nation's problems" (167). And with no choice, "At the end of two years in Florida, with our last two hundred dollars, we pulled up stakes and came North to settle in Briarwood on Long Island . . ." (167). The financial and emotional heartbreak the couple encountered during this period would have certainly exacerbated the earlier disagreements they had had about returning to Harlem earlier. Jackson was now agreeing to return to Harlem, but their financial situation was far more dire than ever before.

Though understandably devastated by their financial losses in Florida, the Great Depression would ultimately destroy Jackson's will altogether. With little savings in hand when the couple arrived in Briarwood, Long Island, they borrowed more money and financed a home. Bennett details how "My husband and I again thought we were on the road to prosperity and happiness. . . . We seemed to be cashing in on the courage that had seen us through our lean years" ("Last Night," 167). Before long, however, Bennett acknowledges:

> Like so many others we had miscalculated on what the future held. The black clouds of the depression were soon to envelop not only the extremely wealthy who could afford to gamble in Wall Street and the unskilled laborer who depended on the prosperity of big industry to make his living, but even that middle class whose position was usually most secure. The bank in which we had deposited our tiny savings had not opened after the Bank Holiday. Most of my husband's patients lost their money in the same bank. Briarwood saw its first breadline. (167)

It was the reality that Bennett and her husband faced in the rural South, coupled with the financial and emotional devastation they soon met in Long Island, that forever changed Bennett's personal and professional focus. Within a few years of returning to the North and not being able to make a go of it in the face of the Great Depression, Bennett grew further apart from her husband. Jackson quickly fell into chronic alcoholism, cheated incessantly on Bennett, started performing illegal abortions, and contracted tuberculosis. Her marriage was in tatters, so Bennett refused to stay with the man she no longer recognized, and she started her life anew in New York City.

Bennett took a job with the New York City Works Progress Administration Federal Arts Project writing articles on the life of the social and economic situation African Americans were facing during the Great Depression. She maintained a separate residence in Harlem, began a three-year-long affair with the artist Norman Lewis, and made peace with her estranged husband just prior to his death in 1935.

It is in her own essay "Harlem Reflection" that Bennett successfully captures the sense of helplessness that many African Americans felt during the Great Depression. Interviewing over "forty odd professional men and women in Harlem for the Department of Education and Information of the Welfare Council of New York City," Bennett could not help but note the irony of the situation. The article "The Plight of the Negro Is Tragic," writes Bennett, was "based on the material I gathered, appeared in quite an emasculated form in *Better Times*, their official organ. What an anomaly—that I should write the story of Harlem during the depression years for a magazine whose name was better times!" ("Harlem Reflection," 173). In her essay, Bennett reports that she "had found that almost no physician in Harlem, almost no dentist or lawyer had escaped a closer contact with poverty than the ordinary middle class white person could ever imagine. One pharmacist, whose drugstore had occupied one of the most prominent corners in Harlem for some ten years, had been forced through the poverty of the community to lose his holdings one by one until in 1935 he was running an elevator in a down-town office building" ("Harlem Reflection," 173). This, continues Bennett, "was a man who had graduated with honors some twenty years before from one of America's leading universities and had studied abroad on a scholarship for several years" (173). Directing the story to her own situation, but without revealing Jackson's name, Bennett recalls how "One physician had become so undernourished through the poverty of this period that he had in his run-down condition contracted tuberculosis and because he was not able to go away to a sanatorium was practicing medicine with T.B. and living at the mercy of fellow physicians" (173). This harsh reality affected Bennett profoundly: "Lawyers, teachers, doctors, and professional people of all walks of life were hurtled together in a maelstrom of misery. I realize, of course, that this was true of all people, Negro and white, but the point I am making is that Harlem—laughter-loving Harlem . . . had now changed the character of its demeanor from that of a minstrel grin to that of a grimace of pain" ("Harlem Reflection," 174). It was these stories that would galvanize Bennett throughout this new phase of her career.

Bennett wrote countless cultural and social articles throughout the 1930s, returned to educational programming, including running the Harlem Arts Guild and Harlem Community Art Center, and served as teacher and administrator at two new educational institutions in New York, the School for Democracy and the George Washington Carver School. Bennett would have most certainly continued in that work had it not been for increased scrutiny by the House Un-American Activities Committee and the twenty-plus years she was hounded by the FBI for unsubstantiated Communist activities. Though Bennett's educational career would eventually end, her poetry continued. In 1939, Bennett submitted a complete manuscript of poetry to Frank Horne at the US Works Progress Administration. Likely because of the pressure on Bennett by the FBI and others, Bennett's book was never published.

In all, over fifty unpublished poems by Bennett have been found to date. The majority of these poems are considerably more politically and socially focused, which is not surprising given Bennett's "reawakening" in Florida and the harsh reality she and others faced in Depression-ravaged New York. As scholar Brian Dolinar writes in *The Black Cultural Front: Black Writers and Artists of the Depression Generation,* "Bennett increasingly identified with the masses struggling to survive" (46). Numerous poems by Bennett written after her time in Florida discuss domestic concerns, such as "The Hungry Ones" (1938), a free verse poem that "speaks of all the poor, struggling people who must deal with finding enough food to eat on a daily basis," to "I Build America," (1938) which brings Americans from all walks of life who have died "building America" (Wheeler and Parascandola, 108–9). There are also poems by Bennett that show considerable concern for international issues such as "Threnody for Spain." The poem, "occasioned by the fall of Madrid" to Fascist-backed general Francisco Franco's forces on March 27, 1938, discusses "the bloody civil war in Spain" from both sides (109). As noted in *Heroine of Harlem Renaissance and Beyond,* in her papers, "Bennett indicated that she published some poems in the left-leaning *New Masses*; however, nothing under her name is listed in Theodore F. Watt's *Indexes to the New Masses, 1926–33, 1934–35, 1936* and Bennett denied at the WP hearing that she 'had ever wrote under a pen name'" (109–10).

Florida was a terrifying, yet galvanizing, moment for Bennett. While the time in the South was short, it would go on to define the second phase of her career. From a sensitive young writer who wrote "private poetry motivated by mood or appropriate inspiration" and "race-conscious public poetry" that meditated on the challenges New Negroes faced while determining their position in the new renaissance, Bennett's public persona following her time in Florida was that of a public figure who advocated fiercely for individuals locally, nationally, and globally who were suffering racial, economic, or social disparities (Govan). On publishing three of Bennett's previously unpublished poems that were written after her time in Florida, scholar Cary Nelson writes that, taken together, "this group of three poems alone mandates a revised understanding of Bennett's career" (Nelson 629).[5] Bennett's writing during her time in Florida, and her later reflections of that period, highlight how the local inequities she witnessed firsthand were part of her own renaissance that would reshape her professional and artistic career.

Notes

1. Though Jackson had not taken any classes with Bennett while he attended Howard University's medical school, the institution frowned upon their relationship and requested Bennett resign.

2. For more information about Bennett's artistic oeuvre, please see Wheeler and Parascandola's 2018 publication *Heroine of the Harlem Renaissance and Beyond: Gwendolyn Bennett's Selected Writings*.

3. Schomburg Research Center, New York Public Library, Gwendolyn Bennett Papers, reel 1. Bennett hand wrote "submitted to *Nation*, 1929" at the top of the typed manuscript. There is no record that *The Nation* ever published the essay.

4. It is not known whether Bennett's appointment at Tennessee State was supposed to last beyond the summer. In "Tennessee Agricultural and Industrial State College: The Bulletin, Catalogue, 1927–1928 Announcement, 1928–1929," Bennett is listed as an Art Education and English faculty member at Tennessee State, suggesting that she might have signed a one-year contract, but finished up after the summer eager to reunite with her husband.

5. The three poems Nelson published were "Dirge for a Free Spirit," "I Build America," and "[Rapacious women who sit on steps at night]."

Bibliography

Bennett, Gwendolyn. "[Harlem Reflection]." *Heroine of the Harlem Renaissance and Beyond: Gwendolyn Bennett's Selected Writings*, edited by Belinda Wheeler and Louis J. Parascandola, 171–74. University Park: Pennsylvania State University Press, 2018.

Bennett, Gwendolyn. "I Have Seen." Schomburg Research Center, New York Public Library, Gwendolyn Bennett Papers, reel 1.

Bennett, Gwendolyn. "[Ku Klux Klan Rides]." *Heroine of the Harlem Renaissance and Beyond: Gwendolyn Bennett's Selected Writings*, edited by Belinda Wheeler and Louis J. Parascandola, 162–65. University Park: Pennsylvania State University Press, 2018.

Bennett, Gwendolyn. "Last Night I Nearly Killed My Husband." *Heroine of the Harlem Renaissance and Beyond: Gwendolyn Bennett's Selected Writings*, edited by Belinda Wheeler and Louis J. Parascandola, 166–71. University Park: Pennsylvania State University Press, 2018.

Dolinar, Brian. *The Black Cultural Front: Black Writers and Artists of the Depression Generation*. Jackson: University Press of Mississippi, 2012.

Dutrieuille, Bernice. "Art Weds Science." *Pittsburgh Courier*, April 28, 1928, 6.

"Eastern Social Circles Agog over Bennett's Suicide (?)." *Pittsburgh Courier*, August 28, 1928, 2.

Govan, Sandra Yvonne. *Gwendolyn Bennett: Portrait of an Artist*. Dissertation, Emory University, 1980.

Johnson, Charles S. *Opportunity: A Journal of Negro Life* (National Urban League) (August 1926): 241.

Johnson, James Weldon, ed. *The Book of American Negro Poetry*. New York: Harcourt, 1922.

Nelson, Cary. *Anthology of Modern American Poetry: Volume 1.* New York: Oxford University Press, 2015.

Ortiz, Paul. *Emancipation Betrayed: The Hidden History of Black Organizing and White Violence in Florida from Reconstruction to the Bloody Election of 1920.* Berkeley: University of California Press, 2006.

Stephens, Robert. "The Truth Laid Bare." *Pegasus* (University of Southern Florida) (2020). https://www.ucf.edu/pegasus/the-truth-laid-bare/.

Wheeler, Belinda, and Louis J. Parascandola, eds. *Heroine of the Harlem Renaissance and Beyond: Gwendolyn Bennett's Selected Writings.* University Park: Pennsylvania State University Press, 2018.

CHAPTER SIX

Negotiating Kitsch and Race in Florida Writing and Art

Hurston, the Highwaymen, and Duval-Carrié

Taylor Hagood

To say the name "Florida" is to evoke the bizarre, the gaudy, the tawdry, the exaggerated, the almost unbelievable. At once beautiful and hideous, Florida is a place of breezy dreams and horrific realities. These elements and extremes congeal in a distinct brand of kitsch that takes on such immediately recognizable forms as alligator heads, shell-covered jewelry boxes, and the lacquered cedar souvenirs on the shelves of roadside stores. Those souvenirs and the many other campy embodiments of Florida's tackiness function on levels not immediately present on their surfaces but knowable on deeper and contradictory levels. As the well-oiled tourist industry of Florida knows, the state's kitsch—a quality, entity, persistence of which so many commodities are mere graven images—even at its ugliest nevertheless compels and in so doing seduces even when it repulses.

It is the darkness of the surface-level brightness of Florida's seductive kitsch that I want to address in relation to African American cultural history. On one hand, kitsch that represents stereotyped and nostalgic African American images, sounds, and cultural production exists in Florida as an extension of a general southern Black kitsch. But Florida also has a distinct African American–*produced* commodity history that can signify as/on kitsch in the form of midcentury landscapes painted by African American artists now collectively called "The Highwaymen." In this essay, I read Zora Neale Hurston's writing in terms of kitsch and triangulate it with the Highwaymen's mid-twentieth-century work and the contemporary art of Haitian-born, Miami-based artist Edouard Duval-Carrié. In so doing, I hope to illuminate Hurston's sensibility in new ways that reveal how she drew on Florida's fund of kitsch as the Highwaymen did and Duval-Carrié does, exposing throughlines and resonances among their works via kitsch and exploring Hurston's own blending of the visual and the literary to identify a central actuating aspect of Hurston's writing not easily articulated by and even opposed to modernism.

Kitsch, like its close cousin camp, can be notoriously difficult to define. Thomas Kulka has ventured a workable definition of kitsch as an aesthetic that evokes highly charged "stock emotions" (28) in "instantly and effortlessly identifiable" (33) ways that do "not substantially enrich our associations relating to the depicted objects or themes" (37). Kitsch aesthetic tends toward the conservative, nostalgic, and uncomplicated, with stereotypes being a species of such a combination. For theorists from Clement Greenberg to Hermann Broch, writing in the heat of modernism's advent, kitsch could readily be defined as the "vulgar" industrial commodification of art or literally the invasion of an insipid Romanticism that amounts to a kind of "evil," respectively.[1] Where "good art" seeks to re-envision the world through complexity and methodological innovation that requires contemplation that slowly achieves full comprehension, kitsch is thought to employ established techniques to create a simple emotion that is quickly ascertained.

Fashioned from positions of empowered cosmopolitan elite male whiteness, such discussions of kitsch both worked under and advanced assumptions that nonwhites and the philistine, industrial-Kool-Aid-drinking working class naturally gravitates to kitsch. From these theorists' viewpoint, people of "bad taste" preferred art in "bad taste." That people of color should be drawn to and depicted within kitsch made sense in such logic; if anything, from such a viewpoint, African Americans were more to be pitied and indulged than were whites who committed de facto crimes against their race by loving kitsch. Moreover, people of color themselves became objectified and commodified *in kitsch*, with African Americans particularly being depicted as smiling watermelon-eaters, mammies, and other stereotypes on postcard images and in the forms of cast-iron banks and doorstops, dolls, and salt and pepper shakers. The glittery plastic surfaces of such products conveyed the elements of kitsch Kulka identifies, playing off nostalgic, racist stereotypes to entice mostly white consumers.

In our present moment, bolstered as it is by postmodernism's suspicion and deconstruction of empowered narratives, it is possible to understand kitsch as occupying a less stable, more troubled, and, in certain ways, troublesome yet also paradoxically empowering place. Some artists embrace kitsch, an example being John Waters, who offers a queering articulation of kitsch: "In order to acquire bad taste one must first have very, very good taste" (qtd. in Ward 6). In a different embracing of kitsch, Norwegian artist Odd Nerdrum promotes a kitsch "movement" that stands directly in opposition to the machinery of artistic norms set in motion by Kant and steadily enforced to the literal point of inescapable circularity in the linguistic philosophy–turned–sociopolitical epoch inaugurated by Derrida. In other words, "art" is a product and producer of modernism, where kitsch is confined to all that is not modernism and that even stands in opposition to it. The likes of Waters and Nerdrum arguably pose the threat that "tasteless" art is not always "bad" art; in fact, "tasteless" art might even have the power to draw people away from the strenuous and ironically quasi-puritanical precepts of "art." As Kulka writes, "Bad taste is neither a necessary nor a sufficient condition for explaining the seductive powers of kitsch" (21).

The element of seduction cuts in multiple directions when race connects with kitsch in African American art, ranging from a racist weapon used against African Americans to something that might be signified on and wielded by Black artists. While highly visible filmmakers and artists may promote kitsch at some peril, a person of color embracing kitsch risks losing major ground vis-à-vis a cultural establishment steeped in values that are essentially modernist. Being taken seriously while exploring kitsch requires serious effort and risks marginalization and expulsion, especially for Black people already marginalized. It might be argued that the arbitration of literature, art, music, and other cultural productions has grown relatively decentered, less white, less straight, but many would retort that the fundamental values of modernist-guided culture and art have not changed much if at all. Black contemporary artists who draw specifically upon African American–based kitsch in order to forge a brave, oppositional kind of art must negotiate such fraught waters. Reviewing such work, popular art critic Charlie Finch writes, "For years and years, African-American art was ghettoized by the liberal elites as nothing but kitsch, neoprimitive sculptures, family scenes from the hood and moody dreamscapes." In describing *contemporary* African American artists employing kitsch, however, Finch discerns a possible authenticity that seeks to allow kitsch simply to be kitsch, as he explains "that African-American artists, now finally in some form of ascendancy, have mined the narrow river of ornament for a new burst of visual expression."

So overdetermined are the hierarchical power dynamics of kitsch that discussing or employing it for artists and critics is highly problematic. Finch is wary of what he sees as African American kitsch:

The sense of Af-Am kitsch as a fundament of the new black art's creative success is still that of a dream deferred: is it the candy-colored
reverie of fantasy or the remembrance of suffocated beauty from the
African-American past? Combining the two for this talented pioneer-
ing cohort of great artists, and all their student apostles, will scatter the
dreams in favor of a new reality, no longer dependent on white patrons
or liberal indulgence.

As hopeful as Finch's Langston Hughes–esque rhetoric may be, it is not altogether clear that these artists are comfortable with a white critic calling their
work kitsch or kitsch-derived. The goals of their production are far more
complex than the relegating (even when the relegator seems to be trying
not to) force the designation of kitsch exerts when applied, as it were, "exter-
nally," from an out-group critic writing with the full force of dominant culture
behind him.

Artists, writers, musicians, and other cultural producers of color therefore must negotiate an array of factors that dominant culture pressures them
toward within an equally strong expectation, pressure, and embracing of
a kind of seduction. Sex combines with nostalgia and surface-level beauty
to effect kitsch's potency, this triumvirate the engine of a seduction kitsch
depends on in order to gain adherents (in the form of buyers or critics) and
to overcome the considerable opposition posed by dominant culture and the
hegemony of art. If dominant culture itself should try to embrace kitsch, then
all the worse, for such appropriation threatens to invade the very idiom and
logic that gives kitsch its unique power. In this double whammy, not only does
a manufactured image or item representing a Black body become a sexualized
and othered "beauty," but when this commodity gets positioned within an
"artistic" setting and viewed with irony and/or awareness (historical, aesthetic,
or otherwise) the originary energy of the object itself potentially becomes
marginalized and silenced. Reframed in a more recognizable critical idiom,
kitsch's catch-22 resembles the essence of Spivak's classic question, can the
subaltern speak? Such a dynamic puts tremendous pressure on Black artists
and writers to negotiate racist stereotypes of hypersexuality.

The Highwaymen found themselves caught in these jolting forces as they
produced and marketed their paintings in a time and place pervaded by
kitsch. Peter Ward writes of kitsch's "garishly diverse seductions" (22) in the
mid-twentieth century, from Andy Warhol's work to Jayne Mansfield's body
and persona, noting that for "many people it was also the first time that they
could afford to buy significant numbers of non-functioning objects to decorate their mantelpiece and walls" (24). Kitsch grew especially widespread in

south Florida's atmosphere in that era, as Gary Monroe writes in his book on the Highwaymen:

> In Miami Beach, during its opulent 1950s and 1960s, more was definitely better. Photo studios stood along Washington and Collins Avenues, where vacationers lined up to have their souvenir pictures taken in front of stylized hand-painted backdrops, usually depicting palm trees and parrots. Along Lummus Park on Ocean Drive, the bases of real palm trees were painted white. Colored spotlights illuminated the trunks, yielding cake-icing hues blending with tropical balmy night skies. Across the street, the art deco hotel architects had all competed to see who could design the showiest faced to attract the most attention. Hotels were named after faraway places, places that people dreamed of or, more likely, had left behind. Ship motifs were very common—masts, streamlining, portholes. Cadillac fins grew bigger by the season. Fantasy came to life. "Kitsch" was part of the environment, my home.

Unsurprisingly, as Finch asserts, "Even the Florida Highwaymen, those anonymous and subtle travelling black interpreters of the 1950s Florida landscape, were dismissed as kitsch."

Finch's statement acknowledges the range of viewpoints of white critics and buyers as well as the intentions of the artists themselves. Both in their original moment and in their later renaissance among collectors and critics, the twenty-six original Highwaymen have negotiated a vexed warren of expectations affected to various degrees by kitsch. During the renaissance that began in the 1990s and continues now, the Highwaymen are problematically portrayed as self-taught folk artists capturing a now-gone "authentic" Florida untouched by later development.[2] A segment of critics and collectors consider the paintings to be "bad" art, as Kristin G. Congdon has noted, yet are caught up in the drawing power of their images and even "forgive" what they might otherwise consider to be kitsch. In their original moment, the Highwaymen produced and marketed in a mode closer to souvenir kitsch than to the established art world, something they were largely forced into because those establishment opportunities were not as open to Black artists. The motivations, inspirations, and intentions of artists are not easily reduced or fully conscious, but both the artistic and entrepreneurial sensibilities of these painters would have grasped the kitsch dynamics in their milieu.

Whether or not these artists individually or collectively saw themselves as working in a kitsch mode, producing their work nevertheless meant engaging in a kitsch atmosphere that made demands on aesthetics, labor methods, and marketing. Insofar as some of the Highwaymen were encouraged by white Florida landscape artist Albert "Beanie" Backus, they were aware of the appeal of his work, which he expressed as, "For a landscape to really communicate there must be a degree of nostalgia attached to it" (qtd. in Firestone and Firestone, 80). Taking nostalgic appeal to heart, the Highwaymen seized on elements guaranteed to make immediate appeal to the senses and dreams of Florida, painting achingly red skies, mounting cumulus clouds, flaming royal poincianas, and other stock elements of romanticized Florida sea- and landscape.[3] In terms of labor, the artists worked quickly, individually, and at times even in assembly-line fashion to produce great quantities of paintings with cheaply obtained materials so they could sell in high volume at low prices. Marketing took place not in galleries but through direct selling that involved driving throughout the state to find individual buyers or businesses such as hotels and doctors' and lawyers' offices looking to decorate their walls.

Most Highwaymen paintings, being landscapes, did not make race overt, yet in the mid-century moment and especially in the ongoing renaissance, the artists' race played/plays a role in buying and collecting. Edmonson Asgill sees race as distinguishing the Highwaymen's aesthetics: downplaying Backus's influence, Asgill asserts that these artists' style manifests "residual traces of a deeply rich African cultural tradition of art: a complete disregard for form, proportion, and reality" (188). Picasso's incorporating elements of African art may have brought him respect, but the Highwaymen have not always been extended the same accord. Meanwhile, even good intentions among buyers and critics are vexed, for some original buyers may have been, with some condescension, merely seeking to "support Black artists" while, as Anthony and Schrock have shown, the promotion of these works has continually reaffirmed racist stereotypes.

Arguably the most compelling of these artists, Alfred Hair, has emerged as so precisely for the ways his life has been presented along the lines of racist stereotypes of seduction, tragic brutality, self-taught skill, entrepreneurial savvy, and American dream ethos. Hair is generally credited with devising the assembly-line method of producing paintings, and he was a good-looking young man with powerful charisma. The story goes that he was promiscuous or was at least thought to be so, which caught up with him on August 9, 1970, at Eddie's Place in Fort Pierce, when Julius Funderbuck shot and killed him. A painting of Eddie's place, by Harold Newton, points to a more introspective and less market-driven approach, arguably a work that in departing from the standard elements is suggestive of the ways other paintings employ Florida kitsch aesthetics. The doctors, lawyers, hotel owners, and other buyers of the first phase of Highwaymen paintings likely had less interest in an African American juke joint as compared with a scene of a quiet central Florida prairie or a palm tree near the beach. In the contemporary moment, Hair seems to fit the stereotype of a hypersexualized Black man killed by another Black man.

Hair might bring to mind Tea Cake, Zora Neale Hurston's memorable character from *Their Eyes Were Watching God*. In a novel otherwise concerned with the nuances of Black women struggling to express in voices that signify on fraught, subtle waves, Tea Cake dances across the stage as a kitsch hero. His entrance into the narrative jars, his looks alone enough to drive all independence away from Janie. She abandons her regular life entirely, giving herself and her time to a man who is liable to run around to juke joints, strum his guitar, and even beat her. Where Janie had been self-reflexive in her dealings with Logan and Joe Starks, she swoons completely into a lusty romance with Tea Cake, morphing the novel from one of a Black woman's successful quest toward independence to something that might forgivably be seen as a torrid romance genre novel.

To discern kitsch elements in a novel requires thinking kitsch beyond the art world to consider what ways kitsch can exist in both content and style of literature. Kulka ventures that "themes" can be kitsch, arguing that kitsch can take the form of clichéd plot structure or in literature that does "not question the basic metaphysical and moral assumptions of human existence" (97). Although in *Their Eyes Were Watching God* Hurston arguably flirts with clichéd plot structure, she most definitely questions the basic metaphysical and moral assumptions of human existence. Yet that line-walking also does not exactly amount to a self-reflexive "artistic" appropriation of kitsch, either. Rather, it seems (to me at least) more true to Hurston's fictional sensibility to understand it as blending celebratory immediacy, including an unembarrassed borrowing of stock emotions, *with* a deep probing of Black female ontology and epistemology, which extends to a larger interrogation of voice that necessarily negotiates Black and non-Black expression.

Such African American in-group/out-group negotiation of expression *is* signifying, as Henry Louis Gates Jr. has so famously argued, which raises a question as to whether or not in Hurston's hands signifying itself might be viewed as a kind of kitsch. At first blush, signifying's deformation of standard English in style and rhythm as well as idiom and denotation strikes far closer to modernism and the movements of jazz. On the other hand, where white modernist writers' language experiments were often shaped by an overarching sense of alienation deeply intoned with melancholy, foreboding, and despair, Hurston's signifying tends to be community-defining and -confirming and characterized by a kind of ironic, semi-comedic, blues style. There is a recklessness in Hurston's ethnographic cataloguing of folk forms, working-class and rural Black life, and language strategies, especially in the heart of the Harlem Renaissance when the Du Boisian Talented Tenth embodied a cool, thoughtful version of Black accomplishment and critics castigated Hurston for depicting African Americans in crude terms that at times confirmed stereotypes. As a matter of fact, Du Bois himself in *The Souls of Black Folk* time and again verged on the sentimental and labored to keep the emotion of African American expression intact without giving in to racist/racialist cliché, and Hurston was not near as ginger with kitsch and its seductive powers. Janie and Tea Cake's relationship can even be read as a fable of kitsch's allure and marketability, a concern for Hurston, who depended in significant ways on white patronage just as the Highwaymen depended on nostalgic white customers.

A similar fable appears in Hurston's "The Gilded Six-Bits." Hurston makes both class and race clear in sentence one: "It was a Negro yard around a Negro house in a Negro settlement that looked to the payroll of the G. and G. Fertilizer works for its support" (86). She then describes the house and yard in terms that arguably mix kitsch's shallowness and nostalgia with an underlying hard economic reality:

> But there was something happy about the place. The front yard was parted in the middle by a sidewalk from gate to door-step, a sidewalk edged on either side by quart bottles driven neck down into the ground on a slant. A mess of homey flowers planted without a plan but blooming cheerily from their helter-skelter places. The fence and house were whitewashed. The porch and steps scrubbed white.
>
> The front door stood open to the sunshine so that the floor of the front room could finish drying after its weekly scouring. It was Saturday. Everything clean from the front gate to the privy house. Yard raked so that the strokes of the rake would make a pattern. Fresh newspaper cut in fancy edge on the kitchen shelves. (86)

The "happiness" of the home is rooted in cheap decorations that, in line with kitsch, identify happiness with being poor so long as that being poor finds a corrective in cleanliness and order.[4]

Into this scene Hurston introduces the element that brings conflict. Missie May and her husband, Joe, live in the house and have a little game they play in which he brings home his pay in silver dollars, some of which he throws into the open door while hiding others in his pockets for her to find. They are perfectly content in this ritual and their life until a man named Otis D.

Slemmons comes to town. Slemmons looks "lak a rich white man" (89) and has "a five-dollar gold piece for a stick-pin and he got a ten-dollar gold piece on his watch chain and his mouf is jes' crammed full of gold teethes" (90). Joe envies Slemmons and hopes to be as rich as he is someday but proclaims, "Ah'm satisfied de way Ah is. So long as Ah be yo' husband, Ah don't keer 'bout nothing else" (91). Unfortunately, Missie May is not so satisfied and falls prey to Slemmons's seductions, themselves based in his apparent wealth. Joe comes home early one night and catches Missie May and Slemmons in bed, and when Joe punches Slemmons, knocking him into a somersault from which he recovers and flees, Joe manages to snatch the man's gold coin watch charm. The coin stands between Joe and Missie May, looming as a symbol of her infidelity that grows more intense when Joe realizes she is pregnant, until one day she realizes it is actually just a gilded half dollar. After the baby is born and Joe's mother assures him that Missie May has not been fooling around, Joe goes to Orlando to spend the coin, which the store clerk affirms is fake. Realizing the coin's cheapness and that Slemmons too was fake and that even if he did not beget Missie May's baby he nevertheless has an authenticity that Slemmons never can have, Joe begins to laugh and buys up candy kisses, which he takes home to all-Black Eatonville where he revives his game of tossing coins into the house for Missie May.

This happy ending could be read as a kitsch device, but Hurston structures the story in order to show the real grief and fraught situation underlying it. Right at the story's end she inserts a moment that casts the dark shadows in the kitsch in full relief, for the white Orlando clerk tells another customer, "Wisht I could be like these darkies. Laughin' all the time. Nothin' worries 'em" (98). This white stereotype of African Americans as happy and laughing contrasts sharply with the many months of worrying Joe has just gone through and renders even clearer the depth of grief-dealt-with in his laughter.[5] Joe's power is that, despite the kitsch of his home's decoration and the kitsch nature of his relationship with Missie May, he himself is not kitsch but is rather actuated by complex emotions he deals with in complex ways, for he has never directly attacked or overtly shamed Missie May (even if she herself feels shame). Joe may have only silver dollars to offer, but they are far more valuable than fake gold coins, and curiously Joe's likening Slemmons to a rich white man relocates the defining of kitsch into a white viewpoint rather than a Black one. It would probably be too much to argue that Hurston fashions the story as an allegory against the dangers of giving in to modernist-defined art that always already marginalizes Black forms of cultural production. Yet Hurston's idea about writing manifests a deep suspicion not only of white defining but also African American writers' efforts to align with white art.

Hurston knew that white values in literature, art, music, and even dance must be negotiated, but her writing often embraces Black values that run in opposition, doing so with awareness and maybe even a degree of irony but also valuing Black values for whatever they may be.

Hurston's highlighting coinage and the commodities it purchases (literally candy kisses) explores the role utilization plays in kitsch—the ways objects can be kitsched—and this dynamic appears in her nonfiction work on voodoo culture in Haiti and Jamaica, *Tell My Horse*. One of the arresting moments of that book is Hurston's discussion of voodoo practitioners' use of images of Catholic saints. Such commodified images may be viewed as constituting a specific kind of kitsch, and Hurston includes a photograph of a voodoo altar filled with them, while also writing the following:

> And right here, let it be said that the Haitian gods, mysteres, or loa are not the Catholic calendar of saints done over in black as has been stated by casual observers. This has been said over and over in print because the adepts have been seen buying the lithographs of saints, but this is done because they wish some visual representation of the invisible ones, and as yet no Haitian artist has given them an interpretation or concept of the loa. But even the most illiterate peasant knows that the picture of the saint is only an approximation of the loa. In proof of this, most of the houngans require those who place themselves under their tutelage in order to become hounci to bring a composition book for notes, and in this they must copy the houngan's concept of the loa. I have seen several of these books with the drawings, and none of them pretend to look like the catholic saints. Neither are their attributes the same. (114)

The brilliance of the dynamic Hurston identifies (or perhaps in Hurston's explanation itself) lies in the ways it uproots the otherwise kitsch aesthetic and recasts it as a far more fluid and conceptual kind of negotiation. The gods, mysteres, and loa ultimately exist as spiritual entities and phenomena, their very invisibility an indication and testimony to their presence and power. The images of saints are simply a making-do, not even dignifying their original source religion and culture enough to be "done over." Moreover, the drawings of the hounci (Hurston does not provide examples of these)—which might seem "in spirit" closer to modernist alienated, individualistic interpretations/ incarnations—are more accurately understood not as being superior to but of a different kind from the lithographs. Hurston thus offers a very different view of mass-produced imagery steeped in voodoo community and practice to which the very philosophical machinery that would differentiate that imagery as kitsch is itself alien and arguably irrelevant. The surfaces of such "kitsch" (I place the term in quotes deliberately in order to signal its alienation from the prevailing concept and align it with Waters's and Nerdrum's viewpoints) glittering in candlelight convey an alterity that lays bare the fragile defining and differentiating concepts between art and kitsch that the modernist era has attempted to place on it. That alterity derives from and depends specifically on Black, African cultural practices and performances themselves outside of the rules of modernity.

This alterity appears as a bold force in the work of Edouard Duval-Carrié. A native of Port-au-Prince, as a child Duval-Carrié moved to Puerto Rico with his family, who were fleeing François Duvalier's administration. After attending the Université de Montréal and McGill University, Duval-Carrié received his BA from Loyola College, Montréal, in 1978. He then lived in Paris, attending the École Nationale Supérieure des Beaux-Arts before settling in Miami. Duval-Carrié has forged a style thoroughly aware of and presenting the torturous legacies of colonialism and slavery historically and in contemporary Haiti as well as the circum-Caribbean, including Florida. As overtly political as his work can be, Duval-Carrié invites the viewer via tactile imagery that makes use of literally plastic surfaces and both two- and three-dimensional images (including items lit from behind) drawn from popular culture and the kinds of Catholic liturgical images in Haitian voodoo practices Hurston identifies. An example is *L'Etrange Monde des Zombies* (see fig. 6.1), which features three-dimensional plastic flowers and glitter combined with painting on aluminum covered over with resin. The enticing aesthetic recalls a touristy kitsch effect, yet it is presenting a cavernous setting with a mysterious figural narrative. Is the green figure imploring the white one? Are they friendly? Should they be read allegorically?

Duval-Carrié's own comments on his work provide a useful gloss for this image. While not explicitly evoking kitsch or citing it as an influence or a mode he engages, he outlines modes of engagement that may be traced back through Hurston and the Highwaymen. Referring to his works as "visual concoctions," he explains the ways he wants his art to address the "miscarriage of the representative political process" in Haiti (Duval-Carrié). "I have scrutinized the successive generations of pathetic leaders and their sordid entourages," he explains. "From the operetta emperor to the demented shaman, they all have surpassed each other in the deepening hole of that grave that they have dug for their all adoring peasantry and urban masses as they are called today. All of this under the glaring sun of the Tropics." Ultimately, Duval-Carrié hopes to access "the fabulous world of spirits, old and new, true and false, real and imagined, made themselves felt at different planes of consciousness" that take

Figure 6.1. Edouard Duval-Carrié, *L'Etrange Monde des Zombies*. (Used with permission from Edouard Duval-Carrié.)

on an array of forms and labels, especially in voodoo symbology. "I have staged them over and over again never tiring of doing so," he writes, and raises a revealing question and answer: "Where will the goddess of love, Erzulie Freda Dahomney, turn up? In the local strip club?!!" Duval-Carrié's is an imagination, therefore, that negotiates kitsch out of a deep concern with varying kinds of movements, meaning, and machinations within material, including industrially produced and commodified objects. In this work and others like it, Duval-Carrié taps directly into Hurston's insights in *Tell My Horse* and the complex "kitsch" negotiations in voodoo imagery and iconography.

In other words, Duval-Carrié takes a more overt but equally kitsch-informed approach to representing legacies of colonialism and cruelty in African diaspora. Particularly interesting is his mixed-media collage *Memory #4* (see fig. 6.2). As with *L'Etrange*, this work is large (58" × 58"), but instead of

Figure 6.2. Edouard Duval-Carrié, *Memory #4*. (Used with permission from Edouard Duval-Carrié.)

using a voodoo aesthetic, it directly addresses images and objects of slavery. Made up of items embedded in resin, the whole of it typically displayed back-lit so that it glows, from across the gallery the image invites as "delightful." But closer inspection reveals bric-a-brac including a cross, an anchor, a key, and pearlesque beads combined with images of African Americans in torture devices, holding guns, and on the plantation, all interspersed with bugs. Here again, the image's power lies in its combining images and effects that might be normally thought of in terms of immediacy and popular assemblage (recognizable as scrapbooking accessories or crafting decorations) with frightening, uncanny, and rebellious images of the history of slavery. Work that seems immediately accessible thus emerges as being far less so, and continued observation reveals layers far deeper than the depth of the resin that prod into the darkest catacombs of the history of slavery, segregation, and racism in the new world. While this work and others in this series represent legacies of slavery more starkly perhaps than Hurston tended to do, they nevertheless incorporate the kitsch aesthetic that functions to draw the viewer in through the eye-catching illumination and polished, seductive gleam.

Hurston walked such a fine line between the immediately "pleasing" and "inviting" and the disturbing and even frightening. It was a brave aesthetic, apt to get her into trouble with her peers as quickly and easily as it has kept her relevant and canonical, since her work resurfaced in literary critical discourse in the 1980s. It is an aesthetic shaped by the unique dimensions of Florida's own history in commodification and in its multilayered dreams driven by an array of forces and forms steeped in stereotypes of race and the imagined seductions of otherness. To understand this aspect of Hurston's approach to literature means understanding the unique confluences of African American life within Florida and the unique contributions such confluences mark within African American literary history.

Notes

1. In addition to Greenberg and Broch, see Benjamin and Hans Reimann.

2. For a nuanced discussion of these expectations, see Anthony.

3. For examples of Highwaymen paintings, see Gary Monroe's chapter in this book.

4. Despite the disposable income that drove the mid-century kitsch explosion later to come, kitsch often keys into lower-income lifestyle nostalgia and taste. Even gaudy displays requiring high monetary sums may be kitsch insofar as they embody a poor person's concept of what to buy when rich.

5. John Wharton Lowe has elucidated humor in Hurston's writing, his most sustained meditation being in *Jump at the Sun: Zora Neale Hurston's Cosmic Comedy*.

Bibliography

Anthony, Amanda Koontz. "Racialized Authentification: Constructing Representations of the Florida Highwaymen." *Sociological Quarterly: Official Journal of the Midwest Sociological Society* 53 (2012): 394–421.

Anthony, Amanda Koontz, and Douglas Schrock. "Maintaining Art-World Membership: Self-Taught Identity Work of the Florida Highwaymen." *Social Currents* 1.1 (2014): 74–90.

Asgill, Edmondson. "The Highwaymen and Other Black Icons." In *Florida in the Popular Imagination: Essays on the Cultural Landscape of the Sunshine State*, edited by Steve Glassman, 185–200. Jefferson, NC: McFarland, 2009.

Benjamin, Walter. "Traumkitsch." *Angelus Novus: Ausgewählte Schriften* 2 (1966): 158–60.

Broch, Hermann. "Evil in the Value-System of Art." In *Geist and Zeitgeist: The Spirit in an Unspiritual Age*, 3–39. Trans. John Hargreaves. New York: Counterpoint, 2002.

Congdon, Kristin G. "Stories About the Highwaymen: Insights About All of Us." *Visual Arts Research* 30.1 (2004): 13–21.

Du Bois, W. E. B. *The Souls of Black Folk*. 1903. New York: Penguin, 2002.

Duval-Carrié, Edouard. "Artist Statement." Bernice Steinbaum Gallery. Wayback Machine
    Internet Archive. September 7, 2020. https://web.archive.org/web/20090217084242/http://
    bernicesteinbaumgallery.com/artists/duval_carrie/statement_duval-carrie.html.
Finch, Charlie. "Is Black Art Too Kitschy?" *Artnet* (13 April 2012). http://www.artnet.com
    /magazineus/features/finch/is-black-art-too-kitschy-4-13-12.asp.
Gates, Henry Louis, Jr. *The Signifying Monkey: A Theory of African American Literary Criticism.*
    Oxford: Oxford University Press, 1988.
Greenberg, Clement. "Avant-Garde and Kitsch." In *Art and Culture.* Boston: Beacon Press, 1961.
    3–21.
Hurston, Zora Neale. *Tell My Horse: Voodoo and Life in Haiti and Jamaica.* 1938. New York:
    HarperPerennial, 2009.
Hurston, Zora Neale. "The Gilded Six-Bits." 1933. In *The Complete Stories,* 86–98. New York:
    Harper Perennial, 1995.
Hurston, Zora Neale. *Their Eyes Were Watching God.* 1937. New York: Perennial Classics, 1998.
Kulka, Tomas. *Kitsch and Art.* University Park: Pennsylvania State University Press, 1996.
Lowe, John Wharton. *Jump at the Sun: Zora Neale Hurston's Cosmic Comedy.* Urbana:
    University of Illinois Press, 1994.
Monroe, Gary. *The Highwaymen: Florida's African-American Landscape Painters.* Gainesville:
    University Press of Florida, 2001.
Nerdrum, Odd. *On Kitsch.* Oslo: Kagge Forlag, 2001.
Reimann, Hans. *Das Buch vom Kitsch.* München: Piper, 1936.
Ward, Peter. *Kitsch in Sync: A Consumer's Guide to Bad Taste.* London: Plexus, 1991.

CHAPTER SEVEN

"Follow Me through Florida"

The Journey of the Black Federal Writers

Pamela Bordelon

There was a time in the not so distant past when America went in search of its roots. This was not an ordinary venture, but one created by the federal government in response to massive unemployment. Beginning in July 1935, the New Deal's Federal Writers' Project (FWP) launched a work-relief program that hired some 6,600 unemployed writers and white-collar workers and set up the research for the American Guide Series that among other things would profile each of the then forty-eight states. In the hands of highly creative and driven intellectuals, the FWP became more than just a relief program. In fact, historians and literary critics would argue that the FWP gave the nation its first credible look at its roots. Federal writers, hired on the government's dime, were sent to every corner of the nation to report what they discovered, what they uncovered, and how ordinary people lived. This was a massive, almost amorphous drive that lasted but four short years as a federal project, sputtered on three more under state auspices, and then disappeared entirely (Kazin, 485–518, 489).

During most of its short life, the FWP remained controversial, an object of public ridicule, even a congressional witch hunt. Misunderstood and maligned, when the FWP finally ended, only a few historians, intellectuals, and writers grasped the full significance of what had been accomplished. It would take many more years for America to wake up and see how clear-eyed the FWP search had been. These FWP writers, based in every state in the union and two territories, had gone in search of grassroots America, taking stock of the nation, searching out unknown history and folklife. They found and interviewed ordinary people, recording their thoughts about their lives, their beliefs, their work. As a part of this process, these federal writers gave America its first credible look at its African American roots. It is this search that interests us most (Mangione, 284–326).

The FWP Black studies program marks a perceptive shift in the American psyche and a clear step toward deeper understanding of what it meant to be Black in America. The New Deal of Franklin Delano Roosevelt led the shift, and for four years, offered bright hope for the nation to better understand its African American past. Nothing before and little after matched the boldness and findings of this effort, as Howard Sitkoff in *The New Deal for Blacks* reminds us. In this small sliver of time, the life stories of aged Black former slaves were written down, Black culture examined, folklore gathered, and Black writers discovered and sustained. All mattered.

The heart of the search was the institution of "Negro Writers' Units," as these Black Writers' Units were colloquially known, that were strategically placed in key southern states. The Black Writers' Unit in Florida proved one of the most fruitful and its outpouring exceptional.

The Launch of the Southern Black Federal Writers' Units

The New Deal's launch of Black Writers' Units was made possible only by the economic crisis the Great Depression had unleashed. This was an economic and social crisis that turned America upside down, opened the way for new approaches, and brought Franklin Delano Roosevelt to the political forefront. When the national economy began its downward spiral in October 1929, no one understood that it would last a decade, or eventually become known to history as "The Great Depression." President Herbert Hoover certainly did not understand, nor did most of the nation. The Republicans continued to pull out old fixes for a new set of problems. Nothing worked. Finally, in complete and utter disgust the voters elected a promising, but unknown leader: Franklin D. Roosevelt, who was the successful governor of New York yet largely unknown in the national arena. Roosevelt in 1932 was still a mystery, a person who many critics considered a lightweight, a shadow perhaps of his more famous cousin Theodore Roosevelt. But the voters responded to his call for action, and change, and experimentation. They knew something had to be done, but what? There were so many unanswered questions, so desperate a need among the unemployed for jobs, for something positive to do. They elected him in the 1932 presidential election, the first Democrat since Woodrow Wilson (Lindley).

On March 4, 1933, amid what looked like the final collapse of the nation's banking system, Roosevelt was sworn in as president of the United States. No one really knew Roosevelt's thoughts as he assumed office or delivered his first inaugural address and underscored the need for "action and action now." He cautioned that "all we have to fear is fear itself." But millions of hopeful Americans, listening over their radio sets, took his words to heart and were buoyed by their promise (Alter, 207–44).

True to his word, Roosevelt went into quick action, shored up failing banks, and gathered about himself the most dynamic and creative advisors he could find (Alter, 198–204, 226–52). Most were ordinary but gifted, proven leaders willing to jump into the fray with bold ideas and with the guts to tackle seemingly endless problems. Among these administrators was a relatively unknown social worker named Harry Hopkins who did not shy away from bold action. As the head of the Federal Emergency Relief Administration (FERA) from 1933 to 1935, and then as head of the Works Progress Administration (WPA) from 1935 to 1938, he experimented with various forms of relief. The FERA dispensed direct grants, but Hopkins believed that the people really wanted work, a sense of purpose, and a way to earn a living. He pressed his ideas on Roosevelt, and eventually the WPA was conceived. This federally administered work relief program, rolled out in May 1935, would change the nation physically and imaginatively. Hopkins's belief that jobs should fit the skills of those on the relief rolls led to the creation of four arts programs: one to hire musicians, another for actors, still another for artists, and finally one for writers. These programs were ethnically diverse, giving Black Americans a chance at relief and uplift (McJimsey).

The Florida Federal Writers' Project

The New Deal's announcement in Florida in September 1935 that the Federal Writers' Project was hiring unemployed writers, journalists, teachers, and the like created a stampede. Hundreds applied for eighty-six statewide positions. Many were turned away, including a number of highly qualified Blacks: former college professors, English teachers, journalists, and college graduates. Qualified Blacks who did get certified for relief and assigned a WPA position found themselves not on the writers' division but on a construction project, where they were handed shovels and told to dig ditches.

In the southern scheme of things, when there were so many whites seeking these highly coveted Writers' Project jobs, Blacks lost out. In Florida, where a great many educated Blacks lived, they were simply informed: "It is too late to receive the aid" (Kellock to Alsberg, January 23, 1936). This was happening all across the South.

Black leaders protested. But no Black leader by 1935 had the clout that Florida's own Mary McLeod Bethune possessed. She was now the highest-ranking Black administrator in the New Deal and the leader of the informal group of New Deal Black advisors known as "the Black Cabinet." Her words counted. She had by sheer force of will risen from poverty, educated herself, opened a school, and then a college. She was passionate about education, knowing it was the key to Blacks' futures. Her own life showed what other Blacks could do (Watts, 261–82).

Born in 1875 in Mayfield, South Carolina, her parents Patsy and Samuel McLeod were former slaves. Growing up, she knew the bare grind of poverty that attended sharecropping Blacks like her parents. After the Civil War, it took the entire family's labor to even survive. Mary McLeod hoed and picked cotton until she was eleven, a hard life for a child. Her one passion was to get an education, for she saw it as the way out of a bleak, hopeless existence. Neither of her parents could read or write, but they both knew the promise of education. Mary McLeod's dream was fulfilled when a local teacher who was starting a school sponsored by the Presbyterian church convinced her parents to release her from the drudgery of the fields and let her get an education. Looking back, Bethune believed she was guided and unique and claims her parents felt the same. She excelled as the school's most dedicated student. Later she was sent to Scatia Seminary's residential program to continue her rigorous education. To help with the expenses, she worked as a domestic and picked up various odd jobs. In 1894, she received a scholarship to Moody Bible Institute in Chicago. Upon graduation, she applied to the mission fields of Africa, and was bitterly disappointed when she was turned down. Undiminished, she would return to South Carolina and Georgia and begin teaching. In 1897, she met and married Albert Bethune, had a son almost immediately, and tried to settle down as a mother and a wife. Yet she could not. Her horizon was not a kitchen or a house, or even a backyard. She felt a call to educate and uplift and enlighten. She had a vision and deep desire to start a school for girls.

In 1899, the couple and their son Albert moved to Palatka, Florida, where the Florida railroads provided jobs and educational opportunities. She ended up in Daytona Beach in 1904, where she started her school for girls. Within two years, it had grown from five to 250 students. Her energy was boundless; her ability to tap the largesse of rich white patrons who lived in the area was renowned. By 1923, her school for girls had merged with the Cookman Institute and became Bethune-Cookman College.

Yet Mary Bethune was not done. Starting in the 1920s, she began traveling across the United States lobbying for Black education, civil rights, and women's issues. She met Eleanor Roosevelt in the late twenties at a luncheon Sara Roosevelt hosted for Women's Club advocates. Mrs. Bethune was the only Black woman in attendance and no other woman wanted to sit near her. Sara

Roosevelt graciously seated the courageous Black woman near her daughter-in-law Eleanor at the head of the table. This event sparked the beginning of a friendship that blossomed after Eleanor Roosevelt's husband became president. By 1934, Mary McLeod Bethune had become critical to New Deal efforts to win Black votes (Watts, 261–82).

In 1932, Mary Bethune had voted Republican, as had most Blacks. Yet as the New Deal unfolded and she moved into a closer friendship with the First Lady, she was impressed with the New Deal's social programs and humanitarian outreach. By this time, Bethune's political acumen, organizational talent, leadership, and ability as a speaker had come to New Dealers' attention. Aubrey Williams, a liberal Southerner who had risen through New Deal ranks, first as one of Harry Hopkins's chief assistants and then as head of the National Youth Administration (NYA), appointed Mary Bethune to the NYA advisory board in 1934. At a select NYA board meeting in the spring of 1935 at the Roosevelt estate at Hyde Park, New York, Mrs. Bethune met Franklin Roosevelt for the first time. Never one to miss an important opportunity, when called upon to speak, she turned on her charm and illuminated her mission: She began, "Now I speak Mr. President, not as Mrs. Bethune but as the voice of fourteen million Americans who seek to achieve full citizenship. We have been taking the crumbs for a long time. We have been eating the feet and head of the chicken long enough. The time has come when we want some white meat." And then she stated her ideas for the future: ". . . The further an individual is down, the more chance he may have to come up. But the Negro cannot find his way to the opportunities that are opening unless he has someone to guide him" (Holt, 193).

Her address brought tears to the president's eyes. Roosevelt thanked her "for the informal knowledge you have placed at our disposal in these important days of beginnings in a new field" and assured his support to "contribute something to help make a better life for your people." He personally liked Mrs. Bethune and bestowed upon her the leadership of the newly created National Youth Administration Office of Minority Affairs. In this capacity, she now had a large voice in New Deal relief (Holt, 193).

In this role, by October 1935 Mrs. Bethune was in an unusual position to do something to help middle-class Blacks in Florida. Many of those turned away from the Federal Writers' Project positions in her state had been graduates of her college. Mary Bethune quickly went into action. Working as she most often did behind the scenes, at her behest Edward Rodrigues, a close confidant, adopted son, and protégé, whom she had installed as head of minority affairs in the Florida National Youth Administration, wrote Henry Alsberg, the national director of the Federal Writers' Project. Rodrigues told Alsberg of Blacks who had applied for the Florida Federal Writers' Project but had been turned away. He pleaded: "I am asking that you, in your wisdom and knowledge of the situation [to] put forth every effort to see that our people receive their portion of such projects." He stressed, "We have an enormous amount of native and skilled talent in the state," and he noted "that there were four colleges through which some of these projects might be conducted adequately" (Edward Rodrigues to Henry Alsberg, October 7, 1935, admin correspondence, Florida, WPA R.G. 69).

Alsberg, a deeply sensitive man, a humanitarian, and a champion of the underdog, assured Rodrigues, "I shall do everything to see that there is no discrimination whatsoever." But at this juncture Alsberg knew that his hands were tied. His national FWP office was an editorial concern. They outlined the research and writing for each state's automotive guidebooks. It was the state WPA offices that handled the hiring of personnel. Carita Corse, the director of the Florida Federal Writers Project, selected her writers from a list of candidates that the Florida WPA office sent to her (Alsberg to Rodrigues).

Although blatant discrimination fired up other Black leaders on the national level, Mary Bethune, through her direct access to the First Lady and her leadership of the Black cabinet, had the most clout. But more than any other factor, Roosevelt's reelection campaign, which was underway and needed the Black vote in a number of northern cities, pushed New Dealers to find Blacks jobs on the FWP. A solution was found. Black Writers Units were implemented (Watts, 261).

In late February 1936, the New Deal increased Florida's FWP quota by ten and authorized an appropriation of $2,000 to hire ten Blacks for a special "Negro Unit." On March 5, 1936, Martin Richardson, J. M. Johnson, Alfred Farrell, Viola Muse, Rachael Austin, Rebecca Baker, Samuel Johnson, and Wilson Rice started covering Florida (McDonough, 153–66).

In keeping with the rigid Jim Crow racial divide, Black writers worked out of an upstairs room at the Clara White Mission in the heart of Jacksonville's Black quarter. Eartha White, an unusual and successful entrepreneur and humanitarian, had bought an old theater and converted it into a soup kitchen and community outreach center. She had extended her largesse to housing the WPA sewing and recreational projects; now the WPA arts projects would join them (Alsberg to Corse, February 20, 1936; Corse to Alsberg, March 5, 1936)

In keeping with the strict Jim Crow separate but equal policy, the Black Writers had no contact with their white counterparts, who were based a few blocks away in the Duval Building in the heart of Jacksonville's business district. "About all we ever saw of them," Stetson Kennedy, one of the white writers, wrote, "was twice a month they sent a runner over to get their checks" (Kennedy interview, January 6, 1989).

Mary McCleod Bethune was made honorary supervisor of the unit, a clear indication of her behind-the-scenes influence and her interest in the Black history of her state. She put the resources of Bethune-Cookman College in Daytona Beach at the writers' disposal. Locating the unit in Jacksonville assured a supply of highly qualified unemployed Blacks whose college, newspaper, and teaching positions had been casualties of the Depression (Bordelon, "Mirror," 133).

The New Deal's hiring of educated Blacks to compile African American histories of their respective states was a bold move indeed, especially in the American South, where these educated Blacks' efforts ran counter to the era's rampant racism, where strict Jim Crow laws were enforced to keep most Blacks "down." A Black man looking sideways at a white woman could get himself lynched. Often the Ku Klux Klan marched in the same rural areas where these Black federal writers collected their information. Despite these real dangers, the people spoke anyway, for they wanted their stories told. Their highly educated and polished brethren in the employ of the federal government who moved among them offered hope.

Despite their small number, all-too-frequent quota cuts, and the short duration that the unit operated in Florida, the Black writers amassed an impressive body of research and writing that in many instances surpassed the quantity and quality of their white counterparts. They did this despite formidable challenges posed by segregated facilities such as the state's libraries, archives, and county records offices. These segregated facilities were off limits to Blacks. If they were miraculously allowed entrance, they received little help and had to work in rooms separate from white patrons. One Black writer on the Dillard project in New Orleans recalled years later to an interviewer that "he had to know the holdings of the libraries because librarians would provide only the materials specifically requested" (Clayton).

Since they were unable to access the few written records that did exist, Florida's Black writers turned instead to the people. While researching the Black experience of Florida towns, they found dozens of former slaves, many of whom still lived near their place of bondage. Now decades past slavery, they had had time to think about bondage, to contextualize it, and sum up its significance to their lives. Speaking with a much younger member of their race, most reacted with deep emotion. In Jacksonville, J. M. Johnson interviewed Eartha White, the well-known local philanthropist, whose mother had been a slave on Amelia Island. She told him of "the old slave market on Forsyth Street about 100 feet east of the ocean" where on a "little crude platform were auctioned off at regular intervals slaves from all over the area." She spoke of the "white-haired old auctioneer," for years a resident of nearby Mandarin, "and explained how he auctioned slaves. He would hold the slaves on the platform, open wide their eyelids to show that their eyes were good, show their tongues, punch the chest and ribs to show that they were solid and wind up his narrative of their qualities in the case of a female, remarking, 'She's a good breeder too'" (Bordelon, "Mirror," 137).

In Jacksonville, Rachael Austin found Margaret Nickerson, a Jacksonville resident who had just turned ninety, a willing interview subject. Obviously comfortable with Austin, a much younger woman whom she called "child," she spoke of the brutality of slavery, of being crippled from overwork, and the savage brutality of her master. The depth of her thought, her careful choice of words, and her calculated delivery show how she valued the importance of what she was saying. Nearing the end of a long life, she wanted to unburden herself, pass her story to the next generation and make them mindful of her sacrifice. Her words show what freedom meant. She told Austin: "Now ef you jest lis'en, I wanna tell you all I kin, but I wants to tell it right; wait now, I don' wanna make no mistakes and I don' lie on nobody. I ain' mad now and I know tain' no use to lie, I'm takin' my time. I done prayed an' got all de malice out o' my heart and I ain' gonna tell no lie on um" (Rawick, XVII, 252).

While researching the African American history of Tampa, Viola Muse reported, "Interesting tales of the days of slavery may be had for the asking from some of Tampa's oldest negro citizens." She found Evelyn Beasley, still living in the vicinity of her enslavement. now willing to talk. Beasley spoke of her mother who had been "forced into companionship with a white slave owner." Muse noted that even though the white slave owner "appeared to have developed a real affection for her that lasted even after the slaves had been freed," Mrs. Beasley's mother always hated her father. The mother left the plantation immediately after freedom was declared, and refused to let Evelyn's father help them (Bordelon, "Mirror," 140).

Although seven decades had passed, Beasley still carried the shame of being the child of a forced relationship, a fact easily identified by her lighter skin. So great was her trauma that she refused to divulge the name of her white father (Bordelon, "Mirror," 140). Chances are Ms. Beasley had spoken to no one of her origins. However, when this young government interviewer offered her a chance to unburden herself to the wider world, she relented.

Sent to document the early history of Pensacola, Martin Richardson encountered former slaves who spoke of the horrors of bondage. A former newspaperman, Richardson had approached community leaders and asked about former slaves living in the area. They led him to four men, including one who was now pastor of a church, who had been slaves in the area. Gathered in a group and interviewed together, perhaps at their church, they told Richardson of a "reign of brutality and cruelty" that in some cases, Richardson wrote, defies description. Richardson noted that "One ex-slave in the telling of it had to pause many times in his emotional recital of things he himself had witnessed." He told of "having seen his mother strung up by her thumbs to a tree limb, stripped to her waist, and beaten until she was unconscious because she refused to answer a summons to appear at the house in her night clothes. . . ." Richardson continued, "This man said that after witnessing this savage brutality, he carried in his mind a firm determination to kill his slave master." The young child was spared what would have been his own certain death when "riotous living and dissipation caused [his owner's death] while the ex-slave was still in his childhood" ("History of the Negro in Florida," 92, 94–95).

The horrors of slavery were uncovered all through north Florida's plantation region, a rich agricultural area where hundreds of slaves had once labored. Alfred Farrell found and interviewed a number of them living in Live Oak, Florida, a small agricultural hub not far from the state capital. Many stayed on after freedom, and their descendants sharecropped. They were willing to talk.

Now in their eighties, these former slaves spoke willingly to a much younger, refined member of their race. Bolden Hall told of a kindly master who permitted his slaves to attend church and noted he occasionally found an "itinerant colored minister to preach." This was not the case for Charlotte Martin, whose abusive master whipped her eldest brother to death for taking part in a secret religious meeting in the woods late at night. Sarah Ross also remembered an owner who abused his slaves so horribly, that as Farrell wrote, "No kind of punishment was too cruel or severe to be inflicted on these souls in bondage" (Bordelon, "Mirror," 134). Farrell's carefully chosen words register his own horror and empathy upon hearing what these aged ex-slaves had endured (FWP Florida, "Slave Interviews," unpublished manuscript, 197–200, quotes 197, 200).

Florida's federal writers had touched a raw nerve. Clearly slavery was the overriding story. With Black interviewers, these former bondsmen had opened up with stunning testimony filled with feeling and insight. The interviews were typed and passed to Carita Doggett Corse. A historian by training, Corse knew their worth. While doing her own research of the Zephaniah Kingsley Plantation on Amelia Island while writing *Key to the Golden Islands* (1932), she recalled later to an interviewer that one of her key sources was a former bondsman living on Ft. George Island, and she remembered how he had supplied her with critical personal details and a wealth of insight into slavery in Florida (Bordelon, "Mirror," 142). Realizing the importance to history that these encounters with former slaves provided, Corse encouraged the Black writers to continue their interviewing. This they did. They typed the exchanges up separately, and combed Jacksonville and the rest of Florida for more informants (Yetman, 534–53).

In March 1937, Corse forwarded a number of these Florida interviews to the national FWP office in Washington. She received an immediate reply from George Cronyn, the project's assistant director, who had passed the Florida narratives to John Lomax, the FWP's folklore consultant. Cronyn wrote Corse, "Mr. Lomax and I found the stories of the ex-slaves fascinating reading. We feel that these will be valuable for future reference and possible publication." Florida's initiative in collecting them, which came from the normal turn of events as the Black writers conducted their exhaustive field work, had unearthed a rich vein of Americana (Yetman, 248–50).

Cronyn assigned John Lomax the task of developing guidelines for other state projects. Lomax was a seasoned collector, having spent nearly thirty years in the field collecting ballads and folk songs. Early in his collecting, he found that southern prisons, filled with Black inmates, were a veritable treasure trove of unusual folk songs. While Lomax's methods of collecting were sometimes suspect—he used the warden's control over his inmates to ensure their participation—Lomax's heart was in the right place. He saw the value of folk song and the need to preserve it. He endured years of ridicule from most whites who felt he was clearly crazy to collect it. Yet his books on folk songs sold, and his talks at colleges were popular.

Lomax received pushback from educated Blacks, who like whites did not believe the folklore and song of poor Blacks should be remembered; in fact, most educated people shunned it. It is to Lomax's credit that he plodded on. Eventually the Library of Congress would supply him with a rarity, a state-of-the-art recording machine, a very large and cumbersome box that he and his son Alan hauled all over the South collecting the folk songs of Blacks. By the mid-1930s, Lomax was the chief researcher to the Library of Congress's Archive of Folk Song and considered a veteran field collector. He took a one-year sabbatical from the Archive to work for FWP (Lomax).

When Lomax read the Florida interviews, he immediately recognized their worth. Here were former slaves speaking with deeply charged emotion about their years as slaves. Henry Alsberg and George Cronyn also saw their significance and wanted to extend the interviewing. Yet despite the National FWP Office's best efforts, there would be a wide discrepancy between the quality of the interviews done with Black interviewers and those done by whites.

Cronyn wrote the directors of the North Carolina, South Carolina, Georgia, Alabama, Louisiana, Texas, Arkansas, Tennessee, Kentucky, Mississippi, and

Oklahoma projects and told them of the new initiative. Lomax drafted nineteen interview questions "to get the Negro to thinking and talking about the days of slavery." Ideally, he hoped the interviewer would develop enough of a rapport with the former bondsman to get him to talk freely, without prodding, "to say what he pleases without reference to the questions" (Bordelon, "Mirror," 135). These directives, meant to help other states, had little impact on Florida's interviewers; editorial comments later merely asked the interviewer to return to their subjects to pursue interesting lines of questioning. Clearly the Florida interviewers had developed their own way of doing things. Lomax's influence over the Florida narratives was restricted to editorial comment.

More than just instigating the national program to interview "ex-slaves," as they were referred to at the time, Florida, with its deeply capable Black interviewers, set the standard. Time proved that Black-on-Black interviews were far superior to those done between a white writer and a former slave. More than race, Florida's Black writers displayed a remarkable empathy, a deep desire to get older Blacks to speak of bondage. They themselves wanted to know.

In his formal instructions to other states, Lomax made this point: "workers should concentrate on one of the more interesting subjects, establish a rapport with them, and draw information from them over several visits. . . ." He cautioned the interviewer not to influence the informant and "not to let his own opinion on the subject of slavery became obvious." Here Lomax was trying to keep biased white interviewers from interjecting their racial views (Bordelon, "Mirror," 135). This was nearly impossible; ingrained attitudes do not just disappear. A group of interviews done in Pensacola by Modeste Hargis, a sensitive and highly educated white woman who bore the distinction of becoming Florida's first woman pharmacist, proves this. She had operated her own drugstore in downtown Pensacola until the Depression forced its closure. Well-connected and educated, she was able to get one of the highly coveted writer positions handed down in the city. More than likely she sought Blacks who had been her drugstore customers and asked them for interviews. An older Black couple consented. At the beginning of the interview she wrote "Richard Lindsay and his wife are typical old time darkies." She added, "They do not talk 'n----r' dialect, but express themselves very nicely." She meant this as a compliment at the time, but today, readers cringe when they read her background comments. Hargis continues, "They were very polite to me, offering me a chair in the tiny front hall. After I was seated, the old man sat down near the table and his wife sat just behind him" (Bordelon, "Mirror," 147). The interview that followed lacked detail and feeling.

It is obvious that former slaves were reluctant to share the raw details of bondage with whites. When Hargis asked Joe Youder about cruelty, he told her some masters "wuz mean" but refused to give any details. He added, "All the slaves worked hard, even the chillun, but most of the slaves wuz treated right" ("Bordelon, "Mirror," 138). Compare her interviews with those of Martin Richardson, who also interviewed Pensacola Blacks, and the difference between white and Black interviewers is obvious (Bordelon, "Mirror," 137).

Lomax directed interviewers to ask about freedom: "Now that slavery is ended, what do you think of it?" and "What did you get after freedom?" Perhaps Squires Jackson best summed it up: "No storm lasts forever . . . even the best masters in slavery couldn't be as good as the worst person in freedom. Oh, God, it is good to be free, and I am thankful" (Bordelon, "Mirror," 146).

Although the national office had every intention to publish the ex-slave interviews, time and funding ran out. Some 2,300 were eventually collected and archived at the Library of Congress. Those done in Florida were intended for "A History of the Negro in Florida," but the book was never completed. The chapters that were compiled from Black writers' field copy, such as "Slave Days in Florida," show how white editors took Blacks' field copy and turned it to their own viewpoints (McDonough, 19–30, 31–38).

In addition to slavery, Florida's Black writers provided invaluable documentation of the contemporary scene: how Florida Blacks were faring during the Depression, how they had organized their own churches, the state of Blacks' education, and prospects for Black labor. Folklore, music, and amusements would round out the picture. But of all these findings, the most disquieting and perhaps most revealing was Martin Richardson's report on Black labor, titled "What the Florida Negro Does." Trained as a journalist, he was a close observer and an expert interviewer. He would present an indictment of the abuses of Black labor in Florida (Bordelon, "Mirror," 147–53).

Sometime, probably in late 1936 or early 1937, during the winter tourist season in South Florida, Richardson set out from his home base in Jacksonville to find out. His topic was labor, but his report was more an indictment of the raw conditions and labor abuses that Blacks in Florida withstood. Almost certainly he was tapping into the $2 million that the New Deal had appropriated to study Black joblessness. Surely Mary McCleod Bethune funneled traveling expenses and perhaps a small stipend as he traveled through the state. As head of the Black Cabinet and head of the Office of Minority Affairs for the NYA, Mrs. Bethune needed documentation such as this to press for more funding for Florida Blacks (Watts, 275).

We will never know the exact motivation for the piece, or if there were any background instructions imparted to Richardson, but funding had to have been found to pay his travel expenses throughout the state. And this is where we find a deep mystery. Carita Corse did not have extra travel funds for Black writers, nor would Corse have agreed with Richardson's eventual findings. Clearly, she was not in the picture. This points to background forces and the long arm of Mary McLeod Bethune.

Richardson's report begins with these dismal figures. "Out of 459,000 black workers in Florida, only half that number were employed even half the year." Jobs in agriculture, citrus production, and the tourist industry were seasonal. He noted that "Relief work, odd jobs, small businesses, and part-time employment . . . have partially made up for the lowered total of normal workers." As Richardson traveled the state, interviewing workers, he added his own observations that, combined with statistics, present a commanding indictment of Black labor in Florida (Bordelon, "Mirror," 148).

Beginning his report in South Florida, Richardson interviewed the workers who serviced the region's seasonal tourist industry. He spoke with bellmen, doormen, elevator operators, waiters, and cooks who told him that salaries were almost nonexistent and that they lived on tips. As Richardson noted, "tips averaged from three dollars a day in modest establishments to ten and fifteen dollars a day in the deluxe hotels." In addition, bellmen, doormen, and elevator operators reaped large returns running "social contact agencies for lonesome guests," "bootlegging after legal closing hours for the hotel bar," and "similar thoughtful enterprises" (Bordelon, "Mirror," 149). He learned that "the most highly paid Black hotel workers were the chefs." In the larger establishments they ran the entire food service operation even though, as he observed, "many of them could not read the menus that they had planned." However with the Depression and disappearance of job opportunities, Richardson found out that Black chefs were squeezed out by whites who demanded their higher-paying jobs. Richardson discovered that by 1937, the number of Black chefs had been reduced considerably, although "there are still several major hotels with Negro chef cooks, bakers, and other kitchen personnel" (Bordelon, "Mirror," 149).

South Florida's mansions offered hundreds of Blacks jobs working in the palatial mansions of wealthy Northerners who wintered in the Miami and Palm Beach areas. These domestic and service workers were paid well during peak season, which lasted from November through May, but not as well as those working for tips in hotels. Yet they, he found, savored the stability of these year-round positions. When their wealthy patrons returned north, they stayed on with fewer responsibilities but moderate pay. Richardson reported:

"As a general rule, domestic work for the tourist population is regarded by the workers as being less tedious, although usually less lucrative than that of hotel work. Hours are long but periods during which the employers are away from the home for protracted periods are frequent. The employment of couples permits a normal family life for the employees that is almost totally lacking in the hotel, road house, restaurant types of domestic employment" (Richardson, "What the Florida Negro Does," 7). Richardson is referring to Black couples—husband and wife teams—who staffed these houses as chauffeurs, house maids, cooks, and gardeners. They told Richardson that the steady employment was worth far more than a few months of work with high tips. When their employers returned to the Northeast, as they always did in the spring, the Black servants remained to maintain the house properly.

Leaving the tourist areas of South Florida, Richardson traveled to the nearby vegetable and fruit truck farming region where he found labor conditions grueling. Here migrant labor lived in hovels without proper sanitary conditions or even shelter. They harvested the state's lettuce, strawberry, celery, bean, and tomato crops, which were destined largely for national markets. The hours, from sunup to sundown, were exploitative. This was the famous migrant area where families arrived in their flivvers. They picked the beans, tomatoes, lettuce, and cucumbers: mothers with nursing babies and several dirty, shabbily dressed children, and the men, looking beaten down by poverty and want (see Bordelon, "Mirror," 150; Richardson, "What the Florida Negro Does," 10).

Richardson wrote that conditions here were by far the most appalling. One picker told Richardson that the people on one farm worked "so hard they look like African wild men." Richardson learned that few Blacks would work on these farms at low wages and that labor became so difficult to secure that in 1936 and 1937, truck farm owners sought the assistance of city and county police who staged clean-ups in the Black communities. A "clean-up" meant any Black man that did not have a job was rounded up and charged with loitering. These unfortunates, slapped with court costs and fines, were thus indebted and forced to work off their debts. Local sheriffs "leased" them to farm owners who paid their debts and essentially made them "peons" or debt slaves. Unable to pay their fines and court costs, they were forced to stay at these abusive jobs until their owners were reimbursed. Those who tried to escape these unfair and harsh conditions often paid for their boldness with their lives (Bordelon, "Mirror," 151). Richardson added, "the alternative of work on the truck farms was a sentence on the chain gang" (Bordelon, "Mirror," 150–51).

Labor conditions for Blacks in Central Florida's citrus growing region were equally exploitative. Grove owners employed thousands of Black workers who were "neither among the happiest nor the most prosperous of Florida's working population." He noted: "Wages are unusually bad in the citrus belt. Labor in the groves, he found, was partly migratory, partly permanent. By pitting these two types against each other, the grove owner in many cases forced wages down to subsistence levels. . . ." Talking to workers, he also found that employers encouraged conflict between white and Negro workers, again to drive down wages (Bordelon, "Mirror," 150).

Moving his investigation to Northwest Florida, Richardson found conditions among sharecroppers and tenant farms were just as exploitative, but not as abusive as those of migrant and forced labor in South Florida's vegetable region. He observed that many of these Black farmers were "living on the identical cotton fields that they or their fathers tended as slaves before Emancipation." In most cases, Richardson observed, "the farms are usually only small scale imitations of the hundreds of acres they once had devoted entirely to production of the valuable, fluffy white bolls." He observed that these tenant farmers and sharecroppers labored as hard as they had as slaves and that abusive child labor was the norm. He wrote: "Children had to work in the fields from the age of six or eight so that the family could break even on the year's work." Yet, he noted, they got no pay in return. Despite long hours, the sharecroppers told Richardson they had handled "no cash money in years" (Bordelon, "Mirror," 151–52).

Moving to investigate turpentine and phosphate workers in Central and North Florida, Richardson documented the most abusive conditions of all. Richardson wrote: "To the evil of low wages in the state must be added forced labor . . ." (Bordelon, "Mirror," 152–53). He entered several turpentine camps and uncovered evidence of the "the infamous commissary system, which forced camp workers to purchase all of their food and commodities at the company store at highly inflated prices." He noted that in turpentine camps in Baker, Duval, and Clay counties, where forced labor had been reported, the commissary system was used to keep the turpentiners in debt and on their jobs. With great difficulty, he found workers who were willing to talk, but who were "so terrorized that they refused pointblank to be seen talking to field workers engaged on The American Guide" (Bordelon, "Mirror," 153). Richardson's report documented the low wages and the alarming state of abuse surrounding contemporary Black labor in Florida, but one wonders about the long-range impact of "What the Florida Negro Does." Did it help lobby for reform? It was just that kind of report.

By the end of 1937, New Deal quota cuts had eliminated all the Black federal writers' positions. The number of white writers had also been cut to the bone. What followed is known to history as "the Roosevelt Recession." The economy sank. Roosevelt was forced to increase WPA hiring in 1938.

In Florida, Zora Neale Hurston was recruited to join the Florida FWP, which she did in April 1938. She lived in Eatonville. Paul Diggs, a community organizer, signed on at the same time. Yet gone was representation of Black writers in the northern part of the state. However, these new hires based out of the Tampa area would round out the northern Florida Black writers' offerings and contribute mightily to the collection's superior quality.

By 1938, Zora Neale Hurston had completed four books, *Jonah's Gourd Vine* (1934), *Mules and Men* (1935), and *Their Eyes Were Watching God* (1937), and in Eatonville, her hometown, finished her manuscript for *Tell My Horse* (1938), an account of her folkloric collection in Jamaica and Haiti. With her book publication months away, and her Guggenheim grant funding exhausted, in March 1938, she found herself in a bleak financial position. She was forced on relief, a desperate move, for it meant that she had to stand in line at a state intake office, speak with an intake worker, swear she owned no property, and answer a long list of humiliating questions. This was yet another example of how like so many times in her life, Hurston had to bite her pride, humble herself, and in this case "go on relief." She told no one, not even her nieces with whom she was living in Eatonville (Bordelon, *Go Gator*, 13).

Despite her misgivings, the Federal Writers' Project pulled from Hurston some of her best work. She wrote her seminal folklore essay, "Go Gator and Muddy the Water," a sampler of relevant Black folklore found in Florida and an explanation of the context from which it sprang. A separate chapter, "Other Negro Folklore Influences," compared Floridian and Bahamian music, dance, and humor. A third essay, again framed as a chapter for the proposed "History of the Negro in Florida," discusses the place of "the Sanctified Church" in the contemporary scheme of Black religion. She ties the Sanctified Church's vibrant worship as seen in their display of dance, song, and music as reflections of the culture. Hurston's presence on the Florida project drew the deep interest of the national office (Bordelon, *Go Gator*).

About the same time Hurston joined the Florida FWP, Benjamin Botkin joined the national FWP office as national folklore editor in April 1938. In Botkin, who was replacing John Lomax, Hurston found a kindred spirit. Both were scientifically trained folklorists; both saw folklore as reflective of the culture. It was Botkin who requested Hurston's report, "Proposed Recording Expedition into the Floridas" (1939), a seminal piece that outlines the background and the variety of Florida folklore worthy of recording. In association with this endeavor, Hurston would participate in "The Jacksonville Recordings" with Herbert Halpert and her boss, Carita Corse. Close listening of Hurston's interview with Herbert Halpert, who was collecting background information about the songs, shows how Halpert "talks down" to her. Given the paternalistic views of white southerners, and in this case Halpert, it is not surprising that the Florida FWP ignored most of Hurston's work, not even including it in the rough draft of "The Negro in Florida" (Bordelon, *Go Gator*, 20–35).

Despite Botkin's patronage from Washington and Alsberg's intervention to make her an editor and raise her salary, the Florida FWP ignored Hurston's capabilities and did not tap her writing ability. We know that she was unhappy from the few letters she wrote to friends who knew she was on the project. At one point she claimed she wanted to "bolt" the project, but her cooler self prevailed and she remained. She needed the salary to finish writing the book that would become *Moses, Man of the Mountain*. She had the comfort of her nieces, whom she dearly loved, and her brother John, who lived in Jacksonville (Bordelon, *Go Gator*, 28–35).

In the end, none of Hurston's FWP writings were identified as her work. Several thumbnail pieces appeared in the Florida guide, but this was done only because the final edit of the Florida guide manuscript took place in the national FWP office in Washington, DC (Bordelon, *Go Gator*, 25–28).

Hurston left the FWP abruptly in July 1939, a victim of "The Eighteen Month Rule," which stated that every federal writer who had been employed for more than eighteen months was automatically terminated. There is little doubt that Hurston was ready to move on. But what she had left for the Florida FWP, and for the world for that matter, was cutting-edge folklore that America and the world would take decades to fully recognize (Bordelon, *Go Gator*, 46–49). The largest part of her work was relegated to the files and languished there until 1999, when it was finally published as *Go Gator and Muddy the Water*.

Hurston's presence on the Florida Project was a deep source of pride to other Black writers. Paul Diggs, who had been hired with her, traveled from Lakeland, a small agricultural hub near Tampa, to Eatonville to frame his celebratory piece "House by the Lake." His revealing description documents the conditions and place where she wrote *Moses, Man of the Mountain* (McDonough, 147–48): "When you turn off of the main highway No.17, you enter a road that is full of winding curves, and flanked on each side by foliage and large oaks which are laden with moss." He takes the reader past beautiful winter homes of the tourists and orange groves until entering the village of Eatonville. He drives past Claude Mann's Filling Station and on the right, one quarter mile down the road, is Hurston's dwelling. He notes the lush vegetation: the oaks dripping with moss and the beauty of Lake Buck, on whose banks her house sits. "It is a weather-boarded house, very spacious, and comfortably arranged in the interior." But remarkably either Hurston was not at home or declined to be interviewed, for he tells us nothing concrete about her (McDonough, 147–48).

Diggs's chief contribution to the Florida FWP would be his Black life histories. By 1938, William T. Couch, who had become Corse's direct boss when appointed regional director of a number of southeastern states including Florida, launched the Life History Project. The idea was to profile ordinary southerners and let them tell others, in their own words, about their lives in particular and the South in general. It was felt that these personal life histories would give the nation a clearer picture of the South and correct distortions like those projected in popular books and Broadway plays like Taylor Caldwell's *Tobacco Road* (Bordelon, "Mirror," 201–36).

Diggs conducted a number of these interviews near Lakeland. One of the most revealing is his exchange with turpentine boss Rich Grey, in which Diggs's skill in getting his subjects to talk is readily apparent. The turpentiners' low life and hardships as the worst paid and most exploited of all state workers is best reflected in this exchange that includes several of Grey's workers.

Rich Grey, who now supervised about forty turpentiners each day as they set out and worked a drift, knew the business inside and out and had worked his way up into this position of trust. Supervisory was one position that earned $2.50 a day, relatively good pay for those days. He tells Diggs that he likes "living out here, as to bein' in town. We's free out here, and being as how I haves what I want, why not!" With great detail and patience he describes his job to Diggs. He admits to Diggs that his workers barely make a living. He mentions the abusive commissary system where the company store sells goods "much higher than they is in Lakeland. . . . too high fer folks what lives here in this camp." Mack McMillan, one of the workers, chimes in: "Yeh, we kin hardly make a go at it, specially when we paying 20' cents a poun' fer white bacon here at the commissary, and the same fer fresh po'k. Worser than thet, butta is 15 cents a stick, syrup comes from 25 cents to 40 cents a quart, and black-eye peas is 10 cents a poun'. We only gits paid oncet evr five or six weeks and by thet time everything you make is done tuk up" (Bordelon, "Mirror," 219).

Given that Diggs, Grey, and the turpentiners were all of the same race, this had a great effect on the substance of the interview. Yet there is still a sense of "censorship." They do not mention that they live in a company house and are charged rent. In the end, Mack McMillan and the turpentiners under Grey make nothing and are most likely in debt to the company. As Rich Grey sits with his workers, he serves as a censor, which keeps them from sharing deeper discontent. Nevertheless, the testimony is unique. Grey apologizes for his bosses, who he explained to Diggs depended on the price they got for turpentine. "What they earn is all according to the price the boss is gittin fer the turpentine on the market." That was "the best we kin do" (Bordelon, "Mirror," quote 219).

Diggs, like Hurston, would be gone in July 1939, victims of the Congressionally imposed eighteen-month rule that stated anyone on the

FWP more than eighteen months was fired. Southern Congressional conservatives had finally had their say. At this time federal sponsorship ended and state sponsors turned away from most national initiatives. With the departure of Hurston and Diggs, the activity of the Black Federal Writers' Unit in Florida ceased entirely, an ignominious end to a bright and startling enterprise.

The Search Ends

For a narrow sliver of time the New Deal had funded a search for America's Black roots. Talented and introspective Black white-collar workers had covered the length and breadth of Florida. They had documented the early history and life of Florida's towns by interviewing persons who lived in those towns. They spoke with former slaves willing to testify about bondage; church leaders told of their grass roots efforts to build Black churches where newly freed slaves could worship and find help. They spoke to and wrote about community organizers, women like Eartha White, who had proven Black entrepreneurs could be successful. And then these federal writers spoke with a wide variety of Black laborers who filled in for their interviewers details no book contained: They testified to all sorts of abuse, of "community sweeps," of conditions now defined as neo-slavery. Richardson had found appalling working conditions for hundreds, even thousands of Florida's Black workers.

As the field copy piled up in the Black Writers' Jacksonville office, it was carefully filed, awaiting compilation into "A History of the Negro in Florida." But the tools to credibly turn their rich documentation into a worthy history did not appear. Time ran out. The New Deal, whose concern for the Black Writers Units had been largely political, turned its back on the Federal Writers Project as Congress grew more conservative. Finally, the Black federal writers ceased working during the summer of 1939.

Looking back there had never been enough time or attention or funding invested in creating an end product. The Black writers' unit, while funded and staffed with writers–good ones—had no real editor, no director of consequence to pull together discordant streams of thought into a unified whole. There was no one committed to understanding *the story*.

Zora Neale Hurston, who could have done it, was given large assignments to cover Florida folklore and investigate recording possibilities for a recording expedition that was sent through the state in June 1939. Hurston did not have the desire to edit the "History of the Negro in Florida." She knew her boss Carita Corse would have the final say, and that the book was being bent to the paternalistic, white point of view.

At some point, Carita Corse, the state FWP director, attempted to shape the Black writers' material. But what she was doing was rewriting *their* history and shaping it to the white paternalistic viewpoint. She judged their field copy slanted, too reflective of what at the time was called "the Negro bias." When Eudora Richardson, state director of the Virginia FWP, pulled together her Virginia Black writers' copy, she explicitly stated that it was too reflective of the "Negro Bias." This was the temper of the times, the way things were in Jim Crow America, where there were few educated Blacks and white dominance was the norm (Richardson, *Negro in Virginia*, xii–xiii).

Corse's white history of Black Florida finally appeared in 1993 as *The Negro in Florida*, a book that would make anyone who truly knew the Black aesthetic cringe. It basically published the reedited Black writers' copy. Those former slaves whose life stories are included were edited to make them more acceptable to the white point of view. The Black point of view is missing entirely; Zora Neale Hurston's superior writing and summation of folklore in Florida is nowhere to be seen.

Once the Project closed, the Black writers' documentation was divided between two archives: the University of Florida, designated the main depository, and Florida Historical Society Library, which is where the motherlode of the Black writers' field copy ended up. Ignored for decades, yet faithfully preserving the Black writers' field copy, this largely untouched treasure trove imparts the truest mirror of what Black life in Florida was really about.

As America battles for its very soul, survival depends on acknowledging the whole truth. And one of the nation's most carefully guarded secrets is the true reality of our Black past—all of it, from slavery to neo-slavery, to present-day police brutality. The right questions are finally being raised in the broad public forum. Nicole Hannah-Jones in *The 1619 Project* laments that "growing up, Black people were largely absent from the histories I read" (Jones, xviii). Finally, America is setting the record straight. Making the Black federal writers' copy more accessible to the general public is a step in that direction. After all, does not understanding the past liberate the future?

Bibliography

All in-text citations of correspondence come from Works Progress Administration Records. Record Group 69. National Archives, Washington, DC.

Alter, Jonathan. *The Defining Moment: FDR's Hundred Days and the Triumph of Hope*. New York: Simon & Schuster, 2006.

Bordelon, Pamela. "The Federal Writers' Project's Mirror to America: The Florida Reflection." Diss., Louisiana State University, 1991.

Bordelon, Pamela. "Zora Neale Hurston: A Biographical Essay." In Zora Neale Hurston, *Go Gator and Muddy the Water: Writings From the Federal Writers' Project*, edited by Pamela Bordelon. New York: W. W. Norton, 1999.

Cantwell, Robert. "America and the Writers' Project." *New Republic* (April 26, 1939): 323–35.

Clark, Winifred Hurston. Interview by Pam Bordelon. June 26, 1993.

Clayton, Ronnie. "A History of the Federal Writers' Project in Louisiana." PhD diss., Louisiana State University, 1974.

Colby, Merle. "Presenting America to the Americans." *Publishers' Weekly* CXXXIX (May 3, 1941): 1815.

Corse, Carita Doggett. Interview by Nancy Williams. March 18, 1976, New Smyrna Beach, Florida. P. K. Yonge Library of Florida History, Gainesville, Florida.

Corse, Carita Doggett. Interview by Robert Hemenway. February 2, 1971, Jacksonville, Florida. P. K. Yonge Library of Florida History, Gainesville, Florida.

Federal Writers' Program Collection. P. K. Yonge Library of Florida History, Gainesville, Florida.

"The Federal Writers' Project." *New Republic* (October 21, 1972): 22–26.

Federal Writers' Project Collection. Florida Historical Society Library, Cocoa Beach, Florida.

Federal Writers' Project. *Florida: A Guide to the Southernmost State*. New York: Oxford University Press, 1939.

Federal Writers' Project. "Negro History in Florida." Unpublished manuscript, P. K. Yonge Library of Florida History, University of Florida, Gainesville.

Fox, Daniel. "The Achievement of the Federal Writers." *American Quarterly* 13 (Spring 1961): 3–19.

Holt, Rackham. *A Mary McLeod Bethune Biography*. Garden City, NY: Doubleday, 1964.

Hopkins, Harry. "Food for the Hungry." *Collier's* (December 7, 1935): 10–11, 61–62.

Hopkins, Harry. *Spending to Save: The Complete Story of Relief*. New York: W. W. Norton, 1936.

Kazin, Alfred. *On Native Grounds: An Interpretation of Modern Prose Literature*. Garden City, NY: Doubleday, 1956 [1941].

Kellock to Alsberg, January 23, 1936. Field reports, Florida, FWP, R.G. 69.

Kennedy, Stetson. *Palmetto Country*. New York: Duell, Sloan & Pearce, 1942.

Kennedy, Stetson. Interview. Green Cove Springs, Florida. August 2, 1988; January 6, 1989.

"Killing the Writers Project." *New Republic* 100 (August 23, 1939): 62.

Life Histories. Southern Historical Collection. University of North Carolina, Chapel Hill.

Lindley, Ernest K. *The Roosevelt Revolution*. New York: Viking Press, 1933.

Lomax, John. *Adventures of a Ballad Hunter*. New York: Macmillan, 1947.

Mangione, Jerre. *The Dream and the Deal: The Federal Writers' Project, 1935–1943*. Boston and Toronto: Little Brown, 1972.

McJimsey, George T. *Harry Hopkins: Ally of the Poor and Defender of Democracy*. Cambridge, MA: Harvard University Press, 1987.

Mormino, Gary. "The Florida Slave Narratives." *Florida Historical Quarterly* LXVI (April 1988): 399–419.

Rawick, George, ed. *The American Slave: A Composite Autobiography*. 19 vols. Westport, CT: Greenwood, 1972–77.

Richardson, Martin D. "What the Florida Negro Does." Unpublished manuscript, P. K. Yonge Library of Florida History, University of Florida, Gainesville.

Schlesinger, Arthur M., Jr. *The Age of Roosevelt: The Coming of the New Deal*. Boston: Houghton Mifflin, 1958.

Sherwood, Robert E. *Roosevelt and Hopkins: An Intimate History*. New York: Harper & Bros., 1948.

Soule, George. "Are We Going to Have a Revolution?" *Harper's Magazine* CLXV (August 1932): 277.

Virginia Writers' Project. *The Negro in Virginia*. Reprint, Durham, NC: Blair, 1994.

Watts, Jeff. *The Black Cabinet: The Untold Story of African Americans*. New York: Crown Press, 2020.

Woodward, C. Vann. "History from Slave Sources." *American Historical Review* 79 (1974): 480.

Works Progress Administration Records. Record Group 69. National Archives, Washington, DC.

"WPA Achievement." *Time* XXXV (August 12, 1940): 64.

Yetman, Norman. "Background of the Slave Narrative Collection." *American Quarterly* (Fall 1967): 534–53.

CHAPTER EIGHT

Interrogating Ethnography
Hurston's Critiques of Ethnographic Convention in *Polk County*

Genevieve West

Despite the similarities between Hurston's frequently studied and well-known ethnography *Mules and Men* (1935) and her drama *Polk County* (1944), the play has attracted relatively little attention from scholars. The ethnography takes readers along as Hurston returns to her hometown of Eatonville, Florida. From there, informants advise her to move south to Polk County, where she finds the Everglades Cypress Lumber Company near Loughman, Florida. In that locale, she adopts the ruse of being a bootlegger on the run from the (white) law in order to gain the trust of the rough, unlettered Black folk for whom the concept of "folklore" was just an everyday way of saying, singing, and doing. *Mules and Men* next takes readers on to Mobile, Alabama, and to New Orleans, Louisiana, but the time Hurston spent in Polk County clearly had a powerful impact. She writes about the experience in her autobiography *Dust Tracks on a Road* (1942) where she devotes five times the number of pages to Polk County as she does to studying Voodoo in New Orleans (689–700). And when she made what would be her final attempt to bring "real" folk drama to the stage, it was to the Polk County segment of *Mules and Men* that she returned with collaborator Dorothy Waring to develop a play slated for production on Broadway (Hemenway, 298). The product of that collaboration, *Polk County* (1944), never made it to the stage in Hurston's lifetime for reasons we can only speculate about.[1]

Only a handful of scholars have examined the play. John Lowe's early study situates *Polk County* in the context of Hurston's other dramatic productions, noting the ways in which Hurston blends genres, as well as mimesis and "magical realism," in the play. More recently, he has put *Polk County* in dialogue with Faulkner's fiction and examined the ways in which she casts Polk County characters as modern primitives who resist social norms (Lowe "Backwoods Modernism"). Elin Diamond has also recently examined Hurston's uses of modern primitives, particularly gestures and folk traditions, in the play. David G. Nicholls argues briefly that *Polk County* "diminish[es] the political implications of the folklore" she first recorded in *Mules and Men* (477), a claim I take issue with later. Keith L. Huneycutt's essay focuses on the collaborative and Voodoo elements of the play as he speculates about why the play was not produced in Hurston's lifetime. My own approach, somewhat like Lowe (in "Backwoods Modernism") and Diamond, returns to the impact of modernist anthropology on the play. Influenced by Michael A. Elliott's *The Culture Concept Writing and Realism in the Age of Difference* (2002) and Daphne Lamothe's *Inventing the New Negro: Narrative, Culture, and Ethnography* (2008), I am intrigued by the relationships between Hurston's creative, more transparently fictive writings and her anthropological work. Read from this perspective, I argue that *Polk County* comments on the genre and practice of ethnography, specifically the relationship between the ethnographer and the community she studies.

The protagonist of *Polk County* is a young woman, Leafy Lee, who enters the lumber camp because she wants to learn to sing the blues. In this way, she functions as an ethnographer or anthropologist who enters a community to learn its traditions. Jean Lee Cole and Charles Mitchell describe Leafy as a "fictionalized version of Hurston herself" in *Mules and Men* where she arrives at the camp in search of "lies" (269). I agree with this statement as far as it goes. But as Hurston moves from ethnography to stage production, the play does more than dramatize *Mules and Men* and blend the genres of ethnography and drama (although it does both). Significantly, the play also pulls back the curtain on processes that unfold early in the ethnographic endeavor. The plot and dialogue reveal what Hurston elides in *Mules and Men* as well as community actions that take place outside the view of the ethnographer, making it impossible for her to report.

Mules and Men focuses the gaze of the ethnographer on the community as an object of study. In *Polk County* Hurston reverses the gaze—and its inherent hierarchy. The revision imaginatively gives readers access to community members' perspectives *on the ethnographer*. In this remarkable revision, the ethnographer becomes a subject of study as much as an observer, and the community exercises a level of agency not immediately apparent in *Mules and Men*. Hurston's use of perspective in the play challenges anthropology's researcher/subject dichotomy and the hierarchy of the gaze. To make this argument, I first discuss Hurston's training as an anthropologist and then turn to the play itself to demonstrate the ways in which Hurston engages and challenges ethnographic conventions. While there is much in the play that remains to be addressed by scholars, I focus on Act I.

Seeing through the "Spy-Glass" of Anthropology

In the 1920s when Hurston undertook the research that would lead to *Mules and Men* and *Polk County*, she was answerable to the wealthy white woman Charlotte Osgood Mason, who funded her research and owned the anthropological material she collected, as well as to her college professors (and professional gatekeepers) Franz Boas and Ruth Benedict. By 1944, long graduated from Barnard and a published anthropologist and novelist, Hurston was freer to trouble key concepts of professional, academic anthropology, particularly those surrounding the power dynamics inherent in the ethnographic project. Diamond suggests that "[she] sifted Boas and Benedict, using one or the other, or neither, as needed" (115). My own argument goes further to examine the way in which Hurston's more explicitly "creative" work in *Polk County* challenges social scientific principles advanced by Boas and Benedict and illuminates challenges of ethnography as a means of study.[2]

The very foundation of the ethnographic endeavor is the ethnographer's ability to observe. That observation requires the scientist to see what unfolds around her. Thus, the ability to see—the nature of the gaze itself—is central. In the opening pages of *Mules and Men*, Hurston employs her often-quoted description of her native folk culture as a tight-fitting dress, a chemise, and her ability to *see* it:

> From the earliest rocking of my cradle, I had known about the capers Brer Rabbit is apt to cut and what the Squinch Owl says from the house top. But it was fitting me like a tight chemise. I couldn't see it for wearing it. It was only when I was off in college away from my native surroundings, that I could see myself like somebody else and stand off and look at my garment. Then I had to have the spy-glass of Anthropology to look through that. (9)

Hurston's "chemise" and "spy-glass" have become touchstones for critics and scholars grappling with her thoughts on folklore and the ethnographic project. Daphne Lamothe describes this passage as Hurston's articulation of modernist double-consciousness: "Anthropological methods provided Hurston with the tools with which to experience the double consciousness that characterizes the modernist gaze—'see[ing] myself like somebody else'— and to experience that condition as self-awareness" (Lamothe, 7). Hurston's "spy-glass" came from her training at Barnard College, once the women's division of Columbia University, where she studied with Franz Boas, often called the Father of American Anthropology, and Ruth Benedict, editor of the influential *Journal of American Folklore*. Written nearly twenty years later, *Polk County* suggests that Hurston was still thinking about the anthropological principles to which Boas and Benedict had introduced her.

Hurston's training in Boasian anthropology rejected the evolutionary thinking that had once been central to the discipline, and it embraced cultural relativism.[3] The means of studying another culture promoted by Hurston's mentors was the participant-observer method, "which privileges the immersion of the participant-observer in the 'field'" (Lamothe, 9). Hurston's work as an anthropologist was complicated by her role as a "native ethnographer" or "auto-ethnographer." Both terms describe someone who studies a group of which they are in some way already a member. In Hurston's case, she was both an insider, an African American in the rural South, and an outsider by virtue of her training as an anthropologist, which at the time generally assumed a white, male ethnographer. Thus, she occupied a liminal space, simultaneously both but fully neither insider nor outsider. Lamothe notes the "[t]he paradoxes, ironies, conflicts, and tensions experienced by native ethnographers" (14). While *Polk County* certainly "problematizes the subject/object dichotomy on which conventional ethnographies depend," we do not see them, in Kath Weston's words, "collaps[e]" in the play (qtd. in Lamothe, 15). Rather, the play challenges the power contemporary anthropology ascribes to the ethnographer's gaze and illuminates the challenges faced by ethnographers in attempting to report accurately.

Boas, whom Hurston called Papa Franz, expected his protégé to approach her subjects from an "objective" and detached perspective, indicated, as Lamothe notes, in Hurston's ability to "stand off" from herself and her culture to see through the "spy-glass of anthropology." That distance would inspire the belief, among scientists and popular readers alike, that her depictions were "objective" and "authentic" (Lamothe, 14). In our own time, we understand that both objectivity and authenticity are problematic concepts, but in Hurston's time they were highly desirable. Reviews of Hurston's novels frequently reflect this interest in objectivity and authenticity.[4] Ironically, it was widely assumed that the "objectivity" of the outsider/researcher would lead to a more accurate rendering of the culture being studied. The view of the ethnographer "carried far more weight for readers of ethnographic accounts than did the views of . . . people on their own lives" (Lamothe, 13).

Although prized in the scientific community, the objectivity required of the ethnographic method resulted in "epistemic violence" by making people into things, into objects of study (Lamothe, 14). According to Lamothe, even outside of anthropological circles, "The gaze, from the perspective of Anglo-American modernism . . . connotes consciousness and the powers to reason, universalize, and objectify that which the viewer surveys" (4). She describes an analytical gaze that measures, extrapolates, and distances the individual viewer from the subject under consideration. Indeed, that gaze is now widely acknowledged in anthropology as colonial in nature. It easily, although perhaps unintentionally, exploits "others" for personal and professional gain in the name of science or understanding. Because the power to determine what does (and does not) appear in the resulting ethnography rests solely with the ethnographer, the scientist is today typically seen as more powerful than the subjects being studied. Lamothe argues that "New Negro writers" like Hurston "interrogate and ultimately critique the colonizing gaze on the racialized subject, intersecting and shifting the presuppositions of both literary modernism and modernist anthropology" (5).

Building on and extending Lamothe's work, I argue that Hurston's 1944 treatment of the ethnographic endeavor in *Polk County* complicates the construction of race as the signal marker for "native ethnographers." In fact, Hurston demonstrates what we talk about today as intersectionality.[5] As in Hurston's other writings, most of her characters are African American. The only white character crossing the stage is the Boss who runs the lumber camp. As we might expect from Hurston, her white characters exist on the margins of the plot and the community in which the action unfolds. In this way she privileges the Black community around the sawmill—its norms, values, and practices. At the same time, Hurston's treatment of the all-Black world in *Polk County* flattens or levels the hierarchical colonial gaze on the "racialized subject" (Lamothe, 5), to reveal more complex, intersectional considerations of identity that affect native ethnographers.

In *Polk County*, the concept of "otherness" is not attributable to race. Rather, Hurston grounds the characters' otherness in region, class, gendered performance, speech, and musical knowledge. While underlying assumptions about the role of race in the construction of native ethnographers suggest that Leafy's race should provide her with entree into the lumber camp, her clothing, speech, and experiences mark her as an outsider. Racial identity alone does not assure her admission to the community.

Hurston learned about this reality facing native ethnographers the hard way. A few years after collaborating on *Polk County*, Hurston wrote about these challenges in her autobiography, *Dust Tracks on a Road* (1948). She recounts her first efforts to collect folklore in the mid-1920s on a grant from Carter G. Woodson's Association for the Study of Negro History: "I went about asking, in carefully accented Barnardese, 'Pardon me, but do you know any folk tales or folk songs?' The men and women who had whole treasuries of material just seeping through their pores, looked at me and shook their heads. No, they had never heard anything like that" (687). Hurston learns quickly that being African American will not alone gain her access to the folkloric materials she seeks. Instead, she must earn the trust of the community, and when she returns on her second trip as an ethnographer, she adopts the ruse of being a bootlegger. Supposedly being on the run from the law does more to gain her the trust of people in the lumber camp than her complexion does (63). Demonstrating the complexity of identity in the field, these intersectional markers of identity create otherness in the play and remove it from the realm of (only) racialized exoticism.

Rethinking Agency and Unity on the Stage

In addition to studying with Boas at Columbia, Hurston also took classes with Ruth Benedict. Benedict served as editor of the prestigious *Journal of American Folklore*, and her *Patterns of Culture* (1934) found a broad audience. While Hurston was a student at Barnard, Benedict was developing the ideas she would advance in *Patterns of Culture*, which was "the best-known single volume of work produced by any anthropologist of the Boas school" (Elliott, 166). Her study develops two related ideas that Hurston responds to in *Polk County*: first, the powerlessness of the individual in the face of culture's powerful forces, and second, the idea of "unified" or cohesive culture. In contrast to her mentor, Hurston reveals fault lines or tensions within the community in a way that challenges Benedict's thinking in *Patterns of Culture*.

Elliott explains that in *Patterns of Culture* Benedict emphasizes the power of culture over the individual and the relative "powerlessness of an individual" in the face of "traditional custom," which shapes the individual in ways that the individual cannot, in turn, shape culture (Elliott, 167). Benedict goes so far as to suggest that a "life-history" "is first and foremost an accommodation to the patterns and standards traditionally handed down in his community" (2–3). Hurston's approach to the individual and to culture is more balanced and measured (Elliott, 167). Her landmark essay, "Characteristics of Negro Expression," emphasizes the individual's power to adapt, revise, and make over cultural practices and material culture. Hurston even says "Discord is more natural than accord," emphasizing the tensions within culture ("Characteristics," 840).

In the first act of *Polk County*, the characters clearly exist in specific cultural contexts, but they also exert a level of agency that allows them to resist cultural norms in ways that Benedict's work fails to acknowledge. Members of the community introduced in the play are hardly, in Elliott's words, "object[s]" of study and helpless "in the face of" cultural forces. Big Sweet's character is a prime example. Her size, strength, and demeanor hardly make her a traditionally feminine woman, but she has nevertheless carved out an identity for herself that challenges cultural norms. She fights men as well as other women, for instance, and defends her man, Lonnie, from another who cheats at cards (*Polk County*, 280–83).

Another example is the way that Big Sweet and other women in the community exert their power through the gaze, which is typically associated with the ethnographer. In the first scene of the play, in a type of exposition, readers meet most of the important characters: Big Sweet, Dicey, Lonnie, and Mah Honey. Readers do not meet Leafy, the protagonist, until she arrives in the following scene. As that scene opens, the community women wait for the men to return from the day's work. This chronology suggests that the community exists before Leafy's arrival and will continue to exist after her departure. As she enters the stage, Leafy—the ethnographer's stand-in—becomes the first subject of study, the first subject of the gaze. Hurston's reversal of the gaze, here directed at the anthropologist figure, troubles the privilege and power frequently ascribed to the ethnographer. Mwenda Ntarangwi's study *The Reversed Gaze: An African Ethnography of American Anthropology* beautifully captures this sense of a traditionally "othered" subject looking at the "scientist" in his term the "reversed gaze," which I adopt here.

The women in *Polk County* reverse the gaze to note Leafy's fair complexion and wonder aloud if she is white or Black. Leafy's polite "How de do" to the women and her reference to Bunch as *Miss* Bunch answer the question about race, as no white women would show Bunch such respect (294). A series of questions follow from Laura, as she tries to determine just who Leafy is and what her motives are. Is she a teacher? Is she married? Laura eventually invites Leafy into her home to wait for Bunch's ostensible return. In fact, Bunch is on hand and listening to every word. While Leafy goes inside out of hearing, the women gather to discuss how to deal with the young interloper. Reversing the ethnographer's gaze, the community women see Leafy and study *her* long before she can study them and their music. Their study of Leafy is based on a number of aspects of identity: her race, her age, her employment, and her marital status. Lamothe argues that "Hurston consistently equate[s] looking and knowledge" (7), but the play problematizes the gaze and the concept of unity through Dicey, who sees Leafy as a threat when the others do not. She incorrectly describes Leafy as a "fan foot," a woman who chases men on payday. Her perception, based on what she sees, is mistaken, a misinterpretation that illuminates the unreliable nature of the gaze itself. If the gaze—the foundation of the ethnographic endeavor—is unreliable, then ethnography as a disciplinary practice can also be faulty.

As the women respond to Leafy, Hurston demonstrates one of the strategies community members might use to protect themselves from a perceived intruder: lying. Just as she calls into question the reliability of the gaze, here Hurston exposes the flaw in the Boasian mandate to report accurately and objectively. When the community lies to an ethnographer, how is the ethnographer to know and report accurate information? Hardly powerless as Benedict's work would suggest, the community members seize their agency to limit access to their people and traditions. Hurston directly addresses this subject in *Mules and Men* when she describes the "feather-bed" approach that African Americans take to dealing with "curiosity." While Native Americans adopt "stony silence" as a means of resistance, "The Negro . . . let[s] the probe enter, but it never comes out. It gets smothered under a lot of laughter and pleasantries" (10). Resistance to the ethnographic gaze, Hurston tells us, can come in many forms. And in the play, that resistance first manifests as lying.

In *Polk County* the community women further exercise their power when they opt to contain Leafy inside the house while they consider their options. Out of view but within earshot, Leafy continues a conversation with Maudella, who had been playing a game of Chick-ma-craney-crow with other children. Leafy goes so far as to ask Maudella to teach her how to play the game, revealing the way in which the participant-observer collects folklore. Suggesting both the anthropological purpose of her visit and her relative youth, Leafy's wanting to learn to play the game "don't sound so bad" to Bunch (296), but neither Laura nor Dicey want to risk Leafy attracting the interest of the men. Dicey argues that Leafy is a "fan-foot" who is after their men, suggesting they run Leafy off before the men return to camp. While Laura and Bunch seem more inclined to permit her to stay, Big Sweet's arrival means they can allow her to make the final decision. After the women apprise Big Sweet of the situation, the scene moves to Laura's house, where Big Sweet puts her foot up on the porch and waits "grimly" for Leafy to appear (297–98). Big Sweet putting her foot on the porch tells readers that she is prepared to "signify," to take a verbally aggressive posture with the visitor who is apparently up to no good.

Hurston explains the significance of Big Sweet's actions in a section of *Dust Tracks*:

> If you are sufficiently armed . . . , it is all right to go to the house of your enemy, put one foot up on his steps, rest one elbow on your knee and play in the family. That is another way of saying play the dozens, which is a way of saying low-rate your enemy's ancestors, and him, down to the present moment for reference. (696–97)

While readers of the play never see Big Sweet signify, her posture forecasts it, and the other women characters gather to watch the show they expect to unfold.

Once Leafy appears on the front porch, the stage notes indicate that Big Sweet "looks Leafy over from head to foot slowly and deliberately, and back again" (298). In looking so long at Leafy, Big Sweet reverses the gaze and takes on the posture that Lamothe attributes to the anthropologist, for she hopes to "construct and contain through observation" of this unfamiliar woman (Lamothe, 5). Looking for cues about what is happening, Leafy glances at the other women, where she finds "hostility or cold indifference" (298). Only then do Leafy and Big Sweet lock eyes. Leafy "grins" at her observer and despite trying not to, Big Sweet finds herself smiling back. Eventually, Big Sweet's body language changes, as she removes her foot from the porch and puts her hands on her hips. The power dynamics in this nonverbal exchange are telling.

Big Sweet's standing akimbo with her hands on her hips is something a mother might do to a child or a posture a friend might strike. It is far less aggressive than putting her foot up on Leafy, the *subject* she is prepared to speak to and on. Big Sweet has the power, symbolized by the reversed gaze, in this initial encounter. She can verbally and physically drive Leafy away from camp if she wants to. The other women will not intercede to help the intruder. Leafy, recognizing Big Sweet's authority, greets the resident's challenge with a smile. Leafy's smile promises that, although she is the outsider or "other," she is not a threat. In the larger culture beyond the camp, Leafy's experience with the outside world might make her the more powerful figure, but not here. On "the job" the community women, especially Big Sweet, claim their power, at least in part through the reversed gaze.

Hurston talks back to Benedict's *Patterns of Culture* in another way as well. Benedict argues that anthropology needs to shift its focus from studying particular cultural traits to "the study of cultures as articulated wholes" with "dominating ideas." Benedict was interested in "integration," in which elements of culture create "a whole" that "is more than the sum of their traits" (47–48). Other anthropologists would directly critique her thinking as an "overstate[ment]"

(Kroeber and Kluckhohn qtd. in Hoyt, 407). Although her approach is more implicit, Hurston's *Polk County* also counters Benedict's claims.

The communities created in Hurston's fiction, drama, and folklore are whole in that individuals and practices are interrelated and function, typically, without interference from without. However, rather than focusing on the "integration" of the whole, as Benedict does, Hurston attends to individuals (Elliott, 168, 176). In doing so, she illuminates the fractures within communities in order to develop a more complex view of culture, one she articulates in her influential essay "Characteristics of Negro Expression" (1934). There, in Elliott's words, Hurston describes "culture as a realm of tension as well as of harmony" (168). When *Polk County* opens, the initial tension is between Dicey and Mah Honey and between Dicey and Big Sweet, where the tensions are individualized. Although Dicey and Mah Honey had a sexual encounter, Mah Honey does not wish to pursue a relationship with Dicey, and in her role as community mediator, Big Sweet counsels Dicey to accept Mah Honey's decision. The other community members join Big Sweet in this effort, demonstrating both Elliott's "harmony" and "tension," when Dicey refuses.

Leafy's arrival, however, introduces a number of complications that operate at both individual and symbolic levels. Elliott explains that in Hurston's thinking, "cultural forms not only reflect but also produce, the medium of conflict between the individual and the group" (168). Thus, in this case, the play reflects and produces tensions within the larger folk community represented, between individuals and their communities. As the plot of the play progresses and Mah Honey takes a romantic interest in Leafy, symbolic fault lines emerge in the community. Individually, there is immediate tension between Dicey and Leafy, but symbolically the two characters represent tensions between insider and outsider, between dark- and light-complexioned women (Dicey has a dark complexion; Leafy has a fair one), and between classes of Black women (Dicey longs for a tough reputation; Leafy is more middle class). Here, too, Hurston fractures the notion of a unified "race" or community of people in favor of more individualized thinking.

Once Big Sweet has decided that Leafy is not a threat to the community, she takes the visitor to her own home. The following scene opens on Hurston again interrogating the relationship between ethnographer and subject. In Scene III, readers see Big Sweet and Leafy exchanging information on education, marriage, love, and virginity. I describe this exchange of information as leveling the gaze as Hurston establishes the contrasts between these two women, largely based on class. Leafy sees Big Sweet, learning about the death of her father, the impossibly high price of being a virgin, and her decision to start "kicking" people's "behinds" (301–2). In contrast, Big Sweet learns that Leafy is twenty-two, has had "more schooling," has remained a virgin, and has never been in love. Having established mutual respect between the two women, Hurston reveals that the ethnographer (Leafy) teaches her subject when Big Sweet learns for the first time about a man asking for a woman's hand in marriage (300). While Scene II makes Leafy the subject of the reversed gaze, in Scene III the gaze is leveled or exchanged as Big Sweet looks at Leafy and the two women exchange cultural practices.

In Scene IV, the final one in Act I, readers see the participant-observer method unfold, but even there, Hurston troubles ethnographic principle as she targets the accuracy expected of the ethnographic gaze. Underlying the mandate for accuracy is an assumption that an ethnographer has access to a complete corpus or body of information. The interaction between the men and Big Sweet demonstrates, however, the extent to which the presence of an outsider affects or changes what information the community members share.

When the men return from work, a group gathers at Big Sweet and Lonnie's home to teach Leafy her first blues song. Repeatedly the men start to sing a song only to have Big Sweet stop them. A song titled "Nasty Butt" is the first that Big Sweet halts because Leafy is "a lady" (304), a class-based term that sets Leafy apart from the other women. The men are "puzzled" but make another attempt, saying "Us don't have to sing under the clothes of them Tampa fanfoots. Let's we sing about a man." That song, too, Big Sweet ends abruptly as the men start to sing lyrics about "Uncle Bud's gals" who "rocks their hips from wall to wall." She truncates yet a third song, "Angeline," about a woman "who rocks and reels behind." Clearly, Big Sweet is objecting to lyrics that sexualize women. Finally the women sing "Careless Love" (307) and the men sing "John Henry" (309), both of which avoid sexualized lyrics.

This final scene of Act I works in several ways. Dramatically, it allows Hurston to showcase two songs, while referencing others that a middle-class northern audience might not be familiar with and might be offended by if sung in their entirety. At the same time, it continues to comment on the ethnographic endeavor. The presence of an outsider, Leafy, clearly affects the behavior of the community and the folk traditions they share. Hurston highlights the community changing its performance in response to Leafy's presence. This impact of the anthropologist/observer on the viewed, of the anthropologist on the community she studies and the performances to which the community agrees to give her access, illustrates the complexity of the ethnographic endeavor and problematizes Boasians' emphasis on objectivity and authenticity. What the ethnographer has access to and reports may be accurate but incomplete if elements of the performance or larger context are concealed. This dynamic relationship between the scientist and her subjects also emphasizes the agency of the community members. They very clearly control what information Leafy has access to.

Singing the Blues to Build Bridges

In *Polk County* Hurston substitutes her search for folklore with Leafy's desire to learn to sing the blues. Nicholls suggests that her focus on the blues indicates her recognition that they have value in the commercial marketplace (477). His reading suggests Hurston's treatment of the blues is exploitative in that she uses them in an effort to profit financially. And, indeed, Leafy does speculate that Mah Honey, whom she designates as an artist, would find a paying audience up North and "make a lot of money" (306). It is also true that Hurston struggled to support herself with her creative work, so a Broadway play about the blues might have been financially attractive. At the same time, as early as 1928, Hurston was thinking about a "real Negro art theatre" (Kaplan, 116). She argues in "Characteristics of Negro Expression" that, "musically speaking, the Jook is the most important place in America. For in its smelly, shoddy confines has been born the secular music known as blues, and on blues has been founded jazz" (841). She even links the Jook, featured in later scenes of *Polk County*, to the Black theater: "The Negro theatre, as built up by the Negro, is based on Jook situations, with women, gambling, fighting, drinking" (842). These statements, published a decade before the play in 1934, ground *Polk County* in Hurston's repeated attempts to bring what she considered "real" Black drama to the stage.

Further, in focusing on the blues, Hurston identified a genre that would bridge interracial and intraracial prejudices. The play teaches northern audiences, Black and white, to appreciate the rural, southern roots of the musical genre and the humanity of its creators. Hurston's play appeared in "a climate in which perceptions of racial difference were intertwined with assumptions of White racial superiority and Black inferiority and that saw little significance in class or regional differences among African Americans" (Lamothe, 13). *Polk County* challenges these notions by establishing that Leafy and those who work in the lumber camp are not all the same. Their differing values fracture "the race" that popular discourses homogenized and Hurston resists in *Dust Tracks* (731–33).

The play also bridges intraracial prejudices based on class differences between southern and northern African Americans. Read from this perspective, the play is highly political in its attempt to undermine racist and classist assumptions about rural southern Black folk. The middle-class Leafy finds that she has much to learn from the folk in the lumber camp, and they in turn learn from her. In this way, Leafy functions as more than an ethnographer figure. She is also a proxy for a northern audience that loves blues songs but doesn't understand them as artistic creations and, based on race and/or class differences, might denigrate the very people who created the form. In this way, Leafy models for the reader the decision to celebrate the blues, as well as the communities and people who create them.

Where Nicholls sees (only) a commercial endeavor, I see a highly political project. Lamothe argues that modern ethnographic fictions "offer their authors the chance to stage the complex dynamics between center and periphery" (9). Extending her claim to include Hurston's dramatic production, we see that in *Polk County* Hurston inverts margin and center as the lumber camp becomes the center, and the outside world the periphery. Leafy and her middle-class audience enter the world of a lumber camp where *they* are the outsiders, their ways are foreign. The audience never leaves the camp and swamps that surround it precisely because these sites constitute the center of the characters' lives. Readers hear about the Sheriff and his jail, as well as the train station, but we never see them.

At the same time, Hurston also challenges the anthropological establishment in her explorations of the gaze and power dynamics. Countering Benedict's work, Hurston endows her characters and community in *Polk County* with considerable agency. That agency allows the community members to resist outsiders and external "patterns" that might contain or limit them. That community also has the power to determine whether to accept new members, to teach those new members, or to expel them. Her use of the gaze in *Polk County* acknowledges it as a form of power. At the same time, she problematizes it. The ethnographer is not the only one who can use the gaze. The community members seize its power, as well. Complicating matters is the reality that the gaze upon which the practice of ethnography depends is not always reliable or complete. The community members, who reverse the gaze to claim their power by gazing at Leafy, do not all agree on what they see in the young visitor, also suggesting the unreliable nature of the gaze. Nor does Leafy have access to all of the blues songs. Her study of the community's musical traditions is limited to what Big Sweet designates as "fittin'" (305), a move that also demonstrates the power of the community to limit the ethnographer's access. Leafy and Big Sweet level the gaze in their exchanges of information and personal histories. To add another layer, readers of the play see the characters' gazing at one another and, thereby, participate in the gaze in an effort to make meaning of the play. Hurston's blending of genres and modeling of the ethnographic endeavor makes explicit—and forces the audience to engage—the layers of viewing, of seeing, of objectifying the "other." In the words of Lamothe, "The hybrid narrative in and of itself is a theoretical site in which knowledge production can be queried and staged. Juxtaposing different modes of representation compels the reader to question how we know what we know" (11). Making the play a study in epistemology, Hurston acknowledges that everyone—in the play and outside of it—is looking at someone else's performance in an effort to interpret and make meaning.

Created later in Hurston's career, *Polk County* offers her most advanced and thoughtful examination of the ethnographic endeavor and her final attempt to bring "real" Negro folklore to the national stage. As a play, *Polk County* presents a number of challenges: a running time estimated to be more than four hours, dreamlike or magical sequences that seem very much out of keeping with the play's larger mimetic aesthetic, and a large cast.[6] The play's similarities to *Mules and Men* may encourage readers to overlook it. However, the different perspectives provided by the two texts prove fruitful when alongside one another. *Polk County*, then, remains a prime but neglected source for those interested not only in Hurston's dramatic productions and her uses of folklore, but also in her work as a social scientist.

Notes

1. Waring's husband, Stephen Kelen d'Oxylion, was to produce the play, but she and Hurston had conceptual differences. When Waring urged Hurston "to keep a 'sort of Gershwinesque feeling' about their Polk County musical, Zora's reply was, 'You don't know what the hell you're talking about'" (Hemenway, 298).

2. The idea that Hurston worked against as well as within ethnographic conventions is not new, nor is the idea that Hurston's fiction influences her ethnographic work and vice versa. See, for instance, Elliott's *The Culture Concept: Writing and Difference in the Age of Realism*, where he argues that Hurston adapted her folkloric training to her writing of *Jonah's Gourd Vine* (1934) and *Their Eyes Were Watching God* (1937), and her fiction writing skills to her anthropological work in *Mules and Men* (169–87). I make a related argument in "Subversions of Boasian Anthropology in Zora Neale Hurston's Great Migration Fiction and Ethnography," forthcoming in *African American Literature in Transition, 1920–1930*, from Cambridge University Press.

3. Boas's rejection of evolutionary thinking was a means of establishing objectivity. Arguing for cultural relativism and against comparing cultures, he believed doing so would allow an anthropologist to view a culture on its own terms, through the lens of its own values (Lamothe, 34–35). Black writers and thinkers of the period, including Hurston, adopted Boas's rejection of evolutionary thinking as a means of challenging white racism and establishing the value of Black culture (Lamothe, 41).

4. For reviews that address issues of authenticity and objectivity in Hurston's fiction, see, for instance, those by Locke, Jones, and Brickell.

5. Intersectionality is a term that describes the ways in which parts of individual identity intersect to create unique subject positions. Discussions of intersectionality have largely clustered around race, class, and gender. In this way, I am not just a woman but a white middle-class woman. Marcella C. Clinard's recent dissertation, "Intersections of Religion and Race

in Women's and Gender Studies: Possibilities for Teaching Introductory Classes," argues for expanding intersectionality to deal with religion. My own scholarship has considered region and rural/urban divides as well.

6. Cole and Mitchell identify the running time for the full play to be four hours (269).

Bibliography

Benedict, Ruth. *Patterns of Culture*. 1934. Boston: Houghton Mifflin, 2005.

Brickell, Herschel. "Books on Our Table." Review of *Jonah's Gourd Vine* by Zora Neale Hurston. *New York Post*, May 5, 1934, 13.

Clinard, Marcella C. "Intersections of Religion and Race in Women's and Gender Studies: Possibilities for Teaching Introductory Classes." PhD diss., Texas Woman's University, 2021.

Cole, Jean Lee, and Charles Mitchell. "Introduction." In *Zora Neale Hurston Collected Plays*, xv–xxiv.

Cole, Jean Lee, and Charles Mitchell. "Polk County (1944)." In *Zora Neale Hurston Collected Plays*, 269–70.

Diamond, Elin. "Folk Modernism: Zora Neale Hurston's Gestural Drama." *Modern Drama* 58, no. 1 (2015): 112–34. DOI: 10.3138/MD.0692.112.

Elliott, Michael A. *The Culture Concept: Writing and Realism in the Age of Difference*. Minneapolis: University of Minnesota Press, 2002.

Hemenway, Robert. *Zora Neale Hurston: A Literary Biography*. Champaign: University of Illinois Press, 1978.

Hoyt, Elizabeth E. "Integration of Culture: A Review of Concepts." *Current Anthropology* 2, no. 5 (1961): 407–26. JSTOR: www.jstor.org/stable/2739785.

Huneycutt, Keith L. "'The Profound Silence of the Initiated': Zora Neale Hurston's Polk County, Dorothy Waring, and Stage Voodoo." *Florida Studies: Proceedings of the 2009 Annual General Meeting of the Florida College English Association*, edited by Carole Policy and Claudia Slate. Cambridge Scholars Publishing, 2010. 39–49.

Hurston, Zora Neale. "Characteristics of Negro Expression." In *Zora Neale Hurston Folklore, Memoirs, and Other Writings*, 830–46.

Hurston, Zora Neale. *Dust Tracks on a Road*. 1942. In *Zora Neale Hurston Folklore, Memoirs, and Other Writings*, 557–808.

Hurston, Zora Neale. *Mules and Men*. In *Zora Neale Hurston Folklore, Memoirs, and Other Writings*, 1–268.

Hurston, Zora Neale. *Polk County: A Comedy of Negro Life on a Sawmill Camp with Authentic Negro Music in Three Acts*, with Dorothy Waring. *Zora Neale Hurston Collected Plays*, 271–362.

Jones, Dewey. "The Bookshelf." Review of *Jonah's Gourd Vine* by Zora Neale Hurston. *Chicago Defender*, May 12, 1934, 12.

Kaplan, Carla. *Zora Neale Hurston A Life in Letters*. New York: Doubleday, 2002.

Lamothe, Daphne. *Inventing the New Negro: Narrative, Culture, and Ethnography*. Philadelphia: University of Pennsylvania Press, 2008.

Locke, Alain. "The Eleventh Hour of Nordicism." Review of *Jonah's Gourd Vine* by Zora Neale Hurston. *Opportunity* (January 1938): 8–12.

Lowe, John. "Backwoods Modernism: Primitive Portraiture in Faulkner and Hurston." In *Faulkner and Hurston*, edited by Christopher Rieger and Andrew B. Leiter, 21–51. Cape Girardeau: Southeast Missouri University Press, 2017.

Lowe, John. "From Mule Bones to Funny Bones: The Plays of Zora Neale Hurston." *Southern Quarterly* 33, no. 2–3: 65–78.

Nicholls, David G. "Migrant Labor, Folklore, and Resistance in Hurston's Polk County: Reframing *Mules and Men.*" *African American Review* 33, no. 3 (1999): 467–79.

Ntarangwi, Mwenda. *The Reversed Gaze: An African Ethnography of American Anthropology.* Champaign: University of Illinois Press, 2010.

Zora Neale Hurston Collected Plays. Edited by Jean Lee Cole and Charles Mitchell. New Brunswick, NJ: Rutgers University Press, 2008.

Zora Neale Hurston Folklore, Memoirs, and Other Writings. Edited by Cheryl A. Wall. New York: Library of America, 1995.

CHAPTER NINE

African American and West Indian Folklife in South Florida

Joyce Marie Jackson

Present-day metropolitan Miami, which encompasses most of Miami-Dade County, is an evolving environment that illustrates the historical flow of cultural ideas between diverse populations. The Black population provides an excellent example of this diversity. The 2010 US Census reported that 472,976 Blacks comprised 18.8 percent of Miami-Dade County's total population. In the City of Miami, 76,695 Blacks comprised 19.2 percent of the city's population. Most of Miami's Black or African American residents cluster in the city's northern neighborhoods. Many of these residents came from the Caribbean, Latin America, and Africa. In this chapter, I will examine some aspects of the folk culture of two African diaspora groups in Miami—African Americans and West Indians. Most of the data was collected from the various communities by conducting ethnographic field research.

The African American Presence

Since they first came to the Miami area in the early nineteenth century, African Americans have responded to a broad range of experiences: slavery, urban migration, disenfranchisement during the Jim Crow era, the struggle for civil rights and economic freedom, and today, a new political activism. Throughout the episodes of their history, African Americans have found ways to educate, strengthen, comfort, inspire, motivate, and entertain their minds and spirits, thereby making it possible to survive and grow beyond the external circumstances of their lives.

A rich and immense body of tradition has emerged from this struggle for survival. African American folk culture includes the songs, verbal lore, crafts, and occupational skills that African Americans brought from both rural agricultural areas and other urban centers. These traditions are composed of more than skills that can be learned by example, such as improvising the lead in a gospel song, piecing a quilt, or break dancing. They also include the concepts, cultural values, aesthetics, and worldviews that make African American folk expression unique. Many of these emerged directly from the values shared by various African societies.

When Africans were transported to the sugar plantations of the Caribbean, then to the cotton plantations and farms in the southern United States, they brought their traditional ways of thinking and living with them. Since many Africans had lived in close and prolonged proximity with European-derived culture, they were able to exercise a cultural selectivity by tenaciously retaining those elements of their African heritage that were most valuable to them. This selective process and subsequent synthesis of African and European elements defines the evolution of a distinct African American culture. In African American folk traditions, however, the African elements are usually more prevalent.

Religion

The culture of urban African Americans reveals much about the boom, bust, and subsequent redevelopment of their communities. Throughout the process of community change, African Americans have selectively chosen to hold on to long-cherished ways of doing things. The rhythm and flavor of African American urban community life takes one in many directions. The church is a good place to begin, for it serves as the most important community institution for newly arrived families. It is also one of the strongest and most enduring transplants to urban life. For many African Americans, the church family replaces to a substantial degree parts of the extended family that were left behind.

African American migration patterns follow well-traveled corridors. People from rural areas leave some relatives and move to urban areas with other branches of their families; over time, others may follow. In this manner, entire communities can be gradually transplanted. Many of the African American churches in Miami were organized with memberships based on rural congregations. Some of the smaller churches are still shaped by members arriving from rural areas in Florida or other southern states. In the early 1920s, some residents of Calvin, Georgia, moved into the West Perrine community and founded the church that became Mt. Moriah Baptist Church. Families from Perry, Georgia, moved into the Goulds community in the mid-1920s, and some still have their church membership at Mt. Carmel Unity Baptist Church.

The church is the place where the raw edges of migrational change are softened, where old flavors and sounds from home are not discarded, but blend in comforting ways in a new urban gospel pot. There you can find the elders who perform Black sacred songs and prayers holding on to a tradition that surely represents continuity not just from the rural South, but from older African roots as well.

One can go to the Church of Christ in the Goulds community and still find a strong traditional unaccompanied song service led by elders who maintain the old, rich pattern of singing a song phrase followed by the congregation repeating that same phrase, a practice which is known as lining-out. One also hears the old patterns with "amen comers" (i.e., a group within the congregation that responds verbally to the sermons and songs) and general congregational singing in unison and heterophony. The call-and-response structure, which is a common performance practice in West African music, is prevalent not only in this folk church setting, but in most African American traditional music. Call-and-response is an alternation between a leader and a chorus, purposefully done so all can join in. Many West African, and thus African American, musical events are of a participatory nature. Their songs—spirituals, hymns, and jubilees—are accompanied by handclapping, foot stamping, and interjection of a shout, cry, or holler from someone who feels the spirit.

In many churches, especially the larger ones, old gospel songs led by the elders in the traditional way have been supplanted by the newer sounds of songs accompanied by electric organs and/or instrumental combos. New songs that serve new needs evolved from traditional ones. Many of them combined the musical structure and poetic forms of old secular and religious songs with new musical and textual ideas. These gospel songs can be heard in Mt. Carmel Missionary Baptist Church and New Macedonia Baptist Church in Liberty City or Glendale Missionary Baptist Church in Richmond Heights.

The highly emotional and spirit-filled music called gospel evolved from the Holiness and Pentecostal churches, and first penetrated more established denominations through the "storefront" Baptist and Methodist churches that permeate areas where African Americans have lived in Miami. Today, denomination is not a determining factor, and one finds gospel music in Baptist, Methodist, Catholic, and Episcopal congregations throughout the communities.

Going out to a "singing" is another urban-based Christian sociocultural event that takes place in churches, schools, community centers, and auditoriums. Singings, "gospel extravaganzas," and "gospelfests" are programs of gospel music, with between two and ten vocal groups performing a few songs each. A minister usually opens the program, and many times it is closed as the "doors of the church" are opened in an invitation to accept Christ as one's personal savior.

Smaller community-based vocal groups often perform along with choirs at singings. These groups are organized in churches and schools, and among occupational, community, and family groups. The Calvary Travelers (mixed group) is an example of a family group that continues to perform in the unaccompanied, or a cappella style. The emphasis is on blended ensemble singing, with group harmonies serving as the only needed arrangements for the solo singing of the lead. Their arrangements include the whole group singing choruses in harmony, with the lead performing words and melody over repeated, harmonized, rhythmic phrases sung by the group. Performances by the Heavenly Jewels and the Disciple Travelers have remained a cappella. However, some quartets and other smaller groups who performed unaccompanied for many years, such as the Stars of Harmony, have added instruments. Although it is not the norm, Miami also has its share of female a cappella quartets, including the Gospel Lyrics, the Goldenaires, and the Wimberly Sisters.

Secular Music

Music, sacred and secular, is a powerful force in all communities, but is perhaps even more so in the African American tradition, since it was something that could be held on to under the most adverse circumstances. When the blues, which is traditionally African American, rural, and southern, came to the urban areas, it immediately took root and became the main song form used for entertainment. The blues of the country fields and small "juke joints" became urban when musicians employed amplified instruments in the 1940s. During that era many such bands could be heard while strolling down N.W. Second Avenue in Overtown—then Miami's "Little Broadway." Today you still hear the familiar sounds of the blues bands in clubs such as Tobacco Road (Miami's oldest extant nightclub), Sensations, and Studio 183. Singers like Charles Wright and Alice Daye have also carried on the tradition. Blues and many other African American folk traditions have survived largely by oral transmission from senior members of the community to the younger generation.

Blues performers provided music for dancing in clubs, at barbecues, house parties, and other social gatherings. The music also served as a means for passing time and making social statements. The solitary, transient lifestyle of many blues singers did not deter them from making use of the call-and-response performance tradition. In the twelve-bar blues, a singer makes a statement or asks a question related to some circumstances of life. The comment or response at the end of the phrase comes not from a chorus of other singers, but from his guitar.

Miami bluesman W. C. Baker was born in the rural outskirts of Live Oak, Florida, between Jacksonville and Tallahassee. At age six, he began to sing the blues while plucking chicken wire strung across an old box made from scrap lumber—his first guitar. Like many country bluesmen who made their first instruments, this was his rite of passage into the blues world.

Baker's first professional engagement as an adult came forty-six years ago at the Big House club in Brownsville. His early life was very transient, and he had to deal with many adverse circumstances caused by discrimination, financial strain, and lost love. Nevertheless, through discipline and cooperation, Baker gradually moved from the lonely life of a transient bluesman to the leader of a well-known Miami blues band called W. C. Baker and the Cooperatives.

A more recent milestone in Miami's Black music culture is its shaping force on the evolution of Southern hip hop and dance music. Miami's most notable mark in this area is the creation of the hip hop subgenre called Miami Bass. As an electronic music, Miami Bass relies on equipment such as drum machines, turntables, mixers, crossfaders, samplers, digital audio workstations, and sound systems. A DJ uses these tools to create a heavy rhythmic foundation of thick, reggae-inspired basslines and upbeat kick drum tempos overlaid with repetitive scratching, sampling, and comedic, raunchy, dance-themed call-and-response lyricism.

Miami Bass originated in the mid-1980s with session musician and recording engineer Amos Larkins II. The music gained local popularity with promoters like Luther Campbell, a hip hop DJ and entrepreneur whose parents immigrated to the city from the Bahamas and Jamaica. After songs like M.C. A.D.E.'s "Bass Rock Express" first were played at Liberty City block parties, skating rinks, and dance clubs, the early 1990s commercial success of the rap group 2 Live Crew introduced Miami Bass to worldwide audiences. Since then, the music has lived on in Miami's underground club and rap scenes and as an influence on other hip hop and dance music subgenres.

Domestic Arts

Neighborhood community centers are another significant place in Miami's African American communities where many aspects of traditional culture can be seen. For many generations African American women in the South have made patchwork quilts for utilitarian purposes. Although quilt making is not a specifically African tradition, it is possible that both the tradition and styles of African American quilts are related to the African tradition of decorative textiles. The quilts made by members of other cultures are more formal and unyielding in design and color than African American quilts.

At the Goulds Senior Citizen Center and the Perrine Neighborhood Community Center, elderly women gather to work on quilts. Not only do they make new quilts, they also frequently repair or restore older quilts for others. For them quilting remains a social event, during which they talk about things that interest them. Because of this social function, it is likely that quilting will survive in African American neighborhoods for a long time.

Pattern names are a part of quilt folklore. The ladies at the West Perrine Neighborhood Center have quilted the "Flower Garden," "Star," "Little and Big Bow Tie," "Square" or "Nine Patches," "Around the World," and "Stove Eye." The ties to West African textile art can be seen in the quilts they refer to as "String" quilts, which strongly resemble the woven fabric and designs of West African cloth.

Virginia Barrel came to the community of West Perrine from Atlanta, Georgia, thirty-nine years ago. She has quilted since the age of twelve, when she learned the craft from her grandmother and mother. Mrs. Barrel comments: "I held the lamp at night, so they could see how to quilt. . . . They used a frame that hung from the ceiling by a cord or string. . . . I made my first quilt at age fourteen with strings left over from other quilts." Some of the women hate to discard anything, and these leftover items provide materials for other crafts. For instance, some use the fabric left from the quilts to fashion rag dolls, as well as dresses for dolls they have made from plastic bleach and detergent bottles. They create yo-yo pillows, pincushions, fabric flowers, and rugs out of old stockings. In addition, they make items from plastic soft drink can holders, aluminum can poptops, and egg cartons. The impetus to make these things comes from the strategy of survival that arose when people had to "make do" by making use of everything.

Doretha Carter, who moved to Miami in 1924 from White Springs, Florida, utilizes many old things. She continues to make her own lye soap because she does not like to throw away her leftover cooking fat and she prefers doing things the old-fashioned way. Carter also preserves fruits such as guavas, mangoes, and oranges when they are in season.

Many women in the community still employ home remedies to cure various illnesses. They gave several examples of remedies for fever, such as drinking fever grass tea or an alcohol, mustard, and turpentine mixture. For the common cold, they recommended a mixture of castor oil, cod liver oil, and honey. If children have worms, they might chew a piece of asafetida. Sores or burns may be treated by rubbing them with aloe vera or tobacco juice.

The West Indian Presence

In the 1890s, Coconut Grove became the first major settlement in South Florida by people of African descent, most of whom were Bahamian. Since that time, thousands of Caribbeans have made Miami-Dade County their home. They continue to add a new and vital dimension to this city by the sea. Large communities of residents born in the English and the French Caribbean are visible within Miami's Black or African American neighborhoods. Most of the city's residents born in Spanish-speaking Cuba and the Dominican Republic live outside of the high-percentage Black areas.

Even though many Caribbean groups have assimilated to the mainstream Miami culture to a certain extent, they maintain a very strong sense of shared identity through several strategies. First, a large number of Caribbean organizations or voluntary associations plan cultural activities and address social, political, and cultural issues. One example of this is the Miami Caribbean Carnival Association. In addition, there are newspapers, tabloids, journals, and magazines that keep the Caribbean community informed about issues and activities concerning them and their respective island nations. Furthermore, just as African Americans continued selected cultural practices when they moved from the country to the city, Afro-Caribbeans have bridged the gap from the island to the mainland by preserving some forms of their homeland's cultural practices that have become symbolic of their ethnic identity.

The West Indian sense of ethnic identity is also reflected in home interiors, which make important statements about the identity of their residents and the way they want others to perceive them. Home interiors often encompass vital aspects of family and homeland history and reflect aesthetic patterns and values that are reiterated in other spheres of life. Far from remaining fixed and unchanging, arts and crafts displayed in the home always incorporate both continuity and change by reflecting their owner's travels to the home country. For example, in a Trinidadian home I observed beautiful embroidery done by the mother and the headdress of an old Carnival costume juxtaposed with a commercial wooden replica of the island of Trinidad, obviously made for tourists. The value of these objects, then, is not found in their function and aesthetic form alone. Clearly, the process of creating the items and the act of possessing them carry significance for community members and make important statements about how they perceive their identity.

Another strategy for reinforcing the traditional culture is the frequent journey home to the mother country. Many travel to their home island several times a year, depending on factors such as family, business, or vacation. Since a large number of people frequently fly to the islands, a number of West Indian–owned travel agencies have been established in the north Miami-Dade vicinity.

Music and Song

One of the most noticeable aspects of West Indian culture in Miami is the music. The remarkable richness of West Indian musical life is partly the product of its multilayered complexity and diversity, which reflects the encounter between European and African musical traditions. European folk music practices, whether of Spanish, French, British, or Dutch origin, have for centuries come into contact and fused with the musical traditions carried by slaves from West and Central Africa to the Americas. The various practices and the way they have combined differ from place to place. However, the fundamental cultural elements in the different colonies paved the way for a creative process of blending and fusion (sometimes referred to as "Creolization") that has had similar results throughout the Caribbean.

In Miami, parties and other social events are held in peoples' homes or in rented halls, and generally involve a deejay who spins reggae, calypso, and soca (an invigorating musical synthesis of calypso with soul and funk elements) records. Occasionally, live reggae bands such as Zero Crew or Spice Roots, and live steel bands, including the Burt Reyes Steel Orchestra or the Rising Star Steelband, perform at the events. Staged dance performances, such as calypso and limbo, may also be featured along with informal social dancing.

In addition to local entertainers, major calypsonians, soca, and reggae stars, including David Rudder, Baron, Mighty Sparrow, Calypso Rose, Steel Pulse, and others, usually appear in concert several times during the year. These social events are often sponsored by a West Indian organization to raise funds for a cause or by a promoter for pure entertainment and monetary profit. West Indians flock to these events. The concerts are a medium wherein they can experience their common bonds, as well as express and solidify their West Indian heritage.

In all the previously mentioned West Indian musical styles—calypso, reggae, and soca—one can hear the synthesis of European and African elements along with indigenous island characteristics. For example, each style is per formed on instruments of European origin and uses the European harmonic system based on the diatonic scale, but the African elements are very strong.

They include the presence of the call-and-response structure, syncopated rhythms, improvisation, strong percussion, the relationship of music and dance, and the music's political as well as collective social nature. While all three styles are dance and party music, reggae and calypso also function as media for social and political commentary.

Musical and extra-musical affinities link the various styles with the individual characteristics of their island nations. Although calypso is performed today on European instruments, it is traditionally performed on steel drums, or "pans" as they are referred to by Trinidadians. The rhythm of the Trinidadian and Jamaican dialects tends to exert a powerful influence on the music and the manner in which it is performed. It does not matter how urban or international these styles have become, they still retain a strong indigenous character.

Although currently a popular style, reggae has its roots in traditional styles of Jamaican music. Elements from the Kumina tradition (religious ceremonies of drumming and dancing, held for the purpose of communion with the spirits of ancestors) are evident in the rhythmic layering of the guitar and keyboards in many reggae songs. Reggae also has an "off-beat" phrasing of the rhythm guitar that strongly resembles that of mento songs. Jamaican mento music is similar to the calypso of Trinidad and Tobago in that it is sometimes comical while still making historical, political, and social comments. However, mento consists of a different combination of instruments than calypso. In addition to guitar and banjo, a rumba box is the percussive instrument instead of a drum. Mento phrasing can also be heard in the accents of reggae trap drummers, although their individual styles vary. Even the dance movements of reggae are similar to that used in mento dancing. This similarity is noted by Louise Bennett-Coverly, a Jamaican folklorist, poet, storyteller, and newspaper columnist. She refers to the dance movements as an "old African step": the "weak knee" or "dipping motion."

Carol Pratt has resided in Miami since 1980, but she still plays mento and other more traditional songs on her guitar, and sings the lyrics she learned during her childhood in Jamaica. Pratt has returned to some of the rural areas where people still practice the old folk songs of Jamaica in order to collect and learn more. She performs them at her church and other cultural events in the West Indian community.

Lucille Ranger-Brown, who has lived in Miami since 1971, is a celebrated Jamaican performer. She performs many traditional Jamaican songs and dances, including work songs that portray typical marketplace scenes, women washing their clothes at the riverside, men working on the railroad, and other aspects of "the old culture like it used to be." Ranger-Brown also recites stories in Jamaican dialect or patois, and intersperses songs and dances in the midst of them. She comments: "We tell stories through folk songs. You see everyday living and we'd make a song or dance out of it. We don't go to school for this."

Narrative

Narrative tradition is another vital aspect of the influence of African traditions on West Indian culture. Storytelling—expressing a concept, moral lesson, or day-to-day experience in dramatic imagery—is one of the strongest retentions of African narrative forms in the diaspora. As in African communities, it is an important means of recordkeeping and transmitting information. Telling stories about animals that exhibit human behavior in familiar situations was a common method of instruction in West African society. A prevalent theme was the confrontation between a small animal, such as a spider or a rabbit, and a large animal, like a lion or a fox. The weaker animal prevailed by using its wit or cunning. Within the context of the oppressed lives of the slaves, the tales took on another connotation—that of the slaves outwitting their masters.

Lucille Fuller, also from Jamaica, has a large repertoire of animal folktales, particularly those about the Anansi (spider) character. She is a very animated and dramatic storyteller who tells tales in Jamaican dialect and uses voice changes to represent each animal. Fuller learned her stories from her grandmother, mother, and father. Now, she recites the stories in schools and in church and community programs.

Foodways

One can see the expression of West Indian identity in Miami through foodways. There are presently many authentic West Indian restaurants, such as the Pantry Restaurant, the Pepper Pot, and Pauline's. Taken as a group, they offer a considerable variety of foods, with the repetition of some dishes that are universally popular in the Caribbean, such as rice and peas. Other popular dishes include curried goat, oxtail stew, "jerk" chicken or pork, Escovich fish, fried plantains, codfish and oiled bananas, conch fritters or salads, callaloo, and ackee with saltfish.

Shirley Sutherland of Tobago is proud of her heritage and traditional cooking. She still prepares the traditional foods of her island home for her family, friends, and West Indian community functions. For example, she cooks bigi, which has spinach as its main ingredient, and coo-coo, which is made from cornmeal, okra, and coconut milk. For special occasions, she prepares a main dish like callaloo, made from dashing leaves, okra, green peppers, pig tails, and crabs.

Sutherland and other West Indians need certain basic ingredients to maintain the authenticity of traditional dishes. Therefore, Miami has many grocery stores that specialize in the essentials for West Indian dishes. Some businesses serve a triple purpose, such as Jamaica Products, Inc., which is a wholesale warehouse, retail grocery, and restaurant. Don Linton and his wife sell cases of canned goods, fresh produce, medicinal herbs, spices, pharmaceuticals, and other Jamaican products to clients in Miami and other parts of the United States.

Smaller West Indian grocery stores and bakeries may provide more than one service. Tai's Bakery, run by a Chinese Jamaican family, also serves hot lunches. The bakery abounds with West Indian breads and sweet treats, like sourdough and coconut breads, fry bake, plantain and coconut pastries, currant rolls, and fruitcakes. Two of the more popular items are the spicy lobster patties and meat pies.

Celebrations

Many Trinidadians from Miami make the annual journey home for Carnival. It is recognized that no single event in the English-speaking Caribbean engenders as much ethnic unity and comradery among West Indians abroad as the Carnival celebration. Not only do they make the annual pilgrimage back for Carnival, but also wherever they happen to be domiciled in large numbers, bands of masqueraders parade in imitation of the event.

Masquerading (mas for short in Trinidad) is an almost universal feature of the widely distributed pre-Lenten festivals, which culminate on Mardi Gras (Fat Tuesday), the day before Ash Wednesday, and the beginning of the Lenten fast. Trinidad is no exception. Early descriptions of the restrained European Carnival celebrations in Trinidad prior to Emancipation mention maskers, and the custom was carried and elaborated by freed slaves. In recent years, many of the older traditional Carnival characters have disappeared, and the hundreds of mas bands that participate in Carnival usually construct costumes on a new and original theme each year.

Llewellyn Roberts, who remembers following old sailor bands around as a child in Trinidad, and who, like most Trinidadians, has participated in Carnival all his life, is committed to continuing similar celebrations through Miami's West Indian Carnival. Roberts, who is a master craftsman, has been designing and building costume headdresses for many years. His specialty is wire bending—the painstaking task of constructing frames of wire that can be shaped with foam rubber, cloth, paper foil, sequins, and paint into a finished costume. Jesse Lampkin, also a wire bender from Trinidad, designs and builds full costumes. He lived in New York for many years and always participated in the West Indian Carnival on Labor Day.

On Columbus Day, Miami's West Indian community turns out to "Jump Up" and "Play Mas": dancing through the streets of downtown Miami to calypso and soca music. The Carnival combines African rhythms, colors, and sensuous movement, with the West Indians' unique flair for hospitality, entertainment, and bacchanal.

Just as Llewellyn Roberts and Jesse Lampkin persistently endeavor to preserve and celebrate their Trinidadian culture, Billy Rolle and Bruce Beneby have played similar roles in the Bahamian community. Billy Rolle is the executive director of the Miami/Bahamas Goombay Festival Celebration, which takes place in early June. His grandfather was one of the first settlers to come from the Bahamas in the 1890s, and his father emigrated around the turn of the century from the family island of Exuma.

Since it began in 1978, the festival has evolved into a large and celebrated event during which Coconut Grove's Grand Avenue turns into Nassau's Bay Street. The internationally acclaimed Royal Bahamas Police Band performs at Goombay events and marches in the parade. In 1989 close to 800,000 residents and visitors packed the Grove for the festival, feasting on traditional Bahamian treats, viewing the arts and crafts, and enjoying the music of Miami's Sunshine Junkanoo Band.

Bruce Beneby was the leader of the Sunshine Junkanoo Band, which consists primarily of his family and friends. He was born in Nassau, but lived in Miami since 1956. There are various theories on the origin of the term Junkanoo. Beneby believed that the term and the celebration of Junkanoo "all began in Africa with a gentleman named 'Johnny Enew,' leader of a band that traveled from house to house, from street to street during certain holidays like Christmas and New Year's, which is when Junkanoo is celebrated in the Bahamas." Every year during the holidays, Beneby returned to Nassau, to participate in his country's traditional celebration, marching in the parade and beating drums.

The Sunshine Junkanoo Band members play horns, drums, whistles, and cowbells. Each year they create a new array of vividly colored costumes with headdresses based on a specific theme. The band has performed at the Goombay festival in the Grove since its inception, and also performs at other festivals and events throughout the state. Bruce Beneby was tragically killed in a hit-and-run accident, but his family and friends are continuing the tradition of celebration.

In conclusion, traditional culture continues to pervade the lives of African Americans and West Indians in Miami. Many traditions, such as those mentioned here, not only provide an enduring foundation for family and community life, but also serve as a source of aesthetic satisfaction for generations of participants.

Bibliography

Gonsher, Aaron. "Interview: Amos Larkins II, Party Rock with a Miami Bass Pioneer." Red Bull Music Academy, 2015. Accessed June 1, 2021. https://daily.redbullmusicacademy.com/2015/10/amos-larkins-interview.

Sarig, Roni. 2007. *Third Coast: OutKast, Timbaland, and How Hip-Hop Became a Southern Thing.* Cambridge, MA: Da Capo Press.

Serwer, Jesse. "Nightclubbing: The Pac Jam, Home of Miami Bass." Red Bull Music Academy, 2015. Accessed June 2, 2021. https://daily.redbullmusicacademy.com/2015/10/nightclubbing-the-pac-jam.

CHAPTER TEN

The Art of the Highwaymen
Superficial Beauty and the Imagination

Gary Monroe

During the 1950s and 1960s, more was definitely better. This was particularly true in tropical Florida, which was then in its early boom days of modern tourism, when air conditioning and insect control made the state more appealing. Furthermore, Dwight Eisenhower's development of the Interstate Highway System and increased car ownership meant that thousands of Americans could easily drive all the way to this Paradise. The golden age of travel brought northerners to Miami quickly and with added cachet. South Florida especially was always about being seen in the best light possible. To this end, some who came by train or bus would take a taxi to the airport and with a sense of glamour board their hotel's shuttle to arrive in style. If you were fortunate enough to stay in Miami Beach's flagship hotel, the Fontainebleau, you could walk down their perfectly placed circular staircase and halt to have your picture taken, perhaps to show off your mink stole, stylish dress, and jewelry. Otherwise, the stairs are functionless, like a bridge to nowhere.

Tourists marveled at the lush foliage, the exotic birds such as the flamingos at Hialeah Race Track, the mangrove swamps and royal poinciana trees, and the Everglades. They could see alligators, manatees, pelicans, and dolphins from rivers and beaches. The now classic hotels of South Beach, mostly done in a tropical version of the art deco style, and often painted in pastel colors, found a minor echo in the many tourist courts and mom-and-pop motels that dotted Florida. Beyond the top attractions such as Cypress Gardens, Silver Springs, Parrot Jungle, Monkey Jungle (where people were in cages and the chimps ran free), Gatorland, and Marineland played on these environmental elements as well. The opening of Walt Disney World in Central Florida in 1971 would only accelerate the fantasy elements of Florida imagery. Folks began to yearn for and respond to the clarion calls of these dreamlike scenes.

At the same time, much of the large African American community of Florida, particularly in Fort Pierce but also in cities and rural hamlets across the state, languished in segregated poverty. In 1954, just as the *Brown v. Topeka Board of Education* decision created the first major attack on the reign of Jim Crow culture, Harold Newton (1934–1994), a young, self-taught artist from Gifford, an African American township adjacent to Vero Beach, just north of Fort Pierce, met A. E. Backus, a talented white regionalist artist, whose nascent career had been interrupted by his service during World War II. While the wider audience for beautiful renditions of landscapes had waned by then in favor of more modernist, experimental, or self-reflexive art, Backus had a steady supply of customers in Fort Pierce itself, where people knew him and loved him and his landscape paintings.

At the time of their meeting, Newton had been concentrating on painting religious subjects. Impressed by his budding talent, Backus persuaded Newton to switch to landscapes, a genre Newton developed in his own way after the initial influence of Backus. His early images alluded, however unintentionally, to the primordial emergence of life.

To make a living through art, but without contacts with dealers, galleries, or shops, Newton hawked his works out on the streets, a pattern subsequent painters like him adopted; hence their ultimate soubriquet became the Highwaymen. The name was given to them long after their enterprise ceased to be financially rewarding. Soon there were two aspiring artists; Alfred Hair (1941–1970) came under the tutelage of Backus, who had been recommended to him by his high school teacher Zanobia Jefferson (1923–2016). Hair had a gift for turning out paintings quickly, which enabled him to sell his two-by-three-foot boards at a cut-rate price, twenty-five dollars. These two Black artists quickly attracted the attention of other young would-be-artists in the area, who were encouraged by Newton and Hair. "Backuses for the working-man," observed collector Tim Jacobs about the cohort's paintings. Indeed, the Highwaymen found their niche, and it seemed massive and unending.

From the mid-1950s through the early 1980s, it was a common sight to see young Black men and one Black woman entering white enclaves, such as offices and businesses, offering a variety of framed pictures for sale. These were alluring landscapes variously depicting the ocean, stretches of open lands with big skies, backwater swamps, and almost always, water, birds, and some type of palm trees. These works, usually painted on Upson board, an inexpensive interior wallboard used in construction, were cheaply framed, and could fit in stacks in the trunks of the artists' cars, which became their roadside warehouses.

I have identified twenty-six Highwaymen, most from Fort Pierce, but also Gifford. In addition to Newton and Hair, they are Curtis Arnett, Hezekiah Baker, Al Black, Ellis Buckner, George Buckner, Robert Butler, Mary Ann Carroll (the only woman in the group), Johnny Daniels, Willie Daniels, Rodney Demps, James Gibson, Isaac Knight, Robert Lewis, John Maynor, Roy McLendon, Alfonso Moran, Lemuel Newton, Sam Newton, Willie Reagan, Livingston Roberts, Cornell Smith, Charles Walker, Sylvester Wells, and Charles Wheeler. Various estimates of their output range from a group total of 50,000 paintings to many times that. Their sales territory gradually extended south toward Miami and north through Daytona Beach, as well as the inland area around Lake Okeechobee. While there are many similarities in their works and methods, there was no organized group; the artists did, however, have a shared style developed through their process of fast painting.

The Highwaymen practiced a vernacular art, one based in a tropical landscape that has been drastically reduced since their era. Whites who bought the paintings could congratulate themselves on helping those in a lower economic sector, while also thinking that they were now patrons of the arts. Mostly, though, owning one of the glowing paintings confirmed one's arrival in Paradise; the images engendered pride. They were trophies of sorts. Hanging them on their walls was an affirmation.

In 1997 I began photographing self-taught artists throughout Florida. It seemed easy enough. I did most of this with color film, which I never thought of using before. I could then send the film to a lab rather than processing them myself, to save time and labor while I thought about being a midcareer artist with all it entails. It was to last a year, sufficient time to reflect on my work.

This new focus on self-taught artists, which came to include the Highwaymen, however, drove home the realization that the raw energy, obsessive nature, and unimpeded visions of the most genuine outsiders paralleled something essential to my own ideas about camera work. I hoped to maintain the spirit that is at the core of their art-making impetus, something easily lost to formal training. There was a sense of freedom, of surging exploration, about these renegade artists' works. They just let it all flow, without a care in the world. I knew that for me and for them, creating art was done alone, in solitude. They weren't relying on a stamp of approval, gallery representation, grants, awards, or exhibitions. Besides, as James Agee wrote in *Let Us Now Praise Famous Men*, "Official acceptance is the kiss of Judas."

My photographs of the Highwaymen artists especially were good enough but lacked something: narrative. I come from the school whose teachers said that the work speaks for itself. Well, it doesn't and never did, and I wonder if they knew this but were more concerned with their own productivity as artists in the macho-ness era in which they studied, rather than philosophizing about the world through art and ideas.

When I came across the paintings of the recently dubbed Highwaymen, they had been working for years in near anonymity. Fascinated by their work, I determined to learn more about them and their culture. What drew me to these paintings of the tropical wilds? What was the brewing groundswell all about? Paintings by the Highwaymen did not resemble paintings by professional or otherwise academically trained artists, nor were they technically in accord with standard notions of representation. They were raw and curious, disrupting cherished traditional modes of representation . . . and something scratched at their surfaces.

A year into this journey, I thought I had done enough research. I could get back to full-time photography with my Leica, strong legs, and a quick index finger. But I was wrong. I had a new calling that I thought would complement my camera work. as I thought through art-making. My aesthetic was realized, and I felt refreshed and vital. But I couldn't put this on hold. There was zero scholarship about the Highwaymen at that time, just rumor and misinformation laced with disinformation. Although I was not a scholar, I went for it. I would write a book.

I wore out two sets of tires in three years while researching *The Highwaymen: Florida's African-American Landscape Painters* (2001). I lost track of the number of drafts I had written; both peer reviewers rejected the version I initially submitted to the University Press of Florida. Good, I told then editor-in-chief Meredith Babb, I can get back to my obsessive photography; writing was starting to get in the way. But she told me to get back to my computer. She was right. The book has been in print now for more than twenty years, and I have subsequently published four more Highwaymen books.

We now see even more in these painters' productions; in today's art climate, Highwaymen landscapes are perfect stage-setters for discussions about environmental fragility, global warming, and especially sea level rise around the peninsula. They continue to generate critiques about glamorizing white people's lives, while the paintings and all they offer remain out of reach of disadvantaged and/or disenfranchised Black youths. Ironically, the young Highwaymen came from tough Southern towns, and made the paintings as the civil rights movement brewed. Concurrently, the paintings have recently stimulated a conversation about the limitations of nostalgia, which is what lies behind much of the popularity of these paintings today.

The truth is that these painters were reared in the surprisingly rich culture of a segregated community; the momentum of the civil rights movement made the artists determined to rise above what seemed to be their social destiny of picking oranges in the groves and beans in the fields. Little if anything about their story plays into the hands of expectation. They favored creating a product to producing art, though it is unfair to say they were not concerned with the quality of their painting. They became, as I see it, artists by default. Unconcerned with white standards of landscape painting, they created a fresh and creative approach to the genre that redefined or even defied an exhausted model.

The bottom line is that there is nothing narrative about any singular image. Especially when it comes to a photograph, there is no story there. An image might look real and pass for the truth, but it is no more fact than fiction, a mere quote out of context. One is simply more interesting and more convincing than another. A painting might not be dissimilar; it conjures, without a second thought, a memory, an ideal, an experience to which one gives meaning by lending a suitable narrative. Anthony de Mello wrote that the shortest distance between truth and a human being is a story. Accordingly, I do not argue with folks who tell me, for example, where on the St. Johns River Harold Newton painted that river bend scene or where Willie Daniels saw the mighty oak tree in the backwater setting. This is because the artists painted in their backyards sans photographs, often working on multiple paintings at a time. They painted rapidly, from memory, and without underdrawings, applying their oils wet-on-wet.

Fast painting led to their distinctive style, but more than style it accounted for their paintings' substances. Without overt artifice, theirs seemed to be an artless art. The quickness with which they painted stripped the images to their barest essentials, distilling the scenes to arrive at archetypes. Here memory and knowledge were teased by the unconscious. Water, the mysterious primordial bog, is a staple in every painting. This recalls Edmund Burke's notion of the sublime, which created a precedent in Western art. Further, their gestural paintings are tempting and suggestive, making it seemingly irresistible for viewers to lend their own meanings to the images, which is mistaken for stories.

During the artists' banner years of the 1960s (their enterprise ceased in the early 1980s), Florida was still a frontier and its appeal particularly registered with those who served in World War II, as the Sunshine State was then a huge military training camp. According to historian Gary Mormino, as many as two million people were stationed here before being shipped off. Imagine a young person on beaches doing calisthenics in crisp winter sunshine, in 72-degree weather. It must have left an indelible impression, for many servicemen were drawn to move their families to Florida after their terms of service were up. The tropical landscape and climate, the lack of congestion, the many lakes, and of course the entrancing ocean, seemed to constitute a new version of the American dream. Property was affordable, if not always as described in sales brochures. Any disillusionment because of humidity, insects, thunderstorms, roaming critters, and properties bought sight unseen that were further from the coast than expected was forgotten. Any regret could be assuaged by hanging a new original oil painting on a cinder block wall and thereby transforming it into a picture window overlooking Paradise. They even smelled good, the oils fresh and glistening. Besides, Florida did not have state income tax.

Initially, the Highwaymen's art was not a Black art per se; the artists painted pictures that appealed to white people. As noted earlier, the Highwaymen learned what was marketable from the successful white regionalist A. E. Backus. His paintings provided a starting point for the cohort, but soon they were interpreting landscapes with their own insights, altering the nature of the imagery with each painting. In the process they disrupted the established craft of traditional painters to arrive at a variation of the accepted visual language of landscape art, creating a challenging if not a more relevant version of the time-tested genre.

Theirs was a lucrative business, one that flew in the face of Jim Crow regulations. True, the artists were limited; they couldn't, for example, cross bridges to the exclusive barrier islands off south and central Florida after dark. They were no doubt viewed suspiciously by the authorities. But their own reports confirm that after being questioned by police officers about their stacks of still wet paintings, they were allowed to go on their way. The Highwaymen also reported that seldom if ever did they encounter racist acts. As Mary Ann Carroll, the sole Highwaywoman, explained, white people were fine with a one-on-one racial encounter.

The paintings were calling cards. The Highwaymen were welcome to show their paintings to people by going to their homes, but they had more success selling paintings to professional businesses, including realtors, doctors and lawyers' offices, retail shops, government buildings, and even banks, where they received permission to line up their paintings in the lobbies, which became a Friday afternoon practice. The bank locations gave them much better presentation points than the sides of roads where most motorists sped by. Besides, they weren't hawking tawdry mass-produced items like chenille bedspreads or velvet paintings. This was genuine art that reflected the beauty Florida's citizens had come to cherish. It did not make sense to them to set up shop along roadsides.

Their paintings were sold framed for two reasons: artwork looks better framed and frames served as spacers, thereby minimizing one painting damaging the one stacked behind it while in transit for sales. Oils require time to cure but since time meant money to these eager twenty-somethings, no Highwaymen paintings were known to have been sold dry. The frames were not actual frames; that would have been cost prohibitive and therefore contrary to their mission of selling affordable art. They were constructed with carpenter's trim and like the boards they painted on, were purchased at the lumberyard. In all fairness, the Highwaymen were not mercenary business-people; money was the way they kept score in their own invented game of success, one in which they beat the house.

Although neither outcome was part of the plan, these untrained painters advanced the idea of landscape painting and bequeathed an important visual legacy of modern Florida. Some estimates place their output at 250,000 paintings. They kept no records, so determining the actual count is speculative; it likely exceeded 125,000 paintings. How many have survived is another story. Successfully navigating through racial discord, collector Ron Woodsy points out that "the artists sold paintings to their nemesis and made history."

Many of the finest characteristics of this school of painting are found in one of the greatest of the Highwaymen, Alfred Hair. Generous of spirit and movie-star handsome, he was the ringleader of the artists who became known as the Highwaymen. He was living his dream while Martin Luther King Jr. was forming his memorialized speech. Only Hair wasn't thinking of equality; he was thinking about money. He possessed the audacity of hope before Barack Obama was born. He was selling resplendent paintings to a white clientele as he drove a Cadillac along a road to riches. Talk about trailblazers! Regrettably, Alfred Hair, the father of six children, was gunned down in a barroom brawl when he was only twenty-nine years old, at a time when he was on top of his game. Still, this remarkable young man generated some of the most impressive art of his group and the times. The other painters were influenced by his talent and his success at creating a new and accessible visual approach to the Florida imaginary.

Alfred Hair did not set out to form a school of art or an art movement but that is what happened. He showed others how to beat the odds Black men faced by learning to paint the Florida landscape; simultaneously, he showed his emulators how to market their artworks. He inspired opportunities and ambition. His quest for wealth led Hair to paint fast, and in doing so he inadvertently came across a process that resulted in a fresher idea of landscape art than was the norm. In this way, he was cutting edge.

Twenty-five years ago these paintings could be found on junk piles, along with yard trash. They sold at garage sales for a few dollars apiece even twenty years ago. Even when they reached eBay, they were under $100 apiece. With

Figure 10.1. Harold Newton, *Untitled*, not dated. Courtesy of The Walker Collection of Florida Self-Taught Art.

my book's release, paintings climbed to fetch $500 each, and then escalated. Like the trajectory of Florida real estate, finer paintings increased in value so that today they can fetch $10,000 and considerably more. Not all Highwaymen paintings were created equally, of course. Generally, the painters let loose, and the oils flowed. Their distinction is as colorists. They did not adhere to theory but painted intuitively, finding their rhythm with palette knives and the forces of tropical experience.

Eight of the painters established the aesthetic parameters of Highwaymen art. Harold Newton and Alfred Hair were central to the group's formation, although there was no organization, rules, or credo. Newton, like Alfred Hair, set the stage for aspiring Highwaymen. As soon as he returned to his native Gifford, in the mid-1950s, Newton embarked on an artistic career. He painted at home, and then traversed the region selling his oil paintings inexpensively. Newton possessed innate skill; he could effortlessly paint with fidelity and verve, simultaneously. His paintings inspired his painter friends, who watched him paint in awe. His works were prototypical images for this artistic cohort, and would eventually become a revered example of vernacular Floridian art.

The paintings of Roy McLendon (b. 1932) are hybrids of Alfred Hair's fast painting and Harold Newton's controlled finesse. McLendon painted with artistic intent prior to meeting Hair. He and Newton were neighbors in Gifford, and McLendon had dabbled in the arts during his youth. Most Highwaymen paintings are devoid of people and worldly concerns; birds are common compositional elements in their scenes, but they don't include animals. McLendon sometimes placed people in the scenes he painted, unlike most of others of the cohort.

Livingston Roberts (1942–2004) was there at the start, when, in 1961, Hair graduated from high school and embarked on his remarkable journey. Hair and Newton established the parameters, and Roberts, McLendon, and James Gibson were the first to join the ranks, making them the original Highwaymen. Roberts made unembellished paintings and he painted without much flair; his art represents the base of Highwaymen representations of the landscape.

James Gibson (1938–2017) was central to the group dynamic when it formed but, unlike the others, nurtured his own professional path. His artwork stood apart, too. He did not use unrestrained long brush strokes, a staple of the Highwaymen's fast painting. Rather, Gibson's paintings were made with flat color depicting simple scenes. However, they were distinguished. His use of Kool-Aid colors accounted for striking scenes that captured, in their own way, the Florida experience and, more so, the exotica of the Florida dream.

Al Black (b. 1945) had a rare gift for convincing people to buy paintings. By the mid-1960s business was so brisk that the artists often employed salesmen;

in turn the sales force stimulated an even greater output of paintings to keep up with the growing demand. Black sold to people who had rejected the other salesmen and painters. Signs prohibiting solicitation or Negroes did not intimidate him. Interestingly, Black learned to paint by repairing paintings that had been left in his care for sale as they might smudge, for example. He did not start creating his own works until Alfred Hair's death in 1970. Until then, he simply could not spare the time to paint. He was making a lot of money from the sales, taking 30 percent from each painting he sold for others. Often, he would double the sales price, which he would keep for himself. Black accelerated the pace of fast painting by selling paintings fast.

Mary Ann Carroll (1940–2019) had to feed, clothe, and shelter her seven children; most of the time she was their sole support. She took an array of laborious jobs, but soon after meeting Harold Newton, she concentrated on honing her own painting skills. By the time her marriage failed she was making a living from the sales of her paintings. As a woman of faith and a busy parent, she did not socialize with the cohort. Instead, her energies went toward singing in the church choir and building her own ministry. Her unusual use of color primarily distinguishes her paintings from the rest of the cohort.

Willie Daniels (1950–2021) was one of the youngest of the Highwaymen. He lived with his family in a house next to Newton's and McLendon's residences. He acknowledged their influence on his own artistic development. Indeed, combining the formal resolve of their styles with the temporal flair he found in Alfred Hair's paintings, Daniels's works came to epitomize the Highwaymen ideal. More often than the others, he employed Al Black to sell his paintings. Often Daniels left his works unsigned; Black would sign them, with his own name, to facilitate sales. Hence, many paintings signed A. Black are really Willie Daniels creations. This practice did not offend the painters; they were grateful that such a practice increased sales. Theirs, as a consumer-driven moneymaking enterprise, was not one based on the conceits of authorship.

As noted, the paintings eventually hung everywhere, in homes and offices; they acknowledged the owners' good sense in choosing to live in a year-round summer clime. Something else accounts for their revival, though. Most sales ceased in the early 1980s and then the art became as anonymous as the artists, as if neither any longer existed. Neither mattered for fifteen years. Most of the artists had full-time employment anyway. Others came and went. But a core group of painters eked out their livings during this time. Some people who had bought paintings in the 1960s and 1970s were wed to them, but most people were not. Then in the late 1990s, the public's appetite for these works returned with a vengeance along with my book's release. People began cashing

Figure 10.2. Willie Daniels, *Untitled*, not dated. Courtesy of The Walker Collection of Florida Self-Taught Art.

out, while a new breed of collector was born. The painters bought supplies and started painting again as if making up for lost time. It was circuslike. Suddenly it was raining money. The forgotten painters were now celebrities. The word Highwaymen entered the cultural lexicon. I fanned the flames by giving some 300 public lectures through the Florida Humanities Council. I achieved rock star status to older collectors, the seventy- and eighty-somethings.

But what I was enthusiastically describing was not what was happening at that time, but what had happened in the past. The contemporary Highwaymen scene is much different, as are their paintings. Just about every weekend in Florida during "the season," some nonprofit group is hosting a Highwaymen event, parading the artists to an adoring audience as they hawk their new paintings. These paintings differ radically from their vintage work; they are still and studied. Most people don't see or care about this. They just want to rub shoulders with the artists, comment about old Florida, and have their pictures taken beside a living legend. The Highwaymen's fame was solidified by their being inducted into the Florida Artists Hall of Fame in 2004. Originally, I nominated Alfred Hair, then asked myself what Alfred would do, and without hesitating I nominated Alfred Hair and the Highwaymen. Some of the artists have charged to sign their name alongside their paintings in my Highwaymen books. The cost for this is often the purchase of a painting.

The driving force, from what I constantly hear, is that the fervor is nostalgia-driven. These paintings remind people of better times, whether real or imagined. Perhaps they were simpler times, though I don't know if times were ever simple but maybe less tense, crowded, and the land way less developed. These are paintings devoid of telephone wires and other worldly reminders; ornamentation in the form of boathouses and sailboats are sometimes included in the scenes. Maybe the paintings represent a return to Eden. Was there ever a better time or an age of innocence? Do they simply take our minds off our woes, like placebos? Or is the fuss all about narrative? Are these paintings springboards for people to express their hopes and dreams, if not to rationalize aspects of their lives? The sketchy, impressionistic nature of the paintings beckons viewers so inclined to lend their own voices to the dialog, to fill in the blanks. Viewers in this way become coauthors as they finish the images in their minds. If life is a search for meaning these paintings contribute to providing a stage for ascribing meaning, or at least drama, to one's life.

We should also remember that the presence of the divine has long been what landscape art has capitalized on with ease. Who could look at the God-given wilds where the ocean is as boundless as big skies and not experience liberation? Of course, these responses are largely culturally constructed. One could say the same about an abstract expressionist canvas; Mark Rothko's color field paintings have always been felt to express a spiritual element, as we see in the Rothko Chapel of the Houston Museum of Fine Arts. Expressing the ineffable is the business of art. Perhaps therefore postwar artists weren't prone to pontification.

Conversely, one could look at a Highwaymen landscape and shrug, or worse. Years ago, the pejorative "motel art" was levied against Highwaymen paintings. I thought, Yeah, why not? What symbolized a Florida vacation better than motels back then, before they became nondescript boxy edifices along the interstate? Classic Florida motels are right up there with orange juice and alligators. If art mirrors its time and place, this art fits right in with motels, an outgrowth from early Tin Can tourism. The paintings don't always fit within the limited range of some people's understanding, or willingness to understand. Even when the paintings were new, they were old; they were old school. Their mentor A. E. Backus was in some respects the end of the line of the American tradition of landscape painting. Though a skilled painter, he practiced an exhausted aesthetic. A hundred years had passed since the Hudson River School explored and painted that region, then ventured westward; some even painted the steamy tangles of a largely unexplored Florida. As tycoon Henry Flagler's Florida East Coast Railway unfurled southward to Key West, the artists made paintings that echoed the sublime notions that characterize the genre here. Flagler brought key artists to his Ponce de Leon Hotel in St. Augustine, where he had an arcade of studios for each to paint and offer paintings to those staying at the resort.

The art world moved on; impressionism, postimpressionism, cubism, surrealism, and abstract expressionism, among many other modes, forged a new understanding of painting. Many of the original fans of Highwaymen art had little if any interest in these new modes of contemporary, idea-driven art, not then and not now. These people cared about being reminded of the familiar and often dreamlike images of the tropics, which seemed to merge with their concepts of the homes where the paintings would hang.

Most exhibitions of Highwaymen art of late have been community-based, in libraries, history centers, and the like. Few art museums have picked up on this art, and most that have have been second-tier. The Museum of Art/ Fort Lauderdale was the first major big city museum to curate a Highwaymen exhibition, in 2006. Under the direction of Irvin Lippman, we looked at the paintings by Alfred Hair and Harold Newton, whose polar opposite artworks serve to bookend the range of the Highwaymen aesthetic. The Orlando Museum of Art mounted a major show in 2020, "Living Color: The Art of the Highwaymen," that maximized the beauty pageant appeal of the art.

Highwaymen paintings are included in Florida's two major private collections of the state's art, owned by the Vickers and Brown families. The Vickers collection was recently acquired by the University of Florida's Harn Museum of Art, and the Browns endowed the Daytona Beach Museum of Arts and Sciences with a new building and their massive collection of paintings. Highwaymen art is of course in countless homes. Some driven collectors have each amassed well over 100 paintings. With the hunter-gatherer instinct fully engaged, the most driven have more than 500 paintings. Finding and buying the paintings has become addictive to many people, be it a result of entering virgin territory to excavate ancient treasures or because it is a kind of lust sport. But at bottom is a love of natural Florida.

Perhaps at the heart of it is that people want to find meaning; curating this art offers order and expression. The most outstanding collection belongs to Lance Walker in Orlando. He got a late start but has canvassed the field relentlessly, on foot and virtually. His goal is to share the art and stories that inform the paintings, of both the artist's individual and shared biographies along with mining what is most germane about their unusual paintings. To do this he converted a work-bay into a pristine gallery in tony Winter Park. Though not open to the public, his private museum is available to nonprofits for their programming.

This unfolding drama about the meteoric rise of the art's and the artists' popularity has sometimes led to cynicism. One collector-dealer said, "It's better than counterfeiting," referring to the ever-escalating value of the paintings, with sales having exceeded $50,000 for a Harold Newton. Someone else said that he hopes his collector-friend isn't the last man standing when the music stops. That was twenty years ago, and the music is louder than ever. The paintings are now in the collections of many museums and private collections. The Smithsonian's National Museum of African American History and Culture was recently gifted eighteen Highwaymen paintings, which curators have accepted but have yet to figure out what to do with this perplexing art. Everyone has been waiting for a feature film to be produced; a documentary is well underway. The Highwaymen's backstory is made for Hollywood; Steven Spielberg couldn't make it up any more effectively as it played out naturally.

Yet as fascinating as the story goes, in the end it is the art that matters. Now it is time for scholars to explicate meanings about the paintings. Processing abstract sensations in terms of concrete thought is fundamental to experiencing landscape paintings. This is not to suggest overlooking the story of the artists, individually and collectively, but realizing how their stations in life led to a fresh and perfectly calibrated art for postwar dreamers. Mostly it has to do with understanding the particular finesse of these paintings.

Art critics are still thinking about the ways in which traditional approaches have merged with an African American sensibility. As noted earlier, the

Highwaymen eliminated features of modern life such as telephone poles and automobiles, and usually concentrated on unpeopled, idealized, mystical, mysterious images of their native state. Their images may be replete with lush flora, florid sunsets, cresting ocean waves, towering palms, or moonlit waters. In so doing, the Highwaymen created an African American version of the tropical sublime. They gave us accessible and affordable art that could soothe, elevate, and yet also provide a transcendent concept of a very real and unusual tropical realm.

For Further Reading

Monroe, Gary. *Alfred Hair: Heart of the Highwaymen*. Gainesville: University Press of Florida, 2020.

Monroe, Gary. *The Highwaymen: Florida's African-American Landscape Painters*. Gainesville: University Press of Florida, 2001.

Monroe, Gary. *Highwaymen Newton and Hair: The American Dream in the Sunshine State*. Fort Lauderdale, FL: Fort Lauderdale Museum of Art, 2006.

Monroe, Gary. *The Highwaymen Murals: Al Black-s Concrete Dreams*. Gainesville: University Press of Florida, 2009.

Monroe, Gary. *Mary Ann Carroll: First Lady of the Highwaymen*. Gainesville: University Press of Florida, 2014.

CHAPTER ELEVEN

"What Is Florida to Me?"

Shadowing, Danticat, and the Florida/Black Imaginary

Simone A. James Alexander

Renowned Haitian American author and critic Edwidge Danticat's relocation to Miami, Florida, in Little Haiti,[1] captures the growing wave of Haitian immigrants relocating from the northeast United States to Miami. A "triple diaspora" from Brooklyn, New York, Miami, Florida, and Port-au-Prince, Haiti, Danticat's presence in her newly adopted home reinvigorated not only the Haitian (immigrant) community but also enlivened the African American literary scene.[2] Having melded easily into the community, Danticat has become a household name and has been dubbed a "national treasure" and beacon of the community by fellow Haitians. Marvin DM-ijean of Minority Development and Empowerment, Inc., in Fort Lauderdale, Florida, gushes with unabashed pride as he welcomes the new, highly desirable resident: "She's becoming a national treasure for the Haitian community as a writer. . . . I'm sure the Haitians in New York are sad to see her leave, but we down here are happy to have her. She's one of our more recognizable faces and heroes."[3] DM-ijean joined other local leaders championing Danticat as an "inspiration to the local Haitian community." As the appropriately titled article "A Little Closer to Home" intimates, Danticat's newly adopted home in Little Haiti has brought her closer to her homeland, Haiti; as Danticat shared with me, proximity to her home country is one of several incentives that influenced her moving to Miami. Endeared by the potential and possibilities of her adopted home community, Danticat coined the apt phrase, "the soul of Little Haiti," to capture the restoration and revitalization of a people and a community: "The soul of little Haiti lives in any community where people have been driven out and displaced."[4] Encapsulating the regenerative spirit, she pontificates: "Little Haiti is what's possible when people plant new roots and try to create a community for the next generation to call home."[5]

Prior to her relocation to Miami in 2002, Danticat served as a visiting professor of creative writing at the University of Miami's Caribbean Writers Institute in the spring of 2000. Most recently, on February 27, 2020, she returned to the University of Miami as the featured speaker of the university's "One Book One U Program."[6] She is also featured prominently and regularly at the locally owned, independent neighborhood bookstore, Books & Books, in Coral Gables.[7]

Danticat's influence extends to her advocacy work, more recently her support of Haitian refugees, resulting in her close affiliation with the Florida Immigrant Advocacy Center.[8] A voice for the voiceless, the abused, and oppressed (community), Danticat advocates for the impartial treatment of Haitians, having witnessed abuse firsthand and becoming a victim by default through the detention and subsequent death of her own uncle Joseph Dantica, who, in seeking asylum in the United States, was detained and subsequently died in custody at Krome Detention Center in Miami. This paradoxical relationship between Haitian citizens and the state is not lost on Danticat.[9] While calling attention to Haitian's creation of a home away from home,[10] Danticat, in equal measure, foregrounds the challenges and struggles the Haitian community faces, namely extreme xenophobia, biased immigration policies, ICE raids and attendant deportations, and gentrification. Calling attention to the rapidly changing landscape, she poignantly ascertains: "The soul of Little Haiti also rests with the ghosts of the places that have already been disappeared by gentrification."[11]

Danticat's relocating to Miami is incentivized further by one of her icons, her literary antecedent and fellow Floridian Zora Neale Hurston, in whose (literal and literary) footsteps she follows—or more accurately, they shadow each other.[12] Decades earlier, Hurston accomplished a reverse journey from Florida to Haiti to study Haiti's rich oral and spiritual tradition and cultural practices, engendering transnational alliance and exchange that Danticat endorses in the following pronouncement: "[Our heroes are] the world's heroes."[13] This sense of collectiveness gives rise to the Florida/Black imaginary, a fact to which Hurston alludes in assessing her penchant for travel, or "wandering,"[14] as she put it, exemplified in her "feet [that] took to wandering" (*Dust Tracks*, 22), evoking her "travel dust": "That hour began my wandering. Not so much in geography, but in time. Then not so much in time as in spirit" (*Dust Tracks*, 67).[15] In the afterword of *Dust Tracks*, Henry Louis Gates attests to Hurston's mastery of the imaginary: Hurston "did make significant parts of

herself up. . . . That which she chooses to reveal is the life of her imagination"
("Afterword: Zora Neale Hurston: 'A Negro Way of Saying,'" 294). In like manner, Danticat engages, even embodies this imaginary, acknowledging never
having met Hurston yet confessing to being "her friend in the head," fittingly
becoming both her kinfolk and her skinfolk (*Dust Tracks*, 231).[16] Along similar
lines, Danticat intimates how even in the afterlife, Hurston encourages us to
imagine: "In this revival she triumphs. I think she made us all stronger bolder
and much more willing to experiment and trusting that if you tell the story
in your voice, others will have to learn that if you tell it in your language, they
will have to learn that language."[17]

In my conversation with the esteemed author on March 1, 2020, in Miami,
Florida, we discussed her move to Miami, the city's role in her life and writing,
the Florida/Black imaginary, and her kinship with her kindred spirit, one of
her most beloved female authors, Zora Neale Hurston.[18]

Simone A. James Alexander: As I mentioned, I'm writing this essay for a
volume titled *Black Hibiscus: African Americans and the Florida Imaginary*.
Thanks for granting me this interview.

You moved from Brooklyn to Miami about eighteen years ago. Actually,
you've lived in the two most populous cities where they are Haitian inhabitants.[19] What occasioned this migration? Was that by design or just coincidence?

Edwidge Danticat: When my parents left Haiti—my father when I was
two, my mom when I was four—my mom had a brother who was living in
Brooklyn, so—and that was the only person my parents knew there, so my
dad moved here [the United States] to join his brother-in-law, who facilitated
things for him because back then there wasn't really a Haitian community, per
se, there were sort of clusters of Haitians. And when my mom moved here,
it was the same, and I think often these migrations work in these patterns,
where you go where you know people. So naturally, that's where I joined them
when I moved to New York. And then in 2002—well the first time I came
down here [Miami] was for the Caribbean Writers Institute in 1990, and then
I started coming more on book tours and for events with community groups
here. Because the community groups, even though there are in different cities—there are organizations that everybody knows—so I remember coming
for things like that. In 1998 I met my husband in Haiti and he was living here
[Miami] and I was living in New York. And he was teaching, he's an educator for younger, elementary school kids. We met when he went to Haiti to
volunteer in a school; it was a school that was started by a linguist named
Yves Déjean who was trying to pioneer teaching children in Kreyól rather
than in French, which is the more standard type of teaching. My husband

was very interested in that and so he went and volunteered for a year, and at the end of the year, in the summer, he volunteered with the Ministers of Haitians Living Abroad. They had a program where they would bring college students from the US, France, Canada, and Cuba to see Haiti, and the idea was that they would fall in love with Haiti and would want to come back and contribute their talents.[20] So, I was—I was—with the New York group like a chaperon, and so that's where we met and then when we got married I moved here [Miami] because there was more flexibility to my work and I was also ready for a change. So that's how I ended up living in Miami.

SAJA: What role does Miami, and in a broader context, the city, play in your life and your writing? I'm thinking in terms of Toni Morrison's concept of "city limits village values." Does that play any role in your writing? For example, is there a village within the city in your writing and what would that village be? In other words, how do you conceptualize the "village" in your writing?

ED: Well, it's interesting for me writing about Miami. It's really the first time that I am writing about a place in which I live, and so when I was in New York that whole time it was mostly writing about Haiti. When I first moved down here that's when I wrote—well, the last book I wrote in New York was *The Dew Breaker*, so by the time I was touring for *The Dew Breaker*, by the time it was published, I was already living here and all the books that followed then stayed in New York, and really this most recent book, *Claire of the Sea Light*, is the first time that I'm writing fiction about a place in which I am located and it still feels strange to be able to just walk past the venues [*laughter*] that you've written about. That never happened to me before, so I do feel like I'm at a place with my relationship to this city where it has caught up with the writing about where I am. The book—the project—that I'm working on now which is a novel is about—set here, set in Miami fully. The people, the characters travel, but they live here and they pull from things that actually happened here. Because I think also, the city is a very fascinating city at the moment because at the height of gentrification it's a place that is so vulnerable to climate change and extreme weather, and now I've sort of waved through all the ups and downs of hurricane season for almost twenty years. So I finally feel like I can draw from what's happening around me.

SAJA: As a follow-up to your referencing gentrification, Miami has been nicknamed "The Magic City." The city recently approved what is referred to as the massive Magic City Innovation District plan, which they tout as a redevelopment project, but is basically the gentrification of Little Miami that will ultimately result in massive dispersals and displacements. I would like to hear your thoughts about Miami being nicknamed such, because Miami is not necessarily a place of wonder as the nickname intimates, but can be perceived, at times, as a place of drudgery, exploitation, and even death. And I'm thinking about your uncle, Joseph Dantica, and the novel you wrote, *Brother, I'm Dying*.

ED: It goes back to . . . I didn't answer the village part of your question. So when I did first move here in 2002, there was a sense of a village to it and what contributed to that was a sort of the insularity of communities. Where people kind of—There are certain neighborhoods and there is—it didn't seem like—at least—maybe ends of the wealthier enclaves where we might have more international set—but in Little Haiti people stayed together, and in Little Havana. So there are—it is a big city of villages in a way, right, because we have so much recent migration here that I think people do carry a little bit of their village with them. You know—there is Dave Barry, who is a local writer, who has a joke where he says everybody in Miami drives by the rules and laws of their own country [*laughter*] and so, and you get the sense that driving is not the only thing people do by the rules of their own country. And sometimes there has been friction too—where people—I mean, I think this city was one of the first places where people were given religious freedom, for example, for animal sacrifice. People went to court and they had to—If you wanted to have a vodou ceremony where you want to sacrifice a goat, people before could get arrested for that. Then there was a case of religious expression. So, the city has—in terms of that village feeling of villages within villages, which contradicts the whole, you know, too. There is always that contrast because it is an extremely stratified city. It is one of the most expensive cities in America, but it has some of the lowest salaries, and it's based on a tourism industry. So you have—there's a lot of exploitation certainly, based on that you have—I think South Florida has some of the largest numbers of millionaires and billionaires or something like that; at the same time, it has such extreme poverty. So, it's a city even when I moved here it reminded me of how people used to talk about New Orleans or after Hurricane Katrina. With New Orleans, it's the disaster that unraveled the barefaced inequality, but here the city has such a glitter. You know, if you—you can go on these tours and they tell us "This is where J Lo lives" and it costs like thirty million dollars. At the same time you have neglected schools and so, and nobody—I feel like very few people are even talking about climate change, right. But at the same time it is really ravaging our communities because the poor communities are more inland and that's where the magic city development comes in. They ["magic city" developers] are there because it's higher ground, and where they plopped that sign is around the community that used to be a trailer park, where they basically drove everyone out. So—I think it's very—cities like Miami, cities where you have the glitter, where you have so much wealth, you know, will always have a hidden face and behind that face are poor Black families, poor brown families, immigrant families. At the same time, it's very easily—because I think—because we don't have state income tax too here, so we have a lot of rich people who come as a way not to have to pay state and income taxes elsewhere. So we have all this wealth and all this poverty.

SAJA: Your uncle died here in Florida, and you ultimately chose this city to continue your life and begin your children's lives. Moreover, you write a lot about death and dying. I mentioned to you earlier that I just recently completed an article on your book, *The Art of Death: Writing the Final Story*, and some of your other work in which the theme of death pervades. The fact that you chose this space mired in controversy, that harbors horrible memories, to plant roots, does this decision reflect continuity, embodying a kind of "afterlife" of your uncle, or is it a contradiction?

ED: I see it as—I don't see it too much as a contradiction because part of the appeal of Miami to us, even to older generations of Haitians, but to me as well, is the proximity to Haiti. So, I know people who have actually done these crazy one-day trips to Haiti because it—you can be in Port-au-Prince faster than you can be in New York City from here, so I think one of the first ways the community grows is, of course, through the migration from Haiti, a lot of it by boat. But there's also this other thing, there are people, like my parents who initially thought, "We're going back, we're going back at some point, when the dictatorship is over. We're going back when things are better." And then a lot of these people at some point realized, "Oh, we're not going back"; so to them, this was the second best thing. The weather, the thing that I think—so that has created a kind of community feeling that feels sort of more intimate than say the New York Haitian community, which is older and bigger. I think because there is such a constant infusion of new people here that you just feel like you're part of a growing community, and there are actually—here, unlike certain other places . . . You know, in New York there are a lot of different places, but here you have the Little Haiti Cultural Center, you have certain restaurants that have become landmarks, and so there's something about it that I felt was appealing and eventually felt like the pace—But really honestly, the biggest draw of this place to me is its proximity to Haiti and also to the other islands which I've gotten a lot of chances to go to more since I've lived here.

SAJA: Is there a sense of an imagined community, in other words, the Florida imaginary and more specifically, Miami as the imaginary, the "magic city"? Moreover, you referenced proximity to Haiti that facilitates your return, going back home. As an immigrant myself that notion of home and the return, going back, is also on my mind, in my imagination. My own mother visits every year, and even while visiting, midway through she craves a return home. Is that imaginary always with us? Is that part of the Caribbean psyche?

ED: Actually, because I meet so many other people from other islands who have that same feeling. You know the weather is similar, and it's an approximation of home and at least you don't have to be freezing, but this week it's cold [*laughter*]. But, I think, I think it's probably colder where you were too. Yeah, I think it's—well, there are many approaches to the Florida, like the imaginary; it could be also the Caribbean imaginary. Some of us see it as something that floats with us—right . . .

SAJA: A floating homeland . . .

ED: . . . That we take with us, and then others who are just like—well, have kind of resigned themselves to finding places to reproduce some of that. Because when people are very honest, they always say, you know what—I don't—they might not have the patience anymore to deal with certain issues back home [*laughter*].

SAJA: I know. Especially social services . . .

ED: Exactly. So then, I think after a while people recognize that stranger in themselves, and so, they're like I'll reproduce as much as I can here. And in South Florida, whatever island you're from, you're not lacking, your people are here [*laughter*]. I think the majority—I think the largest groups are Jamaicans, Haitians, and Cubans—are the biggest numbers, but there is everybody from every other island.

SAJA: I find your concept of the stranger within intriguing, and it somehow speaks to that floating homeland that you talk directly about in *The Butterfly's Way: Voices from the Haitian Dyaspora in the United States* which communicates both familiarity and unfamiliarity, signaling belonging and unbelonging. So, then you're a stranger twice over, at home and abroad—an exilic existence which also lends itself to a nomadic experience. Is home then an imagined space or community, to echo Benedict Anderson, or is it a floating homeland, where it's intangible, never a specific location or locale?

ED: That's also the dilemma of migration, right, and I think that's why some generations, like my parents' generation, almost didn't even see it as their project. The project was for the next generation, for the kids to have a better education because at some point, I think, they just surrendered their dreams. It's like, because if you worked hard enough suddenly you realize that I'm doing it for the next generation. But what happens here, though, which I find very fascinating, is that I started—I wrote something about it that made me look at it closer. Because I once went to—I don't know if you remember this case, but you can look it up. There was a point during the Bush administration when Bush was having some domestic problems. He was being accused of something with judges and the next thing you know, they arrested six guys, who they accused of being terrorists, and there were six

Haitian guys who—and they were accused of being terrorists because they had a plant from the FBI and who was like "Do you want to pledge to ISIS?" Of course they promised them 50,000 [dollars]. So they did [pledge]. One of the guys—they had a trial, and all except one were deported because they had green cards. One of the sons—and this one boy, of one of the men—one night—was always trying to get into trouble because he was very close to his dad and because he wanted to be deported to be with his father. So, One night he went on the highway and got killed. So [the family] had a service for him and that service, and I went to the service—and then to watch that service, and to see the father streamed in with a camera, it was really sad. But at that service, because the boy was very young, and the father was young too, and so—they had two other generations that preceded them—and you see the very difference throughout, and then—but also this kind of—you realize the loneliness of these young people because like that father who was deported, he grew up in a house with a mom who had to work three jobs and she barely saw him. So out of that—we came here to give you this life, but we're not, we're working so hard to keep it for you—that a lot of young people slip into criminality. And so that to me is something that you see more and more—and a lot of the kids who are coming in recent years, and I'm sure in the coming years too, are traumatized because they've seen—they grew up in an era of seeing bodies in the streets, there are gang fights in Haiti. But they never—for a lot of them—have been, have seen Haiti either before the earthquake or like a really peaceful calm country; so they come here and then they are traumatized and their trauma is never addressed. And I think that the man who was deported was a part of that. So there are all these things too, like there's that kind of life in the city as well. Because you—and I've had, for example, in my area, women who get arrested because—they live in public housing, so they have to work; so they'll say to their neighbor—you can do that in Haiti—*siveye*, look out. But then someone calls and then, you know, so things like that—and then in this city, because people might get a false sense that it's like home because it kind of looks in some ways like home, but then there are all these different rules that they learn the hard way. Because at the same time, the kind of community that you're counting on and the kind of community that you assume it's okay to have, the state is telling you, "No, you can't, you can't leave a baby when you go to the market, and like the neighbor—*siveye*—you can't do that, you can't spank your kids, you can't." And so, there's also a lot of people because they don't understand the rules, their children go into foster care. And not to—added to all of that is the problem of status, of people being deported. What do you do with your kids? A lot of kids now, parents now tell them, "If I don't come home this is where you go, this is who you see," because it's a constant reality that they too will be packed on a bus because immigration enforcement is much more aggressive now.

SAJA: It has been said that your move to Miami has revitalized the neighborhood, as well as the literary and cultural scene.

ED: Oh really [*laughter*]?

SAJA: Yes. You are revered. What are your thoughts? Do you feel in some way that this is a huge responsibility, that expectations are high? I would like to quote Marvin DM-ijean of Minority Development and Empowerment: "She's becoming a national treasure for the Haitian community as a writer." "I'm sure the Haitians in New York are sad to see her leave, but we down here are very happy to have her. . . . she's one of our more recognizable faces and heroes."[21] In keeping with the designation of a national treasure, Kristin Tillotson adds: "She's Haiti's best known cultural export in the United States."[22] Please share your thoughts.

ED: I mean—you know it's funny—what I said last night or I think the night before [referring to her lecture at the University of Miami] about my daughter watching the [interview] and goes: "That's the other Edwidge" [*laughter*].[23]

SAJA: So is this the other Edwidge? Will the real Edwidge step forward [*laughter*]?

ED: I think that stuff, it's very nice and generous, but you can't carry that around every day, right. Because I feel like for me, it's always—and maybe that why I've been able to—it has been twenty-five years now and I feel very grateful that I've been able to maintain because it's always for me about the work; that's *the* most important thing, it's the work. And I remember hearing Toni Morrison, God bless her. She had this interview where she says, you know when she was an editor, she was a novelist, and she had these two boys and she said at some point, she had this big list and she looked at the list and she's like, "What is the thing here that only I can do?" Right, and one was, "raise my kids," and the other "write my books, and I will add some service to that." Also—add service as much as you can. If you just put that crown on, it makes it hard to bend over and do the work [*laughter*]. I love, I feel privileged that I get to do something I love so much and I feel like you have to kind of come to it with humility every single time. It's like Maya Angelou says, "You're always starting over." So, you kind of need to be light, you need to be clear, and just like—those things [referencing praises and compliments] are very nice, but you can't come to the page with them.

SAJA: I think your humility has indeed allowed you to sustain. You're one of the most generous, unassuming, and approachable persons, and you've actually developed a reputation of being very supportive of and championing other writers. Having met you years ago as a student, one of the things that remained with me was your grace and humility.[24]

ED: Thank you.

SAJA: There's a messianic aura around you, where you're envisioned, sort of, like the chosen one [*laughter*]. You're coronated here in Little Haiti. I think it is fair to draw a parallel between you and Zora Neale Hurston.

ED: I'll take that because I love her so much [*laughter*]. She's a Floridian.

SAJA: Yes, I know, she's one of your favorite writers who has influenced you tremendously, and you referenced her in your recent memoir, *The Art of Death: Writing the Final Story*. You referenced [Hurston's] mother and your mother in a parallel story. Is there a reason for this parallel? And there are also many parallels between you and Hurston.

ED: I had read *Dust Tracks on the Road* a long time. And talk about a Florida writer! I remember when I first moved down here I so wanted to go where her grave was, even though it was—with the Alice Walker essay—but I never managed to find it. But I would go almost every year to the festival they have for her in Eatonville, Florida, and they often had it around my birthday. So they stopped having it, but I think they are restarting it. But I had always— Well, my attachment to her goes a long way. Because I read her in high school. I read *Their Eyes Were Watching God*, and it felt—because I was new to America, I was still four years in, and reading in Advanced Placement—when you're in high school. I had so much trouble understanding other texts. But I remember reading that; initially, when you open it, it's intimidating; I thought, "Oh, I'll have to sign it out [at the library]." But it felt like creole to me; I feel like I really get this. And then I went to Barnard where she went. She was the first Black woman to go to Barnard, so her face was everywhere, and there were often these very interesting pictures, so I literally felt like she was following me; now I'm following her to Florida [*laughter*].

SAJA: Shadowing, right—

ED: The way she writes! And it's interesting when you reread things with your own parallel experience. because I remember reading that autobiography[25] and like everybody—and people make you obsess with the inconsistencies: "Oh, she's not really that age . . . She's thirty years younger." I'm like, "Good for her. Some people would have given up." So, but—when you read it in the classroom, you get all that extra information. When I read it after my mother died, the mother part was what stuck with me, and then I realized that I had missed how much she carried this guilt around of not doing for her mother what the mother said. And then she said, "She told me not to let them turn the bed." I was so blown away by the rituals, "that you face the sun," like certain things you do for the dying, and that she was trying to document in

her mother's case. So reading it through that veil like a motherless daughter—
I just read that whole thing very differently and I think I was clinging to, even
the story of her birth, you know, I was seeing now through her relationship
with her mother and all the trouble she went through after her mother died.
She suffered, but which led her to go on the road. And—so that's—it was to
me—I was completely reading it now almost like these kinds of fairy tales
where the child suffers after the mother dies, except she takes onto the road
and becomes who she is because of that loss, in part. That was a rereading for
me through that lens, and I think—and that's where that whole book, just like
the process of writing it, was a search for comfort. And one of the ways that
I comfort myself after some big tragedy, or some problem, is through either
reading or writing. And so, you know, I started clinging to that version of
her life. I don't think her mother gets a lot of say or attention. She gets *Jump
at the Sun*, which is usually people's entry into her mother. And [Hurston] is
such an unsentimental woman [*laughter*]. I can imagine her travelling with
that gun. You know, she's like—I can't wait to see her make a movie. And she's
still producing. I have to get her story collection [*Hitting a Straight Lick with
a Crooked Stick*].[26] I'm glad they did that bio[27] because I remember at some
point—because I loved going to the festival, I remember going to the festival.
I'd met someone—

SAJA: And here is the afterlife at work. What I wrote about your recent
work is the afterlife, and here she continues to produce in the afterlife, producing posthumously.

ED: I was always surprised that—I was always surprised because I remember even in a book they did about her, with letters and documents—it's a book
for kids, but you can open things, and I remember once looking at some of
the archival things that were listed and it seemed like she had a lot of unpublished work. So, it always confused me why that stuff wasn't published. So it's
wonderful to see she has some plays that were never produced or published;
so maybe those are coming next because of *Barracoon*, that did so well, that
now you have the story collection. And, yeah—

SAJA: I'm thinking about the afterlife in relation to your own mother, her
instruction to you, as she grappled with her impending death, about not wearing open-toed shoes to her funeral. This intimate moment between mother
and daughter (imitative of the exchange Hurston had with her mother) is quite
intriguing. She is giving instruction about [funeral] rites from beyond the grave.

ED: She was very much like that; she was telling my brother, "Go to this
place and get this suit" [*laughter*]. She was very—I think that's—it's what we
all like to do, parenting. Parenting never ends, whether it's in your head—or

because often you think—and even people say, "As my mother would say." That's the thing that was planted in you.

SAJA: Yes, there is continuity or embodiment. You're experiencing the pain vicariously when reading your work. Many of the issues resonated with my own childhood and growing up with my mother's instructions. I return to the mother-daughter relationship often. I want to return to Hurston a bit. I'm curious—and you did say that your books are not Florida books, per se, but I was thinking about *Brother, I'm Dying* as sort of a Florida book.

ED: Oh that's true. You're right, you're right. You're right. Yeah.

SAJA: Even though you mapped the two spaces where you lived, New York and Florida, Florida is central to the narrative.

ED: You're so right. That book is the bridge. That's all right. Yeah! You're so right. Yes.

SAJA: Exactly, bridging life and death. I see it as an interesting correlation. I'm thinking about *Brother, I'm Dying* as a Florida novel that parallels or reso-nates with *Their Eyes Were Watching God*. So along these lines, would you say that your Krome Detention Center is Hurston's marsh?

ED: Hmm. Yes, it could—like a parallel. Yeah, yeah! But I feel like Hurston had so many marshes. She didn't just have one [*laughter*]. It's almost— if somebody is going through a hard time and I talk about it, my mother would say this is their *kalvé*, their Calvary. I feel like she had so many, but— and then she overcame. But even in—one of the things that I thought about her writing about Haiti—I thought when I came across that writing, and I know a lot of people contested some of it because they didn't—but I keep—I always feel grateful that she was there. I feel like that brings us even closer. She knew my home.

SAJA: You embody—something about your writing makes you feel that you're living the experience. My students have this visceral and knowing response to your texts. For example, *Breath, Eyes, Memory* is haunting, but there is something attractive, compelling about the haunting.

ED: Thank you. Thank you. I mean aside from kind of, wanting to, always really wanting to live with myself, not living the horror of it, but always like really, I have to see it before I can write it. And really wanting to and trying to write things that I felt like compelled to. And so if you're haunted, I'm even more happy and compelled to write, which is why I—[*laughter*].

SAJA: You keep coming back for more and more [*laughter*].

ED: It's like the longest exorcism ever [*laughter*]!

SAJA: The last piece I wrote was so much fun; it was cathartic, and it was all about death. In that piece, I categorized some of your work as "death narratives."[28]

ED: But I think—I think also part of that is having had the experience of wakes, and the closest I think—I've read—I read once, I can never forget—remember the title, but I read it again when I was writing one of the stories in *Everything Inside*,[29] is an Irish wake. Right! And so, I feel, the closest thing I've seen to a Haitian wake is an Irish wake. Because—the contrast, and to grow up—now it has calmed down; it's a little more complicated. But the wakes used to be this huge party the night before the funeral, and as a kid you're just completely overwhelmed by that [*laughter*]—Like "What's going on?" [*laughter*] And the next day, everybody is on the ground, throwing themselves about and they're distraught. But the night before—it's usually not the immediate mother-father person, but the community comes together in joy. And so, I just, for me, the two [revelry and grief] were inexplicably linked. And then when I got older, I just realized, "Oh, you can only feel that—you can feel that at church because people think 'we'll see each other again.' Or you can feel that in this other space where you feel like there is some continuity." Because if you—I always felt, even in my very young mind, you couldn't have this level of joy if you thought this was completely over. And it was almost like the joy was part of the sendoff for that person, it's your last opportunity to celebrate them. And so for me that's the thing, and you know, people are like "Ah, you talk about death all the time." But it's just—that is the part of it that I felt like, I never had the luxury—maybe because of where I grew up in that particular neighborhood. I never had the luxury of thinking I'm never gonna die. But it was always, "Oh, but if I die, there's gonna be this big party" [*laughter*].

SAJA: They'll celebrate you. Fortunately, you're celebrated in life now.

ED: So, and then, so that was the thing—it just didn't—the thing that people in my family were always most worried about was suffering. "I don't want to suffer." But because—also because my uncle was a minister it was like every minister—and I always used to think that every minister had three sermons, the Good Samaritan.

SAJA: I saw [the fear of suffering] in your depiction of your mother's death. The graphic details of your mother's experience of dying. It was haunting and difficult to read, but yet there's that—the hunger to know. It was difficult to read the scene chronicling her experience with the cancer treatment, reminiscent of Lorde's experience in *The Cancer Journals*.

ED: I realized my mom always—even when I was writing *Brother, I'm Dying*, she said, "Don't. Take me out of it." She didn't want to be in, and in a way it's funny because it kind of helped in narrowing the structure because it became about two brothers. But at the end, I think my mother, at the end, really wanted to be seen. And even when she was saying, "Give the doctors your book," you know, she wanted to be known in her fullness.

SAJA: She was celebrating you. Advising you to give the doctors your book; in essence, acknowledging, I'm proud of my daughter who is continuing a legacy.

ED: But part of it—and I saw it as an extension of, it was kind of celebrating me, but it was more like, "I made that."

SAJA: That's my production. She's an artist in her own right.

ED: I think it was very much connected. Because when you're—I realized this with my mother and my father. You really—that hypervulnerability— you're so reduced, and so you're physically reduced, you're in pain, maybe— and at the same time, my mom was always trying to protect me from her [pain]. I never could gauge her level of pain because I think she didn't want me to be in pain watching her in pain. So, I think, part of that too—at the end, I think she wanted to be seen in her fullness, and I think when you're that sick you feel—you know that there are big chunks of you slipping away, and so because of that, then you want to reclaim certain things, you want people to know who you are.

SAJA: Yeah! That you existed; that you lived!

ED: And I feel she at that point, she was really—then I would sit by her because there are—sitting for long hours at the bedside of someone who's sick and you're waiting for them to wake up—And that was the first time she said, "Don't write about me." She didn't even say "Don't take my picture." We took her picture. I was always taking pictures of her feet, like I said in [*The Art of Death: Writing the Final Story*]. But she didn't really mind us, unlike my dad, at the end, who said "Don't take my picture," because he was really skinny. My mom was too. But I think she wanted to be seen.

SAJA: I also thought it was remarkable her making peace in her final moments. Her articulating the inevitability of death, that we all have to die someday.

ED: But—she was always like—I was telling—someone we know passed away recently, and one of my brothers said, "Oh, I wonder what mom would say?" And I said, "I know exactly what she would say." She was like: "Well, them today, me tomorrow" [*laughter*]. That was always her thing. She was never really sentimental about it [*laughter*].

SAJA: It's inevitable, right, why fight the inevitable.

One of the things—going back to your mom. There's a Haitian creole expression, *pye poudre*, which is translated as travel dust and which I juxtapose with Hurston's travel dust. In *The Art of Death*, you write: "My mother's travel dust took her from Port-au-Prince to Brooklyn" [166]. Likewise, Hurston's travel dust afforded her travels from Eatonville to New York to Haiti. In like manner, your travel dust took you from Port-au-Prince to Brooklyn and now here [Miami]. Can you conceptualize your travel dust? Specifically, have your uncle's death [in Florida] and your mother's [in New York) reactivated your travel dust? And how so?

ED: My travel dust is limited because I'm strapped by two kids [*laughter*]. I'm kind of following their travel dust—it's kind of—you surrender to the next generation. But—yeah—what I do see, it's—I have so much admiration for that generation of my family. Imagine in your thirties you wake up and you're just going somewhere; I never know, you know, what's gonna happen. So there was, I think, I think, my mom, my mom definitely had travel dust, in the sense [that] she went on every trip with me that I invited her to. We went to Japan. We went to all the different islands on book tours. She—we did a lot of travelling together, which I'm really happy about. My father was—we tried one trip, and when he got there he wanted to go home [*laughter*]. My dad was this person who—he wanted to go somewhere to say he'd been, and then go back to his life. My mom was—I remember her on the fast train in Tokyo. She just loved to travel, she loved to travel! So we went on a lot of trips together. And she did—at the same time, she did a cruise every year with her church lady friends. And so, often she's like "I'm coming to Fort Lauderdale," so she loved being away. And I think she felt like it was her reward after, and it was wonderful to see her have that pleasure. So, actually that made me—I used to think how wonderful if my girls would want to travel with me on the space ship that's coming. "Oh, maybe they'll want to go to Mars with me, you know" [*laughter*]. And so that—and she was wonderful company. I remember I would introduce her at all my events. So, that I felt like that was something—but she didn't travel for fun here [migrating to America]. She came to work. And we never, so when I was a kid, we never had vacations [because] we couldn't afford it; so as kids—so, we did one, two bus trips with our church, one to Washington, DC, and one to Lake George in New York. There were two days, two Saturdays in the whole summer and the rest of the time, we were home. And so, so vacations for her—travel wasn't even an option.

SAJA: Is there a ghost/shadowing of sorts that propels you? You mentioned Hurston—

ED: I don't call it a ghost. I feel like it's, I do always feel like I'm reaching for something beyond my reach, and that's an important feeling to have. I think there's always something to unravel, but I do like—but there are moments when I feel whether it's true or not, there is a sense of—I think in all kinds of creativity that—of course—it is beyond what we all see. There's something else coming through. Because I remembered, and I write about it in the book. I remembered when my mother was dying, I was hearing this wailing person outside—you know—I described in the book, and at that moment, whatever it was, just feeling the sense of like—as C. S. Lewis says in *A Grief Observed*, of like a veil being pierced. Right, and it's just like—and I think art and spiritually just kind of put us closer to that veil because we're used to—we have the practice of observation. We have the practice of—there's a part of you that's sort of maybe more open. And so, yes, I feel sometimes like—because sometimes I reread certain things, and I'd say, "But where did that come from?" I do think part of it is being an artist, being a vessel in many ways, and there are things that, not to make it sound too mysterious, come true.

SAJA: Even though you write about death. In the article I am writing, I'm developing a theory of necro-transcendence. Listening to you speak now, I'm convinced there's an afterlife in all of your writing. Death is not the end.

ED: Oh yeah! I think it's because too—maybe it's— Spirituality is always connected to ancestry for us as Haitians because often, you know—people don't say it as much anymore—but people would say so and so if they die, and we have all these—several expressions. So if someone is *lòt bò dlo*, on the other side of the water, it means they've migrated or they died, or like la Guinea, which is like Guinea (referring to the country)—

SAJA: Like Guinea, where Martine travels after death in *Breath, Eyes, Memory*.

ED: Exactly. So, it sounds like a physical—it sounds like Guinea in Africa, so it is like a physical space. So there is always that sense of it. I think it is an overall diasporic space, more so with—you surrender to the air, in honor of the idea of flight and I think that overall contributed a lot to our survival, because otherwise, I think a lot of us would have given up, and our ancestors would have given up if we thought this was all there is—and whatever your next thing is, your descendance or your transcendence. But this is not the end.

SAJA: I thought about necro-transcendence in relation to doubling and repeating, continuity. And I'm rereferring here specifically to *Untwine*, the twins, Giselle and her sister, Isabelle, the one who passed away.

ED: Yeah, yeah!

SAJA: As an aside, the last name, Boyer [referring to *Untwine*], is this an autobiographical or semi-autobiographical reference [*laughter*]?

ED: I used to have a list [*laughter*]. The other day one of my nieces—because I have twin nieces who are the youngest—and the other day, their mother said: "Oh, you stopped doing that thing where you use our names," because she wants me to use the girls' names. And I just haven't had a chance. Boyer, I like because it—my husband's people always ask if he's a descendent of the Boyer who gave away money to the French and got into problem with the Dominicans. He's like, "I don't know" [*laughter*]. For some reason, I met a lot of African American Boyers too. There's an actual Peter Boyer who is a white man. So—and I actually used Boyer again in *Everything Inside*. So I'm like, "Hey, I like it!" I didn't take it on for myself, but it's not a bad name.

SAJA: I really appreciate you taking the time to meet with me. Your work is very accessible and a pleasure to read; my students share a similar sentiment as they love reading you as much as I do. Please stay as humble as you are! Thanks again! Highly appreciated!

Notes

The title of this essay is an appropriation of the first line, "What is Africa to me," of Countee Cullen's famous poem, "Heritage." Caryl Phillips succinctly articulates that Cullen and fellow African American artists were "dreaming of Africa, of repairing the rupture in their personal and social history that had been caused by the institution of slavery" (10). Phillips reiterates that this history, in large part, was imagined. Despite Edwidge Danticat's ambivalent relationship with Florida—some of her personal encounters with the city of Miami position Florida as a "place of make-believe," to echo Phillips, where the unthinkable happens, especially to those most vulnerable—it is "a crucial building block in [her] identity" (Phillips, 11). Fittingly, in her essay "The Soul of Little Haiti," imitative of Cullen's "Heritage," Danticat aptly delineates what is Little Haiti/Florida to her and Haitian and African Americans in general.

1. The well-established and -populated Haitian neighborhood of the Edison/Little River section of Miami has earned the nickname Little Haiti.

2. In her recent short story collection *Everything Inside*, Danticat refers to Thomas, the male protagonist of "The Gift," as "double dyaspora from both Park Slope, USA, and Pacot, Haiti" (84).

3. Quoted in Alva James-Johnson, "A Little Closer to Home," *South Florida Sentinel-Sun* May 7, 2003. https://www.sun-sentinel.com/news/fl-xpm-2003-05-07-0305060402-story.html. Accessed October 4, 2020. Founded in 1996, Minority Development and Empowerment, Inc. is an organization that promotes a legacy of empowerment to Caribbean peoples and other minority groups. See https://www.handsonbroward.org/organization/001A000000mmjkPIAQ.

4. Edwidge Danticat, "The Soul of Little Haiti." https://www.miamiherald.com/news/local/community/miami-dade/downtown-miami/article235553577.html. Written September 29, 2019, at 4:00 a.m., Danticat provides painstaking details about "the soul" of Little Haiti in the eponymous essay, "The Soul of Little Haiti."

5. Danticat, "The Soul of Little Haiti."

6. The "One Book One U Program" was established to aid in the exploration of issues of diversity and inclusion through the reading of a selected text by the university community followed by a signature event with the author of the selected text. Danticat read from her acclaimed novel, *Brother, I'm Dying*. I attended this phenomenal event and had the good fortune and pleasure to sit down and chat with Danticat two days later on October 1, 2020.

7. Uncoincidentally, this conversation took place at this community bookstore, Books & Books, arguably a testament to Danticat's strong sense of community, her community-oriented mindset.

8. Located in Miami, Florida, the Florida Immigrant Advocacy Center (FIAC), founded in 1996, provides legal representation for immigrants, aims to influence policy decisions, and challenges patterns and practices of abuse. See https://community-wealth.org/content/florida-immigrant-advocacy-center.

9. Here I am referring to both the state of Florida and the nation-state, the United States that has a long troubled history with Haiti, including its occupation of Haiti from 1915–34.

10. While this discourse focuses primarily on Little Haiti, the Haitian diaspora as a whole is referred to as the 11th department.

11. Danticat, "The Soul of Little Haiti."

12. I read the reverse journeys accomplished by Hurston and Danticat as exemplary of shadowing: following in each other's footsteps and leaving footprints. Shadowing is prevalent as their paths converge in other instances. For example, they both attended Barnard College in New York, Hurston in 1925 and Danticat, decades later, in 1986. Danticat also calls attention to Hurston's use of Black vernacular speech and rituals that impress upon her and function as a marker of shared identity in her own writing and life; she also draws a parallel with Hurston's relationship with her mother and her own relationship with her mother, focusing on rituals, their dying and eventual deaths. For a more detailed account, see *The Art of Death: Writing the Final Story* (New York: Graywolf Press, 2017). Other parallels between Hurston and Danticat are Hurston's father, similar to Danticat's surrogate father; Joseph Dantica, who raised her until she joined her parents in New York, was a Baptist minister. Little Miami, a Black immigrant enclave, is exemplary of Eatonville, one of the first self-governing all-Black municipalities in the United States. Like the Haitian population that wrestles with state violence and questions of citizenship, Eatonville witnessed a rollback of hard-won legal and citizenship rights for African Americans, an increase in state and state-sanctioned violence against Black citizens, and flourishing of negative images of Black people in popular culture.

13. Danticat reminds us: "Little Haiti is also in the street names and murals celebrating our, really, the world's heroes. The soul of Little Haiti lives within all of us. It lives in you." Danticat, "The Soul of Little Haiti."

Hurston's fascination with Haitian vodou culminated in her travelling to collect folklore and familiarize herself with the practice of vodou (*Dust Tracks on a Road*, 168–69). Hurston's trip to Haiti and Jamaica in 1936 and 1937 was funded by a Guggenheim Fellowship to conduct research on folk and religious practices in the region. While there, Hurston completed her most famous novel, *Their Eyes Were Watching God*.

14. Incidentally, Hurston titled a chapter in her autobiography, *Dust Tracks*, "Wandering."

15. While Hurston's travel dust finds her journeying from Florida to Haiti, Danticat's travels take her from Haiti to Florida.

16. I adopted and adapted this phrase from Hurston. In *Dust Tracks*, Hurston expresses that she harbors "no race prejudice of any kind; rather [her] kinfolks, and [her] 'skinfolks' are dearly loved" (231).

17. Here Danticat refers to the film *Jump at the Sun*, as a revivalist celebration of Hurston's life. We further bear witness to Hurston's afterlife at play, as her out-of-print books became available after her death. As Danticat reminds us: "New generations discover the legacy of Zora Neale Hurston . . . the woman who had consistently been on the wrong side of history is now embraced by the world as a leading figure in American literature" (*Jump at the Sun*).

18. This conversation with Danticat took place the day after I attended her lecture, "One Book, One U: Keynote with Edwidge Danticat" on February 27, 2020, at the Kislak Center at the University of Miami's Center for Humanities. Danticat, fittingly opened her lecture discussing the "boat people," adding that although her uncle, Joseph Dantica, was "not one of the boat people per se, he came legally to the United States on a visitor's visa," he still suffered a similar fate of those escaping terror, only to be confronted with state terror. She also brilliantly articulates that "families are made and unmade by immigration and separation."

19. Florida has the highest population of Haitian immigrants, followed by New York.

20. The trip was designed as a recruiting tool. Danticat observes: "[it] had been beautifully and ambitiously named: *Vakans pou yon demen miyò*: Vacation for a better tomorrow" ("For Love and for Life," unpublished).

21. Alva James-Johnson, "A Little Closer to Home," *South Florida Sun-Sentinel*, May 7, 2003. https://www.sun-sentinel.com/news/fl-xpm-2003-05-07-0305060402-story.html.

22. Kristin Tillotson, "Edwidge Danticat: Daughter of Haiti," *Star Tribune*, October 17, 2013. Accessed December 20, 2020. http://www.startribune.com/edwidge-danticat-daughter-of-haiti/222606581/?refresh=true.

23. Here, Danticat refers to the episode on *60 Minutes* about her uncle Joseph Dantica's death. Brought to tears while watching the episode with her daughter, who also started to cry, Danticat questioned why she was crying and she responded: "Because the other Edwidge—the one on the screen—is crying." She mistakenly thought that the Edwidge on the screen and the "real" Edwidge were different individuals. "Detention in America," *60 Minutes*, CBS, May 25, 2008. https://www.youtube.com/watch?v=hEmjfbZZqIc.

24. I had met Edwidge a few months earlier, but I was reintroduced to her by Maryse Condé at an event at Columbia University, where Condé was being honored and where she taught for several years and is now professor emerita. At this juncture in our conversation, Danticat veered off topic to inquire about Condé, commenting on the rapid pace at which Condé continues to publish, adding that she had just finished reading Condé's novel, *The Wondrous and Tragic Life of Ivan and Ivana*.

25. Danticat refers here to Hurston's memoir, *Dust Tracks on a Road*.

26. This new collection, *Hitting a Straight Lick with a Crooked Stick*, which consists of thirty-one of Hurston's short stories, eight of which are newly recovered, was published posthumously in January 2020.

27. The biography referenced here is Valerie Boyd's *Wrapped in Rainbow: The Life of Zora Neale Hurston*.

28. Here I am referencing my forthcoming article, "Losing Your (M)Other: Edwidge Danticat's Narratives of Un/Belonging and Un/Dying."

29. *Everything Inside* is Danticat's 2019 collection of stories.

CHAPTER TWELVE

Black and Blue in Florida

Moonlight's Poetics of Space and Identity

Delia Malia Konzett

With its unique racial and culturally diverse settler history, Florida stands out as a highly productive region for the articulation of a subaltern America.[1] A border peninsula, the state has a rich transnational and migration history, involving both US southern migration of former slaves and Black offshore migration from the West Indies, where slavery had been abolished in the 1830s. Whether we think of its various indigenous populations (particularly the Seminoles) or its various hybrid Latin American and Latin Caribbean cultures (particularly its more recent Cuban and Afro-Cuban influx), Florida can be characterized as a culturally diverse space in constant flux. For writers and filmmakers, Florida similarly evokes fantasies of difference such as the Black township of Eatonville captured in the writings of Zora Neale Hurston; its tourist and imaginary appeal to writers such as Ernest Hemingway or Wallace Stevens, or films including *Key Largo* (1948), *Some Like It Hot* (1960), *Midnight Cowboy* (1969), *Body Heat* (1980), and *Scarface* (1983). Miami's twenty-first-century demographics—the city's nickname is "the capital of Latin America"—has even led to the paradoxical phenomenon of reverse acculturation, requiring white Anglo settlers to assimilate to immigrant and nonwhite cultural influences rather than imposing national norms. Alejandro Portes and Ariel C. Armony describe Miami's "amazing transition from a place ruled by a tight Southern-style elite to one where former exiles and their offspring gained the upper hand to one where that hegemony had to cede place because of the ceaseless arrival of capital and people from other countries and continents."[2]

The African American and Black Bahamian community contributed significantly to the historical formation of Miami and Southern Florida, helping to incorporate the city of Miami and build the railroad crucial for the region's economic development.[3] Unfortunately, its relevance has since been eclipsed by Jim Crow segregation and post–civil rights migration. The constant refugee flows made up of Cuban and other Caribbean, Latin American, and global immigrants, consisting mostly of educated elites fleeing political oppression, contributed to the region's buildup of significant foreign global power and financial capital.[4] Nevertheless, the recent denationalization of Miami and Southern Florida makes it a quasi–foreign border territory within the United States and also presents a new opportunity for African Americans trapped for decades in entrenched local practices of geographic and socioeconomic segregation informed by the legacy of US slavery and systemic racism.

A Region in Flux: Black Florida, *Moonlight,* and Its New Global Context

Barry Jenkins's *Moonlight* and its depiction of Miami's Black neighborhood Liberty City articulates foremost a new global context of denationalization and deterritorialization. Also known as "Model City," Liberty City was built during the Great Depression in response to the poor urban housing conditions in Miami's neighborhood of Overtown. Barry Jenkins and screenwriter Tarell Alvin McCraney, having both grown up in the housing projects of Liberty City, draw on this experience in a unique and fresh approach. In *Moonlight*'s alternate world, the Black inner-city experience, often narrowly relegated to US national narratives of racial confinement, underdevelopment, and ghettoization, emerges in a wider global context, generating a rich global symbolic currency of Blackness. The cultural disconnect associated with urban Black youth hence becomes open to new transnational communicative lines, much like the global vernaculars of Black music—jazz, blues, R&B, and hip hop. Similarly, Jenkins and McCraney depict their imagined Florida with a blend of social realism and a poetic perspective on identity, creating a coming-of-age narrative in the intersectional world of queer inner-city Blackness. *Moonlight* not only changes the perception of its depicted location via a global focus on Black identity and culture but inflects it additionally with an augmented representation of its frequently omitted gender and sexual politics, particularly its homophobia.

This essay explores the setting of Florida as a global and diverse space in the film *Moonlight* and its evocative poetics or aesthetics of identity, one distinct from a more sharply defined politics of identity. My discussion focuses on forms of representation that break with film conventions of realism, advancing instead a different and alternate aesthetics of location and identity. The film's defamiliarized mise-en-scène, which includes set design, location, costume, acting, lighting, and certain aspects of cinematography and editing, reimagines the mediation of conflicting racial, social, gender, and sexual identities in the symbolically rich landscape of Florida. As will be shown in close readings of significant scenes, the film's blend of codes of setting, character, and action paints a complex portrait of a gay Black Florida with radically new social and cultural affiliations. A further consideration of the trauma of natal alienation deriving from the legacy of slavery leads us to a better understanding of the main protagonist's dissociation from his community. The ensuing journey of self-discovery involves a newly acquired sense of dwelling and what it means to inhabit a location and a world. The film casts this quest for identity in terms of a queer utopia, one in which being Black is intersected with that of being gay. The locations of Miami and Florida are crucial for the protagonist's quest and transformation, as they implicitly support him on his journey in the form of a moral or guiding landscape.

Breaking with American Realism: From Local Ghetto to Global Lifeworld

The film's vision, while informed by the director's and playwright's local background as former residents of Liberty City's housing projects, radically breaks with the US ghetto genre or hood film to which it seems superficially indebted. This genre, prevalent in the 1990s, delivered many of the stereotypical images that document life in the Black inner city. "Hood films," according to Paula Massood, "narrate the coming-of-age of a young male protagonist and the difficulties of such an undertaking in the dystopian environment of the inner city."[5] *Moonlight*'s storyline similarly depicts a young Black male eventually turning to the street crime that surrounds his upbringing. However, the film depicts this growth trajectory with ruptures and breaks, seen particularly in the film's three chapters and its elliptical narration.[6] In addition, the film adds unconventional elements such as a gay melodrama and a pervasive quiet ambience that stands in contrast to the vocality of the ghetto genre. The soundtrack similarly breaks with the loudly scored hip hop music of ghetto films and consists mostly of a mix of classical scoring and retro R&B songs. Hip hop, when used, is remixed in a Southern style known as "chopped and screwed" which, according to Barry Jenkins, slows down the hypermasculine bpm (beats per minute) rhythm to highlight its lyric poetry and pain.[7]

Traditional US ghetto drama predictably delivers what cultural anthropologist Oscar Lewis identifies as the seemingly inevitable replication of a "subculture of poverty" in his studies of a variety of global slum environments.[8]

Poverty, Lewis argues, has to be distinguished from a "culture of poverty" that is marked by chronic underemployment, dysfunctional family structures, lack of communal cohesiveness, provincial entrapment and disconnectedness, and a general sense of despair. Some of the markers of this cultural poverty, according to Lewis, are a setting of "cash economy" and a "persistently high rate of unemployment and underemployment at low wages" with society failing "to provide social, political, and economic organization . . . for the low-income population."⁹ Moreover, "the dominant class . . . stresses the possibility of upward mobility and explains low economic status as the result of individual personal inadequacy or inferiority."¹⁰ The culture of poverty, says Lewis, "represents an effort to cope with feelings of hopelessness and despair that arise from the realization by the members of marginalized communities . . . [and] the improbability of their achieving success in terms of the prevailing values and goals."¹¹

While not openly siding with any sociological position, *Moonlight* does indeed address the existential despair and communicative disconnect of the urban ghetto. As the film's cinematographer James Laxton explains: "*Moonlight* is not necessarily a realist movie by any stretch of the imagination. . . . It's sort of the delicate balance of providing images that allow an audience to feel like they're watching a real experience. But presenting it in maybe a way that's providing a larger lens to look through."¹² At the same time, it no longer exclusively focuses on specific markers from the hood genre such as excessive displays of Black-on-Black violence, ongoing white police intervention, and a pervasive sense of criminality. Elements of the genre identified by Massood as its "nihilistic strain,"¹³ its "image of the contemporary city overrun with poverty, violence, and drugs,"¹⁴ and its "entrapment, violence, and a concern with the role of space and time in the lives of young black men,"¹⁵ are still residually present in *Moonlight* but are significantly estranged and redirected in its visual message.

The ghetto genre's gritty docudrama had pretty much run its course in the early 2000s and peaked with the TV series and police procedural *The Wire* (2002–8) and its voyeuristic excursions into the Black inner city of Baltimore. While *Moonlight*'s storyline does not entirely avoid social commentary, the filmmakers realized that its narration needs to be complicated in order to carry a much wider trans-local and transnational significance. Spike Lee's *Do the Right Thing* (1989) and its nonrealist Brechtian elements of estrangement offers an early example of how the inner-city story can be told differently. Additionally, Jenkins and his cinematographer James Laxton were intrigued by global arthouse filmmakers Claire Denis (*Beau Travail*, 1999), Wong Kar-wai (*In the Mood for Love*, 2000; *Happy Together*, 1997) and Hou Hsiao-Hsien

(*Three Times*, 2005), all of whom produced important local films set in Djibouti, Hong Kong, Buenos Aires, and Taipei, respectively.[16] These films only minimally document their depressed social environments and provide no grand aerial shots or city vistas, focusing instead on an aesthetics of the everyday and unremarkable found in overlooked sets and locations, lighting, color, and mundane interactions.

Apart from its obvious violations of Hollywood formulas, such as presenting an all-Black a gay melodrama, *Moonlight* gives close attention to less-than-spectacular sets in favor of the marginal and peripheral. The French New Wave film movement, particularly François Truffaut's *400 Blows* (1959), has shown that peripheral and unremarkable environments of Paris imbued with the focal perspective of a child can challenge codes of social order and socialization reproduced in mainstream films in creative and unexpected ways. In similar spirit, *Moonlight* reverses the structure of arthouse and the ghetto film. In the words of the director Jenkins, it is not a question of enhancing the arthouse film with hood elements, but rather its opposite, what Jenkins describes as "bringing art house to the hood."[17] This new and different presentation of a locale formerly depicted in gritty documentary or over-the-top blaxploitation style produces the film's original defamiliarization of the Black inner city with its accompanying problems of urban housing, depressed neighborhoods, and systemic racism that have become the routine terrain of sociological fascination, observation, and speculation. One such defamiliarized code concerns the nature of dwelling and what it means to inhabit a location.

Natal Alienation versus Proper Dwelling

Reading Martin Heidegger's essay "Building, Dwelling, and Thinking" (1951) against the grain of its inbuilt white monolithic claims, one discerns an unorthodox approach to the problem of postwar housing shortages. Reversing cause and effect, Heidegger states that "the proper plight of dwelling does not lie merely in a lack of houses."[18] Rather, "the proper plight of dwelling lies in this, that mortals ever search anew for the essence of dwelling, that they must ever learn to dwell."[19] By redefining the question of housing from one of structural scarcity into one of existential dimension, "learning to dwell," Heidegger urges that all design and architecture address the holistic existential needs of a community first and not merely provide for quick and practical housing solutions: "Building and thinking are, each in his own way, inescapable for dwelling."[20] The implicit ecological concept of dwelling would also point in the direction of Lewis's concept of the culture of poverty characterized by despair that stands in need of existential redemption. Jenkins's

Moonlight similarly explores the existential homelessness of his main protagonist in a way that requires a new reflective perspective of learning to live
authentically as a gay Black male rather than hiding behind heteronormative façades of masculinity and power. In order to do so, Little/Chiron/Black
requires the help of his community to reestablish his legitimate residency in
Liberty City.

The film opens with a contrasting shot pattern introducing the main protagonists Juan (Mahershala Ali) and Chiron aka Little (Alex R. Hibbert) in
distinctly different ways. We are first introduced to Juan behind the wheels of
his blue Chevy Impala with a golden crown adorning his dashboard, underscored by the upbeat retro-music of Boris Gordiner's "Every N----r Is a Star."
This visual presentation shows Juan somewhat humorously as the king of the
ghetto and breaks into its R&B soundtrack with the harsher hip-hop sounds
usually associated with street gangs. As he monitors the drug business on the
street corner, his soldier is seen in a dizzying 360-degree surround shot talking to a needy customer, whereas Juan is all the while standing quietly on the
side. In his interaction with his seller, Juan exhibits patience and concern by
not requiring an immediate payout from the closed drug deals and asking
about the health of his mother. While physically imposing, Juan comes across
as a paternal caretaker who relies on communicative and social bonding with
his corner man. The dizzying shot of disorientation is mostly reserved for the
drug business but is not applied to Juan directly as he figures as a stable coor-
dinate in an otherwise chaotic environment.

Walking back to his car, Juan is cut off by a group of running boys. In the
next cut, the camera switches to shaky handheld images following the child
protagonist Chiron being chased and called derogatory names such as "f----t
ass" and "gay ass," forcing him to seek refuge in an abandoned and boarded-
up housing project littered with drug paraphernalia. Inside a dark apartment,
Chiron crouches on the floor covering his ears, attempting to keep out the
sound of the boys' yelling and banging on the door. In narrative film, the mise-
en-scène typically represents the state of mind of the character, and Chiron
comes across as fearful, abandoned in darkness, trying to block out sounds of
reality. This representation weakens Chiron on multiple sensory levels, as he
is not in control of the shot (shaky handheld images) and is instead fearfully
crouched inside a dark apartment attempting to block out the soundscape of
the film with its ocean's surf and Gordiner's nondiegetic upbeat Black pride
song. Chiron/Little is thus established as essentially homeless or "unhoused"
in contrast to the more stable and confident Juan.

Concerned about the bullied young boy, Juan tries to open the door and
eventually takes down a wooden panel that boards up a window, letting bright

sunlight penetrate into its dark interior. He attempts to engage Chiron but is met with stoic silence. As Simone Drake points out, this reticence and silence stands in stark contrast to typical portrayals of "black manhood" as "always already vocal, reactive, and heteronormative." *Moonlight*, Drake notes, instead offers up "a protagonist who says little and, with the exception of one reactive act of violence, also does little throughout the film."[21] Louise Wallenberg links this silence more directly to Marlon Riggs's *Tongues Untied* (1989), a Black gay documentary film or manifesto, where silence is addressed as the sonic identity of queerness: "Silence is my cloak. It smothers. Silence is my sword." "Coming home," as Wallenberg notes, "for both Chiron and Riggs, means accepting and embracing being black and gay," hence indicating a return to language, vociferously articulated in Riggs's film and "rather subtly" in *Moonlight*.[22] Juan continues talking to Chiron even though he is met with silence and proceeds to open the front door from inside, allowing more light to penetrate the house that can be seen as a representation for the young protagonist's dreary world about to be changed by this encounter.

The depiction of Chiron in the opening scenes of the film also carries resonances of the continuing legacy of slavery, defined by Orlando Patterson as a form of social death. "Archetypically," Patterson writes, "slavery is a substitute for death."[23] A more lasting feature of slavery, according to Patterson, concerns its natal alienation as a symbolic instrument of authority and control: "Alienated from all 'rights' or claims of birth, [the slave] cease[s] to belong in his own right to any social order."[24] Chiron, living in Miami's Liberty City district, is characterized by this legacy of slavery as he is a person without a proper family legacy. His reticence turns him into a social statistic—a young Black boy being raised by a single mother who refuses to speak his name—and indicates he suffers from a type of social death. Chiron's sexual orientation further adds to his sense of alienation and illegitimate residency in Liberty City. The mise-en-scène of the abandoned house underscores the lack of a proper dimension of dwelling, to use Heidegger's term. It also recalls British director Steve McQueen's short film *Deadpan* (1997), a remake of a Buster Keaton stunt in *Steamboat Bill Jr.* (1928), with the front façade of the house repeatedly collapsing—the film is presented in a loop—onto the Black director, who emerges unscathed by standing in the location of the window's opening. For American audiences, this short film drives home the problematic relation of African Americans to housing, whether in the sense of suffering from housing shortages, substandard dwellings, redlining, and more importantly, a profound sense of spiritual homelessness and disconnect from the national community.

Trying to engage Chiron, Juan takes him to a diner but is unsuccessful in making him speak and disclose his identity. He eventually takes him home where his girlfriend Teresa (Janelle Monáe) treats Chiron to a home-cooked fried chicken dinner and slowly, patiently coaxes him into speaking. When Little discloses his real name Chiron, with Little being merely a derisive nickname, she replies: "I'm gon' call you by your name then. Where you live, Chiron?" This care and respect elicit Chiron's response of living in Liberty City with his mother and that he doesn't have a father, to which Juan replies, "that's all right." He is invited to spend the night, and the next morning the camera shows Chiron sleeping comfortably in a bed with a white shirt, blending into the background of white linen and pillows. He is lit in a soft bright light with white curtains fluttering gently in the breeze. Underscored by somber instrumental string music, the scene visually illuminates Chiron by surrounding him with whiteness and light. This image of home radically differs not only from the abandoned home Juan has just rescued him from but Chiron's own home that he shares with his mother. Juan and Teresa become in this respect part of Chiron's newly found elective family, foretelling their profound influence on his upbringing. In the next scene, Chiron is driven home, and we see him playfully engaging the air with his hand and making wave movements. This image stresses mobility and a sensuous engagement with his surroundings. Associated with the fluttering curtains, Chiron's wave movements also provide a subtle graphic foreshadowing of his trip to the ocean.

Before the crucial scene of Chiron's visit to the beach with Juan, the film shows Chiron and his peers playing soccer with a makeshift ball in an elaborate panoramic shot scored to the music of Mozart's "Vesperae Solennes," highlighting in quasi-religious ambience the humanity of the young Black boys facing the roving camera. The music is punctuated by the loud horn of a passing freight train, pulling back from metaphysical sentimentality into one of poetic tension. Chiron is also shown breaking away from this ideal community when playing soccer, highlighting his marginalized position. Kevin (Jaden Piner), his close friend, joins him and advises Chiron to show more toughness so as not to become the obvious target for bullying. This tension between guarded toughness and proper dwelling in a community will be seen throughout the film with Chiron both blending in and separating himself from his surroundings. Nothing appears entirely deterministic in his world, as it would be in the case of ghetto films and their milieu studies of inevitable social decline and dysfunctionality. Rather, his choices remain open to good and bad decisions, with Chiron learning how to dwell within an evolving narrative and biography.

The film's coming-of-age story ultimately brings the uprooted boy into a closer relationship with the landscape of Florida that surrounds him, aiding him in the learning process of self-discovery and growing maturity. A central scene in the film—a scene of instruction—is Chiron's trip to Virginia Key Beach with his paternal mentor Juan. Whereas the earlier scene of Chiron playing soccer in a field with his peers does not show the ocean but rather marks the hard horizon with a freight train, the beach scene evokes a poetic opening found in the fluid and liquid element of water and its seascape meeting the horizon of the sky. Historically, African Americans and Black migrants were not granted access to Miami beaches during the era of Jim Crow segregation. Fisher Island, once owned by Dana A. Dorsey, southern Florida's first African American millionaire, for a short time provided access to the beach, but it was sold in 1919 to the white land developer Carl G. Fisher and hence subjected to similar segregation rules. One remaining historical exception was the barrier island Virginia Key (accessible since 1947 via the Rickenbacker Causeway), "known as 'the Black Beach' and shunned by whites accordingly."[25] The images of the freight train and the beach recall in indirect fashion the founding history of Southern Florida with Black labor building the railroad and laying claim to both land and water.

After Chiron shows up in Juan's garden with its lush foliage and banana trees, they head to the beach, which is shown with palm trees stirred by the ocean's breeze and swim towels fluttering in the wind (linking up with the earlier visual image of the billowing curtains). As Juan and Chiron enter the ocean, Nicholas Britell's mildly dissonant and polyphonic chamber soundtrack—evoking the minimalism of Philip Glass's music—creates a sonic contrast to the scene in which Juan teaches Chiron how to float and swim, literally and metaphorically empowering him how to become secure in his surroundings. The shaky handheld camera, recalling Chiron's first anxious shot in the film, shows him now fully immersed and floating in the ocean—"you're in the middle of the world, man," Juan says encouragingly while supporting his head and body—and then cuts back to an earlier scene with Chiron still fully dressed, testing the boundary of beach and ocean in a long shot. This scene is accompanied by Juan's voiceover that mixes with the surf of the ocean and the wind, hence giving his voice a quasi-natural authority and letting the landscape of Florida speak: "Let me tell you something, man. There are black people everywhere. Remember that, okay? No place you can go in the world ain't got no black people. We's the first on this planet." It is here, during this memorable voiceover, where the film makes a crucial switch from the more local world of the African American experience to the global connectedness of all Black people, the Black diaspora, while laying claim to the planet as its first settlers.

For the beach scene, the Arri Alexa XT digital camera, used by Laxton throughout the film, is taken into the ocean, allowing the viewer to stay at eye level close to the characters with the waves lapping against the camera.[26] The filmmakers also chose a Hawk V-Lite anamorphic lens that stretches a small aspect ratio screen to a widescreen format, usually featured in 35mm films focusing on panoramic landscapes such as the Western film. As Laxton explains:

> The attempt was to promote those emotions, not just to present them, but to promote them to a place where you can sense the intensity by which Chiron's character is going through these things. What it means to that character to be bullied, to have to deal with these sexual questions that he's going through in his teenaged years. Our idea was to present them visually with that same amount of intensity. Which for us meant *anamorphic lenses* that express this heightened sense of existence that I think audience members sometimes associate with bigger tent pole films but were presenting this sort of nuanced subtle story but with that same heightened value.[27]

In *Moonlight*, with its many close-ups and domestic scenes, this widescreen format is used counterintuitively but adds to the effect of the audience's intimate proximity to the enlarged characters, blending into the landscape of Florida. The characters thereby participate in the landscape in the possible sense of dwelling in and belonging to a world.

The camera then cuts into a close-up of Chiron and Juan, with the latter stating: "I been here a long time. But I'm from Cuba. Lot of black folks in Cuba, you wouldn't know that from being here, though. I was a wild li'l shorty, man, just like you. Runnin' around with no shoes on when the moon was out." The tight two-shot of Chiron and Juan reveals swaying palm trees in shallow focus with the sound of the ocean and wind continuously pervading the scene. In this aestheticized and archetypal treatment of Florida's beach, the landscape assumes a moral dimension, blending the horizons of mortals, immortals, earth, and sky in the language of Heidegger's description of human dwelling. This dimension of proper dwelling is updated by Juan into a vision of a Black utopia via an anecdote: "This one time . . . I run by this old . . . this old lady. I was runnin', hollerin' . . . cuttin' a fool, boy. This old lady, she stopped me. She said . . . 'Running around catching up all that light. In moonlight black boys look blue. You blue. That's what I gon' call you. Blue.'" Asked by Chiron whether his name is Blue, Juan replies: "Nah. At some point you gotta decide yourself who you gon' be. Can't let nobody make that decision for you." The instructive comments by the old lady teach Juan that Blackness is not a predetermined biological definition or a fixed concept of identity—hence black can transform into blue when seen under moonlight.

Juan's "catching up all that light" plays off the cinematic aspect of controlling the light and being the center of the camera's/cinematographer's attention, as was shown in the earlier scene when Chiron is illuminated on the bed at Juan and Teresa's residence. And though Juan rejects the given name Blue, he follows the old lady's implicit advice of not taking things at face value. This vision of self-determination is likewise passed on to Chiron and is enlarged into the utopian vision of a global Blackness not defined by hegemonic cultural concepts. Louise Wallenberg's discussion, placing the film into a legacy that includes Isaac Julien's *Looking for Langston* (1989) and Marlon Riggs and Essex Hemphill's *Tongues Untied* (1989), gives the term "blue" the additional meaning of the blues associated with both African American history and the repressed gay identity in Chiron. Both precursor films, made during the height of the HIV pandemic, Wallenberg claims, "celebrate and advocate a black and gay experience and make visible and audible a black and gay legacy."[28] Accordingly, *Moonlight* articulates a Black gay utopia and thereby significantly inflects and alters a concept such as Heidegger's notion of dwelling construed exclusively within a white European heteronormative context.

Queerness and Toxic Masculinity

With its intersection of a queer and Black identity coming to the fore, the film also distances itself from and revises more traditional portrayals of a monolithic Black community as evident in the Black ghetto film genre. Jenkins himself has acknowledged his indebtedness to Marlon Riggs's *Tongues Untied* (1989), a vanguard activist poetic documentary that openly challenges the representational containment of Black queerness: "Black men loving Black men is the revolutionary act. Snap!" Though presented in a different generic format, *Moonlight* frequently echoes *Tongues Untied*. One poetic reflection in Riggs's film concerns the trauma of not being at home in one's community as a gay Black man:

> I cannot go home as who I am. When I speak of home, I mean not only the familial constellation from which I grew but the entire black community. The black press, the black church, black academicians, the black literati, and the black left. Where is my reflection? I am most often rendered invisible. Perceived as a threat to the family, or I am tolerated if I am silent and inconspicuous. I cannot go home as who I am. And that hurts me deeply.[29]

From the perspective of Jenkins's film, Heidegger's concept of dwelling, while existentially relevant for the film's narrative, similarly remains stuck in an archaic metaphysics of dwelling concerned solely with a single homogeneous people. The film's narrative ruptures, its many ellipses, and its frequent use of nonsynchronized audio show instead that proper dwelling comes with a sense of disturbance, discontinuity, and diversity. In Slavoj Žižek's updated Lacanian terms, the core of all meaning and identity retains an irreducible absence or split that can lead both to the production of utopian desire and anxiety. For example, in the case of Hitchcock's cinema, Žižek claims that "the imaginary balance changes into a symbolically structured network through a shock of the Real."[30] Similarly, *Moonlight*'s narrative contains multiple shocks of the Real, such as Juan's death (never shown nor explained); the growing drug dependency of Chiron's mother and his discovery that Juan is her dealer, thus destroying the idealization of the elective father figure; the bullying culminating with his best friend Kevin punching him in front of his peers; Chiron's violent revenge upon the instigator of the mobbing incident that lands Chiron in juvenile prison; and his eventual turn to street crime (elliptically explained) as a drug dealer resembling Juan, borrowing his image in his use of a flashy vintage car (Oldsmobile Cutlass Supreme) with a crown adorning the dashboard as well as the use of teeth grills. Yet, in spite of these frequent irruptions of the Real, the film maintains a symbolic balance of hope and growing assurance, and hence a sense of achieved dwelling featured in the final diner scene. In the medium of film, this task involves finding a balance between realism and possibility, between contingency and freedom. As in the case of Zora Neale Hurston's fiction, particularly *Their Eyes Were Watching God*, the landscape of Florida in *Moonlight* always supports rather than overwhelms the main protagonists Chiron and Kevin, allowing them to reach a provisional sense of belonging to a community in spite of serious challenges.

The film delivers in this sense a deeper definition of Black youth culture as advanced by Orlando Patterson. According to Patterson's structuralist definition, "culture is the product of two interconnected sets of processes."[31] The first component of culture involves "collectively constructed knowledge about our world that is unevenly shared and distributed among given networks of persons."[32] The second component resides in cultural knowledge that "is grounded in, and emerges from, pragmatic usage."[33] Thus, it "is in the interactions of cultural users that cultural knowledge is transmitted, produced, reproduced, and changed."[34] In the world of *Moonlight*, the transmission of a semantics of culture originates with Chiron's mother but also Juan and Teresa as supplementary parental figures. The uneven distribution is illustrated with Chiron's mother, Paula (Naomie Harris), whose burden as a single mother and her drug addiction limits her network of persons and pushes Chiron into the position of an introverted latchkey child. Juan and Teresa, however, significantly augment his sociocultural network, linking him in the beach scene to a global Black population, hence opening a utopian horizon. This opening of possibilities is produced and enacted with Kevin in various encounters, both sexual and violent, that finally lead to a new perspective or recontextualization that places Chiron's life into relief. Cinematically, the use of closed frames is reserved in multiple shots for Chiron's mother and her apartment while open frames are depicted in the beach visits with Juan and Kevin, the second one reproducing the first encounter with a significant other.

Juan in many ways gives the green light to Chiron's sexual orientation as he not only accepts its practice but clearly understands and explains its rejection by the community to Chiron. When asked by Chiron what the term "f----t" means, Juan explains: "A f----t is . . . a word used to make gay people feel bad." The stress here is placed on the pragmatic dimension of language and its performative use of power over others. The earlier addressed complex of natal alienation comes into play as well in this communally applied pressure to discourage the pursuit of a sexual orientation that does not produce a biological child. It is interesting to note that Juan and Teresa do not have children and hence adopt Chiron as an elective child. *Moonlight's* world resists an imperative of realism and toxic masculinity, producing instead a radical counter-image of its community based on nonheteronormative concepts of family, operating with new networks of support and interaction. Chiron's sexuality temporarily goes underground, whereas Kevin hides his preference behind heterosexual norms. In the film's final outing of their repressed sexual identity, as well as the envisioning of a family life outside traditional norms, much of the initial pressure placed on the single mother (represented in her drug addiction) is also relieved.

The single mother is both a factual reality and filmic cliché of urban communities where males suffer from systemic un- and underemployment and hence are not considered eligible for marriage. As Jody Miller sums up the research of sociologist William Julius Wilson: "Urban Black women are disproportionately responsible for the economic well-being of their families. This is particularly the case given the growth of single-mother households in poor urban communities, exacerbated by decreases in the 'marriageability' of black men in these settings."[35] Miller, however, disagrees with frequent sociological portrayals that depict Black women as somehow less subject to victimization than their male counterparts, analyzing the "concentrated poverty, and violence" as "a primarily male problem that requires *young men's* negotiation of the 'code.'"[36] Jenkins's film likewise stems against this one-sided portrayal in films by giving considerable attention to Paula and her transformation from loving but stressed and exhausted single mother sliding into drug addiction to a rehabilitated drug user now helping those in similar distress. The film's final beach scene also features a group of mostly Black teenage girls playing in the surf at night, assembling in a space of freedom rather than one of domestic confinement or the urban streets associated with drugs and prostitution (where we encounter Paula at one point). In its queering of gender roles, particularly those that have become commonplaces in ghetto films, *Moonlight* envisions a redistribution of gender roles in the community that lead to more sustainable forms of social interaction.

"Hello Stranger"—On the Way to Florida

As this essay has tried to illustrate, the "culture of poverty" associated with inner-city Black life and its representational vehicle of the ghetto film is reconfigured in *Moonlight* via aesthetic defamiliarization and queering, leading to new perceptions and redistributions of social and communal roles that attempt to heal the community in a self-reliant manner. Outside interventions, systemic or individual white saviorism, do not belong to the self-regulated world of *Moonlight*. Rather, local settings play a significant role and one could argue that the various Florida settings are as important as the characters. To be sure, these settings are not extreme. Miami Beach, for example, is not featured in commercial manner as in De Palma's *Scarface* (1983) or other high-powered scenic Florida films (*Transporter 2*, 2005; *Miami Vice*, 2006) and popular TV shows (*Miami Vice*, 1984–89; *Burn Notice*, 2007–13). However, the presence of Miami and Florida as a transformative and potentially moral landscape is invoked quietly but profoundly in the film's lush and atmospheric cinematography. As James Laxton explains: "The use of natural and ambient light throughout the film mixed with small warm fill lights and touches of color play on the film's dream-like sense of reality."[37] For example, Paula's agitated indoor portrayal with harsh closed framing also includes a surprising pink color, one more associated with the colorful art deco buildings lining South Beach and its tropical locale. In doing so, the film shows how the landscape of Miami and Florida penetrates even the gloomiest home and offers a possibility for redemption in its exotic and upbeat colors.[38]

The film's diner scene finally brings Kevin and Chiron's relationship fully into focus, one that had earlier taken a sexual turn on a Miami beach, before souring due to homophobic bullying that coerced Kevin's participation. Chiron has since started a new life as a drug dealer in Atlanta when Kevin (André Holland) telephones him out of the blue. Kevin apologizes for the events that had transpired and confesses that he had spent some time in jail where he was trained as a cook, his current profession. Chiron/Black (Trevante Rhodes) is shown now as a muscled-up adult, working out with weights, toting a gun, and wearing teeth grills and a do-rag. During Kevin's call, this hypermasculine image reveals cracks as Chiron is on the verge of tears. Kevin tells him of a jukebox at his workplace where customers select songs and confides that "one dude" played a song that reminded him of Chiron. Asking him to visit him at his restaurant, Kevin promises to cook for him.

The jukebox, a device that stores music and memories, is a global commodity that provides a certain sense of home, leisure, and belonging in public spaces. Wong Kar-wai's film *Chunking Express* (1994) features a jukebox prominently, expressing longing and desire in a bar scene triggered by Dennis Brown's reggae tune "Things in Life" with the telling lyrics "It's not every day we're gonna be the same way." Jenkins has been influenced by with Wong's films, including *In the Mood for Love* (2000), which features an atmospheric diner scene of two star-crossed lovers richly imbued via the soundtrack of Nat King Cole's "Quizàs, quizàs, quizàs" ("Perhaps, perhaps, perhaps"). In Jenkins's *Moonlight* version of the diner scene, atmospheric retro R&B music is similarly evoked to relax the scene, while also articulating its hidden desires and bringing them to the fore.

Just prior to this pivotal scene before driving from Atlanta to Miami, Chiron makes amends with his mother who is now residing at the Peachtree Drug Rehabilitation Center. Like the phone call from Kevin, it brings out a softer side in Chiron that he had previously shut out. The initially tensely expressed emotions eventually overwhelm Chiron as he embraces his repentant mother in a scene of forgiveness, leading into Caetano Veloso's rendition of "Cucurrucucu Paloma," a song that equates the cooing of a dove with lovesickness, death, and romantic desire. In an homage to Wong Kar-wai's *Happy Together* (1997), a film about a mismatched gay couple temporarily stranded in Buenos Aires, Argentina, the film emulates Wong's road trip scene to the stunning Iguazu Waterfalls scored to Veloso's music. His soft Brazilian-style ballad arranged with strings is also memorably used in Pedro Almodóvar's *Talk to Her* (2002), where Veloso has a cameo appearance singing this song to a gathering of a mesmerized listeners. For cinephiles, the song carries associations with queer desire directly articulated in *Happy Together* and more generally in the works of the gay Spanish director Almodóvar. Veloso's music constitutes an appropriate choice for a sound bridge that accompanies Chiron on his road trip from Atlanta to Miami highlighting lovesickness and queer desire. Driving along the green treelined highway, Chiron is featured in a tracking profile shot beginning with the crown on his dashboard, moving to his arm bejeweled with a gold band, and a profile shot showing his heavy gold neck chain, teeth grills, and diamonds adorning his ears, giving him a new air of majesty, while recalling his mentor Juan. A subsequent dissolve fades into an overhead shot of his car driving into a nighttime beach scene with young Black teenagers, mostly girls, playing in the surf, before the camera tilts upward toward the sky and catches the moon and its emanating light. This brief homage to Julie Dash's *Daughters of the Dust* not only stresses an open space for young Black teenage girls as a balance against toxic masculinity, but also evokes Dash's distinct self-assertion of the Gullah culture and its African roots thriving off the coast of South Carolina, the new homeland for displaced and former natally alienated slave communities.

The diner scene marks in many ways the inaugural moment of Chiron's possible escape from natal alienation and homelessness. As he passes the entrance to the diner, he is graphically matched with a big sign that reads "Open," indicating an opening or a way out. The scene recalls the earlier dining scene with Juan and Teresa, during which the introverted child opened up and disclosed his name. Juan is evoked in Chiron's appearance, now looking much like his mentor. Teresa's presence is reenacted by Kevin, who invokes "grandma rules"—"you ass eat, you ass speak"—urging the reticent Chiron to speak and open up. Teresa had done so similarly and stressed in her house rules that no drooping-head attitude was permitted. Kevin further brings back memories of Juan when he serves Chiron a Cuban dish, which the camera shows in close-up and slow montage during its careful preparation, underscored by somber and plaintive chamber music reminiscent of Shigeru Umebayashi's string arrangements for Wong Kar-wai's *In the Mood for Love*. The sequence closes with a cut to Chiron browsing through the jukebox before sitting down for dinner, hence associating him with the soundtrack. Jenkins also intended the scene as an homage to Hou Hsiao-hsien's first sequence of his film *Three Times* taking place in an intimate pool parlor.[39] Hou's scene was filmed with slow panning shots capturing the main characters going in and out of the frame, as the camera surveils the setting. *Moonlight* similarly uses this panning technique and establishes the restaurant as a location and ambience facilitating the reunion of Chiron and Kevin. In its not-so-hidden homage, the scene is central to the film's third narrative segment and is supported by three songs and the sound of the diner's doorbell, shown initially and at the end in close-up, ringing twice. A third customer bell is audibly heard during the tense conversation about Chiron's current life as a drug dealer and accentuates the scene. The diegetic songs range from Aretha Franklin's "One Step Ahead," to Edge of Daybreak's "Our Love," and culminate in a shot showing Kevin selecting Barbara Lewis's "Hello Stranger" at the jukebox. The song's progress from a sense of despair—"I'm only one step ahead of heartbreak / one step ahead of misery"—to a more reassured sense of hope—"Wait for me, as I wait for you

/ then nothing will go wrong with our love"—to a sense of relief and the possibility of love: "Hello, stranger / (ooh) It seems so good to see you back again / How long has it been? / (ooh) Seems like a mighty long time."

The diner scene, set in a country-style restaurant with cozy curtains and faux Tiffany lamps, is not without some tension as Kevin is visibly upset that Chiron is engaged in "trappin'" (drug dealing) and asks him "why you got them damn fronts" (teeth grills). At the same time, the scene also features significantly held close-ups when their eyes first meet at the diner counter focused intently on the mutual gaze as a form of direct communication and openness. In a second significant exchange of looks, Kevin explains his reason for cold calling Chiron in Atlanta being due to "a dude" playing a certain song, namely Lewis's "Hello Stranger." This sequence shows Kevin walking to the jukebox to make his point and then standing next to it gazing off frame in the direction of Chiron for considerable time, leaving an empty space for the imagination to fill before returning to the close-up reverse shot. This shot especially indicates that there is room for reimagining and recasting Chiron's identity in the gaze of Kevin.

Arriving at Kevin's apartment, tellingly located near the beach, Chiron stares down a path lined by palm trees leading to the ocean front and its audible sound of the surf. Upon entering Kevin's modest apartment, Chiron says "this is real, man," bringing the film's narrative back from the romantic diner scene to reality. An ongoing tension is sustained as Chiron is shot against an entry door with a barred, albeit decorative, window whereas Kevin is shown in the open space of the kitchen. Kevin tells him that the simple life is working better for him, as it carries none of the anxiety that had come with the life of crime: "It's a life. I ain't never had that before . . . I ain't got no worries, man." He also mentions his son, whose picture he had shown to Chiron earlier, as a fixture in his new life. Kevin's reformed identity leads to an acceptance of family, though he is separated from the birth mother, and is a partial overcoming of natal alienation. In a question that echoes Paula's question to Juan, Kevin asks, "Who is you, Chiron?" pressing him to own up to his real identity. This question leads the conversation eventually to an abrupt confession by Chiron that Kevin was the only person who had ever touched him intimately, a story element that stands in stark contrast to the stereotypical depictions of promiscuous gang life and Black hypersexuality.

After a long silence with a long shot showing Kevin and Chiron facing one another, the shot switches to nighttime with Kevin cradling Chiron's head on the sofa. Though not addressing this film or scene specifically, José Esteban Muñoz's comments eerily summarize its embedded meaning of a queer utopia:

Queer utopia is a modality of critique that speaks to quotidian gestures as laden with potentiality. The queerness of queer futurity, like the Blackness of a Black radical tradition, is a relational and collective modality of endurance and support. The gesture of cradling the head of one's lover, a lover one has betrayed, is therefore not an act of redemption that mitigates violence; it is instead a future being within the present that is both a utopian kernel and an anticipatory illumination. It is a being in, toward, and for futurity.[40]

The quotidian element of the queer utopia is already shown in the earlier montage sequence when Kevin lovingly prepares food for Chiron. The portent cradling shot at the apartment eventually cuts to a final shot with young Chiron/Little standing at the beach at nighttime with his back turned to the viewer before quickly turning his head towards the viewer. Coming full circle, the narrative recovers Juan's story with the moonlight illuminating his body and giving his skin tone blue accents. The shot also recalls the ending freeze frame of Truffaut's *400 Blows* where the young child Antoine turns his head toward the camera at the beach, looking at the audience in silent protest. This shot is modified by Jenkins, as his protagonist faces the audience but looks upward toward the sky, opening up a utopian horizon. Ryan Coogler's *Black Panther* (2018) brings back the young actor Alex Hibbert in a brief cameo in its final scene as a young Oakland kid witnessing the arrival of a spaceship on his basketball court and then turning to T'Challa (Chadwick Boseman), asking him the question repeatedly brought up in *Moonlight*, "Who are you?" thus linking utopia and identity.

Jenkins's *Moonlight*, as was shown, skillfully masters the language of global cinema and expands the film's ghetto story to a new audience, broadening the horizon of its Black queer utopia. Much like Ang Lee's *Brokeback Mountain* (2005) that queered the Western genre, Jenkins revises the ghetto genre and has its utopian poetics prevail at the film's ending. The film illustrates Heidegger's concept of dwelling, read here against the grain of its monoethnic and heteronormative ideology, and points to a newfound sense of home that resides in being on the way to home, namely the "essence of dwelling, that they must ever learn to dwell,"[41] thereby addressing the legacy of slavery and its natal alienation. Broken family relations are newly reconstituted as elective affiliation and community rather than more deterministic biological bonds. The landscape of Florida—Miami, its playgrounds, lower-income neighborhoods, beaches, lush foliage and colors, and cozier domestic dining scenes—support this type of utopian dwelling. Various transportation routes such as highways and causeway bridges, the Metrorail or jitney, and a selection of conspicuously retro vehicles give the film both a sense of mobility, of moving forward, while retaining a form of shelter. Though due its photographic medium the film may make Florida appear as a realistic setting, the defamiliarization of its presentation reminds us of its framed nature as an imagined world, a new global sensorium, or as Juan reminds Chiron when swimming in the ocean: "You're in the middle of the world."

Notes

1. I would like to dedicate this essay to my late mentor Angel Medina, Emeritus Professor of Philosophy at Georgia State University.

2. Alejandro Portes and Ariel C. Armony, *The Global Edge: Miami in the Twenty-First Century* (Berkeley: University of California Press, 2018), 16–17.

3. See Marvin Dunn, *Black Miami in the Twentieth Century* (Gainesville: University Press of Florida, 1997). See also Paul S. George's concise essay "Colored Town: Miami's Black Community, 1896–1930," *Florida Historical Quarterly* 56, no. 4 (April 1978): 432–47.

4. Portes and Armony explain the rapid acculturation of Cuban refugees: "The Cuban upper classes that landed in the city as a consequence of the successful Communist revolution on the island were not only accustomed to power back home, but, in addition, were quite familiar with American politics and culture" (*The Global Edge*, 9). Similarly, Miami "opened the city to the world and welcomed the flows of capital from Brazil, Argentina, Nicaragua, Venezuela, and Ecuador as each of these countries came, in turn, under the sway of populist regimes" (*The Global Edge*, 18).

5. Paula Massood, *Black City Cinema: African American Urban Experiences in Film* (Philadelphia: Temple University Press, 2003), 147.

6. In an interview, Jenkins refers to Taiwanese filmmaker Hou Hsiao-Hsien's *Three Times* (2005) as a crucial film influencing the tripartite story structure of his own film. See "Interview. Moonlight becomes him: Barry Jenkins's journey from a Miami housing project to the Oscars," *The Guardian*, February 7, 2017. https://www.theguardian.com/film/2017/feb/07/moonlight-barry-jenkins-director-interview. Accessed July 2, 2020, 1–5, 3.

7. Barry Jenkins explains this idiosyncratic use of hip hop music: "It's this Southern form of hip-hop called 'chopped and screwed,' where the voice is really deep and it's really slowed down and lines are repeating. . . . Hip-hop is usually moving at such a high bpm that you don't catch that not only is this poetry, but it's really pained. If you chop and screw it, you allow all of that pain to come through" (44). In "Interview with Barry Jenkins by Nicolas Rapold," *film comment* 52, no. 5 (September-October 2016): 44–45.

8. Oscar Lewis, "The Culture of Poverty," *Scientific American* 215, no. 4 (October 1966): 19–25.

9. Lewis, "The Culture of Poverty," 21.

10. Lewis, "The Culture of Poverty," 21.

11. Lewis, "The Culture of Poverty," 21.

12. James Laxton, "Inside the Cinematography of *Moonlight*: The Images That Inspired James Laxton," https://time.com/behind-the-visuals-of-moonlight/. Accessed July 2, 2020, 2/8.

13. Massood, *Black City Cinema*, 147.

14. Massood, *Black City Cinema*, 148.

15. Massood, *Black City Cinema*, 153.

16. See "Interview. Moonlight becomes him," 3–5.

17. See "'Moonlight' Director Barry Jenkins on Bringing 'Art House to the Hood,'" Interview with Ashley Clark, *Vice*, October 20, 2016. https://www.vice.com/en_us/article/gqkdnq/moonlight-director-barry-jenkins-on-bringing-art-house-to-the-hood. Accessed July 6, 2020, 8–18.

18. Martin Heidegger, "Building Dwelling Thinking," in *Basic Writings* (New York: Harper, 2008), 343–64; 363.

19. Heidegger, "Building Dwelling Thinking," 363.

20. Heidegger, "Building Dwelling Thinking," 362.

21. Simone C. Drake, "He Said Nothing: Sonic Space and the Production of Quietude in Barry Jenkins's *Moonlight*," in *Are You Entertained? Black Popular Culture in the Twenty-First Century*, ed. Simone C. Drake and Dwan K. Henderson (Durham, NC: Duke University Press, 2020), 252–67; 253.

22. Louise Wallenberg, "'Let Us Roam the Night Together": On Articulation and Representation in *Moonlight* (2016) and *Tongues Untied* (1989)," in *Hollywood at the Intersection of Race and Identity*, ed. Delia Malia Konzett (New Brunswick, NJ: Rutgers University Press, 2019), 301–17; 311, 313.

23. Orlando Patterson, *Slavery and Social Death: A Comparative Study* (Cambridge, MA: Harvard University Press, 1982), 5.

24. Patterson, *Slavery and Social Death*, 5

25. Portes and Armony, *The Global Edge*, 26.

26. "Another strategy in accentuating the film's unique feeling is using a single Arri Alexa XT camera through the whole shoot. 'The whole thing was one camera,' says Laxton. 'We never had two cameras actually.'" Laxton, "Inside the Cinematography of Moonlight," 5–8. "In the midst of this pivotal moment of self-discovery there's a real awareness of the camera as the water is lapping against the lens" (Laxton, 4).

27. Laxton, "Inside the Cinematography of Moonlight," 5–6.

28. Wallenberg, "'Let Us Roam the Night Together,'" 313.

29. Marlon Riggs, *Tongues Untied*, documentary film, 1989.

30. Slavoj Žižek, "Alfred Hitchcock, or, The Form and its Historical Mediation," in *Everything You Always Wanted to Know about Lacan (But Were Afraid to Ask Hitchcock)*, ed. Slavoj Žižek (London: Verso, 1992), 1–12; 7.

31. Orlando Patterson, "The Nature and Dynamics of Cultural Processes," in *The Cultural Matrix: Understanding Black Youth*, ed. Orlando Patterson and Ethan Fosse (Cambridge, MA: Harvard University Press, 2016), 25–44; 25.

32. Patterson, "The Nature and Dynamics of Cultural Processes," 25.

33. Patterson, "The Nature and Dynamics of Cultural Processes," 25.

34. Patterson, "The Nature and Dynamics of Cultural Processes," 25.

35. Jody Miller, "Culture, Inequality, and Gender Relations among Urban Black Youth," in *The Cultural Matrix: Understanding Black Youth*, ed. Orlando Patterson and Ethan Fosse (Cambridge, MA: Harvard University Press, 2016), 370–91; 371.

36. Jody Miller, "Culture, Inequality, and Gender Relations among Urban Black Youth," 373.

37. James Laxton, "Inside the Cinematography of Moonlight," 6–8.

38. "That pink light behind her in that scene and within the film generally helps to express another side of her," says DP James Laxton. "I think the color pink can have a lot of associations but I think one of them can be beauty. On set it rounded out this character in this moment that is very dark and very intense. She's yelling at her son. But it allowed us to understand that she's a whole character as well." Laxton, "Inside the Cinematography of Moonlight," 6–8.

39. Jenkins answers the question of influence as follows: "*Three Times* by Hou Hsiao-hsien. That had a three-romance structure—a triptych. There is an homage to *Three Times*, the first story in the pool hall. When Chiron first walks into the diner, we're on the dolly, and then he sits

at the counter, the camera pans, and we find André; André walks in the back of the kitchen, camera pans back, André comes down the little alley, and then we do the portraits. Because in the first story, Hou Hsiao-hsien is in the pool hall; camera's perpendicular to the scene, just dollying back and forth, and just panning." "Interview with Barry Jenkins by Nicolas Rapold," 45.

40. José Esteban Muñoz, *Cruising Utopia: The Then and There of Queer Futurity* (New York: New York University Press, 2009), 91.

41. Heidegger, "Building Dwelling Thinking," 363.

CHAPTER THIRTEEN

Civil Rights by *Moonlight*

Liberty City and Miami's Social Justice Histories

Valerie Babb

Despite its crucial importance to civil rights history, contemporary Florida has largely been erased from discussions of Black progressivism. Civil Rights with a capital C and R, as in the civil rights movement, can overshadow the smaller struggles represented by lower-case letters. Their histories are embedded in many sites within Florida. When one thinks of spaces central to Black social justice advocacy, Selma or Birmingham are readily remembered as iconic sites, St. Louis is recalled as home to the Old Courthouse where Dred and Harriet Robinson Sanford Scott's case was heard, Topeka for birthing the *Brown v. Board of Education* decision, and Memphis for being the site where Martin Luther King Jr. delivered his prophetic "I've Been to the Mountaintop" speech at the Mason Temple Church the evening before his assassination. Liberty City, Miami, might not spring readily to mind in this assemblage, but its built landscape embodies many of the markers of Black cultural history: settlement, enslavement, migration, segregation, deterioration, and contested urban renewal. It is not surprising, then, that Liberty City would inspire two of its native sons, Barry Jenkins and Tarell Alvin McCraney, to use it as setting for a combined coming-of-age and civil rights narrative. The film *Moonlight* (2016), directed by Jenkins and based on an unpublished play by McCraney, offers a loving yet ambivalent portrait of Liberty City as a site reflecting Black histories and avowing queer civil rights.

The Liberty City represented in *Moonlight* grew from a nexus of three geographical spaces: Overtown, also known as Colored Town or negro town or the Central Negro District; the Liberty City neighborhood, a stretch of once "white land" that became home to a Black neighborhood, and the Liberty Square Housing Project. Looking at the interactive histories of these spaces is essentially a course in the arc of the struggle for Black enfranchisement. They embody histories of enslavement, segregation, promise, decline, and hope.

Miami became Miami in 1896. The Black community by then was a diaspora of formerly enslaved peoples of the Carolinas, Georgia, Alabama, and their descendants, as well as from the Caribbean, primarily the Bahamas but also Jamaica and Haiti.[1] In the year it was incorporated, one third of the affirmative votes to do so came from Blacks, but it was evident that post-Reconstruction hopes were rapidly being crushed by hardening segregation laws limiting where Blacks could live and Jim Crow violence enforcing these limits. Some of the Black population initially came to work agricultural jobs, but by the 1890s the big draw was the construction and operation of the Florida East Coast Railway, for which leased Black convict labor did much of the construction. By the 1920s, Miami's building boom became the great draw. Residential segregation meant that much of the Black populace were relegated to the central negro district, what became known as Colored Town in the 1920s, and Overtown in the 1940s. With the population of Colored Town continually expanding and with restrictive racial covenants leaving residents with nowhere to go, the resultant overcrowding was to be expected. Funding for infrastructure—paved roads, streetlights, sanitary facilities, hospitals, schools—rarely made it to the district, diverted instead to white areas. Most of the wooden houses were small, frail, and subject to wind and fire. Few had indoor plumbing. These conditions became politically significant once diseases such as tuberculosis and smallpox began to spread, because, as we will later see, stemming the spread of disease to the white households that employed Colored Town's residents in domestic service became a major reason why the Liberty Square projects were established. To outsiders' eyes, Colored Town was a cesspool of racial malfeasance, but within the circle, Colored Town was a thriving cultural mix of Black life.

As in many Black communities, churches became the townhalls and centers of life, and ministers prominent advocates. Baptist, Methodist, Seventh-day Adventist, and Episcopal were among the congregations representing the variety of the neighborhood's residents. As is frequently the case, the pious existed side by side with the profane, and groups such as the Civic League of Colored Town fought to disband a red-light district replete with bootlegging and the prostitution whites purged from their own areas by driving it into Colored Town. But there were other businesses in Colored Town including grocery and merchandise stores, insurance companies, the Mary Elizabeth, an eighty-eight-room hotel with elevator and fire sprinkler system deemed by some as the finest Black hotel in the South. The *Miami Times*, established by Bahamian Henry Ethelbert Sigismund Reeves, was South Florida's major Black newspaper and is still published by the family today. Fraternal organizations were numerous, as were civic and business organizations. Reflecting its diaspora, Guy Fawkes Day parades were annual occurrences until the 1930s, when City of Miami officials outlawed it, thinking it was improper for Blacks to burn a white man in effigy.[2] Jazz and entertainment establishments gave the area the nickname "Harlem of the South," while the movie houses and the renowned Lyric Theatre contributed to Colored Town being known as "Little Broadway." Excursions to other Black communities in Coconut Grove, South Miami, and Little River, were the social events of the day, and by the mid-1940s, Miami's Black residents frequented the Virginia Key Beach, a Dade County Park designated specifically for their use. In a later reincarnation, the beach would become the setting for a key scene in *Moonlight*. As construction workers, draymen, stevedores, porters, blacksmiths, laundresses, nursemaids, and domestics, Black hands built the spaces and facilitated the life in Miami from which they were barred.

Colored Town sat in the heart of Miami's growing business district, and as the pace of the financial center's development quickened, the space for Black living quickly diminished. Black mobility became a threat to greater white Miami, and those seeking to leave Colored Town for other areas were met with keen resistance; however, some were allowed to settle in Brownsville, Richmond Heights, and, of interest to this essay, the Liberty City neighborhood. An interesting tension developed: whites wanted Blacks out of the way of Miami's central business district, yet still wanted them sequestered somewhere. Liberty Square emerged as a solution. Ostensibly born of New Deal desires to create housing for the poor, the project also revealed how indelible social segregation was. Liberty Square becomes a symbol of the ways government policies acceded to racist attitudes demanding separation. The brainchild of the Southern Housing Corporation, the development was envisioned as a "negro colony" created to solve Colored Town's overcrowding and unsanitary conditions. The proposal soon ran into a snag, however, because the projected site was just five miles north of the business district and too close to white residents in larger Liberty City. Eventually, however, the attractiveness of federal New Deal dollars and the construction jobs they might bring won out.[3]

When young Chiron (Alex Tibbert) hides from homophobic bullies in the opening sequence of *Moonlight*, he does so in the faded pastel units with boarded-up windows of what was once Liberty Square. Completed in 1937, Liberty Square was the earliest Florida public housing project built for Blacks. It was located west of the heart of the Black community of Liberty City and represented a New Deal vision of Black paradise—within limits. It would be nice to think that the largesse leading to construction of Liberty Square stemmed from concern for those living in overcrowded conditions with dangerous health hazards (and no doubt there was some such sentiment). But the public record reveals that the greater concern was for how those conditions would affect white employers of those living in Colored Town. Would one want the handyman coming into one's neighborhood to be afflicted with smallpox? Would one want to risk one's children with a caretaker or cook who had tuberculosis? Development plans clearly indicated racist notions of Blacks as a second-class caste. A swimming pool was scuttled because it might spread syphilis; prospective tenants would have to have their belongings fumigated; washtubs in kitchens were given larger space so that those washing for white employers would have enough room to work. The Black advisory group appointed during the project's construction suggested naming it "Utopia" or Toomeyville after prominent Black attorney T. R. Toomey, but the all-white advisory committee, perhaps threatened by the racial pride signified by both, settled on Liberty Square, a nomenclature suggesting enclosure within a larger space. A 1936 *Miami Herald* editorial went so far as to provide assurance to its readers that while the government generously was assisting Blacks out of squalor and disease, "they were being placed in clean, comfortable yet unelaborate quarters," further attesting that there "are no frills at Liberty Square, but there is sanitation and light and air and harmony of simple architecture. There is room to expand, room for children to play, provision for elemental community life" (George, 58, 60). Even in paradise, Blacks were still being constrained to the "elemental."

If Liberty Square was a symbol of implicit New Deal segregationist practices, it also was a site of Black aspiration. It would produce future Black Miami civic leaders, teachers, police, and civil servants. Wealthy Blacks who desired and were able to afford single-family homes built across the street from the development.[4] The early residents of Liberty Square remember community, being able to leave doors open, beautiful personal gardens, a neighborhood where everyone watched everyone else's children. But they also remember the wall, which appears nowhere on federal architectural plans, built to separate Blacks from the all white suburb of Liberty City. Remnants of the wall, ranging from four to six feet in height, are still visible as concrete slabs lining the sidewalk along Northwest 12th Avenue north of Martin Luther King Jr. Boulevard. Liberty Square residents recall parents telling them they couldn't go to the "other side of the road" because the other side was for whites (Shumow).[5] The segregation walls of Liberty City may have represented barriers to Black mobility, but Orchard Villa Elementary School represented the dismantling of those barriers. It was the first integrated school in Miami-Dade County, five years after the 1954 *Brown v. Board of Education* decision.

By the 1960s the paradise that many envisioned Liberty Square to be was rapidly slipping away, and its fortunes became closely tied to those of the Liberty City neighborhood. Once white developers saw Liberty City as desirable, they began purchasing land from Black families, and Black homeownership plummeted, being replaced with rentals. Once the route of the new Interstate 95 was decided, the homes and business district of Colored Town now called Overtown were demolished. Many of the economically challenged former residents moved to rentals in Liberty City and to Liberty Square, which became the most densely populated project in Miami. Many factors were to contribute to the decline of Liberty Square: changing employment opportunities once domestic jobs disappeared, the growing impoverishment of women and children residing there, the impact of welfare policies, Cuban immigration, Black middle-class flight, drugs, gun violence, and race riots. Greater Liberty City succumbed to much of the national racial unrest of the 1960s, when a 1968 riot exploded during the Miami Republican National Convention. Liberty City was again the site of race riots in 1980, when an all-white jury acquitted the police officers charged in the 1979 beating death of Black insurance man Arthur McDuffie, foreshadowing conflicts in 1992 that arose after policemen were acquitted in the brutal beating of Rodney King, and those that rolled across the nation in 2020 in the wake of the murders of Breonna Taylor, George Floyd, and many others. A hundred million dollars' worth of property damage resulted, much of it in Liberty City and Liberty Square.[6] The view from the outside was that this was not a neighborhood of people, but a drug-infested, criminally dangerous ghetto. As journalist Nadege Green notes: "Words matter, how you describe places and how you reference them because then it becomes like a tag, you know. Again when you normally hear about Liberty City, it come with a preceding adjective, crime stricken, crime ridden" (Shumow).

Like many Black neighborhoods that were abandoned in the 1960s, Liberty Square and Liberty City would become desirable again, but to different communities. In 2016, the Miami-Dade County Commission awarded a $300 million redevelopment contract to one of the largest and most powerful developers in South Florida, Related Urban Development Group, chosen by then Mayor Carlos A. Giménez. A 2019 editorial in the *Miami New Times* summed up the responses of many former residents and could be seen to echo the responses of other Black communities facing redevelopment: the project "signals the gentrification of another historically Black neighborhood." The editorial went on, "Nearly 80 percent of the project's second phase is aimed at non-public-housing tenants. The result: displacement of many longtime Pork 'n' Beans residents" (Campbell).[7] The name "Pork and Beans" became a barometer, shunned by some upwardly mobile Black Miamians who see a new vision for Liberty Square, yet still embraced by those who called it home even in the most difficult of times.

What the nexus of Overtown, Liberty Square, and Liberty City shows is the struggle for Black civil rights writ on the built landscape. The enslaved seeking an existence beyond the peculiar institution settled the environs, but by the 1890s their desire for full citizenship already was being firmly curtailed. The result was Colored Town, a living neighborhood where residents labored, established schools, religious institutions, and businesses, one that was strangled by racial segregation. Public representations framed it to reflect contemporaneous views of urban Black pathology despite evidence of its promise of Black modernity in the 1900s through 1920s. Black participation in their own Promised Land of Liberty Square was also sharply curtailed in the 1930s and 1940s when the Miami Advisory Committee on Housing forbade the placement of a Black manager for the project. Segregationist attitudes would be built into Liberty Square itself with the "race wall," which like the Berlin Wall still stands today in testamentary fragments. With the film *Moonlight*, Liberty City again serves as a setting for a new civil rights advocacy. As well as telling a coming-of-age story and advocating for queer right to be, *Moonlight* sheds light on contemporary policies of anti-Blackness that have allowed a community to disintegrate. The techniques of the movie would have been impossible without the place—the faded colors of the former Liberty Square homes in contrast with the vibrant color of the oceanfront in the movie's cinematography, the play of children not far from drug dealing, all show a community of contrasts. In his portrait of Liberty Square and larger Liberty City, Barry Jenkins combines the haunting of a progressive past vision with threads of present despair. As setting, the area reveals a series of dualisms that constrict the characters: order-disorder, power-impotency, legibility-illegibility.

Moonlight is based on Tarell Alvin McCraney's unproduced play *In Moonlight Black Boys Look Blue*. McCraney describes Liberty Square as "the confluence of madness and urban blight" but still "incredibly beautiful. It is still a neighborhood." Jenkins also describes Liberty Square's visual beauty: "It's beautiful, right? When the sun comes out, it just pops" (Jones). Both comments seem contradictive to the way Liberty Square is portrayed in the movie as a drug-riddled, violent neighborhood. But this contrast represents the very existence of Blackness in the United States, characterized by the tense duality Ralph Ellison voices in the "The Blackness of Blackness" sermon in the Prologue to *Invisible Man* (1947): Now black is . . . an' black ain't . . . Black will git you . . . an' black won't . . . It do . . . an' it don't . . . Black will make you . . . or black will un-make you" (10). Black demands for a broad spectrum of civil rights results from the contradiction of belonging yet not belonging, being central to creating what became the United states yet being socially and politically excommunicated within it. Contradiction runs throughout *Moonlight*, from its opening, "i. Little," where present-day action contrasts against the past history and hope of Liberty Square. Young Chiron (Alex Hibbert) evades bullies by entering the pastel remnants of homes, and the scene evokes the search for safety and sanctuary of its early hopeful Black residents that was at the heart of the dwellings' establishment. Through darkened hallways filled with crack pipes he steps on broken glass until he is rescued by Juan (Mahershala Ali), the father figure, mentor, and ironically dope supplier who both gives him solace by telling him he may be gay but he is not a "f----t" and sells his mother the crack that incrementally destroys Chiron's family, the damage denoted by the piece-by-piece disappearance of their apartment furnishings as his mother tries to support her drug habit. Juan, who is from Cuba and tells Chiron that there is no place in the world where Black people aren't, thereby gives Chiron an expanded vision of his world beyond the limits of Liberty Square. Juan effects a psychological desegregation, perhaps his most important gift to the young boy. Chiron, even at an early age, is able to sense that bleakness and bullying are not all there is to life. Juan provides the opportunity to know of a world beyond Liberty Square, important because the first step to asserting the right to be is realizing that there is a world where one is allowed to be.

For young Chiron, this realization concretizes when Juan teaches him to swim, telling him as he holds him floating on his back promising that he has him, "You're in the middle of the world, man."[8] The scene is set at Virginia Key Beach, where in 1945, civil rights activists engaged in a "wade-in." Lawson B. Thomas an attorney who would later become a judge coordinated the posting of bail for those who might be arrested, and the local NAACP alerted the press and police. Rather than risk publicity and future court challenges, local authorities designated the beach "Virginia Key Beach, a Dade County Park for the exclusive use of Negroes." Accessed only by public and private boat, it became a mainstay of Black social life. Sadly, Virginia Key Beach followed the arc of much Black space after desegregation. Black use declined as citizens were allowed to go to more accessible beaches, and the beach itself suffered erosion from storms and a lack of upkeep. By the time Jenkins shoots the scene there, however, the Virginia Key Beach Park Trust has taken over its maintenance, and some of the original edifices—the bathhouse, carousel by the sea, and concession stand—have been designated landmarks.[9]

The first part of *Moonlight* focuses on redemption via imagining a place beyond. The second, "ii. Chiron," focuses on the social power in the word *institution*. This segment of the film reveals how hard it is to fight institutionalized forces, whether they be segregated and underresourced education, the growing feminization of poverty, or racially biased narcotics laws that led to the Jim Crow carceral practices Michelle Alexander identifies in her book *The New Jim Crow* (2010).[10] In early scenes when we meet Chiron's mother Paula (Naomie Harris), she wears the uniform of a medical office assistant or a lab tech. It disappears in subsequent scenes as her addiction and the resultant family poverty deepens, leaving her to use sex to finance her habit. In Liberty Square where she lives, as early as the mid-sixties the number of women raising children on their own began to increase, and the opportunities for employment and education began to decrease. The traditional outlets that had sustained the neighborhood—domestic jobs and civil servant work—had all but disappeared as Miami's demographics shifted and a 1970s American economy demanded skilled rather than unskilled labor. In addition to losing his mother, we learn that Juan has died, and the teenaged Chiron (Ashton Sanders) only has Teresa (Janelle Monáe), Juan's woman friend, as his remaining, minimal lifeline. He becomes untethered, sleeps on the Miami Metro in lieu of going home, and is at the mercy of institutional forces beyond his control. Jenkins sets the major portion of this section in a school, and in the all-Black student populace we see the segregation of majority-student-of-color populations in under-resourced schools that increasingly characterizes public education and entrenches the circumstances many describe as leading to the school-to-prison pipeline.[11]

In the scene that serves as the film's climax, a trapped Chiron walks along a fenced balcony, afraid to exit school as he looks down on his tormentors who are waiting to beat him.[12] The torment is further increased as Kevin (Jharrel Jerome), the one peer who has been kind and sympathetic to him ever since they were younger children, brags about being sent to detention for having sex with a female student, "banging her back out." Chiron is physically and emotionally caged. His pacing back and forth before the fence and the pain in his face represent his anxiety about both surviving bullies and reconciling his emerging sexuality. The subsequent beating is made even more painful because it comes at the hands of Kevin, who is too afraid of falling out of conformity and bows to the instigation of the main bully, Terrel (Patrick Decile). After the beating, Chiron's exchange with principal Williams (Tanisha Cidel) who mouths platitudes about being a man and pressing charges, comments on just how useless institutionalized education is in helping those students who do not "fit." "Listen, son, listen," she begins, continuing "I know it's

254Valerie Babb

hard. Believe me. I'm not trying to disrespect your struggle." Throughout the exchange Chiron painfully fidgets, and his refrain is "You don't even know." Jenkins fades the sound to silence, and we see the principal's mouth moving but hear no sound, making palpable the hopelessness in this visual representation of empty words. The images of confinement are prophecy when Chiron later snaps and is arrested at school for breaking a wooden chair over Terrel's head, leaving him immobilized. Education has long been viewed as a path to Black progress, but in more contemporary moments, with schools failing Black learners, it seems more a dream deferred.

Educator Bettina Love has observed, "We have a series of failing and interdependent systems: Educational justice is connected to economic justice, racial justice, environmental justice, religious justice, queer justice, citizenship justice, and disability justice" (Ray). These intersections are all present in *Moonlight*, illuminated through the struggles of a queer young man. Even within Black communities that are hyperaware of the need for social justice, the presence of those on many points of the sexual continuum is known but not always acknowledged, let alone valued. McCraney makes this point. Growing up in Liberty City, he observes, "there was a dearth of gay people in the media but there were gay people within my neighborhood. There were transgender people within my neighborhood. The way in which the community interacted with these people was so peripheral and marginalizing that I didn't get a chance to know how they could be integrated into the world around us. That's on us as a community and us as people. It's important for us to be representational as people in communities and not get this xenophobic idea of living in this homogenized world" (Maglott). *Moonlight* reimagines Liberty City and Liberty Square yet again as symbolic social justice sites. Once signifying past hopes, a "Paradise" in a segregated Miami, and even though weakened by failed urban policies, Black flight, and the decimation of the crack cocaine epidemic, in the film it now speaks to the need for the intersecting calls for social justice that Love references.

The third segment of *Moonlight*, "iii. Black," is both homecoming and question mark. A now grown Chiron (Trevante Nemour Rhodes) returns to Miami from Atlanta, another seat of Black advocacy, and for the first time in his adult life contemplates the possibility of a future. He reconciles with his former friend Kevin who now works in a restaurant where he cooks a "Chef's Special" for Chiron. The meal he lovingly prepares—pollo a la plancha, grilled chicken breast topped with onions, paired with a mold of white rice, a side of black beans, and in a final flourish chopped cilantro falling slowly atop the dish like snowflakes—uses foodways to mirror the cultural diversity of Miami, but also the threat Cubanness poses to Blackness within new social configurations.

Chiron teases Kevin, "Oh, so you Cuban, now?" to which his friend responds, "Only in the kitchen, papi." Kevin is navigating a personal and work identity that suggests the necessity and difficulties of cultural adaption. The scene suggests many questions, including what civil rights means in a diverse community, and how a variety of Blacknesses are to be understood. Black was a term that conveniently created a composite of Haitians, Jamaicans, Bahamians, and Black Cubans, among many others, in service to solidifying a white identity in South Florida. To think of Miami as a hemispheric South complicates the Black-white binary of racial construction within the United States, but the realities of that artificial divide are still very real. Race continues to trump ethnicity in measurements of Miami's poverty.[13] Inland areas belonging to poorer Black and Latinx communities are particularly vulnerable to what is being termed climate gentrification as coastal areas occupied by a less diverse and more affluent populace become more susceptible to flooding. These tensions are harbingers of increasing questions of what the impact will be of race and migration to conceptions of belonging in Miami.

In the final scenes of *Moonlight*, Chiron and Kevin link past and present. Chiron fills in the gap of his personal history in answer to Kevin's question, "Who is you, man?" Chiron responds, "When we got to Atlanta, I started over. Built myself from the ground up. Built myself fifteen hard." When Chiron asks Kevin about himself, the latter responds, "I wasn't never really worth shit," and continues, "Never really did anything I actually wanted to do. It was all I could do was to do what folks thought I should be doing. I wasn't never really myself." Both seek to build authentic selves answering to their own interiorities, even if they are unsure what form those selves will take. In essence, both reference rebirth, and interestingly many have credited the movie with causing a renaissance in Liberty Square and Liberty City. Barry Jenkins notes, "When we shot at night, parents would come out and tell me 'We don't usually let our kids out after dark, because there are no street lights, but since you all got your movie lights, it's a lot safer.' Kids would come on the set and sit at the video monitors and watch me work and point at me and tell each other, 'He grew up here!' I could tell from their faces that seeing me—this Black dude walking around all this machinery, calling action—was an eye-opening experience" (Rodriguez). This idea of neighborhood renaissance may be both blessing and curse. Like the end of the movie that doesn't answer what Chiron's will fate be, the impact of Liberty Square redevelopment on Black histories has yet to be seen. Many residents fear an erasure of not only their past but their current presence. As of 2019, 1,455 apartments have been built on the parcel site of Liberty Square, and retail space for a 40,000-square-foot national grocery chain store, office space, and recreational facilities, are being planned, but who this redevelopment is for remains contested. Is it for a community who has always been there or a community developers and government want to see there in the future? Hattie Walker, who lived in Liberty Square from 1948 to 1965, stresses, "The young people don't know it, they don't know what they have. And if we don't fight to keep it, you know, it's gone. And it's not a whole lot of history that we have in Miami, dealing with the black community" (Shumow). Van Williams adds, "If you talk to the older generation that been through this area, they . . . still got a passion for this area, cause this area nurtured them and fed them and made them who they are. So, you always want to keep that intact and say this is my community, this is where I came from, this is what made me who I am" (Shumow). So many of us answer the question of who we are by answering where we are from. Zip codes, for better and worse, whether we embrace or reject them, influence development because place indelibly stamps identity. If, as McCraney observes, "A community is only as strong as the stories it tells about itself" (Adams), it will be imperative to retain the stories that gave rise to *Moonlight*. This is the latest iteration of Liberty Square and Liberty City as signifiers of Black advocacy. In the contemporary moment they represent the dilemma of many spaces prominent in Black cultural history—Harlem, West Atlanta, Bronzeville, Chicago: how to navigate the future without losing the past.

The premise of this collection of essays, that Florida's many ethnic communities have given the state a vibrant mix, which has affected Southern, national, and hemispheric cultures, takes a particularly cultural turn in *Moonlight*. Overtown, Liberty Square, and Liberty City followed the cultural arc of Black dreaming, loss, and rebirth, and the film sheds light on the power of Florida as cultural space sparking Black imagination. Tarell Alvin McCraney and Barry Jenkins are the latest artists following in the footsteps of Zora Neale Hurston and James Weldon Johnson, making manifest how central the landscapes of Florida are to Black cultural creation and sustenance.

Notes

1. For more on Colored Town's diasporic population, see N. D. B. Connolly, "Colored, Caribbean, and Condemned: Miami's Overtown District and the Cultural Expense of Progress, 1940–1970," *Caribbean Studies* 34, no. 1 (January–June 2006): 3–60. https://www.jstor.org/stable/25613509.

2. For a consideration of Miami's early Black diaspora, see Raymond A. Mohl, "Black Immigrants: Bahamians in Early Twentieth-Century Miami." *Florida Historical Quarterly* 65, no. 3 (January 1987): 271–97.

3. Paul S. George and Thomas K. Petersen offer a detailed history of the construction of Liberty Square in "Liberty Square, 1933–1987: The Origins and Evolution of a Public Housing Project, *Tequesta* 48 (1988): 53–68. Also see John A. Stuart, "Liberty Square: Florida's First

Public Housing Project," in *The New Deal in South Florida: Design, Policy, and Community Building, 1933–1940*, ed. John A. Stuart and John F. Stack Jr. (Gainesville: University Press of Florida, 2008).

4. For one example, see "Lindsey Residence 1335 NW 67TH STREET," Designation Report, Historic and Environmental Preservation Board, City of Miami, September 1, 2009.

5. For an additional history of the patterns of segregation in Miami, see Raymond A. Mohl, "Whitening Miami: Race, Housing, and Government Policy in Twentieth-Century Dade County," *Florida Historical Quarterly* 79, no. 3, Reconsidering Race Relations in Early Twentieth-Century Florida (Winter 2001): 319–45. http://www.jstor.org/stable/30150856.

6. Manning Marable explores the underlying cultural histories of these events in "The Fire This Time: The Miami Rebellion, May 1980," *Black Scholar* (July–August 1980): 2–18. DOI: https://doi.org/10.1080/00064246.1980.11414129.

7. "Pork 'n' Beans" was a nickname coined in the 1990s as the development's poverty grew. For another take on the redevelopment (though the figures for housing allocations are the same), see "Years in the Making, First Phase in Historic Redevelopment of Liberty Square Is Completed," WLRN, NPR, July 2, 2019. https://www.wlrn.org/local-news/2019-07-02/years-inthe-making-first-phase-in-historic-redevelopment-of-liberty-square-is-completed.

8. Barry Jenkins, Tarell A. McCraney, Adele Romanski et al. *Moonlight*, 2017. All quotes from the movie come from this source.

9. Gregory Bush offers a fuller history of Virginia Key Beach in *White Sand, Black Beach: Civil Rights, Public Space, and Miami's Virginia Key* (Gainesville: University Press of Florida, 2016). DOI: https://doi.org/10.5744/florida /9780813062648.001.0001

10. In addition to *The New Jim Crow*, Michelle Alexander has frequently noted the racist underpinnings in the war against drugs, particularly the nemesis of Liberty City crack cocaine in many outlets: "A few years after the drug war was announced, crack cocaine hit the streets of twenty inner-city communities. The Reagan administration seized on this development with glee, hiring staff who were to be responsible for publicizing inner-city crack babies, crack mothers, crack whores, and drug-related violence. The goal was to make inner-city crack abuse and violence a media sensation, bolstering public support for the drug war which, it was hoped, would lead Congress to devote millions of dollars in additional funding to it. . . . The results have been predictable: people of color rounded up en masse for relatively minor, non-violent drug offenses. . . . In this way, a new racial undercaste has been created in an astonishingly short period of time—a new Jim Crow system. Millions of people of color are now saddled with criminal records and legally denied the very rights that their parents and grandparents fought for and, in some cases, died for." "The War on Drugs and the New Jim Crow," *RP&E Journal* 17, no. 1 (Spring 2010). https://www.reimaginerpe.org/20years/alexander.

11. For studies on inequity in Black public education, see E. R. Meiners, *Right to Be Hostile: Schools, Prisons, and the Making of Public Enemies* (New York: Routledge, 2007); Anthony J. Nocella et al., eds., *From Education to Incarceration: Dismantling the School-to-Prison Pipeline* (Lausanne: Peter Lang, 2014); and Bettina Love, *We Want to Do More Than Survive: Abolitionist Teaching and the Pursuit of Educational Freedom* (New York: Penguin/Random House, 2019). Damien Sojoyner takes a slightly different approach to the issue in *First Strike: Educational Enclosures in Black Los Angeles* (Minneapolis: University of Minnesota Press, 2016).

12. Though shot on location at Miramar High School, the school that served as an inspiration for adolescent Chiron's ultimate breakdown is McCraney's old school, Mays Middle School.

13. See Alan Aja et al., "The Color of Wealth in Miami," Kirwan Institute for the Study of Race and Ethnicity at Ohio State University, Samuel DuBois Cook Center on Social Equity at Duke University, and Insight Center for Community Economic Development, Ohio State University, February 2019.

Bibliography

Adams, Tim. "Moonlight's writer Tarell Alvin McCraney: 'the story needed to be out there.'" *The Guardian*, February 5, 2017. https://www.theguardian.com/film/2017/feb/05/moonlight-writer-tarell-alvinmccraney-observer-interview.

Campbell, Luther. "Liberty Square Redevelopment Will Erase Another African-American Neighborhood." *Miami New Times*, July 16, 2019. https://www.miaminewtimes.com/news/liberty-square-redevelopment-is-another-signof-gentrification-for-miamis-black-neighborhoods-11219779.

Ellison, Ralph. *Invisible Man*. 1947. New York: Vintage, 1989.

George, Paul S., and Thomas K. Petersen. "Liberty Square, 1933–1987: The Origins and Evolution of a Public Housing Project. *Tequesta* 48 (1988): 53–68.

Hannah-Jones, Nikole. "From Bittersweet Childhoods to 'Moonlight.'" *New York Times*, January 4, 2017. https://www.nytimes.com/2017/01/04/movies/moonlight-barry-jenkins-tarellalvin-mccraney-interview.html.

Jenkins, Barry, dir., Tarell A. McCraney, Adele Romanski, et al. *Moonlight*, 2017.

Maglott, Stephen A. "Tarell Alvin McCraney." *Ubuntu Biography Project*. October 17, 2017. https://ubuntubiographyproject.com/2017/10/17/terell-alvin-mccraney/.

Ray, Betty. "The Crisis in Black Education: Reaching Students Where They Are." Interview with Bettina Love. *Edutopia*, February 28, 2017. https://www.edutopia.org/article/crisisblack-education-reaching-students-where-they-are-betty-ray.

Rodriguez, Rene. "Miami Plays a Starring Role in the Glorious 'Moonlight.'" *Miami Herald*, October 21, 2016. www.miamiherald.com/entertainment/movies-newsreviews/article109699627.html#storylink=cpy.

Shumow, Moses. *Liberty Square: Power, History, & Race in Miami* (film, 2016). https://www.youtube.com/watch?v=qlmhlyd8bZY.

CHAPTER FOURTEEN

The Role of Florida in Colson Whitehead's *The Nickel Boys*

John Wharton Lowe

Pain has an element of blank.
It can not recollect
How it began, or if there were
A day when it was not.

It has no future but itself,
Its infinite realms contain
Its past, enlightened to perceive
New periods of pain.
—Emily Dickinson

Colson Whitehead's Pulitzer Prize–winning *The Nickel Boys* (2019) constitutes an aesthetic departure on his part, as in this novel he eschews the various forms of the magically real that animated his prior works. It is a lean text of only 213 pages, but it packs an explosive charge that remains with the reader.

The novel, which takes place in the 1950s and 1960s, begins slowly—forty-five pages are devoted to the central character Elwood's early years in Tallahassee, his rapt following of the civil rights movement in the pages of *Life* magazine and the *Chicago Defender*, and his dreams of attending college.[1] He loves to read, works hard at a menial job, and devours the first volume of an encyclopedia he wins in a contest. The fact that he only has access to "A" entries (the remaining volumes were part of a sales dummy copy and are blank) is a metaphor for the roadblocks he will constantly encounter, but this amazing absorption of this volume's entries shows his potential. His virtues are noted by the community, who seem to single him out as "the one" who can escape poverty and demonstrate the potential of the race. This hope dies, however; Part One concludes when the ride he hitches with one Rodney turns out to be in a stolen car, which leads to his sentencing to the Nickel reformatory. This initial plot bears a resemblance to Ernest Gaines's masterwork, *A Lesson Before Dying* (1993), which like this novel, takes place mainly in a carceral space. There too, a young Black boy, similarly abandoned by his parents and raised by a relative, is convicted of a crime he didn't commit; however, Gaines's protagonist faces the electric chair. By contrast, it might seem that a spell in the Florida reformatory would be temporary, and not life-threatening; however, the Dozier reformatory—originally officially known as "the Florida Industrial School for Boys" on which Whitehead bases his novel—has been revealed as a place where disobedient boys were tortured and sometimes murdered and buried in unmarked graves. The school was renamed the Arthur G. Dozier school after a superintendent appointed in 1946, who was gone before the fifties and sixties inmates who have written about the school were incarcerated. Records show, in fact, that in the early decades of the "school," young boys were hired out in chain gangs alongside hardened criminals. Whitehead may have been drawn to this story because of the veil that the survivors of Dozier have ripped off its sickening history, and to the ways in which the story uncovers an unsuspected aspect of the Sunshine State, which is often not thought of as part of the tragic racial history of the South. Indeed, this part of North Florida is statistically alarming; Michelle Alexander notes that "in interviews with one hundred residents of two Tallahassee, Florida, communities, researchers found that nearly every one of them had experienced or expected to experience the return of a family member from prison" (196).

Whitehead provides a roadmap to the research he did in notes appended to the novel. He clearly made extensive use of Roger Dean Kiser's *The White House Boys: An American Tragedy* (2009) and Robin Gaby Fisher's *The Boys of the Dark: A Story of Betrayal and Redemption in the Deep South* (2010). A review of these and related works helps us to appreciate how Whitehead sifted actual history with the creative and ordering power of his imagination, producing a laser-like narrative of revelation and judgment. It is notable that Fisher's title doesn't pinpoint Florida, but rather makes the state part of the "Deep South," with all the ominous implications of the soubriquet—a notable point, since Florida is often thought of as "not really Southern." However, we remember that the Dozier facility was located in an isolated, tropical setting, hard by a swamp and a tropical river. Throughout *The Nickel Boys*, we see a constant interplay between Whitehead's fictional constructs, real facts about

Florida's racial and carceral history, and the role of the state's topography and climate in quotidian life.

The Fisher book provides much local detail; one of the school's victims grows up by a lake shaded "by palmetto palm and oak trees. Rattlesnakes and sinkholes posed the biggest threat to the . . . folks who lived on the lake" (3). The location of such facilities is intentional; as Michelle Alexander notes, prisons are a rare sight as they are often intentionally placed far from large cities. "Prisoners," she observes, "are thus hidden from public view—out of sight, out of mind" (195).

The Dozier "school" was located near Marianna, about sixty-six miles west of Tallahassee in the Florida Panhandle. Opened on the first day of a new century in 1900, it was finally shut down in 2011. Throughout its history, parallels with the brutal aspects of slavery arose. This is not an accident; as Fisher relates, when the Civil War erupted, Jackson County was plantation country, like most of North Florida, which had 61,000 slaves. The Confederate governor of the state, John Milton, resided on a plantation near Marianna; he killed himself when the outcome of the war became clear. In 1903 inspectors found children at the reformatory in leg irons; brutal punishment was exacted on the frequent runaways, sometimes including death, just as in slave times. Torture and beatings were carried out in the notorious "White House," a small concrete structure still standing today, where miscreant boys were tied to a bed and severely beaten, sometimes resulting in permanent physical alterations or even death. Scores of graves located in what was called "Boot Hill" have been exhumed, providing evidence of these crimes. Malnutrition and infections were common. The abuses of the school had been known for some time, but when the state ordered yet another official investigation in 2008, hundreds of survivors came forward to tell gruesome stories, finding connections on the Internet. The most extensive narrative came from Roger Dean Kiser. His story, however, differs from the initial experience of Whitehead's main character, Elwood; Kiser was abandoned by his mother, abused by relatives, and sent first to an orphanage and then to Dozier, where he was taken many times to what he calls "the White House torture chamber" (27). Kiser's account of his time at Dozier begins with a graphic description of his first White House beating, when he lapses into unconsciousness. Repeatedly, the boys are warned not to tell or they will wind up in Boot Hill's unmarked graves. Like Elwood, Kiser had a close friend, David, the counterpart to Turner in the novel. Whitehead draws a parallel between Elwood and Turner; the former was raised by his grandmother, the latter by his aunt.

By contrast to Elwood and Turner, Kiser and his buddy David both were initially in an orphanage and were then sent to Dozier together. Kiser doesn't shy away from describing sexual predation and the effort to avoid "the rape room" (called "Lovers Lane"), topics that are addressed only slightly in Whitehead's novel. Even so, the equation of physical pain and sexual violation cannot be ignored, and the rooms assigned for beatings and rapes have an equivalence in their use in the work of "ravishment": "[P]ain must be recognized in its historicity and as the articulation of a social condition of brutal constraint, extreme need, and constant violence; in other words, it is the perpetual condition of ravishment" (Hartman, 51). Kiser, assigned for work in the hospital, sees many victims of White House beatings and/or rapes brought in for treatment.

Perhaps the most striking parallel between Kiser's account and Whitehead's, aside from the White House episodes, is the boxing match Kiser describes, which becomes a climactic event in Whitehead's story. Forced to box, which he hates, Kiser nevertheless wins many matches and is named "the champ." The forced combat between the boys also clearly echoes both Richard Wright's *Black Boy* and the "battle royal" segment of Ellison's *Invisible Man*. An event Whitehead doesn't employ, but that Kiser reports, is that of a young Black boy who is punished by the laundry supervisor by being tumbled to death in a dryer. In one of the most chilling episodes in Kiser's book, he recounts how the boys would save the cream that topped milk bottles and shake it to make butter. One day a woman visitor comes into the dining hall where one boy is doing this and she screams that he is masturbating. He is taken to the White House and never seen again.

An appendix to Kiser's account notes the racial segregation in the institution (on which Whitehead concentrates) and notes that the conditions of the Black dormitory were far worse than in the white one; the Black inmates were forced to work until dark each day, sleeping two to a cot without mattresses, often without blankets, a condition reminiscent of both the middle passage and slave quarters. We also learn that the facility had a deceptively attractive appearance, with large brick buildings situated in well-kept grounds, hard by the Chipola River, and surrounded by tropical foliage and swamps, masking the deteriorated interior and the terrors it contained. Kiser's book concludes with the stories of other inmates, who mention the roaring giant industrial fan in the White House that was operated to drown out the screams of the tortured, something that Whitehead uses to great effect. The real-life torturers, mentioned by many survivors, were Robert Hatton and Troy Tidwell; Hatton's beatings were worse because Tidwell only had one arm.

Again, there are patterns in the life of the "school" that echo those from slavery. When boys run away, the entire town knows it as a piercing siren goes off, and bloodhounds are released. Local farmers join the hunt, desiring fifty-dollar bounties (Fisher, 43). The boys were told that if the hounds didn't get them, the swamp would. Swamps, of course, were often sites of refuge for runaway slaves. Toward the end of the novel, Whitehead pushes this further, describing the white men who run Nickel: "Their daddies taught them how to keep a slave in line, passed down this brutal heirloom. Take him away from his family, whip him until all he remembers is the whip, chain him up so all he knows is chains. A term in an iron sweatbox, cooking his brains in the sun, had a way of bringing a buck around, and so did a dark cell, a room aloft in darkness, outside time" (190). So we are not far away from nineteenth-century atrocities that Whitehead amply illustrated in *The Underground Railroad*. It is as if that book haunts this one, just as the memories of Nickel/Dozier torment the former inmates years after their release.

Michael O'McCarthy, one of Dozier's survivors, has wondered if the cruelties were allowed to continue over the years because the boys were seen as "throwaway children," a phrase that summons up the late critic Patricia Yaeger's study of the "throwaway body" in her path-breaking study of southern culture and literature, *Dirt and Desire*, and a thematic that Whitehead also employs. On the other hand, however, the inmates had an *economic* value. As Fisher states, the school "was an industry, requiring employments, goods, and services, in an out-of-the-way place . . . People in town needed their jobs . . . you just had to look the other way" (77), a micro-summary that is still applicable to the macro prison-industrial complex so tellingly excoriated by Michelle Alexander in *The New Jim Crow*.[2] Fisher thus devotes much attention to the workers at Dozier, who desperately need their jobs. Most, however, had no training and often themselves came from the same impoverished, uneducated culture as their wards. By dehumanizing the boys, they excused treating them brutally; the abuses went undetected for so long partly because of the complicity of the surrounding townspeople in protection of a local "industry," but also because of the isolation of the facility. Thus as late as 2008, when Dozier was finally shuttered, the staff treated the boys as prisoners rather than as disturbed and needy children (Fisher, 141). To his credit, Fisher makes his exposé come alive by providing explicit examples of individual boys, such as Robert "Bobby" Straley, who, like Roger Kiser, came from a dysfunctional family, and weighed only 105 pounds when he was admitted to the facility in 1963. Once again, the evil focus is on the school director Robert W. Hatton, who administered most tortures, aided by the one-armed Troy Tidwell. The book begins with the beatings of four boys thought to be planning an escape. Like Roger, Bobby passes out and becomes traumatized for life.

There is much more of the Florida landscape in the Fisher account, as well as a portrait of the deceptively picturesque town of Marianna, called "the city

of Southern charm. . . . Antebellum homes, nestled on small, verdant squares
. . . a Confederate monument stands tall on the Jackson county courthouse
lawn . . . With a population of 6,200, Marianna looks like a picture postcard
for quintessential Americana, with people who care about God, country, and
family. It is also a city with a shameful past" (51–52), a history revealed by all
these accounts as the dark underside of the sublime Florida imaginary. In *The
Nickel Boys* Marianna becomes the town of Eleanor.

Both cautious and crafty, it is Elwood's buddy Turner who plots an eventual escape that will avoid the usual goal of runaways, the swamp; instead,
he uses their knowledge of the town to plan a temporary refuge in a vacant
house in town, where they can steal clothes off a line and head north on stolen
bikes. Marianna, by contrast, doesn't receive detailed treatment in the nonfiction accounts, although the town is made culpable in Dozier's persistence
because of their economic dependency on the jobs there.

The Fisher book comes to a climax when the state agrees to a memorial
service involving the White House Boys at Dozier, and the *Miami Herald* is
preparing an exposé of the school's past. When Robert Straley is interviewed,
he is shocked and horrified to learn that not only is the brutal Troy Tidwell
still alive, he is being honored by the Marianna Rotary Club with the Paul
Harris Fellow award for a lifetime of "Service above Self" (186).

Fisher's account concludes with four testimonials: first, the story of Ellis
Adams, who was sent to Dozier at the age of ten; he, too, was beaten unconscious at the White House. Like many others, Adams led a troubled life after
his release; before he died, he told his wife that many boys were killed and
buried on the grounds. His widow, Monica, sent Robert Straley a four-page
testimonial that Ellis wrote before his death. Next we hear from Michael
Tucker, who was beaten in the White House three times; on one of these occasions he was forced to hold down another victim, whose first name coincidentally is Tucker: "Our common name gave us a certain bond" (217). Then
we get the story of an African American victim, Willie Horne, who is put into
solitary confinement in "the hole" for months; Horne witnesses the murder of
another boy in the White House. A final example comes from the eighty-year-
old sister of one George Owen Smith, whose body, authorities at Dozier told
his mother, was found under a porch in Marianna where he had hidden after
running away. Eventually, however when they visit Owen's grave, another boy
tells them that the two of them had run away; when pursuing cars reached
them, Owen ran across a field and was felled by a shotgun blast, the same ending that Whitehead reprises for his novel.

The *Herald's* exposé of the horrors at Dozier was published on October
19, 2008, preceding a ceremony that was held in front of the White House

on Tuesday, October 21. The structure was officially sealed, and a memorial plaque was placed there by the Florida Department of Juvenile Justice. After the event, Robert Straley learned that no one had found the notorious "rape room," but after a search around the overgrown perimeter of one of the buildings, a trap door hidden under weeds is found that leads to steps that go to this den of terrors, which has been undiscovered for years.

Reform schools may be seen in many cases as prep academies for prisons, as many boys grow up to become convicts. They also have much in common with orphanages. We remember here that when Newt Gingrich was formulating his "contract for America," he drew up a plan whereby the progeny of unwed mothers would be taken from them and placed in orphanages.[3] Gingrich was also all in favor of expanding the prison-industrial complex, which as Michelle Alexander has shown, exploded in the 1990s, with support from both Republicans and Democrats. The then-popular "three strikes and you're out" laws resulted in life sentences for felons who had committed minor crimes. Thus, a nation pondered the containment of a problem—a pollution for some—of Blackness, first by shipping children to orphanages and reformatories, or alternately, in "strict" and impoverished ghetto schools, before locking adults up in jails and prisons. In all these formats, surveillance, work, isolation, and punishment are hallmarks of "houses of correction." Michel Foucault comments on the acceptance of such institutions and on the similarities between them: "how could the prison not be immediately accepted when, by locking up, retraining and rendering docile, it merely reproduces, with a little more emphasis, all the mechanisms that are to be found in the social body? The prison is like a rather disciplined barracks, *a strict school*, a dark workshop, but not qualitatively different. This double foundation—juridic-economic on the one hand, technical-disciplinary on the other—made the prison seem the most immediate and civilized form of all penalties" (233), especially, we might add, in a racist-capitalist society, where "civilization" all too often means confinement and concealment of the poor.

As Whitehead and both Kiser and Fisher document, the Nickel/Dozier school practiced a strict pattern of surveillance and punishment. Students passed through an endless series of "inspections" and were watched everywhere, from the cafeteria to the bathrooms and showers. In order to be effective, Foucault tells us, the system of surveillance must be understood in its significance by the observed. The brutal punishment of the boys—particularly the extreme form meted out in the White House—was hidden from view. But all the boys knew and feared the White House because they had seen the maimed bodies of its victims, had heard about those boys who died during the torture and were buried in anonymous graves in "Boot Hill." As Foucault notes, "the effectiveness of punishment results from its inevitability. When it takes the form of torture, several rules apply: it must produce a certain degree of pain, which may be measured" (33), and this is the case at Dozier, where the strap falls a certain number of times; and it must mark the victim, which is certainly the case with the Nickel boys. The cries of the boys under torture comprise part of the ritual. As Foucault notes, "the fact that the guilty man should moan and cry out under the blows is not a shameful side-effect, it is the very ceremonial of justice being expressed in all its force" (34). But the cries are to be heard only by the torturers; the giant industrial fan, however, turned on to drown out the cries, becomes a stand-in for them, as the other boys know this sound means one of them is bearing the blows in the White House.

Whitehead's achievement in this narrative is his grim determination to face and critique the nature of pain, particularly pain inflicted on others, both as an expression of power and as a pathway to power. At the same time, following after the publication of multiple reports of the horrors inflicted at the Dozier school, Whitehead adds his voice to a chorus of truth; as Elaine Scarry notes, "Physical pain has no voice, but when it at last finds a voice, it begins to tell a story, and the story that it tells is about the inseparability of 1) The difficulty of expressing physical pain; 2) the political and perceptual complications that arise as a result of that difficulty; 3) the nature of both material and verbal expressibility or, more simply, the nature of human creation" (Scarry, 3).

Looked at in another way, the events recounted in the novel depict a pattern of linked trauma, both individual and communal. When we remember that the story is seemingly being told by Elwood, the repeated victim of abuse, we see an illustration of Cathy Carruth's oft-cited statement that the facing and telling about traumatic events in one's life can be restorative. On the other hand, it is clear at the end of the novel that Elwood hasn't been able to fully recover from the trauma that he suffered, and that the physical and emotional wounds he received are still with him, testifying to what lately has been called "slow violence."

Fundamentally, however, all transgressions pointed to in the novel—be they at the hands of the guards, the other staff, or more broadly, the state and juridical institutions—inevitably converge on the body. As Ta-Nehisi Coates has memorably put it, "the sociology, the history, the economics, the graphs, the charts, the regressions all land, with great violence, upon the body" (Coates, 10).

To put this another way, what Whitehead does in fictionalizing the tragic history of Dozier makes it come alive in a coherent, gripping way. Building on the accumulated narratives of actual inmates found in the Fisher and Kiser accounts, he creates characters whose fates are in question throughout most of the book; their relationships and strategies—both for the incarcerated and their keepers—are developed intricately and cumulatively, generating a propulsion and a series of concluding climaxes. In the nonfictional accounts, the memories of former inmates, now adults, are usually framed by locating them in their current lives. This is not the case in *The Nickel Boys*, which keeps the reader, like the inmates, locked inside a confining narrative that mimics the enclosures of the compound. The boys are not spared, and neither is the reader. Whitehead chooses to set the story in the sixties, perhaps because this time at the facility ironically parallels some of the great achievements of the civil rights movement. More importantly, however, it enables him to equip his central character, Elwood Curtis, before his confinement, with a recording of *Martin Luther King at Zion Hill*, whose messages challenge and sustain him during his days of captivity; the quotes from King, however, provide a modulation of love and hope against the ongoing current of depravity and cruelty that dominates the novel.

The institution was originally located on 1,200 acres of forests. Two brick dormitories, a half-mile apart, were built—one for whites, the other for "coloreds." Corn, sugar cane, vegetables, and cotton were grown, and some inmates were put to work making bricks, ostensibly to teach them a trade. But even at the beginning, the school was more like a prison; in 1903, boys were found shackled in irons, and a 1910 investigation uncovered a history of brutal beatings. In 1914, six boys were burned in a fire. In the early twentieth century, some of the boys were hired out by school administrators to work alongside adult convicts. Over the years, the enrolment ballooned, and in 1956, the school was overcrowded, with 698 students and 128 staff members, which made it the largest such facility in the nation. This worse-than-Dickensian place of torment existed for 109 years, closing in 2011; incredibly, even after its sordid history was revealed and the White House was closed in 2008, operations continued for three more years.

Elwood's heroic qualities do not come from his rearing by his grandmother, who has no truck with sit-ins and protests, which she sees as "a young person's game." "Act above your station, and you will pay . . . Her father had paid for not stepping out of the way of a white lady on Tennessee Avenue. Her husband, Monty, paid when he stepped up. Elwood's father, Percy, got too many ideas when he joined the army so that when he came back there was no room in Tallahassee for everything in his head. Now Elwood . . . that Martin Luther King record . . . nothing but ideas" (34). The key quote from King that animates Elwood: "*We must believe in our souls that we are somebody; that we are significant, that we are worthful, and we must walk the streets of life every day with this sense of dignity and this sense of somebody-ness*" (26–27).

As was the case with real-life Dozier, the façade of Whitehead's Nickel institution is a lovely lie, much like the overall image the keepers maintain for the outside world. Elwood's first glimpse—and ours—is positive: "He expected tall stone walls and barbed wire, but there were no walls at all. The campus was kept up meticulously, a bounty of lush green dotted with two- and three-story buildings of red brick . . . cedar trees and beeches cut out portions of shade . . . It was the nicest-looking property Elwood had ever seen—a real school, a good one, not the forbidding reformatory he'd conjured" (47). But the interiors are dirty and in bad repair: "outside was one thing and inside another." Thirty cots crowd one room. Soon, he is warned about escapes: "If the housemen don't run you down, and the swamp don't suck you up . . . They call in those dogs from the state penitentiary" (48). And the very first night, Elwood hears a roaring, which we learn is the industrial fan set in motion when boys are taken "out for ice cream," a euphemism for brutal beatings in the White House. There are local touches; the icy cold water the boys shower in has the smell of rotten eggs, as does much sulphureous water in northern Florida.

Elwood's first brutal beating comes as a result of taking up for a boy being bullied. "The beating room had a bloody mattress and a naked pillow that was covered . . . by the overlapping stains from all the mouths that had bit into it . . . Splatter on the walls where the fan had whipped up blood . . . the strap was three feet long with a wooden handle, and they had called it Black Beauty" (69). Because he passes out, he can't say how many licks he got. He comes to in the hospital, where he learns of Nickel's troubled institutional history. Its printing plant and brick factory make money for the state, and tourists pay to attend the Christmas lights festival. In the hospital, Turner fills him in on the horrors of the school and how to avoid them. Elwood starts applying lessons he learned from his one encyclopedia volume, such as Archimedes's dictum that violence is the only lever big enough to move the world.

Whitehead, like many of the survivors of Dozier, returns to the physical fact of the whip repeatedly, describing the notch in it that snags and slices the boys. As Scarry observes, both "weapon and wound can be used associatively to express pain"; and indeed, pain, she adds, almost cannot be apprehended without the idea of the weapon, and the word pain has its "etymological home in 'poena' or 'punishment' . . . Intense pain is world-destroying" (16, 29). Moreover, this infliction of pain also demonstrates the power of the oppressor, and is designed to "unmake" individuality and the human (20). The inscription of the whip on flesh becomes visible to the other inmates and a sign of both warning and dominant power.

Whitehead adds still other details that we don't find in the books written about Dozier; for instance, in a variant on convict labor, Elwood and Turner are farmed out for local work, like painting Mrs. Davis's house, ironically with Dixie White paint. Turner tells Elwood and us that in earlier times, boys were farmed out for long periods of time as virtual slaves to white families, living in basements; "beat you, kick you, feed you shit" (93).

A key event in the book is the annual boxing match, which, as we have seen, was a feature of the actual Dozier. When the rough Black inmate Griff is chosen to fight as the representative of the Black students, who have held the boxing title for fifteen years, he seems an inevitable winner, but is told by the supervisor, Maynard Spenser to take a dive if he comes up against the "great white hope," Big Chet, in the championship fight. The boxing festival is quite extensive, employing three rings and is attended by local whites. Director Hardee is master of ceremonies. Griff loses track of the bout segments and inadvertently defeats his opponent. That night he is taken to the iron rings embedded in two trees and beaten to death—he is never seen again.

Here Whitehead employs one of his dramatic flash forwards: "When the state of Florida dug him up fifty years later, the forensic examiner noted the fractures in the wrists and speculated that he'd been restrained before he died." The narrator comments: "Most of those who know the story of the rings in the trees are dead by now. The iron is still there. Rusty. Deep in the heart-wood. Testifying to anyone who cares to listen." Indeed, this sentence could be the motto for the novel, which offers a fictional testimony to the very real suffering of the Dozier boys. Here we might recall a key passage in Orwell's *1984*, when O'Brian asks, "'How does one man assert his power over another, Winston?' Winston thought. 'By making him suffer,' he said. 'Exactly. By making him suffer. Obedience is not enough. Unless he is suffering, how can you be sure that he is obeying your will and not his own? Power is in inflicting pain and humiliation'" (Orwell, 219), and so it proves in this novel.

As noted, the sexual predation we know took place at Dozier is obliquely treated by Whitehead until late in the novel, with reference to bigger inmates "punking" weaker ones, but is said to have been practiced by the abusive Nickel, for whom the school was named, and the school's psychologist, Dr. Campbell; "Lover's Lane" is referred to as a place where boys are raped, a subject treated much more fully in the nonfiction accounts of the school mentioned earlier. In Part Three of the book, however, Whitehead gives an account of one Clayton, who is raped by the house father of Roosevelt dorm, Freddie Rich.

Ironies abound; Jaimie, the Mexican inmate, is said to have conducted him-self "in accordance with the Nickel handbook's rules of conduct—a miracle, since no one had ever seen the handbook despite its constant invocations by the staff. Like justice, it existed in theory" (188)—a statement that Michelle

Alexander has shown to be true of the entire US criminal system, a macro-cosm of which the Dozier school was a microcosm.

Part Three of the novel—which comprises the last seventy-seven pages—begins with a huge flash forward to the 1980s and the now grown Elwood's life in New York, where he runs a successful moving company. But his good fortune is clouded by his Florida past, and damages his relation with his girl-friend Denise, whom he met at night school getting his GED. From then on out, Whitehead alternates between the life of our New York Elwood and his last days at Nickel; while Elwood now is prosperous, he is never really free of the memories of Nickel, especially when he runs into or hears from other inmates, like Chickie, who at the reformatory was regularly punked, and then started punking smaller boys himself. Chickie's subsequent life has been a disaster, and he tells Elwood about other inmates: "This one was a crook, that one lost an arm in Vietnam, another one was strung out . . . it was like a pic-ture of the Last Supper, twelve losers with Chickie in the middle. That's what the school did to a boy. It didn't stop when you got out. Bend you all kind of ways until you were unfit for straight life, good and twisted" (165). A key quotation from Dr. King recurs to Elwood as the novel moves to a conclusion: "*Throw us in jail, and we will still love you. Bomb our homes and threaten our children, and as difficult as it is, we will still love you . . . beat us and leave us half-dead, and we will still love you. But be ye assured that we will wear you down by our capacity to suffer, and one day we will win our freedom*" (172). Once inspired by these words, now Elwood thinks "What a thing to ask. What an impossible thing" (173).

Instead of adopting King's strategy, Elwood keeps a record of all the places he and Turner have helped sell Nickel supplies in town; he writes the *Chicago Defender* about abuses but receives no reply. Elwood's records, which include revelations about the White House and Griff's disappearance, more clearly indicate that he sees the outrages at Nickel in more than a personal way; his cries for justice are for all the school's victims. The title of the novel, after all, is plural—this about the Nickel *boys*, not just Elwood.

Turner volunteers to give the record to the white inspectors, whose visit has caused frantic touch-ups at the school, which create a kind of Potemkin vil-lage quite different from the school's reality. The result? Elwood is taken to the White House again for another brutal beating, followed by solitary confine-ment; this causes him to join Turner in an attempted escape, made necessary by Turner overhearing that the guards will take Elwood "out back"—meaning kill him. Whitehead sums up the boy's thinking succinctly: "The world had whispered its rules to him for his whole life and he refused to listen, hearing instead a higher order. The world continued to instruct: Do not love for they will disappear, do not trust for you will be betrayed, do not stand up for you will be swatted down. Still he heard those higher imperatives: Love and that love will be returned, trust in the righteous path and it will lead you to deliverance, fight and things will change" (195). The boy's escape is tight with tension and keeps the reader distraught with fear and hope. It is Turner who plots out their eventual escape; avoiding the usual goal of the swamp, they plan to take temporary refuge in a vacant house in town they know, steal some clothes off a line, and head north on stolen bikes.

Because I hope all of you will have the chance to benefit from this somber but profound story, I won't disclose the nature of the unexpected and ingenious ending; suffice it to say that Whitehead finds a way to make the narrative radiate in multiple directions at its conclusion, combining tragedy and transcendence. Elaine Scarry has stated that physical pain does not simply resist language but actively destroys it, bringing about an immediate reversion to a state anterior to language, to the sounds and cries a human being makes before language is learned" (4). It is to Whitehead's credit that he gives an extended and eloquent communal voice to those who have come to be known as "the White House Boys," elevating their suffering into a monument to their endurance and compelling humanity.

Notes

1. Although Whitehead logically elects to narrow the parameters of his story to the reformatory, he is aware of the complex civil rights movement that played out in Tallahassee, the state capital, in the fifties and sixties; Elwood, the central character, plays a small role in these events early in the novel. The Tallahassee Bus Boycott began in 1956, and the integration of Florida State University in the city comprises another stirring story. The city's historically black university, Florida A&M, is also located in Tallahassee and students there played an important role in mounting demonstrations. For a full presentation of these events, see Rabby.

2. As Ernest Drucker notes, in 2011 US prison budgets had swallowed up many much-needed public funds, in order to pay an average of $25,000 per year for each inmate, or $60 billion annually. The largely privatized prison-industrial industry "offers new investment opportunities on Wall Street for operating 'for-profit' prisons" (Drucker, 46–47). However, as John Pfaff has demonstrated, private prisons account for only a small portion of the nation's carceral facilities; the responsibility for creating and running them falls on the state. As Pfaff reports, once states have invested in correctional facilities, it proves hard to rein in the spending, as public officials benefit from large prisons, which bring jobs to their districts, and to the public-sector unions that represent the guards. Whitehead, of course, is dealing with this aspect of incarceration on the micro rather the macro level but he takes pains to show how local communities come to depend on these institutions for financial reasons.

3. For details on the "Contract for America," see Gillespie and Schelhas, *passim*.

Bibliography

Blakemore, Erin. "Archaeologists Finally Know What Happened at This Brutal Reform School." http://smithsonianmag.com/smart-news/archeologists-finally-know-what-happened-brutal-reform-school-180957911/.

Carruth, Cathy. *Unclaimed Experience: Trauma, Narrative, and History*. Baltimore: Johns Hopkins University Press, 1996.

Coates, Ta-Nehisi. *Between the World and Me*. New York: Spiegel & Grau, 2015.

Drucker, Ernest. *A Plague of Prisons: The Epidemiology of Mass Incarceration in America*. New York: New Press, 2011.

Fisher, Robin Gaby, with Michael O'McCarthy and Robert W. Straley. *The Boys of the Dark: A Story of Betrayal and Redemption in the Deep South*. New York: St. Martin's, 2010.

Foucault, Michel. *Discipline and Punish: The Birth of the Prison*. Trans. Alan Sheridan. New York: Pantheon, 1977.

Gillespie, Ed, and Bob Schelhas, eds. *Contract with America: The Bold Plan by Newt Gingrich, Rep. Dick Armey and the House republicans to Change the Nation*. New York: Times Books, 1994.

Kiser, Roger Dean. *The White House Boys: An American Tragedy*. Deerfield Beach, FL: Health Communications Inc., 2009.

Montgomery, Ben, and Waveney Ann Moore. "For Their Own Good." *Tampa Bay Times*, April 19, 2009.

Nixon, Rob. *Slow Violence and the Environmentalism of the Poor*. Cambridge, MA: Harvard University Press, 2011.

Orwell, George. *1984*. New York: Signet, 1961.

Pfaff, John. *Locked In: The True Causes of Mass Incarceration—and How to Achieve Real Reform*. New York: Basic Books, 2017.

Rabby, Glenda Alice. "Out of the Past: The Civil Rights Movement in Tallahassee, Florida." PhD diss., Florida State University, 1984. Ann Arbor: University Microfilms.

Scarry, Elaine. *The Body in Pain: The Making and Unmaking of the World*. New York: Oxford University Press, 1985.

Whitehead, Colson. *The Nickel Boys*. New York: Doubleday, 2019.

Yaeger, Patricia. *Dirt and Desire: Reconstructing Southern Women's Writing, 1930–1990*. Chicago: University of Chicago Press, 2000.

The Storm, the Telling

Lyrae Van Clief-Stefanon

The soloist has been going off for four minutes and thirty-eight seconds. She has just finished winding her left arm around in a circle as if she might stir a tornado out of the air in the church, snatch it from the ether, and fling it out into the congregation. After giving an emphatic knee-bounce on her high-heeled pumps, and popping back up into her solid, shoulder-width stance, she belts the imperative, "Tell your storm!" with a hair-shake, her closed hand now hanging loosely at her side, as though she had gathered the storm again, as though she held it by the tail.

"I Told the Storm," the song she sings, appears four times in a row on my favorite playlist, a constant anthem in the months of the shutdown. When my best friend came to visit at the end of August 2020, before the Covid-19 surge made such a visit almost unthinkable, I played it for him as we sat at the orange picnic table on my blustery deck. Index finger in the air, I sang along so he could catch the lyrics: *Wind, stop blowing / Flood, stop flowing / Lightning, stop flashing / Breakers, stop dashing! / . . . That's what I told the storm.* That index finger?—: yeah, I laugh about it myself. A gesture requesting a pause. A raised index finger says, "Wait." Asks attention: "Hold on. Listen." In the wrong company, a raised index finger might seem imperious. In the right company, the company of one's beloveds, the same bit of sass suggesting "I've got the floor" or "I am about to tear this part up" enchants. In the Pentecostal church I grew up in, a raised finger combined with a lowered head was a signal that said humbly, "Excuse me." It was customary for a woman, if she were to exit during service, to hold an index finger up in the air as she walked out, marking her departure as respectful, begging pardon. I grew up noting the loveliness, the poetry of such gestures, blending my experience in the church with things I learned out "in the world." That a finger in the air, for example, was a test of wind direction; the body, a weathervane. Touch your tongue to your pointer finger; hold it up; note where the skin feels most cool.

Before he moved to take a job at another university, my best friend and I would frequently visit a scenic overlook just off campus that offered distant views of Ithaca's hills. There we would meet to laugh and sing and talk and meditate, so regularly that we took to calling the spot "the church." One day, caught up in praise at the very beauty of our lives in that moment, we noticed a rapidly approaching storm and decided to ask it aloud to change direction so we could continue enjoying the sun and view for a little longer. When the storm changed course, we were struck with joy! The spirit of this memory between us, I held my finger in the air and sang to him on my deck last year—: *Death can't shake me / [Trump] can't make me / Bills can't break me / Disease can't take me / You can't drown me / My God surrounds me / That's what I told the storm.*

•   •   •

Conduct your blooming in the noise and whip of the whirlwind, Gwendolyn Brooks commands in the final line of "The Second Sermon on the Warpland," whirling me back toward the wild and joyful noise that is the poem's repeated imperative—: *Nevertheless, live.* Before ever reading Brooks, I first got this lesson on living in my mother's house and, at my mother's insistence, in the house of God, in my father's house. The work of believing, of being, of doing and not just hearing the word—: early made challenging by violence :—through and despite challenge, sustains, inspires, and quickens. Its word-work becomes bodywork. Its mind-work, play. My delight in that play—: a blooming faith.

In the video, just after the soloist has thrown one finger in the air and sung, "My God wins every battle and I am a victor!" the songwriter approaches, sidestepping up to the soloist on stage. Seeming to take his appearance as cue to wind the song to a close, the soloist steps aside, handing the microphone to the songwriter; but he says to her, "Stay right there." The music never stops. (Y'all know how we do.) He motions for the choir director and for another singer he has brought forward, and they revise the song on the spot. The soloist standing by listens as the songwriter, singing along to make a three-way harmony with the choir director and this other singer, adds new lines to the mix—: *I'm more ~ than a conqueror ~ and overcomer ~ I'm a survi~vor!*

"Yes!"

It flies out of the soloist's mouth before these harmonizers even get to the end of the line.

•   •   •

I do not want to think about sexual assault.

I never want to write about sexual assault again. Right now, instead, I want to write about Hurricane David—: the storm that struck Florida in 1979, the worst year of my early memory, the year I wrote my mother a note to tell her a family member had been molesting me. That storm killed 2,069 people in Dominican Republic, Dominica, Puerto Rico, and the United States It spawned ten tornadoes in Florida. But I did not know these stats at that time. I was eight. I vaguely remember warnings on the news urging Florida residents to evacuate as the hurricane approached. We lived in Daytona Beach. I remember we taped masking tape X's across the sliding glass patio doors that led to the carport. I remember piling mounds of pillows and blankets into the bathtub where my younger brother and I would sleep that night. But most vividly, I remember my mother letting me walk outside with her into the eye of that hurricane. I will never forget its atmosphere of eerie stillness, the green sky of the storm's eye :—: how that moment remains, strangely, one of my most treasured moments and memories of childhood.

What did I begin to know (about my mother? :—: about myself, about the world, the weather) in that moment? *Knowledge puffeth up but charity edifieth* (I Cor. 8:1). I am writing toward an understanding not academic but edifying. To write courageously means I must share my heart.

I'm a survivor. The declaration cannot but strike me. When the trio in the video stretches their harmony toward it—: how do I write about *the church* of my childhood without harming further those who have been harmed by and within such spaces? How do I hold the lives of those who did not survive? How do I write what is :—: true to storm and sanctuary—: I survived. I did not lose my life. But bonds of family, faith, feeling shifted with the revelations of that year. Standing in the eye of that storm, I entered a space of threat and dare I would later come to recognize and value as—: *let me had been* :—a temporal space marked by way of adynaton

•   •   •

The first time I sang a solo in church must have been the same year Hurricane David struck Florida. 1979. Was it before or after the storm? At that point, my family still attended Church of God By Faith, the little Pentecostal church I remember as a hot, tight box of tension and joy, discipline and brilliance. In this church of my memory, hard wooden pews snagged my stockings and hurt my sit bones; striking Black voices lifted song; swaying Black bodies packed closely in a haze of shared breath, scent, and spirit. It was simultaneously a space of revival and survival, of high fashion, of nourishment, of drama, of eruptive ecstatic dance and piercing sermon—: *He that is mighty has done unto me great things, and holy is his name*—: a bit of scripture, embedded in memory, encapsulating the simmering atmosphere.

When I stood before the pulpit and opened my mouth to sing, I knew too much and felt too well the lyrics of my song—: *Trouble in my way, I have to cry sometimes. So much trouble, I have to cry sometimes. I lay awake at night, but tha's alright ~, 'cause I know that Jesus ~*[1]] Jesus! He will fix it! [*af ~ ter-while*] Af~ ter-whi~ile. . . . [[2] I must have been eight, but my deep alto surprised the Mothers, Deaconesses, and Sisters of the congregation. After service, a throng of women encircled me, pressing me to themselves, remarking, "You sure let the Lord use you today!" And I wondered angrily how it was they didn't understand—: how the word "use" stung me! I felt ashamed. Even now, a woman of almost 50,] and now 50 [I feel accusatory. Were they pretending not to know? How could they not know have known?

It is impossible for me to watch the interactions in the internet video of "I Told the Storm" without the taint of suspicion. I catch myself, eyeing each gesture with scrutiny, watchful for the pain belying each interaction.

●   ●   ●

It is also impossible for me to watch the performance without sheer wonder—: at Black creative force embodied as song, as poem, as breath, as tongue and interpretation, as *noise and whip*, as :—: storm & eye. The choir, a predominance of Black women dressed in Black, follows the choir director, elevating the impossible weight of the line—: *when God speaks* :—she, with raised arms, they, with raised voices. She taps out the song's beat (feet balanced on daintiest kitten-heel mules!). When the soloist in the video taps an open palm to her chest as she sings, "*No weapon formed against me shall prosper*," amplifying the sense of feeling the Word of the lyric, the vibration seemingly flows through her hand directly into the hand of the choir director. Although the two stand with their backs to each other, the soloist's physical indication of personally claiming a Word-inflected courage, taking heart coincides with the choir director's gestural call for heart-based amplification. One motion flows unbroken into the other, like a feeling passed between them. The choir director does not see the gesture; she catches it. To believe in this, the living, moving Word challenged what my mother and those in the congregation deemed "worldly" thought and encouraged instead a delight to read in such spaces how the spirit moves; how one "catches" the Holy Ghost. To illustrate such pulse and passage required study—: to substantiate it, faith. *In the beginning was the Word and the Word was with God and the Word was God*, my favorite passage of scripture reads; from there I trace a lifelong love of poetry. What passes between soloist and choir director as permeability of flesh to word in action, my girlhood in my mother's house and in the church taught me in community to read and value, taught me to love. *Knowledge puffeth up but charity edifieth*. This was reading around which I might build a life.

• • •

In another video of "Telling the Storm," a different soloist interprets the song in the setting similar in size and atmosphere to the church in which I grew up. About two and half minutes into the video she adlibs the words, "I told my storm ~ everything that I'm going through." Improvising in this way she shifts the narrative. The storm becomes a confidante. She continues in this vein, relaying to the church how she told the storm itself, "Trouble don't last always." With her testimony, addressing the storm itself, she shifts the atmosphere.

• • •

"Build with lithe love," Gwendolyn Brooks writes in the final complete sentence of "The Sermon on the Warpland." From that sentence, the poem moves to its conclusion via an expanding fragment, beginning with "with" and defining "lithe love." *With* appears six times in the final strophe of the poem, first assuming the capitalized imperative energy of the verb "Build," then ushering in by way of anaphora a series of similes that culminate in an intensifying chiasmatic description of "our black."

Build with lithe love. With love like lion-eyes,
with love like morningrise,
with love like black, our black—
luminously indiscreet;
complete; continuous. (451)

A reciprocity imbues our Blackness with litheness. There is a bend I am looking for here—: the image of the palm trees, bent but not breaking in the tearing wind in mind. Where do I find it in the materials the poet deems more fitting for building than weathering steel—: in the homophone and the port-manteau. Lion-eyes and morningrise. What to make of the visible marking of the space between, the black dash that links lion-eyes? What of the closing of space in the portmanteau that follows? The rhyming calls attention to the two, insists upon it; I can't but notice. Brooks first links two words, closing the space between them in a way that suggests another soundalike word (*lionize*) breaking open. What does it mean to show the lions in the space of this poem? This reading finds the violence of venatio spectacle broken open to convert an imprisoning, celebratizing gaze into an intense looking back, a looking back in kind with love.

● ● ●

The wind moves the room
bumps gust, makes the word's presence
heard and felt. I want more
time with the wind. I want to be
taking time to notice
its gusty hello. What is
attention? I have spent 90% of
the past year alone. The wind calls
my attention to the building.
The room in which
I listen—: What is shelter?
the wind asks. I choose to feel
vulnerable and free, to be
in the presence of everyone here,
to share these beginnings possible as wind . . .

Notes

1. I cannot describe the experience of singing this solo, nor the ways the choir members' voices interacted with my own, without the intervening open interval and tilde. I punctuate my work to make visible processes that made me a doer of word.

2. I need to poem the Tennessee Whig etymology of *afterwhile*.

Bibliography

Brooks, Gwendolyn. "The Sermon on the Warpland." *Blacks*. Chicago: David Company, 1987.

About the Contributors

Simone A. James Alexander is Professor of English, Africana Studies, and Women and Gender Studies, affiliate member of the Russian and East European Studies Program and Latin America and Latino/Latina Studies at Seton Hall University. She is the author of the award-winning monograph *African Diasporic Women's Narratives: Politics of Resistance, Survival, and Citizenship* (University Press of Florida, 2014; reprinted 2016), which also received Honorable Mention by the African Literature Association Book of the Year Scholarship Award. She is also the author of *Mother Imagery in the Novels of Afro-Caribbean Women* (University of Missouri Press, 2001) and coeditor of *Feminist and Critical Perspectives on Caribbean Mothering* (Africa World Press, 2013). Her current projects include *Bodies of (In)Difference: Intimacy, Desirability, and the Politics and "Poetics of Relation"* and *Black Freedom in (Communist) Russia: Great Expectations, Utopian Visions.*

José Felipe Alvergue is the author of three books of poetry, most recently *Scenery*, which won the Poets Outloud Editor's Prize from Fordham University Press. His poetics and scholarship have appeared in numerous journals and magazines, and his work engages the intersections of aesthetics and politics, embodiment and performance, and transnationalism. He teaches at the University of Wisconsin, Eau Claire.

Valerie Babb is Andrew Mellon Professor of Humanities at Emory University where she teaches in the departments of African American Studies and English. Her publications include *A History of the African American Novel*, issued by Cambridge University Press; *Whiteness Visible: The Meaning of Whiteness in American Literature and Culture, Ernest Gaines*; and the coauthored *Black Georgetown Remembered.*

Pamela Bordelon is an independent scholar and the author/editor of *Go Gator, and Muddy the Water: Writings from the Federal Writers Project* (1999). Her LSU dissertation, "The Federal Writers' Project's Mirror to America: The Florida Reflection" (1991), has been widely cited by scholars. She is currently at work on a study of interviews given by formerly enslaved Black southerners.

Taylor Hagood is Professor of American Literature at Florida Atlantic University, where he was also the 2013–14 Lifelong Learning Society Distinguished Professor of Arts and Letters. From 2017–19, he directed Florida Atlantic University's Study of the Americas Initiative, and he was the 2009–10 Fulbright Professor at Ludwig-Maximilians-Universität-München in Munich, Germany. His books include *Secrecy, Magic, and the One-Act Plays of Harlem Renaissance Women*; *Faulkner's Imperialism: Space, Place, and the Materiality of Myth*; *Following Faulkner: The Critical Response to Yoknapatawpha's Architect*; and *Faulkner, Writer of Disability*, which won the C. Hugh Holman Award for Best Book in Southern Studies. He coedited *Undead South: The Gothic and Beyond in Southern Literature* and *Swamp Souths: Literary and Cultural Ecologies*. His biography *Stringbean: The Life and Murder of a Country Music Legend*, is forthcoming in 2023. He is currently writing a biography on Florida novelist Theodore Pratt and a book on rural aspects in the work of Zora Neale Hurston, Ernest Gaines, William Faulkner, Jim Harrison, and other writers.

Joyce Marie Jackson is Chair of the Department of Geography & Anthropology and former Director of African & African American Studies at Louisiana State University, where she holds the James J. Parsons Endowed Professorship. She has directed the LSU in Sénégambia and Haiti Academic Study Abroad Programs. She has curated numerous art and historical exhibitions along with J. Nash Porter, the documentary photographer, including a Smithsonian Institution exhibit, "New Orleans Mardi Gras Indians: Exploring a Community Tradition from an Insider's View." Currently Dr. Jackson is editing *Blacks in the Red Stick: The African American Presence in Baton Rouge*. She has produced a documentary film, *Easter Rock*, which was premiered at the Ethnografilm Festival in Paris, France. Her awards include the Brij Mohan Distinguished Professor Award for Social Justice and a National Endowment for the Arts and Rockefeller Foundation Fellowship. She recently received the 2021–22 Lifetime Contributions to the Humanities award from the Louisiana Endowment for the Humanities.

Delia Malia Konzett is Professor of English, Cinema Studies, and Women's and Gender Studies at the University of New Hampshire. She is the author of the monographs *Ethnic Modernisms* (Palgrave Macmillan, 2002) and *Hollywood's Hawaii: Race, Nation, and War* (Rutgers University Press, 2017). She recently edited the anthology *Hollywood at the Intersection of Race and Identity* (Rutgers University Press, 2019). Her research focuses on issues of race, aesthetics, and questions of representation in cinema. Essays in film journals and books cover such topics as race in *Casablanca*, settler colonialism in Pacific melodramas, John Ford's Orientalism, and yellowface and minstrelsy in the Charlie Chan series. Her current research looks at race in the films of Stanley Kubrick.

Jane Landers is the Gertrude Conaway Vanderbilt Professor of History at Vanderbilt University. She is Director of the Slave Societies Digital Archive and since 2015 has served as the US member on UNESCO's International Scientific Committee for the Slave Route Project. Landers's award-winning monographs include *Black Society in Spanish Florida* and *Atlantic Creoles in the Age of Revolution*. She is the coauthor or editor of five other books and numerous articles on the history of African and Indigenous resistance in Florida and the Atlantic World. Her research has been supported by the John Simon Guggenheim Foundation, the National Endowment for the Humanities, the American Council of Learned Societies, the Andrew W. Mellon Foundation, and the British Library Endangered Archives Programme, among others. She has served as President of the Conference on Latin American History and Founding Chair of its Atlantic World Section, President of the Forum on Early-Modern Empires and Global Interactions, and President of the Latin American and Caribbean Section of the Southern Historical Association. She currently serves as Chair of the Committee on International Historical Activities of the American Historical Association.

John Wharton Lowe (1945–2023) was Barbara Methvin Distinguished Professor at the University of Georgia. He also taught at LSU, the University of Munich, Harvard, Saint Mary's College, and Columbia. His books include *Jump at the Sun: Zora Neale Hurston's Cosmic Comedy*; *Bridging Southern Cultures*; *Louisiana Culture from the Colonial Era to Katrina*; and *Calypso Magnolia: The Crosscurrents of Caribbean and Southern Literature*, which won both the C. Hugh Holman Award and the Sharon L. Dean Award. The recipient of the MELUS Lifetime Achievement Award, Lowe was President of the Society for the Study of Southern Literature, the Southern American Studies Association, MELUS, and the Louisiana Folklore Society.

Gary Monroe, an acclaimed photographer, is the lead authority on the group of Black Florida painters known as the Highwaymen; he has written five books and presented some 300 lectures about them and their now iconic artwork, including *The Highwaymen: Florida's African-American Landscape Painters* (University Press of Florida, 2001), followed by *Extraordinary Interpretations: Florida's Self-taught Artists* (University Press of Florida, 2003). Monroe's photographs of old-world Jews of South Beach in Miami led to an acclaimed book. Subsequently, he photographed Haitian refugees in Miami's Little Haiti, supported by a Dade County Arts grant. He was subsequently awarded two Fulbright fellowships to photograph in Haiti (1984, 1989). Aided by another grant, he photographed elements of Walt Disney World. He has since photographed other Florida theme parks; this work was exhibited and published as *Florida Dreams* (1993). More photographs were published of fundamentalist groups in *Cassadaga: The South's Oldest Spiritualist Community*. He has taken pictures in Israel, Great Britain, Spain, Mexico, Trinidad, Brazil, Russia, Cuba, France, Poland, Egypt, India, and other countries.

Noelle Morrissette is author of *Anne Spencer Between Worlds* (University of Georgia Press, 2023), *James Weldon Johnson's Modern Soundscapes* (University of Iowa Press, 2013), and editor of *New Perspectives on James Weldon Johnson's "The Autobiography of an Ex-Colored Man"* (University of Georgia Press, 2017). She is Program Director of African American and African Diaspora Studies and an Associate Professor of English at the University of North Carolina at Greensboro. She has written several essays about Johnson's cultural and literary milieu and is author of the introduction to the Barnes and Noble Classics edition of James Weldon Johnson's *The Autobiography of an Ex-Colored Man* and other writings.

Paul Ortiz is a Professor of History and Director of the Samuel Proctor Oral History Program at the University of Florida. He is the author or coauthor of five books, including *Emancipation Betrayed: The Hidden History of Black Organizing and White Violence in Florida from Reconstruction to the Bloody Election of 1920*; and most recently, *People, Power: History, Organizing, and Larry Goodwyn's Democratic Vision in the Twenty-First Century*. Ortiz's book *An African American and Latinx History of the United States* was identified by *Fortune* magazine as one of the "10 books on American history that actually reflect the United States." He has published essays in *The American Historical Review, Latino Studies, Cultural Dynamics, The Oral History Review, Kalfou, Florida Historical Quarterly*, and many other journals. He has also worked as an organizer with the United Farm Workers of Washington State, the Farm Labor Organizing Committee, and many other unions and community organizations. He is a former president of the Oral History Association and a National Archives Distinguished Scholar in 2022–23.

Lyrae Van Clief-Stefanon is Associate Professor of English at Cornell University. She is the author of *Open Interval*, a 2009 finalist for the National Book Award and the LA Times Book Prize; *Black Swan*, winner of the 2001 Cave Canem Poetry Prize; as well as the chapbooks *Leading with a Naked Body* with Leela Chantrelle and *Poems in Conversation and a Conversation* with Elizabeth Alexander. She has been awarded fellowships from Cave Canem, the Lannan Foundation, and Civitella Ranieri. She has written plays and lyrics for The Cherry, an Ithaca arts collective, and in 2018 her work was featured in Courage Everywhere, celebrating women's suffrage and the fight for political equality, at National Theatre London.

Genevieve West is Professor and Chair of the Department of English, Speech, and Foreign Languages at Texas Women's University. A scholar of Zora Neale Hurston's work, West has contributed to prestigious academic journals such as *African American Review, Amerikastudien/American Studies, Receptions*, and *Women's Studies*. She is the author of *Zora Neale Hurston and American Literary Culture*; the editor of Hurston's Harlem Renaissance stories, *Hitting a Straight Lick with a Crooked Stick*; and coeditor with Henry Louis Gates Jr. of *"You Don't Know Us Negroes" and Other Essays by Zora Neale Hurston*.

Belinda Wheeler is an independent scholar and the editor of three books: *Heroine of the Harlem Renaissance and Beyond: Gwendolyn Bennett's Selected Writings; A Companion to Australian Aboriginal Literature;* and *A Companion to the Works of Kim Scott*. She has previously taught at Clafin University.

Index

Page numbers in italics indicate figures.

Abraham, 6
Adams, Ellis, 264
Adams, John Quincy, 83
Adams, Monica, 264
aestheSis, 72n2
African Americans. *See* Blacks
African Methodist Episcopal Church, 6, 61–62
Africans, 64; diaspora, 134–35; enslaved, 4, 16; exploration, 7; heritage and folklore, 176–82; religions, 24; of Spanish Florida, 83; Yamasee Indians, 31–55
African-Yamasee alliance, 45–46, 47, 83
Afro-American Life Insurance Company, 10
Afro-Caribbeans, 182
Afro-Cubans, 13–14; diaspora, 3; jazz, 14; religion, 13
Afro-Floridians, 14
afterlife, 216
Agee, James, 191
agency, 172
agricultural jobs, 247
Alabama, 13, 147, 247; bus boycott in, 11
Alachua County, Florida, 68; Community Remembrance Project, 76
Alachua plantation district, 83
Alexander, Lewis Grandison, 106
Alexander, Michelle, 253, 257n10, 260, 261, 263, 265, 269–70
Alexander, Simone A. James, 25
Ali, Mahershala, 230, 252
alienation, natal, 229–35, 241, 242
Allied Forces, African Americans in, 12
Almodóvar, Pedro, 239
Alonso, 40

Alsberg, Henry, 142–43, 147, 154
Altamaha, 36, 37
alterity, 133
Alvergue, José Felipe, 17
Amelia Island, 144, 146
"amen comers," 178
Americaneity, 65
American exceptionalism, 56, 57, 58–59, 60, 65
American Guide Series, 138
Anansi/spider trickster tales, 22, 185
Anastasia Island, 46
Anderson, Benedict, 212
Angelou, Maya, 214
Anglo slave system, vs. Spanish slave system, 37, 43
Anthony, Amanda Koontz, 128
anthropology, 162–65, 172
anti-Blackness, 58, 59, 60, 63, 64, 66, 69–71, 72n6, 73n11, 73n18, 251
anti-Black violence, 74–89; designed to thwart progress, 82; upsurge of, 80; whitewashing of history of, 74, 75
Anzaldúa, Gloria, 72n3
Apalachicola River, 5
Aponte, Pedro, 47
Archive of the Indies, 36
Arena Stage, 21
Argüelles, Antonio de, 47
Arkansas, 147
Armony, Ariel C., 225, 243n4
Arnett, Curtis, 191
Arri Alexa XT digital cameras, 233–34
art, 4, 23, 24–25; of the Highwaymen, 189–205; racist stereotypes and, 128